D0640554

UNWIN UNIVERSITY BOOKS

The Profession of Government

46

By the same author

INTRODUCTION TO FRENCH LOCAL GOVERNMENT
THE PREFECTS AND PROVINCIAL FRANCE
THE LIFE OF BARON HAUSSMANN
(*with J. M. Chapman*)

BRITISH GOVERNMENT OBSERVED

The Minerva Series of Students' Handbooks
General Editor: Dr. Brian Chapman

RUSSIAN POLITICAL INSTITUTIONS
by D. J. R. Scott

INTERNATIONAL INSTITUTIONS
by Paul Reuter

FREE ELECTIONS
by W. J. M. Mackenzie

THEORY IN POLITICS: AN INTRODUCTION
by Wilfrid Harrison

INTERNATIONAL ECONOMICS
by Kurt Martin

The Profession of Government

THE PUBLIC SERVICE IN EUROPE

BRIAN CHAPMAN

Professor of Government

University of Manchester

LONDON

UNWIN UNIVERSITY BOOKS

FIRST PUBLISHED IN 1959
SECOND IMPRESSION 1963
THIRD IMPRESSION 1966
FOURTH IMPRESSION 1970

ISBN: 0 04 351002 7

UNWIN UNIVERSITY BOOKS

George Allen & Unwin Ltd
40 *Museum Street, London W.C.*1

PRINTED IN GREAT BRITAIN
BY UNWIN BROTHERS LIMITED
WOKING AND LONDON

PREFACE

This book is a contribution to the study of comparative government; it is an attempt to write a text book for a subject which does not yet exist.

Certain hurdles may not have been cleared. First, in many countries in Europe the study of public administration has been dominated by lawyers. The political scientist will not find in printed sources much assistance in answering the questions he wants to ask. The only solution is to live in each country and do some original work. The reader of this book should therefore be warned against the obvious dangers of partiality, prejudice, and personal assessments. To people reading about their own country critical friendliness may easily appear to be plain unfriendliness. If all foreign readers feel this, I have probably succeeded in being just.

Second, of the various possible methods of presentation, I have chosen that which emphasises the advantages of a single author. A country by country survey is best done in a symposium dominated by a powerful editor; an encyclopaedia of detailed facts, either by a research team or by someone who has been guaranteed long life. A single author can dominate his material in a way impossible for an editor, and choose the points he wishes to attack in depth. Provided he chooses the right subjects there is a unity of treatment not possible in a symposium.

Third, each subject dealt with in this book justifies a separate book for each country. In order to make the material manageable and intelligible it has had to be drastically compressed. I hope that nothing of major importance has been lost in the process. In general, the method I have used has been to state the standard practice where there is one, and to draw attention to other examples which seem to be important, exceptional or very interesting.

Fourth, only a professional linguist can work competently in eight languages. Not being a professional linguist I have always preferred to be accurate rather than elegant in translations. Whenever there is any likelihood of difficulty or confusion I have left the names of institutions in their original language. Attempts to translate are more often misleading than helpful.

It would be quite impossible properly to acknowledge all the help I have received in the preparation of this study. It would have been quite impossible without the generous assistance of a fellowship of the Rockefeller Foundation. I am deeply indebted to a great number of public officials, scholars, and politicians in many different countries for their unfailing kindness, patience, and courtesy. It would be invidious to single any out by name, and probably most of them would not thank me for doing so. But without their friendly co-operation I could not have produced this study, and I have been very conscious of my debt to them even when I have been most critical.

I owe a particular debt to my colleague and friend Professor Mackenzie, who not only suggested this study to me, but also did his best to make it logical and coherent. I am also greatly indebted to Mr. Grove of the University of Manchester, Professor Langrod of the French Centre National de Recherche Scientifique, and M. Chapel of the Institut International des Sciences Administratives for reading the manuscript most assiduously, helping me to avoid errors, and making many valuable suggestions which I have tried to incorporate in the text. None of these gentlemen can, of course, be held in any way responsible for the errors of fact, style, or taste which still remain. What I owe to my wife cannot be disclosed. During the years of travel, research and writing she has been my constant companion, most loyal collaborator, and dearest friend.

CONTENTS

PREFACE page 5

HISTORICAL INTRODUCTION 9

PART ONE. COMPOSITION
1. The Extent of the Public Service 47
2. Recruitment 74
3. Training 99

PART TWO. CONDITIONS OF SERVICE
4. Rights and Duties 133
5. Security of Tenure 145
6. Pensions 153
7. Discipline 158
8. Promotion 164

PART THREE. CONTROL
9. The History of Control 181
10. The Structure and Personnel of Administrative Courts 199
11. The Powers of Administrative Courts 206
12. The Ombudsman 245
13. Financial Control 260

PART FOUR. POLITICS AND PUBLIC
14. Politics and Administration 273
15. Public Service Trade Unions 296
16. Public Officials and the Public 308

BIBLIOGRAPHY 323

INDEX 345

Historical Introduction

This preliminary chapter will be a general outline of the way modern public services have developed in Europe, tracing the emergence of questions which will be dealt with later in this book. It will seek to put modern problems into a historical perspective whereby they may be more easily understandable and their general nature appreciated.

It may appear somewhat artificial to begin a study of modern public administration with a discussion of Roman law and Roman institutions. But there are parallels between Roman and modern European administrative institutions, and Roman law has exerted a great influence on continental jurists and is the fundamental European tradition.

THE ROMAN STATE

From the point of view of law two Roman principles are important. First, the head of the state received his powers from the people. Even the virtually all-powerful Roman Emperors remained the representatives of the state, and held and exercised their powers in the name and interests of the state.[1] Ulpian said, 'Quod principi placuit, legis habet vigorem: utpote cum lege regia, quae de imperio eius lata est, populus ei et in eum omne suum imperium et potestatem conferat.'[2] By the time of Diocletian and Constantine the Emperor had come to exercise his powers in his own name and by virtue of his own quality as prince. Yet even as late as Justinian the Institutes still refer back to the lex regia as the original act which invested the ruler with powers of state delegated to the prince by the people.[3]

[1] A. Esmein and Génestal: *Histoire du Droit Français.* 15th ed. Paris, 1925. p. 60.
[2] Digests, I, IV, i.
[3] Institutiones, I, II, 6.

The corollary to this which the Romans also accepted was a distinction between the private and public personalities of the head of the state. In practical terms this meant a distinction between the financial resources of the state (the aerarium), the imperial treasury of the head of the state (the fiscus) and the personal resources of the head of the state (the patrimonium). Augustus is held to have distinguished between these different resources and to have recognised a moral obligation to devote the first two to the needs of the state alone.[1] In the later Empire good emperors continued to stress this distinction, and on occasions talked as if they were legally bound by it, but eventually it disappeared as all forms of property and revenue came to be regarded as Caesar's, and as the distinction between the public and private personalities of the head of the state was lost.

These legal distinctions have a direct bearing on the modern state.

The structure of the Roman Empire was also a source from which later jurists and statesmen were to draw lessons. At the centre of the web of administration was the Emperor himself in whom were vested both legislative and executive functions. Many executive functions were delegated to the praetorian prefect, who emerged as a type of first minister of great dignity. His powers came to be so extensive that Augustus created a second post so that they should offset each other; but under Tiberius there was again a single prefect.[2]

When, after a long process of evolution, the centre of the Empire moved to Constantinople, the number of praetorian prefects was increased to four: each dealt with a geographical area—the East; Illyria and Thrace; Italy, Africa and western Thrace; and Gaul, Spain and Brittany. Vicarii under their authority ruled the dioceses, and under the vicarii were legatii or praesides, responsible for the administration of the provinces; the whole administrative structure hinged on the praetorian prefect, who centralised in his person the powers of government, including the supreme judicial function. This judicial personality was vested in the praetorian prefect personally, and could be

[1] Duff: *Personality in Roman Private Law*. Cambridge, 1938. pp. 59–60.

[2] See H. F. Jolowicz: *Historical Introduction to the Study of Roman Law*. Cambridge, 1932.

exercised wherever he was, even outside his own area of jurisdiction.

For some time the prefects' decisions were sovereign; that is, no appeal was possible, not even to the emperor. Diocletian and Maximus, however, allowed a right of appeal against oral decisions of a prefect within two years, but only as a petition of grace (facultas supplicandi non provocandi) and on the grounds that the law had been misapplied (si contra jus se laesos affirment).

In addition to his judicial function, one of the prefect's most important powers was to determine the fiscal contribution due from each province; he could levy the taxes but not impose new ones. Much of the financial administration, however, lay outside the prefect's control. The imperial finance minister (comes sacrarum largitionum) and the imperial domain minister (comes rerum privatarum) were not subordinate to the praetorian prefects. The fundamental importance of financial administration seems to have been recognised very early, and there has been a long tradition of giving it a specially autonomous status.

The other principal officers of state in the later Empire were the chamberlain (praepositus sacri cubuculi); the magister officiorum, responsible for all the services in the Empire relating to law and order and for the protection of the imperial palace; the first secretary of state (primicerius notariorum), responsible for the archives and for formal records of imperial acts, decisions and deliberations; and finally the magistri militum, responsible for military affairs. Originally military powers were vested in the praetorian prefects, but they were prudently separated from his civil functions to a point where the magistri militum had powers in the military sphere co-extensive with the prefect's powers in the civil field. Experience showed the undesirability of one man possessing a monopoly of military powers, and for this reason several magistri were appointed. They served both in the prefectures and in the imperial palace.

The emperor had two advisory councils. The auditorium dealt with the emperor's judicial functions and advised him on appeals and points of law; the decisions were prepared by assessors and ratified or amended by the emperor.

The structure of the Empire is interesting for several reasons. In the first place the hierarchy from the provinces through the dioceses to the central government is a system clearly modelled on military organisation, and so is the bestowal of executive authority throughout the chain of command to officers dependent on and responsible to the central government. The long-lasting success and the logical clarity of the administrative structure could not fail to impress the statesmen and jurists of later generations when once again the achievements of the Roman Empire came to be known.

A second interesting feature is the early division of government into its major constituent parts. Military affairs are clearly distinguished from civil affairs, each with its separate hierarchy. Within the field of civil affairs, finance is regarded as a separate branch of administration, as is also the administration of justice. The remaining branches of internal civil administration tend to be the responsibility of the 'police' authority, with powers over all those matters likely to affect the good order of the Empire. From an early stage 'police' administration came to have a much wider connotation than it does in modern English usage, and in many European languages it is still used in the original broader sense, to cover not only the maintenance of public order, but also fields such as maintaining highways, victualling the city, supervising markets, combating plagues and pestilences, and so on.

In the Roman administrative system one can therefore distinguish four of the five main pillars of administration: military affairs, finance, justice and police. The fifth, foreign affairs, was in theory conducted by the head of the state through his personal representatives, and was less formalised as an administrative organisation. Even though negotiations were often in fact conducted by military gentlemen, foreign affairs were no doubt easily distinguishable from military affairs. These five divisions are to be found in the first reorganisation of the French administration in 1790, and the modern pattern of administration developed with the breaking down of the 'police' function into its component parts; transport, health, education, agriculture and trade.

THE FEUDAL STATE

With the breakdown of the Roman Empire in Europe, the subtle concepts of the Roman jurists and the sophisticated administrative organisation disappeared. Indeed, for several centuries Europe had only faint memories of a coherent, unified body of law. In France and Spain the chief documents embodying the Roman tradition were the Lex Romana Visigothorum and the Breviarium Alaricianum. Justinian's code had some importance in Italy after he had reconquered the peninsula, but it was never introduced into France and the West, and the Corpus Juris is not heard of between 603, when it is mentioned by Gregory the Great, and the middle of the eleventh century.[1]

It is also true to say that the idea of any but the most elementary public services seems also to have disappeared. The most significant feature of the Dark Ages was the enormous increase in oral law at the expense of written law. During the tenth century even the text of the law of the barbarians and the Carolingian ordinances cease to be mentioned, and the only valid law seems to have been custom law.[2] The very basis of civilised Roman society, the concept of property, virtually disappeared during the early feudal ages; and only in Italy perhaps was there any litigation on the subject. Instead, litigants sought the protection of 'the good old law', and invoked the 'saisine' or 'Gewere', or 'the memory of men as far back as it goes'.[3] Communal self-help rather than organised administration was the key to early feudal society. After the fall of the Carolingian empire even organised defence became a local responsibility. Men were forced back on one of the most primitive forms of association, the search for a chief who would protect them at the price of personal homage and fealty.[4] The feudal concept of lord and vassal had long been known to the primitive Germanic tribes, successors to the lands abandoned by the Romans. The Carolingians attempted to use this personal bond to ensure cohesion and loyalty amongst their

[1] H. F. Jolowicz: 'Revivals of Roman Law.' *Journal of the Warburg and Courtauld Institutes*, vol. 15. London, 1952. pp. 88–98.

[2] M. Bloch: *La Société Féodale: la formation des liens de dépendance*. Paris, 1940. p. 174.

[3] Loc. cit. p. 183.

[4] An idea excellently conveyed in the Anglo-Saxon poem 'The Wanderer'.

very small group of 'public' officials. They regarded these officials as being under the special 'maimbour' of the emperor, and more and more frequently they were recruited solely from men who had sworn loyalty 'by mouth and hands'. The very concept of the state disappeared together with the concept of public service. By the time of Louis the Pious (AD 778–840) no office at court and no post of command was given to a man until he had performed the rites binding him as personal vassal to the monarch.[1] Only in Italy was there no trace of homage 'by hands and mouth'; only there was there a level of juristic culture which could accept binding obligations without sanctifying them with formalistic rites.

Feudal society affected public administration in two ways. On the one hand it was hierarchic, based fundamentally on the concept of 'Mannschaft'. Public officials were therefore the vassals of the prince; the reverse of this coin was the slight contractual element in the relation, since the prince could be held to have some responsibility towards his vassal, notably to protect him and to dispense justice. This duty was explicit in several coronation oaths. A right to resist the prince was recognised in early mediaeval law, but it was not so much a contractual right as one based upon the duty of the private man to foster some ideal, objective legal order.[2] The Church, for instance, taught that everyone had a duty to build the Civitas Dei, and the danger of clerical justification for a secular right of resistance was well appreciated by the princes. While little written law existed, however, princes were able to combine a platonic responsibility to God and the Law with a practical absolutism, limited by lack of organised resources.

The concept of imperium was replaced by the more characteristic feudal concept of concordia. Only in the field of justice did the original idea still persist. Even when the Capetian kings were reduced practically to nothing, men still clung to the idea that the king was responsible for ensuring peace by justice.[3]

The provision of services, generally of the most rudimentary kind, was for the most part the responsibility of local seigneurs,

[1] M. Bloch: op. cit. p. 245.

[2] F. Kern: *Kingship and Law in the Middle Ages*. Trans. by S. B. Chrimes. Oxford, 1948. p. 21.

[3] L. Duguit: *Les Transformations du Droit Public*. Paris, 1913. p. 4.

though occasionally towns and cities were strong enough to achieve a qualified independence. The public services provided by the prince were administered on his behalf by officers of his own household. No clear distinction could be drawn between the private and public personalities of the monarch. His palace officials were in law and practice his personal servants. Household officers of high standing such as the chancellor, the chamberlain, the marshal, doubled the rôle of personal attendant and advisor on special aspects of public affairs. These high officers, and the assemblies of notables, were the forerunners of modern government, but were changed out of recognition by the rise of the absolute state, and later by the French Revolution.

THE ABSOLUTE STATE

The modern administrative state is in most countries the direct descendant of the absolute monarchies of the sixteenth, seventeenth and eighteenth centuries. These monarchies were the result of different local circumstances, but two common features were the development of a money economy and the emergence of a new middle class. Both monarchs and middle class found that the established feudality obstructed their growing importance, and in several countries they formed an alliance to oust the old aristocracy from their monopoly of positions in government and the public service. The new middle class stepped into the vacated posts, and incidentally provided the monarch with allies against recalcitrant nobles.

The new jurists of the absolute monarchs—the letrados, the légistes, the curiales,—spread and glossed the newly discovered treasures of Roman law. They argued that public power had been granted to the monarch by a mythical lex regia, and that the people, once having done this, ceased to have any control. They transferred the imperium to the monarch, and by an ingenious use of the Roman law concept of property they identified the monarch's imperium with the individual's private property. The 'right' of sovereignty, they argued, was vested in the monarch. The state then was 'owned' by the monarch, and sovereignty belonged to him personally; he alone could legally exercise it, transmit it to his heirs, or otherwise dispose of it.

This argument is advanced frequently in different countries during the seventeenth and eighteenth centuries. In France, in 1640, for instance, Loyseau wrote: 'Le Roi est parfaitement officier, ayant le parfait exercice de toute puissance publique... et il est ainsi parfaitement seigneur, ayant en perfection la propriété de toute puissance publique. . . . Aussi il y a longtemps que tous les rois de la terre ont prescrit la propriété de la puissance souveraine.'[1]

A century later the famous Prussian cameralist, Justi, irritated by the doctrines of the Enlightenment, wrote: 'The enemies of the supreme power, and especially of absolutism, whom we are accustomed to call the Monomarchi, adopt as their chief principle the theorem that the whole people is above the ruler, and hence may either call him to account for acts prejudicial to the welfare of the community, or may resist him. From such damnable principles came the unhappy tragedy of the unfortunate Charles I of England, and from the same cause Henri III came to his death in France. Nothing is more detestable than these ideas which are evidently contrary to the nature of a republic and open the door to all sorts of uproar and disorder. . . . We should limit the supreme power much too narrowly if we should make it consist merely in laws, penalties, ordinances, etc. To the means and the powers of the state belong not only all sorts of goods both fixed and movable within the boundaries of the country, but also all the talents and abilities of the persons who reside in the country. The reasonable use of all these things, then, and the prerogative of such use is therefore the supreme power.'[2] Sovereignty was the right to command, and those commanded had a duty to obey. Laws were the tangible expression of the will of the monarch, and there was no higher authority to which further appeal could be made.

The scope of public services underwent radical transformation. Whereas during the middle ages the king had been primarily responsible for defence (though dependent for supplies on local rulers) and for justice, in the new world of the sixteenth and seventeenth centuries there was a remarkable increase in the services undertaken by the Crown. For the first time since the

[1] Loyseau: *Traité des Offices*. Paris, 1640.

[2] Quoted in A. Small: *The Cameralists*. Chicago, 1909. p. 325.

Romans, finance, justice, foreign affairs, internal affairs and defence were clearly distinguished from each other with specialised administrative services. With its new power, the Crown assumed new responsibilities, and what had been matters for local regulation became matters of royal concern. The Crown intervened in social and economic fields; for example, Poor Law Acts in England, Louis XIV's extension of the salt tax, or Frederick William's introduction of stable food prices and state guarantees.

Both the administration of justice and armies were nationalised, and it was the royal commission rather than personal status which now conferred authority on a man. The exploitation of new lands overseas required investment on a scale beyond the scope of private individuals, and monopolies of new sources of wealth strengthened the Crown correspondingly.

The feudal assembly, the curia regis, was replaced by new privy councils, in which the monarch could have both the secrecy and the personal preponderance necessary for the exercise of monopoly powers, and as the Crown assumed responsibility for new public services, their administration—when it could not be imposed as a duty on subordinate authorities—became the responsibility of committees of the privy council.

The first country to elaborate an extensive system of administration by committee was Spain. A Consejo Real existed from 1402 and was reorganised by the Catholic kings in 1426 to deal with administrative matters. The Consejo de Estado seems to have been in existence by 1526[1], and was used by the Emperor Charles V in the most important affairs affecting the Empire. A complicated system of councils developed, some of them, like the Consejo de Aragon, or those of Flanders, Italy, Burgundy and Portugal, having a regional competence, and others, such as the Consejo Supremo de Guerra, the Consejo de Hacienda, the Consejo de Cruzada and the Consejo de la Inquisición, organised functionally. These councils possessed both judicial and administrative powers, and the Consejo de Estado, presided over by the monarch, was the supreme tribunal for all matters affecting the realm.

[1] Luis Jordana de Pozas: *El Consejo de Estado Español*. Madrid, 1953.

This polysynodal system was for long regarded by foreigners with admiration. The Abbé de Saint-Pierre was expelled from the Académie Française in 1719 for having 'voulu diminuer la gloire du feu Roi (Louis XIV) et d'avoir dit dans cette intention plusieurs choses très injurieuses à Sa Mémoire'. His offence was to point out the advantages of the Spanish system of administration compared with the system in France.[1]

Prussia furnished an even more striking instance of the way the privy council developed from a policy-making body to an administrative organ. National public services were for the most part administered as off-shoots of the privy council, while in the eighteenth century the policy-making functions of the privy council were assumed by the cabinet, which evolved from the Kammer of the Elector. The judicial committee, the postal secretary, the general domain directory, and the college for ecclesiastical affairs, were all permanent committees of the privy council which came to assume detailed administrative functions.[2] War administration came to establish itself as a completely independent administrative structure reporting directly to the Elector and having only tenuous contact with the privy council. In the course of the eighteenth century the composition of the privy council changed, and it became a committee of heads and directors of the administrative services rather than a controlling and policy-making body.

In Sweden it was held that joint control of administrative services and policy-making would lead to tyranny.[3] The new constitution of 1720 specified, therefore, that members of the Council of the Realm (policy direction) could not be members or heads of the administrative boards (collegia). The only exception to this rule was the chancellor, and it is from this office that the modern prime minister has descended. The presidents of the administrative boards were specially appointed and protected from detailed interference from the Council of the Realm.

[1] Discours sur la Polysinodie, ou l'on démontre que la polysinodie ou pluralité de conseils est la forme de ministère la plus avantageuse pour un roi et pour son royaume. Quoted in Jordana, loc. cit.

[2] R. H. Dorwart: *The Administrative Reforms of Frederick William I of Prussia.* Harvard, 1953. p. 187.

[3] G. Hesslén: *Public Administration in Sweden:* Swedish Institute, Stockholm, 1954. p. 7.

The secretariat of the Council of the Realm was composed of special government offices. There were three or four secretaries who had a general responsibility for following and supervising the work of the administrative boards. The secretaries—who are still called departmentschefer—came to be the king's personal advisors, and during the nineteenth century developed into the modern type of parliamentary minister. The royal administrative boards have, however, retained much of their administrative independence, and regard the minister as their eighteenth-century predecessors regarded the secretaries. The ministries themselves are small groups of immediate advisors to the ministers. The minister, in turn, is a member of the Council of State, the advisory body to the monarch which performs the same functions as the cabinet in other countries. Swedish administration is a striking survival of the administrative state of the eighteenth century; it illustrates an alternative line of development to the one which other countries in fact followed.[1]

Most modern ministers are descended from the king's secretaries. Thomas Cromwell in England and Floribert Ribertet in France were the great pioneers in these offices, whose origins can be traced back to the king's scribes of the twelfth and thirteenth centuries. The absolute monarch found in them a ready reserve of talent and discretion, generally amenable to his will, frequently from modest origins, and able to assist in the modernisation and centralisation of the state.

There were always more secretaries of state in France than in England. In 1547 there were four in France and the office was already firmly established. In both countries they exercised both policy-making and administrative functions. In France the powers of the Crown were divided up on both a functional and geographical basis, and each of the four secretaries had a functional and a geographical sphere of responsibility. The Secretary of State for Foreign Affairs dealt with foreign powers and correspondence with ambassadors, and in addition supervised the affairs of Guenne and Gascony, Normandy, Berry, Champagne and Brie, and Dombes. The secretary of State for the King's Household dealt with religious affairs, pensions, and 'lettres de cachet', and supervised such a wide range of provinces

[1] Gunnar Heckscher: *Svensk Stats Förvaltning i Arbete.* Stockholm, 1952. p. 26. seq.

that he may reasonably be regarded as an embryonic Minister of the Interior[1] The Secretary of State for War dealt with military affairs, posts, and the maréchaussée, and supervised the frontier provinces. The Secretary of State for the Marine dealt with naval affairs, consulates and fishing; he had no jurisdiction over provinces in France but was responsible for the colonies.

In addition to these secretaries of state there were the Chancellor and the Comptroller General of Finance; in France, as in Rome, the financial administration throughout the country was virtually autonomous and marked off from the rest of the machinery of government.

Spain followed closely in French footsteps. Before Philip V there was only, as his title suggests, one Secretario del Despacho Universal, who centralised for the king's attention the recommendations and proposals put forward by the councils for decision by the Crown. In 1705 a second secretary was created with responsibility for naval affairs. After a further reform in 1714 there were four secretarios-ministros, one for Justice, one for War, one for India and Naval Affairs, and one Ministro de Estado. Here again a special appointment was made for financial affairs, the Intendent de Hacienda. The French system was adopted of intendants in the provinces directly subordinate to the central government, and these considerably strengthened the ministers. As the ministers' power and prestige increased they absorbed both policy-making and administrative functions and the older councils declined. By 1750 the Marquis de la Enseñada roundly called for the councils to restrict themselves to purely judicial matters. Policy was formulated now by a small secret Consejo de Cabinete composed of ministers and any favourites the King wished to call in.

Two other features of the absolute state were important as forerunners of the modern administrative state: centralisation of field services, and the organised recruitment of civil servants. All absolute monarchs tried to centralise the local affairs of the provinces, partly to break the strength of the aristocracy, partly to increase their own material power. The case of France, at the time regarded as the most successful of the centralised states, was in fact by no means conclusive. France was built

[1] A. Esmein and Généstal: op. cit. p. 375.

up of individual territories acquired by marriage, conquest and treaty. Local institutions and legal systems were chaotically dissimilar, and there was not even a standard weight or measurement common to all France. Under Richelieu, and later under Louis XIV, strenuous efforts were made to concentrate the affairs of the provinces in the hands of the intendants, sent out on royal warrant to the provinces with very considerable powers covering taxes, tutelage, war supplies, recruitment, public works, and so on.[1]

Yet they did not entirely succeed as a centralising force. The old institutions were not transformed, and the intendants had to work through competing and overlapping provincial bodies. The sale of office was general throughout the public services, so that the Crown had little control over office holders whose title was regarded as private property which could be transferred at will by sale or inheritance. This system also created vested interests within the public service itself. It was largely responsible for the economic and financial decline of France in the years preceding the Revolution.

About the middle of the eighteenth century, there was a general tightening of the administrative structure throughout western Europe. In Austria the final victory of the princely power over the traditional territorial authorities came in the reign of Maria Theresa, when an organised structure of local authorities was built up, dependent upon the central government. The basis for this had been laid under Maximilian I in the sixteenth century, when Regierungen were set up with full-time officials in Crown lands, but this earlier experiment lacked central direction.[2] This was rectified by the Maria Theresa reforms, which included the establishment of central administrative organs, the Geheimer Rat, Hofrat, Hofkanzlei, and Hofkammer, with jurisdiction not only over Crown lands but over the whole Empire. Austria, though not Hungary, was unified under central direction in a single state. In 1742 a Haus- Hof- und Staatskanzlei was set up for unified direction of foreign affairs; followed in 1749 by a supreme judicial court,

[1] Fr. Olivier-Martin: *Précis d'Histoire du Droit Français*. Paris, 1945. p. 345. seq.

[2] Maximilian I's reforms of the Austrian administration were deliberately based on the system of government he found in Burgundy when he succeeded to Charles le Téméraire. See Hartung: *Zur Frage nach den burgundischen Einflüssen in Oesterreich*. Vienna, 1921.

and a directorium in publicis et cameralibus for the internal affairs of the German and Bohemian Länder. This last office was replaced in 1762 by the Vereinigteböhmisch-Oesterreichische Hofkanzlei. Financial administration came under the central direction of the Hofkammer.

These reforms also introduced the Gubernien in the provinces themselves under the direction of the central administration; subordinate to them were Kreisämter, who supervised the administration of the towns, the lower courts, and police. But later in the century the attempt by Josef II to weld the whole Empire, including Hungary, into a single centralised state based on thirteen artificial Regierungsbezirke, was successfully resisted by the old Land authorities, and his successor was even forced to restore some of the old constitutions abolished by Maria Theresa.[1] He was however responsible for improving the work of the public service by insisting on speedy and impartial decisions, and he introduced the idea of a proper scale of pensions for public officials who had satisfactorily completed their period of service. He also began a rational system of noting public officials, to be used for promotion and disciplinary purposes.[2]

These reforms were partly copied from the successful attempts in Prussia by Frederick William I to rationalise the whole administrative structure of the state. In Prussia, by 1740, only the judicial system remained largely on a territorial basis. The civil administration of the Crown lands and the military administration in each province were combined in a Kriegs-und-Domänen Kammer, whose internal structure closely resembled the pattern of collegial administration to be found in the central government.[3] Under the supervision of these combined provincial chambers, Steuerräte, appointed by the central government, controlled the administration of the towns and communes, while the provincial chambers were themselves supervised by the General Directory in Berlin. The whole administrative system, covering all the Prussian territories, was directly subordinate to the King. Local customs

[1] L. Adamovich: *Grundriss des Oesterreichischen Verfassungsrechts*. Vienna, 1947. pp. 5–8.

[2] E. C. Hellbling: *Oesterreichische Verfassungs-und Verwaltungsgeschichte*. Vienna, 1956.

[3] E. R. Uderstädt: *Die Ostpreussische Kammerverwaltung, ihre Unterbehörden und Lokalorgane*. Königsberg, 1911.

and local autonomy were overridden whenever they conflicted with the new administrative machine.[1]

The Prussian monarchs realised from an early stage that a centralised state, with a complex and extensive administrative system, required specially trained civil servants. The development of such a corps was the greatest example Prussia gave to Europe during the eighteenth century.

Professional public servants directly responsible to the King and in the literal sense servants of the Crown were needed for several reasons: to break down the autonomy of the provinces, to act as a counterweight to the aristocracy, and to form a strong chain linking together the scattered territories of the Prussian state. In the first instance they were sent out for purely military affairs, for recruiting, billeting, victualling, and so on. They were also responsible for military security and provost duties, and inevitably they gradually encroached on the ordinary fields of municipal and provincial government.[2] These Crown officials found themselves forced into financial and tax administration to raise revenue for military purposes, and by 1713 there were quite clearly recognisable military-police and military-finance administrations staffed by Crown public officials.

From 1650 onwards rules were gradually formalised regarding recruitment, but the principal steps to form a highly trained body of civil servants were taken under Frederick William I. He created chairs of cameralistics at Halle and Frankfurt, and the holders had the specific duty to provide the training necessary for future public officials. The holders of these chairs frequently came from the higher administration themselves, and as much, if not more, emphasis was placed on the practical requirements of the administrator as on the theoretical work properly the function of university professors. Nevertheless, some of the books on cameralistics produced during the eighteenth century have a charm of their own for the student of public administration, and they are for the most part refreshingly free from abstract juridical argument.[3]

[1] R. H. Dorwart: op. cit. p. 196.

[2] R. H. Dorwart: loc. cit.

[3] A discussion of the origins of administrative 'science' to be found in G. Miglio: *Le origini della scienza dell'amministrazione*. Milan, 1957.

The major steps in organising recruitment to public office were embodied in two ordinances of 1722 and 1748. The central administration and other high officials were required to propose to the King the names of suitable candidates for appointment. The ordinance of 1722 laid down that the names of suitable non-commissioned officers should be proposed by the Adjutant-General to the King for nomination to subordinate posts.

During the eighteenth century conditions became increasingly rigid, and the General Code of 1794 summarised Prussia's achievements in this field. The merit system for appointment covered all types of post, and the general principle was that 'special laws and instructions determine the appointing authority to different public service ranks, their qualifications, and the preliminary examinations required from different branches and different ranks'. Entry to the higher public service required a university degree in cameralistics, which covered agricultural economics, estate management, financial law and administrative law. After their degree course candidates spent a period of practical training in the field, at the end of which they underwent a further oral and written examination. If they successfully cleared these hurdles they were not guaranteed a state post, but could reasonably expect to obtain one.

Unfortunately, by 1794, the Prussian organisation had degenerated into a caste system. Earlier Prussian kings left on the public service some of the distinctive marks of the Hohenzollern family; rigour, austerity, an ideal of service. But the creation of such an administrative corps d'élite bred exclusiveness, contempt for outsiders, and social caste, and one of the results of this was to make selection for the higher service a form of co-optation. Co-optation to office is a method of recruitment secretly desired by highly organised civil services; this was reinforced in Prussia during the nineteenth century by social discrimination, aloof paternalism, contempt for politicians, and the idealisation of the omnipotent authoritarian state.

This was partly offset by the renewed vigour injected into the municipalities and provinces by Baron vom Stein's reforms of 1808. It has been well said that the strength and vivacity of local government in Germany provided an outlet for civic energies which in England found their rightful place in parliament and national politics. But the vigour of local life could not entirely make up for the lack of popular participation in national government, and an authoritarian public service fostered the German belief in government by experts. This had some unfortunate results.

THE NAPOLEONIC STATE

Vom Stein's reforms were in fact stimulated by the collapse of Prussia before the attacks of the Napoleonic armies. With the French Revolution of 1789 and the advent of Napoleon in 1800, Europe entered a new age. Both events radically transformed the whole basis of public administration. The French Revolution changed the concept of the state itself, and with it the nature of public office and the status of public officials. Napoleon created a rational system of administrative organisation closely resembling the organisation of the Roman Empire, and this became a model for many European countries. He also revived the distinctive mark of the Roman legal system: bodies of codified law, logically ordered, and each code providing in its special field an exhaustive formulation of principles, conflicts and penalties. During the nineteenth century, codified law spread throughout Europe, and greatly affected the judicial and administrative arrangements of the countries which adopted it.

With the French Revolution and Napoleon, the nature of the state was fundamentally reformed. By 1789 in the more advanced countries the concept of the prince had already been to some extent replaced by the less personal concept of the Crown, which emphasised continuity and was a convenient way of distinguishing imperium from patrimonium. But the French Revolution was a big step forward in the depersonalisation of the state. The French theorists took over one version of the patrimonial state and replaced the king by the nation. The country was no longer the patrimony of the king but the patrimony of the nation, and the state was the machinery which the nation set up for its own government and to organise its public services.[1]

[1] The institutional changes at this time are dealt with in detail in J. Godechot: *Les Institutions de la France sous la Révolution et l'Empire*. Paris, 1951.

The status of the public official changed at once. He was no longer the servant of the Crown or the prince, he was the servant of the state, and indirectly of the nation. He became an instrument of public power, not the agent of a person. He acted according to the law, and not according to the wishes of an individual, and his allegiance was to the law because the law was the expression of the will of the nation. Whereas previously it had been difficult to make any clear distinction between public and private law, the depersonalisation of the state encouraged a rapid growth in the field of public law concerned with the organisation, duties, and rights of the 'public power'. There were no longer any inherent prerogative powers vested in a person, but only such powers as the nation itself might commit to the holders of public office to ensure the continued existence and good government of the country.

In practice this new doctrine was in several ways more ruthless than those of the ancien régime. A comprehensive state claimed a monopoly of loyalty, and if the concept of citizen confers more abstract rights than the concept of subject, it also presupposes a more organic society than the older world with its traditional loyalties to locality, corporation and trade. Some of the practical disadvantages of the attractive political theory of the General Will were not at first fully appreciated.

The practical application of these new doctrines to the administrative field was wholly beneficial. Within the state all citizens were equal, and all were therefore entitled to hold public office without reference to creed, colour or race. The sole test to be applied by the state was merit. Furthermore, public services were public, and it was the duty of the state to provide them. The needs and duties of communities could be calculated logically on the basis of this new equality, irrespective of local differences; and this meant that local authorities could be standardised and local privileges and exceptions abolished.

The Napoleonic administrative state was a strong, coherent, closely articulated affair. It closely resembled the administrative system first elaborated by the Romans. It too had many military features. A clear chain of command, duties clearly and definitively apportioned between authorities, a firmly established administrative hierarchy with the head of the state at the apex; specialised corps were created, authority was depersonalised, and individual officials were assigned explicit duties with personal responsibility both to their superior and to the law.

Central government was divided into the five basic units of Finance, Foreign Affairs, War, Justice and the Interior. The Interior covered a wide field of administration, public works, police, education, church affairs, control of local authorities, agriculture, trade, and so on. Each ministry was organised into divisions and bureaux, each specialising in one branch of the ministry's work, and some ministries had offices in the provinces. At each level of government there was a state executive authority with general responsibility for the maintenance of public order, health and morality; the mayor in the commune, the sub-prefect in the arrondissement, the prefect in the department and the Minister of the Interior at the top of the hierarchy. The pattern of authority was in the form of an hour-glass, with authority descending from the central government to the prefect, and from the prefect to other state officials and to the departmental and communal authorities.

With the hard logic of the military mind Napoleon insisted on the personalisation of authority. When civil servants were servants of the Crown they held that they simply advised the king, and were not personally responsible for the consequences of their advice. It was for the king to accept or reject it. Systems where public officials are servants of the Crown breed anonymity, administration by committees and generalised authority. Napoleon, on the contrary, insisted that even if advice was the function of several, responsibility for every action should be taken by one man who could be clearly distinguished: the emperor for the affairs of state, the ministers for the affairs of their ministries, the prefects for the affairs of the state in their Departments, and the mayors for the affairs of the communes. Public power was not the prerogative of one man, the monarch; it was apportioned between the high servants of the state, and they were held responsible, before their superior, the law, and the nation, for the exercise of their powers. There is little room for executive committees in the Napoleonic system. And this insistence on personal action and personal responsibility is one of the hall marks of the best French administrative tradition.

Another Napoleonic idea of organisation reminiscent of the Romans and the army was a belief in the need for an able general staff and skilful specialists. The ministers and their staffs might be compared to ordinary troops, and some of the specialists needed in public administration were the same as those needed in military administration: for instance, highway engineers and mining experts. Napoleon inherited from the ancien régime a notable specialist corps already used in both military and civil administration, the Inspection générale des Ponts et Chaussées, a corps of civil engineers responsible for highways, bridges, docks, harbour works, and all kinds of public works. Napoleon created another highly trained body, the Corps National des Mines, for the mining and explosive industries. Both these great specialist corps had their early training in the Ecole Polytechnique, which was also the training establishment for future officers in the specialist corps of the army. He also added a purely civilian corps of high grade specialists, the Inspection des Finances, attached directly to the Minister of Finance.

For his general staff Napoleon reshaped the old Conseil du Roi and created the Conseil d'Etat. Through this council he controlled the whole administration. To it he sent administrative and legislative problems, and from it he obtained expert advice on all questions of government business. It was a purely advisory body as far as the Emperor was concerned, but it had substantial control powers over the other administrative services. The Revolution rightly considered that the judiciary was too conservative properly to be entrusted with the task of supervising executive actions, and yet the alternative was for the executive to be judge of its own acts, a definition of the Polizeistaat. The Conseil d'Etat filled the lacuna: it was part of the executive, but independent of the active administration.

The Conseil d'Etat was also used for training promising young men for the highest posts. They came from a far more varied social background than did the Prussian senior civil servants, and their training and experience were designed to fit them individually for bearing the burdens of high office. Napoleon looked for administrative generals as well as for military generals. The history of the French Empire shows how well he succeeded in both fields.

The democratic element in the selection of higher personnel should be insisted upon; the Napoleonic system was one of nomination, not co-optation, and nomination could be effected by objective tests of merit. Pupils at the Ecole Polytechnique, for instance, from which came many of the most prominent administrators, scientists, scholars and generals in the nineteenth century, gained entrance on the strength of their intellectual merit in science and mathematics. This conferred on its graduates a prestige of quite a different kind from that conferred by caste or social class, and since it promised prospects of the highest posts in the state it attracted not only the brightest of the middle class but also those members of the upper class who happened to be both ambitious and able. This has contributed to the fact that in France, to be a grand commis d'Etat has for long been one of the most honourable professions; a tradition established under the ancien régime.

Few countries in Europe were unaffected by the new organisation.[1] Administrative arrangements can be copied more easily than political institutions, particularly when they are couched in clear and comprehensive terms. Codified law, a simple and rational organisation of local government, the personalisation of state authority, and councils of state with judicial powers, were ideas which began to affect all countries. But whereas French administrative leadership was readily accepted, there were natural reservations about France as a political model; for a growing number of liberal thinkers had reservations both about revolutionary government and about autocratic government. The rulers of Spain or the states of Italy or Germany were naturally inclined to adopt the Napoleonic state with only minor modifications. But new countries like Belgium, or older countries as they became more democratic, looked to England rather than France as the best example of constitutional government. It was, however, extremely difficult to fuse English political principles with French administrative institutions. The first, and perhaps the best compromise was the French Orleanist constitution of 1830, which retained the Napoleonic system of administration,

[1] Undoubtedly the clearest exposition of the Napoleonic system of government is Alejandro Oliván: *De la Administración publica con relación a España*. First published 1843. A new edition by E. García de Enterría appeared in 1954.

but divided political responsibility between executive and legislature along the lines suggested by a study of British practice. The British concept of the Crown was, however, greatly toned down, and although the executive had substantial reserves of authority, the king as head of the state was simply one constitutional organ among several. The nation remained sovereign.

THE ADMINISTRATIVE STATE

Between 1830 and 1870 the administrative state began to assume its modern form.

In Austria, the complications of the multi-national empire had prevented the complete establishment of the centralised state, the first steps towards which had been taken under Maria Theresa. There was opposition from the aristocracy and from the Länder with their own constitutions. After the 1848 revolution, the Stadion constitution of 1849 began an era of increased centralisation in the whole Empire, and a German-dominated imperial bureaucracy was extended throughout the Länder. Stadion wished to compensate for the increased centralisation by according a greater degree of autonomy to local authorities, in rather the same way as vom Stein's reforms in Prussia. Internal administrative problems were complicated during the nineteenth century by the Hungarian question, but in the Austrian territories Stadion's concept of 'double track' administration predominated. At each level of government, responsibility was divided between local elected representatives and officials appointed by the central government, the Kreishauptleute and Bezirkshauptleute. The lower the level of government, the greater the autonomy of the elected representatives.

The German element increased steadily within the administration throughout the century. By 1914 in the imperial ministries of War and Foreign Affairs, 815 of the 1,446 officials were German, a proportion of 56% as compared with the 24% German element in the total population of the empire. In the Austrian internal administration 81% of all the posts in central government were held by the German ethnic element.[1]

[1] Ed. K. G. Hügelmann: *Das Nationalitätenrecht des alten Oesterreich.* Vienna, 1934. p. 280.

In the German Empire, too, after 1870, there was deliberate discrimination against Alsatians, Danes and Poles, who were the principal minority groups. In both Germany and Austria there was marked political discrimination against liberals and social democrats, with the result that the administration, and particularly the higher ranks, were dominated by extremely conservative elements. A Prussian law of 1852 gave the government power to suspend from office and transfer to the retired list any officials occupying strategic posts; these included the under-secretaries of state, directors of ministries, regional and provincial governors, state prosecutors and chiefs of police. The reform was designed to ensure complete conformity of policy between the political and administrative direction of the country. After 1862 Bismarck used the law to get rid of 1,000 officials suspected of liberal sympathies. Loyalty to the Prussian state was not enough; he demanded loyalty to the Prussian government of the day. After 1871 the principle was extended to the under-secretaries of state and directors of ministries of the Empire's central administration.

It was widely recognised that a government needed to have confidence in the support and sympathy of the senior administrators. In several countries this led to an unhealthy turnover at the top, with successive changes of government. But despite abuses it came to be generally admitted that while patronage was an undesirable basis of recruitment for the bulk of the public service, there was something to be said for special arrangements for those posts which were, by their nature, partly administrative and partly political. Only in Britain is this view seriously challenged, and on grounds which require closer examination in a later chapter.

It was during this period that the conditions of service of public officials were first seriously considered. They laboured under two disadvantages. First, their relations with politicians were difficult. They were members of the government machine, and therefore politicians controlling that machine were tempted to use them as electoral agents, or at least to expect their political support. The prospect of promotion or dismissal ensured the official's adherence to the views and interests of the minister, and many minor posts were frankly filled as rewards for political services. The second disadvantage was that public officials were completely dependent on their immediate administrative superiors. The principle of hierarchy weighed heavily on the lower grades, but was almost as tyrannical even at the middle and higher levels of the service. The principle behind recruitment, promotions, dismissals and discipline became an urgent question, more urgent in some countries than others.

In Prussia, for instance, there was not much difficulty about the political activities of public officials, since they constituted a highly conservative and authoritarian group in harmony with the aspirations and sentiments of successive governments; hierarchic discipline was very strong indeed. In France, on the other hand, a reasonable arrangement seems to have been devised fairly early on to deal with questions of discipline and hierarchy,[1] but relations between politicians and public officials were a minefield. In Italy the stern and aloof Piedmontese bureaucracy which had assumed administrative leadership after unification, was swamped first by the politicians of the South, and later by their political nominees and place seekers.[2] Only the northern monarchies avoided these difficulties. In Britain there was a convention that an officer of the Crown was protected from arbitrary dismissal. In Sweden, a provision of the 1809 constitution protected the official from dismissal except after court proceedings.

THE SOVEREIGN STATE

After 1870, the problems of political intervention and the conditions of service of public officials merged into broader questions of political theory and constitutional law. Clearly the position of public officials largely depends on what kind of employer the state is. This leads to consideration of the general nature of the powers exercised by the state and the basis of its 'sovereign' powers. And if it has 'sovereign' powers, can the citizen get any redress if he suffers as a result of the exercise of those powers, and within what limits is the state

[1] H. Monnier: *France Administrative*. Paris, 1841. vol. II. p. 56.

[2] S. Spaventa: *La Giustizia nell'Amministrazione*. Turin, 1949. p. 96, and M. Minghetti: *I Partiti politici e la Ingerenza loro nella Giustizia e nell'Amministrazione*. Bologna, 1881. pp. 128–9.

'responsible'? These were the questions which preoccupied jurists and administrators in the late nineteenth and early twentieth centuries.

The German and French schools of jurists approached these basic questions from quite different points of view.

There is perhaps something in Heine's theory that the Germans are royalist by nature and the French republican. This did not refer to any particular public virtue on either side. Heine simply meant that a country which is royalist by nature believes in the people who are in authority, and trusts the individual placed in a position of power. The republican character of a nation, on the other hand, is expressed in a trust in the law and distrust of individuals, especially those in authority; suspicion of authority incites these people to continual criticism, mockery and opposition, to keep all men of influence and power in their place. Heine's view of the French and German characters is borne out by the legal controversies of the late nineteenth century.

Until the middle 1860's German jurists continued to teach the doctrine of the patrimonial state in which public power was the personal right of the prince. In 1865 Gerber propounded a counter-doctrine which had great influence on later German writers. He held that the state was itself a juridical person distinct from the person of the prince, and it was the state which was the sovereign body; the prince and the nation were simply organs of the state. The influence of Hegel is preponderant. 'The state is the juridical form for the collective life of the people, and this juridical form belongs to the original and elementary type of the moral ordering of humanity. The juridical observation of the state first grasps the fact that in it the people arrive at a collective consciousness and acquire a capacity to will; in other words in the state the people come to have a juridical personality. The state, in that it protects and demonstrates all the forces of a people directed towards the moral realisation of the common good, is the highest juridical personality known to the juristic order . . .'[1]

The state is one and indivisible and comprises three elements: a territory, a people and a government. It is the sole and original repository of sovereignty. The governors of a country are not

[1] C. F. Gerber: *Grundzüge des Deutschen Staatsrecht.* 3rd. ed. 1880. p. 3.

the representatives of the nation, they are the organs of the state. There is no legal relationship between the organs and the state any more than there is between an individual and his several senses.

Jellinek gave this pernicious doctrine its fullest expression. 'Sovereignty (Herrschaft) means to command unconditionally and to be able to exercise irresistible force; it is the public power (Staatsgewalt), a power of will which is never determined except by itself, and that is precisely sovereignty.' But as a result of this unconditioned and unconditional power the state can determine as it wills the extent of its own powers and of the individuals subordinate to it: consequently it is impossible to determine its limits.[1]

This doctrine had important implications for public administration. As Perthes said, 'acceptance of public office has no contractual basis . . . a person chosen by the head of the state is required to accept that employment, and there is no more question of taking his consent into account than there is when he is required to pay taxes or perform his other duties as a citizen.'[2] Laband and Meyer tried to introduce a contractual element into acceptance of public office, but nevertheless held that once appointed the relation between civil servant and state was best explained by the old concept of lord and vassal. Bluntschli tried to escape from this dilemma—which was inescapable—by fabricating a special law, the 'lex specialis', distinct from both public and private law.

Politically, the German doctrine justified concentration of power in the hands of the head of the state, which served the interests of the German emperors. It also justified the executive acting not in the interests of individuals within the state, but in the interests of the state itself, since the executive was in a better position to determine what these were than any other organ of the state. Public administration, therefore, did not exist to provide services for the public, but to serve the ends of the state itself.

This transcendental view of the state unfortunately spread to other countries; in Italy, for instance, under Orlando's influence, it came to dominate the schools of law. Even Switzerland

[1] W. Jellinek: *Allgemeine Staatslehre*. 1900. p. 161, 190 seq.

[2] Perthes: *Der Staatsdienst in Preussen*. Berlin, 1885. p. 55.

was not immune, though a doctrine more opposed to the Swiss constitution and Swiss political practice it would be hard to imagine. The only beneficial result of these theories was that it was easier to fit into them Gneist's insistence on special administrative courts than it would have been with the previous doctrine of the patrimonial state.[1] But this depended in part on creating a theory of self-limitation imposed by the state on itself.

French jurists reacted strongly against the German school of jurisprudence. They began from a fundamentally different premise: that the sovereign was the nation, not the state, and that the nation delegated its powers to its representatives, the governors of the country. This gave the politicians a primacy over the public officials totally unlike the position in the German states. Esmein, in many ways closest to the German jurists, held that the state was the juridical personality of the nation, and that it was necessary to have a permanent and ideal repository of sovereignty as a basis for public power distinct from the individuals in office at any particular moment.

Both Hauriou and Berthelémy (H) moved away from even this limited notion of state sovereignty. For Hauriou the concept of state personality was only necessary where the state had transactions with other parties. Sovereign power was no longer the essence of public law. There would always be a power to dominate, but it was no longer a subjective right possessed by the state; it was above all a social function. Berthelémy took this a stage further. He said: 'Acts of authority performed by the administration do not involve the notion of a juridical person in whose name they are performed. The notion of personality is only indispensable when it is necessary to represent the state as a legal subject. It is a great mistake to regard the use of power as an exercise of rights. The officials who command do not exercise the rights of a sovereign; they perform functions, the totality of which, if you will, constitutes the sovereign power.'[2]

It was left to the most famous of the positivist jurists, Duguit, to complete the demolition of the transcendental state. 'I maintain,' he said, 'that the notion of the state, the public

[1] The history of administrative courts is dealt with more fully below, p. 186.

[2] H. Berthelémy: *Droit Administratif*. 7th. ed. 1913. pp. 41–2.

power, being able to impose sovereignly its will because it has a nature superior to that of its subjects, is imaginary and has no basis at all in fact. This supposed sovereignty of the state cannot be explained either by divine law, which involves a belief in the supernatural, nor by the will of the people, a gratuitous, unproved and unprovable hypothesis. I maintain that the state is quite simply the result of a natural differentiation, sometimes perfectly simple, sometimes extremely complex, between men of the same social group; and from this there comes what may be termed public power, which cannot be made legitimate by reference to its legal origins, but only to the services it renders according to the rule of law. From then on the modern state appears more and more as a group of individuals working together for the realisation of the material and spiritual needs of the participants under the direction and control of the governors. Thus the notion of public power is replaced by the notion of public service; the state ceases to be a power which commands and becomes a group which works, and those in authority can legitimately use it only in order to ensure general co-operation.'[1]

From this it follows that the great mass of law is really nothing but the rules for the organisation and functioning of the public services. 'La loi est avant tout la loi d'un service public.'[2]

Governors and agents are no longer masters of men exercising a sovereign power, an imperium, over their subjects. Nor are they the organs of a corporate personality which commands. They are the administrators (gérants) of the affairs of the collectivity.'[3]

This part of Duguit's argument refers back to a distinction, probably first made by Edouard Laferrière in the 1880's, between two types of public official, the 'political' official and the purely administrative one. From the time of Vivien[4], the distinction between administration and politics had been recognised, even in Prussia. For different reasons it became necessary to distinguish between those officials whose acts were acts of public power, for which there could be no legal

[1] L. Duguit: *Traité du Droit Constitutionnel*. 3rd. ed. Paris, 1927. vol. I. p. ix.
[2] L. Duguit: *Les Transformations du Droit Public*. Paris, 1913. p. 53.
[3] L. Duguit: loc. cit. p. 54.
[4] Vivien: *Etudes Administratives*. 3rd. ed. Paris, 1859. vol. I. p. 220.

redress except by grace, and those officials whose activity was strictly comparable to work done in private employment, and liable to damages in private law. This was the classic distinction between actes (and fonctionnaires) d'autorité, and actes (and fonctionnaires) de gestion. In the 1920's it was realised that this distinction was arbitrary, and its practical effects harmful. The Conseil d'Etat then abandoned this distinction and was able substantially to extend its protection of the citizen against administrative activities.[1]

The distinction between fonctionnaires d'autorité and fonctionnaires de gestion was much discussed in connection with the question of the political activities of public officials. A wave of syndicalism affected the public sector, more perhaps than the private sector, at the end of the nineteenth and the beginning of the twentieth centuries. The mass organisations of state workers like postmen, school-teachers and clerks, regarded themselves as part of the administrative proletariat, with the right to organise against their employer, the state. The state was, in fact, worse than the ordinary employer, for in addition to being the economic master it was also the political master, with power legally to penalise and discipline its employees in a way a private employer could never do. In Belgium, France, Spain and Italy, trade unions of public officials, for the most part illegal, sprang up. They maintained that state business was just like any other form of business organisation, and that their employers were simply the senior public officials. Their leaders wanted the public law relationship between the state and the civil servant abolished, and replaced by a collective labour contract like that used in industry. In its extreme form public service syndicalism wanted appointments, promotions and selection of leaders to be decided by a vote, either restricted to the officials directly concerned, or to the officials concerned plus those citizens who had an interest in the proper functioning of that administration. Authority would then come from below, not from above, hierarchy would be replaced by autarchy, and an equilibrium of power would be established between superior and subordinate. Obedience would come from a common recognition of the public will. Public officials would all be employed on a purely contractual

[1] See below, p. 239.

basis, and conditions of service and the administrative organisation would be determined by common agreement between those concerned.[1]

The syndicalist programme was the political expression of a general movement among public employees to be freed from many of the limitations placed upon them because of the jurists' mystification of the notion of the state. Public employees demanded freedom from supervision of their private lives, freedom to participate actively in public and political affairs, freedom to express themselves freely in the press, in speech and at meetings, even when their opinions were contrary to those held by the political leadership of the country. Out of the office they demanded the same freedom as as any ordinary citizen. Inside the service they demanded higher salaries, pensions, shorter hours, and promotion within the career to be determined primarily by seniority and decided by promotion committees on which the unions were represented. Disciplinary measures they wanted taken out of the hands of individual superior officials, and made the responsibility of disciplinary committees with full employee representation; also that each public service should have a properly established consultative committee with power to control the decisions of administrative superiors and to advise the heads of the service.[2] This illustrates very clearly the basic interests of the rank and file of public officials. By the end of the second world war most of their demands had been met so completely that in many countries the public service was fast becoming a self-governing corporation.

THE PUBLIC SERVICE STATE

In the inter-war period there were significant changes in several countries. In both Italy and Spain the syndical activity of the civil service trade unions, the corrupt relations between politicians and administration, the use of public office as a reward for supporters, and the chronic underpayment of employees to offset the unwarranted number of people

[1] Harmignie: *L'Etat et ses Agents*. Louvain, 1911. pp. 237 seq. 274 seq. 321 seq.

[2] O. Ranelletti: 'Il sindicalismo nella pubblica amministrazione.' *Annali della R. Università di Macerata*, 1927. vol. II. pp. 28–60.

employed, all contributed to sap the vitality of democracy.[1] In Italy the transition to an authoritarian régime was relatively easy, and more castor oil was spilt than blood. The new régime kept public service unions firmly under control, the executive ceased to be really responsible to any other state organ, membership of the Party became a condition of public office, and it became impossible to argue about conditions of employment. In Spain the transition, when it came, was bitter and prolonged, and not until the beginning of the second world war was an authoritarian régime firmly established. But when it was, the public service underwent the same transformation as in Italy, and became a docile, domesticated, underpaid, overstaffed and inefficient bureaucracy, whose members tried to protect themselves against the external pressures of a single party government by dutiful and unimaginative performance of duties.

In Germany during this period the problem of the relationship between politics and administration became acute. Twice 'the neck of the civil service was broken'; once in 1918, and again in 1933. Under the Empire, civil servants had been encouraged to sit in the Diet, provided they supported the government of the day. The conservative parties greatly benefited from the talent they acquired in this way. But with the declaration of the Republic in 1918, the public servant had squarely to face his moral duty: his oath to the monarchy, his duty to the state, his personal political alignment. It is probably true to say that not more than a handful of public officials were republicans; but only one Prussian public official is known to have resigned when faced with the moral issue.[2]

The Weimar Constitution made matters worse. Article 130 laid down that 'public officials are servants of the community, not of the party', which made sense in the German tradition. But this was followed by, 'freedom of political opinion is guaranteed to all public officials'. These two provisions were found to be incompatible. Despite an attempt in 1922 to

[1] These are the conclusions of the Commissione Parlamentare di inchiesta sull'ordinamento delle Amministrazione di Stato e sulle condizione del personale. Report, 1922. Spanish conditions are described in J. Fabregas del Pilar: *Politicos y Funcionarios*. Madrid, 1932.

[2] R. Mende: *Notes on the political activities of civil servants in Germany*. Frankfurt, 1950.

require every public official to 'uphold the authority of the republican state in the execution of his duties and to refrain from activities incompatible with his position as civil servant of the Republic', the strain on the loyalties of the public official was too great. Membership of the political party in power became an important element in promotion and careers. The public service lost the esprit de corps which had held it together under the Empire, and did not manage to find any alternative sentiment to replace it. When Hitler came to power in 1933 the integrity of the service had already been corrupted.[1]

The Austrian administration remained relatively unaffected by political change, even though the country had been reduced to the rump of the old Empire. The public officials most affected by the political upheavals were those employed in city government, especially in Vienna. But the central administration managed to impose its will on successive ministers. The bureaucracy constituted too important a mass vote for any of the parties to risk upsetting its members: 'nothing can be done to the public official, because each political party is seeking to win the heart of the individual public official and the vote of the body of officials'.[2] The new democratically elected ministers were in the hands of their Hofräte, who charmed them with their discretion and expert knowledge and won their allegiance. Their mastery in their own fields of work made parliament very loath to cross swords with them. When necessary the strong public officials' associations could block measures which affected their members' interests (for instance, the amalgamation of the National and University Libraries in Vienna), or extort special privileges for them (for instance, substantially reduced travel rates on railways).[3] Even under Hitler the Austrian administration managed to retain some independence, and to keep its pride and special status.

Other more fortunate countries had the leisure to face up to some of the thorny problems associated with the growth of the public service to cover the extended social services. The ideas and machinery of nineteenth-century administration

[1] A view of the administration from the inside during the Weimar Republic is: F. Friedensburg: *Die Weimarer Republik*. Berlin, 1946. First published 1934. The author was a Regierungspräsident for much of the period.

[2] W. Rode: *Oesterreichs Beamtenpyramide*. Vienna, 1927. p. 24.

[3] W. Rode: loc cit.

proved inadequate for modern needs. Sweden, Holland and Denmark were able to pursue a tranquil course, partly because of their modest size, partly because they already had a sound administrative basis and were able to cope with new problems within the existing framework. Only control of the expanding public services called for major changes. Denmark, after the second world war, borrowed from Sweden one of the most effective methods of control yet devised[1]; while Belgium, who had recognized during the 1930's that her traditional methods of control through parliament and the courts was not enough, and had made various unsuccessful attempts to solve the problem, finally turned after the second world war to her neighbour France, and borrowed the notion of the Conseil d'Etat.[2]

Belgium, in fact, became preoccupied by the whole question of civil service organisation in a broader context, and just before the second world war a civil service statute was promulgated and a new and more formal recruiting organisation created. But it was not until after the war that these reforms began to have any practical effect, and even then, for various reasons, the effects were limited.[3]

France, too, had her problems.[4] The Conseil d'Etat, which provided the citizen with more far-reaching remedies against the state than in any other European country, boldly explored new and unchartered fields of administrative jurisprudence, until it had unchallenged supremacy in this field.[5] Even the British were effected by the pre-eminence of the Conseil d'Etat, and looked with fresh eyes at the institution so badly misunderstood by Deicy.

In another field France made up lost ground. Until 1939 only the Germans had given to the problem of training public officials the consideration it called for. At intervals from 1848 onwards recommendations had been made in France to set up a school of administration for training public officials, in particular those destined to fill the highest posts. In 1871, a

[1] See p. 245.

[2] See p. 196.

[3] For a résumé of attempts to reform, see: V. Crabbe: *Les Commissions de Réforme administrative en Belgique*. Institut Belge des Sciences Administratives, 1954. See p. 78.

[4] Excellently described in W. R. Sharp: *The French Civil Service*. New York, 1931.

[5] See p. 229.

private organisation, the Ecole Libre des Sciences Politiques, was set up, and this provided admirable pre-entry training for the grands corps de l'Etat. But its selection had a marked social bias, its graduates gradually acquired a monopoly of the best posts, and this damaged the rest of the service, and moreover provided no answer to the general problem of recruitment and training. After the second world war, therefore, a commission recommended the foundation of a state school of administration, the Ecole Nationale d'Administration, responsible for the selection and training of all the higher public service. Its place in modern French administration will later be discussed in some detail.[1]

In France, as in Belgium, the civil service unions achieved their aim of recognition as part of the machinery of government. They were, in fact, illegal during the 1920's, though informally recognised. The pressure of the unions and their supporters in the political parties grew, and achieved success with the promulgation in 1946 of a General Statute of the Public Service which could reasonably be regarded as a charter embodying the aims of the civil service unions.[2]

Finally, in Italy, there was an intensive movement to reform public administration in the years after the war. The Constitutional Assembly wrote exhaustive reports on the subject, and a special office of reform was set up to make proposals.[3] Its work was published in 1953, and the following year the government was given power to prepare a new statute covering the whole field of public employment, with special provisions concerning careers. This was promulgated in 1956, and forms the present basis for public service law in Italy.

This chapter has attempted to pick out and explain the principle problems and developments of public administration

[1] For a summary of the position in Europe just before the war, see: R. Didesheim: 'La formation et le recrutement du cadre administratif supérieur.' *RISA*, 1939. pp. 279–316. For the ENA, see p. 115.

[2] This did not bring satisfaction, however. See M. Ragon: 'Le CGT et la fonction publique.' *Revue Administrative*, 1950. p. 39. And p. 133.

[3] Presidenza del Consiglio dei Ministri: *Stato dei Lavori per la Riforma della Pubblica Amministrazione*, 1948–1953. 3 vols. Rome, 1953.

in western Europe. It should serve as an introduction to the rest of the book, putting into perspective those issues which call for closer attention: the training and recruitment of civil servants, their conditions of service, relations between politics and administration, methods of controlling administrative acts. It also shows the emergence of the civil service in Europe as a distinct profession, with most of the distinguishing features of the classical professions: self-recruitment, self-discipline, self-government, and sustained efforts to prevent outsiders from interfering in its internal affairs. But it is unique in that its members deal with the whole range of public affairs, and not only one particular aspect. There is, indeed, an innate contradiction in the concept of a profession of government which gives rise to many peculiarities and paradoxes that will have to be touched upon.

Three important matters are not dealt with in this book. First, no attempt is made to cover in detail the British public services. To do so would have overburdened the text to little purpose.[1] Instead, I have drawn on British experience in general terms, examining British preconceptions in the light of continental ideas and experience.

Second, statistics are not used in this book. At the outset it seemed possible that a study of civil service statistics might reveal interesting points of comparison, particularly regarding personnel policies and standards of living. But the material available is at present quite inadequate for such a study. It is extremely difficult to obtain from each country strictly comparable, up-to-date figures, and quite impossible to get them over a long enough period to show trends. Even if this material could be collected, attempted comparisons would probably be highly misleading in many cases; definitions vary, and so do budgeting and accounting methods. Standards of living are notoriously difficult to compare, and there seems little point in listing salary scales (which would in any case be out of date within six months) in various currencies and with no possibility of relating them to national cost of living figures. Of one point there is no doubt, and it is of interest to the English reader: the British civil servant has a far higher salary than his opposite

[1] A comprehensive account of British central administration already exists: W. J. M. Mackenzie and J. Grove: *Central Administration in Britain*. London, 1957.

number in any European country, and he enjoys a considerably higher standard of living. This is true for all grades.

Lastly, there will be no theoretical discussion of the nature of the state and the legal relationship between civil servants and the state. The reason is that this would require a book in itself. It would involve a comparative analysis of the constitutional and public law of the countries dealt with here at a high level of abstraction and couched in juristic terms. My own position is that I feel Duguit's view of the relations between the civil servant and the state is the most satisfactory advanced so far; it seems to me the most realistic, humane, and free from mumbo-jumbo. This personal preference is likely to colour some judgments in this book. It is responsible, for instance, for a preference for regarding civil servants as servants of the state rather than of the Crown, for an antipathy for prerogative and sovereign powers, and for a desire to demythologise the process of government.

PART ONE

COMPOSITION

CHAPTER 1

The Extent of the Public Service

In the most logical system of public administration there would be a clear division between local and national services; the national services would be operated by central ministries, and local services would be run by local administrations. There would then be a clear distinction between national public officials and local public officials. The first would be covered by the British term civil servants, the latter by the term local government officers.

Unfortunately in no country is it as simple as this, and the purpose of this chapter is to attempt to describe the difficulties inherent in the concept of 'the public service' in western Europe. The classical pattern has to be modified in two ways. First, many services run on a national basis by state authorities have a special status which marks them off from the normal ministerial structure; the personnel of these public services may or may not be regarded as public officials.

Second, the operation of some national services has always entailed some of its servants working far from the centre scattered over the country. For instance, judges at assizes, customs officers in ports, tax collectors in provincial capitals, army commanders in garrison towns, foreign diplomats abroad, are all regarded as part of the country's national services, and are nominally recruited and paid by a central government authority. Some countries have gone further than this, and have on grounds of national policy insisted that certain powers, in particular the police power, are of their nature state powers, and that any local authority exercising such powers does so subject to state control. When exercising those powers an official becomes in part a state official.

The development of modern public services has been rapid,

and not generally well thought out. The result is that few countries have a coherent pattern of public services. New services have been created without considering which of the traditional forms of administration would best suit their particular needs, and sometimes traditional forms were rejected as unsuitable even though the alternative forms used had at least as many faults.

We examine first the traditional form of administration by ministry, then the newer national authorities which have escaped from the ministries, and finally the various manifestations of national government inside local government authorities.

GOVERNMENT BY MINISTRY

Ministries are still the nucleus of central administration in every country. In the past there were normally five great ministries, each responsible for one of the primordial fields of government. These were the ministries for Foreign Affairs, Justice, Finance, Defence and War, and Internal Affairs. The first four ministries had reasonably clearly defined fields of administration, and the public services they provided fitted into a coherent pattern. The fifth ministry had the residual powers of government, as ministries for Home Affairs and of the Interior still have everywhere in Europe today. The powers of government not explicitly assigned to or assumed by another central authority fall under the jurisdiction of this ministry.

In the past this meant of course that it had very extensive powers. It was responsible for transport, highways, education, trade, agriculture, church affairs, for the poor, for law and order. With the modern growth of public services some of these residual powers have increased in importance and split off from the ministry of the Interior to become special departments, and later separate ministries. Today most countries have separate ministries of Education, Agriculture, Transport, Trade, and so on.

Then there is a third category of ministries which deal with services not envisaged before the new social pressures of the nineteenth century: National Insurance, Pensions, Social Security, Health. Some countries have gone further along these lines than others; some have tried to restrict the number of new ministries by keeping related fields of administration under a single composite ministry.

The smallest central government is to be found in Switzerland with seven ministries: the Political Department (foreign affairs), the Department of the Interior, the Department of Justice and Police, the Military Department, the Department of Finance and Customs, the Department of Public Economy, and the Department of Posts and Railways.[1] The Finnish government has eight ministries, not having a special department for posts and railways, but having one for education and another for social affairs.[2] The Portuguese government consists of twelve ministries: the ministries of the Interior, Justice, Finance, War, the Navy, Foreign Affairs, Public Works, Colonies, Communications, National Insurance, National Education, and Public Economy.[3]

Sweden has the most advanced and complex system of public administration based on ministries. The constitution specifies that there must be not less than eight departments of state whose ministers form the nucleus of the cabinet. These eight original departments of state have now grown to eleven. They are the ministries of Justice, Foreign Affairs, Defence, Social Affairs, Interior, Communications, Finance, Education and Ecclesiastical Affairs, Agriculture, Commerce, and Supply.

These ministries are very small, some of them having no more than a dozen or so officials who are in effect the personal staff of the minister. The reason for this is a pronounced dualism in the Swedish system of government: the political direction of the country is in the hands of the cabinet assisted by the staffs of the different ministries: the bulk of administration is the responsibility of about sixty royal boards. Every ministry, except the ministry of Foreign Affairs, has a number of these royal boards attached to it. The ministries of Social Affairs, Interior, Communications, Finance and Commerce have the largest number of royal boards attached to them. The ministry of Social Affairs, for instance, has the Royal Social Board in charge of unemployment insurance, child welfare,

[1] G. Sauser-Hall: *Guide Politique Suisse*. Lausanne, 1947. p. 170. seq.
[2] V. Merikoski: *Précis de Droit Public de la Finlande*, Helsinki, 1934. p. 33.
[3] M. Caetano: *Manual de Direito Administrativo*. 4th. ed. Coimba, 1957. p. 360.

and poor relief, the National Pension Board for disability, sickness and old age pension schemes, the National Institute of Insurance for accident insurance, the Labour Council Board for administering factory and labour legislation, the Labour Board for dealing with labour disputes and arbitration, and the Labour Market Board for administering the labour exchanges. The ministry of Communications has a group of extremely strong and important royal boards: the Royal Postal Board, the Royal Telegraph Board, the Royal Railway Board, the Road and Waterways Commission, the Hydro-electric Board, the Board of Public Works, and the National Meteorological and Hydrological Institute.

Each royal board has its own statutory powers contained in its Letter of Instruction. These Instructions specify the work for which the royal board is to be responsible, lay down the size and extent of its administration, sometimes impose conditions to be observed in recruiting qualified members of its staff, define the responsibilities of the various members of the directing board, and they nearly always make the board responsible for following work in related fields in other countries.[1]

Within the terms of their Instructions the royal boards are very independent. In the slow and methodical tradition of the Swedish parliament, advice and opinions from all relevant sources are collected before legislation. The opinion of a royal board is always sought before legislation affecting its field of activity. Its advice is given independently of the ministry, and may sometimes conflict with the ministry's views. It seems important to the Swedes that when parliament legislates it should be in full possession of all the facts and all views, and should not rely solely on a ministry's evaluation of facts, as the latter may suppress discordant evidence, and assess divergent expert opinion to suit its own view. But the system has obvious disadvantages for civil servants with a passionate desire for anonymity.

The royal boards are dependent on the ministries for their finance. Each board drafts its own budget and presents it to the ministry, which alone is authorized to present estimates to par-

[1] D. Philip: 'L'Administration Centrale Suédoise.' *Revue Administrative*, 1954. pp. 679–83.

liament. This can be a source of disagreement, and the budget may conceivably be used as an instrument for ministerial tutelage. Letters of Instruction specify that the royal board shall act subject to the overriding control of the minister, who shall be able to give general directions. This indeed seems to be the minimum control practicable.

On the whole relations between the boards and the ministries are handled with tact and discretion. Disagreements clearly arise from time to time, but these are for the most part settled through discussions between the director general of the board and the state secretary at the ministry. Parliament has no direct authority over the boards, but a major disagreement between board and ministry could have political repercussions if differences are not smoothed over informally. Parliament theoretically has to ask the minister's permission before calling a board's director general as a witness, but in practice it often communicates with him directly. If a director general feels strongly about a disagreement with his ministry, it is not impossible for him discreetly to provoke a member of parliament to ask questions.

The Swedish method of absorbing major public services into the standard forms of central administration is to be found elsewhere in Europe. This is particularly true for the railways and the post office. As early as 1902–3 the Swiss Federal Railways were formed by the amalgamation of four major private companies. The Federal Railways are under the direct supervision of the department of Posts and Railways, within which the railway administration has the status of a general directorate with a large measure of internal autonomy. The general directorate is composed of three senior officials and there is also a conseil d'administration whose members are nominated by the Assemblée Fédérale from distinguished figures in public life.

In Germany both posts and railways are run on similar lines. In some German Länder the railway network was from the beginning a state undertaking. Prussia and Saxony took over their systems from private companies in difficulties. After the 1918 war the railways were brought under federal control, partly because of post-war transport difficulties, and partly because of reparations. A public company was formed under the control of the federal Minister of Transport. After some vicissitudes its position was finally determined in 1951 by the Federal Railway Law which made it into a federal authority under the supervision of the Minister of Transport with some autonomy and a governing board nominated by the government.

Its personnel are regarded as state officials, except for a large group of manual employees who are covered by agreements between the trade unions and management. 180,000 of the 550,000 personnel employed are, in the full sense of the word, Beamten, and have the rights and duties laid down in the Federal Civil Service Law of 1953.[1]

The German postal services are also run by a federal authority, whose staff are Beamten; it has rather less internal autonomy than the railways; for example, it has no separate governing board.

A very special public service is the Waterstaat in Holland, the organization responsible for the construction and maintenance of the dykes and polders. This comes under the ministry of Public Works.[2] Already the first constitution of 1815 stated that 'the Waterstaat will remain one of the country's primary interests; it will be directed by a special administration nominated by and under the control of the Sovereign Prince'. The present organization leaves responsibility for detailed administration to the elected executives of the provinces, while ministry of Public Works engineers act as technical superintendents.

Holland is divided into five Waterstaat regions, with at the head of each an engineer-in-chief. The regions are divided into sectors, with an engineer in charge of each. The engineers-in-chief are in direct and continual contact with the provincial authorities, and the sector engineers with the syndics of the polders and the municipalities in their areas. They are concerned with checking the work of the local authorities, with giving technical advice and assistance, and with making recommendations to the ministry after local enquiries. In time of imminent danger the state Waterstaat services under the

[1] W. Friedmann and H. Hufnagel: 'The Public Corporation in Germany.' In symposium: *The Public Corporation*, ed. Friedmann. London, 1954. p. 140 seq.

[2] A. G. Maris: Le 'Waterstaat.' *RISA*, 1951. p. 3 seq.

engineers-in-chief assume exceptional powers, and have complete authority over all dykes, drains and protective works.

The Waterstaat works closely with the rest of the Directorate General of Roads and Bridges, since roads themselves in Holland form an important part of the protective system.

The officials of the state Waterstaat, including the engineers, are all civil servants; those employed by the provincial authorities and by the syndics of the polders are provincial or private employees. No other country has an organization quite like the Waterstaat, probably because no other country is faced with the same type of problem as the Dutch.

OTHER STATE INSTITUTIONS

The traditional European method of dealing with new public services has been either to create a new ministry or a special directorate with some degree of autonomy attached to a ministry. When this was not possible or desirable the alternative has been to set up an autonomous public law authority. This type of institution originated in Germany where the öffentliche Anstalt has long been a common form of public administration.

The öffentliche Anstalt has two special characteristics: first, it can be set up at every level of government, from the municipality to the federation. Second, it has no general competence; it is created by statute for a specific purpose, and may not go beyond the terms of this statute. It is 'an aggregate of personal and institutional elements which are vested in a public administrative institution and permanently dedicated to a specific public purpose'.[1]

Its public law status has important consequences. It is now generally accepted that the relations between an öffentliche Anstalt and third parties are governed by public law, and in certain fields, such as contracts and liabilities, this gives it certain privileges. An additional consequence is that its officials are regarded as public officials, and they have the full status of Beamten, with special rights and duties. These institutions have however become so numerous that in order to avoid too great an increase in the number of Beamten many of the posts are classified as öffentliche Angestellten, which is a recognised civil

[1] Mayer, quoted by Friedmann and Hufnagel, loc cit.

service category, but does not carry the same status, prestige, or rights as Beamten.

Oeffentliche Anstalten range from universities, museums, polytechnics and radio stations to social insurance boards, credit and mortgage banks, and national insurance companies. They are always subject to the overall supervision of the public body which created them; in all important cases this is a Land ministry.[1]

The French établissement public is in many ways similar to the German öffentliche Anstalt. In French law a distinction is made between the établissement public and the régie. The établissement public, like the öffentliche Anstalt, is an institution of public law possessing some degree of autonomous administration. Public services run en régie, on the other hand, are operated directly by the public authority. French jurists regard the administration of justice, or the administration of the tobacco monopolies found in many countries, as services run en régie[2]. In the normal way people employed in either a régie or an établissement public are public officials; those in institutions are state officials, those in institutions created national by local authorities are communal or departmental officials.

These distinctions gave rise to no great problem once the famous Blanco case decision of 1873 had laid down the sense henceforth to be given to the term 'a public service'.[3] The difficulties that have arisen in the last decade originate in the status of the new nationalised industries which are clearly providing national public services, but which for various reasons have been given a statutory basis half way between public and private law. There is a serious difficulty about the notion of 'public service' because the ways in which the French Railways, gas and electricity undertakings, banks, the Renault works, and mines have been made into state controlled public services have little in common with the traditional juridical forms. It has been suggested that these services might constitute a special category of industrial or commerical services, using an ostensive definition that industrial and commercial state public services are those 'which function under the same or similar conditions

[1] K. E. von Turegg: *Lehrbuch des Verwaltungsrechts*. Berlin, 1954. pp. 81–7.
[2] A. De Laubadère: *Traité élémentaire de Droit Administratif*. Paris, 1953. p. 37.
[3] See p. 238.

as private industrial or commercial companies'. As a definition it has been severely attacked by the best jurists. It clearly cannot make any valid distinction between the French Railways and the Post Office.[1]

But the definition of the term 'public service' has important practical results where the civil service is concerned. The employees of these national industrial and commercial services are specifically excluded from the terms of the civil service Statute of 1946. Consequently they have obtained the social and financial benefits associated with private enterprise, while at the same time their bargaining strength has been so great that they have obtained virtually the same rights to pensions, security of tenure and special disciplinary procedures as the civil service proper.[2] This has caused bad feeling amongst the mass of civil service employees. The discrepancies are very marked. A typist in the civil service who in 1956 got 475,000 francs a year with a pension of 240,000 francs, would, had she been employed by a nationalized industry, have got 600,000 francs and a pension of 420,000 francs. The salary structure is such that in the gas and electricity industries alone there are over 500 people with salaries at a level reached by only a handful of the most senior officials in the whole civil service. In addition there are private enterprise benefits which no civil servant ever obtains. A senatorial commission of enquiry found that a director of the electricity industry whose official salary in 1956 was 2,179,000 francs in fact drew a gross salary of 4,109,000 francs after various benefits had been added.

The French in fact nationalized their industries almost as irrationally as the British. Not only is this sector the untidiest branch of public law, which will take all the logic of French jurists many years to unravel; it is also a piece of political incompetence which has had serious results on the morale of the lower ranks of the French civil service.

French nationalizations took the form they did for both financial and political reasons.[3] The financial reasons advanced were that these national industrial and commercial enterprises

[1] Loc cit. pp. 616–17.

[2] R. Fusilier: 'Le statut du personnel des entreprises nationalisées comparé au statut des agents de la fonction publique.' *Revue de Droit Public*, May, 1956.

[3] R. Gardellini and P. Couaillier: 'L'intervention de l'Etat dans le domaine économique.' *Revue Administrative*, 1952. pp. 244, 254 and 454.

had to be free from treasury control and their finances had to be based on a system of commercial accounting. This was always an unsatisfactory argument: there was nothing to prevent parliament giving a statutory basis to special accounting procedures if it wished. Furthermore, while gas and electricity enterprises were in municipal hands they conformed to the normal rules of public accounting, and at the time no criticism was made of their lack of commercial ability. Moreover there are clearly no special duties which distinguish these and most of the other industries from the highly complex operations of the postal services.

Political pressure came from both Left and Right. The Right, hostile to all forms of public enterprise which provide no immediate benefit to private industry, was even more hostile to such services being state services. The caricature of the civil service which the Right has always painted, ended by being taken seriously by its authors. On the Left the communist trade unions, while insisting on nationalization, held that it should not entail an increase in the size and power of the state's machinery of government. 'By nationalization,' said the CGT, 'we mean that national property should be put under the control of those directly interested, the producers and the consumers.'[1] This dichotomy between State and Nation has a long history in French political thought and in this case was strengthened by the obvious political advantages which might accrue to a strongly organized political trade union movement.

The result of these pressures is evident in the present structure of the nationalized industries in France. Despite consistent attempts by ministries to increase their control, these enterprises have built up a new form of feudalism and treat with each other and with the government as equals. By persistent efforts parliament has succeeded in bringing them under much closer public control than in Britain, but they remain a formidable economic force which is only barely kept in check. Should they become financially independent of the government they may well prove impervious to outside pressure and direction. Meanwhile no satisfactory answer has been given to the question why the bulk of their employees should not be regarded as an

[1] R. Drago: 'French Public Corporations.' In Symposium: *The Public Corporation*, ed. Friedmann. London, 1954. pp. 108–37.

ordinary branch of the public service, recruited and paid in the normal way.

We have covered the Swedish and German methods of absorbing public services as far as possible into the traditional system of public administration, the Dutch hybrid Waterstaat, and the inconsistencies of the French nationalizations. Far removed from all these is the Italian and Spanish system of leaving public services in private hands while bolstering them with extensive state assistance through special institutions. The Spanish system is a direct copy (adapted to local conditions) of the Italian system, which alone will be dealt with here.[1]

The origins of the Italian system lie partly in the peculiarly predatory nature of Italian capitalists, partly in the depression of 1929, partly in the policy of economic autarchy of the Fascist régime. In the first decades of the twentieth century a small number of extremely influential finance groups gained control of the major banks and the most important industrial groups. The resources of the industrial companies were used to extend the speculative activities of the banks and the finances of the banks were used to back newspapers, political groups, subsidiary companies, and co-operatives which would assist the banks in obtaining further benefits from the state or the taxpayer.[2] When, in the post-war era, a series of spectacular crashes shook the Italian economy, the state was incited to step in with moratoriums and guarantees to protect these societies from the consequences of their own mistakes. No Italian government has ever been able to stand against these groups which are few in number but which control large sectors of the labour market. The threat of large-scale unemployment (in addition to that which always exists) has always sufficed to obtain state co-operation.

At various times, through various institutions, and under various governments, the state has acquired large holdings in different sectors of the national economy. Its shareholdings have either come through advances made to companies in difficulties, or through taking over more or less bankrupt firms whose

[1] It should be noted, however, that in every country the state has holdings in private companies, sometimes amounting to almost the entire paid-up capital. There are several instances given in Friedmann: *The Public Corporation*, op. cit.

[2] E. Rossi: *Lo Stato Industriale*. Rome, 1953. pp. 56–7.

work was regarded as nationally important, or through the support given ab initio to industries proposing extensions in fields which the state thought interesting. For instance, all the capital goods required for the operation of the East African transport system were provided by the state free of charge to the private company which had undertaken to operate the service.

Such is the extent of the Italian State's share in the national economy that if its true powers were exercised Italy could be transformed overnight, without further legislation, into the most advanced socialist society in western Europe. The state has holdings amounting to 99 % of the coal industry, 85 % of the anthracite industry, 80 % of ship building capacity, 80 % of the air transport system, 80 % of the production of pig iron, over 50 % of the telephone industry, the production of natural gas and of mercury, substantial interests in steel production, the motor car industry, railway construction, and a variety of interests which are hard to determine in the chemical industry, and in the tourist, hotel and cinema trade. It also controls some of the most important banks.[1]

These holdings were controlled mainly by the Directorate General of State Domains in the Ministry of Finance, and by a special body, the Instituto per la Ricostruzione Industriale (IRI). But other ministries had interests as well, and the legal, economic, and political position of all the various companies and enterprises in which the state had a direct or indirect interest was so complicated that when La Malfa, as minister without portfolio, reported on them in 1951, he described the whole sector as 'una selva infinita'.[2] By that time the minister had arrived at over a thousand different undertakings, not counting provincial or communal ramifications which would have pushed the number into several thousands. Their status, their structure, the forms of control to which they were subject and their place within the machinery of government were utterly incoherent. Some were public bodies, some private firms, some technically autonomous state institutions. The legal status of

[1] G. Cosmo: 'Le Partecipazioni economiche dello Stato.' In *Quaderni di Cultura e Storia sociale.* January, 1953.

[2] Relazione La Malfa: *La Riorganizzazione delle Partecipazioni economiche dello Stato.* Rome, 1952.

some of these enterprises was so obscure that the courts were continually giving widely divergent judgements as to their position. Firms in exactly the same business were purely by historical accident in some cases under the Directorate General of State Domains, in others under IRI or under other different ministries. The control exercised over different industries varied from a purely formal approval of accounts to the nomination of directors, while sometimes the statutory instruments defining the form control should take had never been made at all. In several cases the state owned the entire capital but the firms remained private firms; for instance, the Cogne works of the Val d'Aosta with its subsidiaries is entirely state owned and the shares are vested in the Directorate General of State Domains; the Domains also holds all the shares in the Metane gas company, in the Cinematographic Industry, in the company which owns Cinecittà. The whole stock of the Banca Nazionale del Lavoro is held by the Treasury. Critics have claimed, apparently with some justification, that there were two reasons for these absurdities. First, that by maintaining these firms as private companies they could be administered directly by the ministerial directors without giving parliament any chance to intervene and check their operations. Second, that by having this wide variety of enterprises in their hands senior officials were able to appoint themselves and their colleagues to lucrative directorships as state nominees. The Roman bureaucracy has a bad name in Italy, and some of the wilder accusations are probably untrue, but it certainly seems clear that some officials had become important figures in industry in their own right. It is undoubtedly true that in certain ministries, such as the Treasury, Finance and the Interior, senior officials regard appointment as directors as almost a vested right, and the additional salaries, bonuses, expense accounts, and so on, form an important part of the emoluments of high administrative office. Eight of the thirteen directors of IRI itself are officials. Of these eight the Auditor General, the director general of State Domains, and the director general of Industry are presumably appointed for their professional competence, but the others are members of the ministries of Posts and Telegraphs, Merchant Navy, Labour and Defence; they are not apparently appointed because of special knowledge useful in administering

IRI affairs, but simply because they have reached a certain rank in their respective departments.[1]

To meet criticism the government decided to introduce a measure of reform, a bill to set up a new ministry to take over all the state holdings. The bill was steered through parliament by a jurist who had previously been in charge of the post-war reform of Italian central administration. The bill became law in 1956, and the new ministry of State Holdings was created in 1957.[2] Its task is to act as holding agency for state shares in all branches of industrial and commercial activity and to assume responsibility for their supervision instead of the ministries. Fears were voiced in parliament and the commissions that such a ministry in the hands of civil servants would rapidly become a top-heavy bureaucracy, interfering in all aspects of economic life. To avoid this as far as possible, the law lays down that the ministry is to have only a secretary general and not a director general, a title traditionally associated with a large and extensive department. Furthermore, the ministry is simply divided into two inspectorates, one for administration and one for economic affairs. As a final obstacle (it is hoped) to bureaucratic elephantiasis, the law lays down the maximum number of one hundred staff to be employed in the ministry. Another fear was that the ministry would act as a honey pot for all the opportunists in the civil service who might hope that an early footing in such a ministry would lead to interesting posts later. It was clear that the parliamentary commission distrusted the senior members of the administration at least as much as the middle-ranking officials who might merely be seeking rather more rapid promotion. Anticipating manoeuvring from many ministerial directors, the parliamentary commission wrote into the law the provision that the three posts of secretary general and inspectors general at the head of the new ministry could, for an initial period of five years, be filled by people from outside the service. The persons appointed could be instantly removed without cause; only in this way could proper political responsibility be ensured. Similarly, with an eye to the pretensions of lower officials, the commission laid down that the other posts in the new ministry were to be filled by competitive

[1] E. Rossi: op. cit. p. 129.

[2] R. Lucifredi: *Sul Ministero delle Partecipazioni statali.* Rome, 1956.

examination between already established officials. It is hoped that the new ministry will be able to absorb some of the best elements of the defunct ministry of Italian Africa.[1]

LOCAL AND REGIONAL GOVERNMENT

All European countries have subordinate levels of administration in which state officials are employed, and there is rarely a clear distinction between local and central government.

Throughout Europe the province or department is a standard area of administration for all state services which require a field service. Better communications have meant that some state services operate on a regional basis, but these regions are groups of provinces or departments, and their boundaries do not cut across provincial borders.

In each province therefore a considerable number of state officials work for central government administrations: tax collection, education, communications, police, social services, agriculture, public works, health, and so on, have their own representatives and permanent staffs.

This section is primarily concerned with the status of central government officials in local government, but a digression is perhaps necessary at this point. Of all the state services operating throughout a country the most delicate to organize properly are the police forces. Every country has to face the dilemma that a national police force is more efficient than a group of autonomous local police forces, but that a thoroughly efficient national police force can become the most vexatious form of tyranny. The police is a unique public service and the extent to which it is under impartial outside control affects not only the day-to-day lives of citizens but also the whole atmosphere of government. Something must be said of this problem.

No country in Europe organizes its police system independently of ministerial control, although, of course, the Nazis did so. Nor are there nowadays any separate ministries of Police as there were in Fouché's time.

Instead, police forces are nowadays either organized under a

[1] There is also a Minister for State Holdings in Germany; but his task is to dispose of the companies which were confiscated from the Nazis at the end of the war or which had no legal owner. Their value is about 6 billion marks.

central ministry, the ministry of the Interior or the ministry of Justice; or they are put in the hands of local authorities subject to some central control. There are also, however, intermediate arrangements in which there is a centrally organized police service for certain functions, and local authority police forces for all the rest.

(i) The federal states of Germany and Switzerland have an extra level of police organization, the federal police service. In both countries this is a small group of officers drawn from state or cantonal police services without direct recruitment. They are never concerned with the elementary form of policing, the maintenance of public order, but with more specialized functions: criminal investigation of particularly widespread and complicated crimes, the compilation and registration of criminal identification records, special forensic medicine research, counter-espionage, the provision of specialists at the disposal of local forces, and relations with the international police commission. In Germany the federal police service comes under the federal Minister of the Interior but has its headquarters in Wiesbaden; in Switzerland it constitutes a special division of the ministry of Justice. The federal ministry of the Interior in Germany also has a special police office which co-ordinates the work of the federal police, makes general regulations for overall police legislation throughout the country, and controls the activities and deployment of the *Bereitschaftspolizei*.

(ii) The countries with a centralized police force are mainly those in the Napoleonic tradition: France, Italy, Spain and Portugal. Some German Länder have a predominantly centralized police service, and for special reasons Denmark has too. The principle behind the centralized police force is twofold. First, that the state has (and ought to have) a monopoly of coercive power, and this should never be entrusted to persons not subject to the control of the state. Second, that small communal police forces are open to corruption and are inevitably inefficient. Thus, local communal or town police forces are subject to the control of the mayor or some other state authority, and their responsibility is limited to maintaining order in the area, to the prevention of crime, and to ensuring the orderly execution of the law. Beyond this the state police forces intervene.

The state police forces are normally of two kinds, again closely following the Napoleonic model. First, there is a country police force which not only polices rural areas but also acts as a military police organization in time of war, and provides contingents of military police for normal peace time provost duties; these are the *gendarmerie* in France, the *guardia civil* in Spain and Portugal, the *carabinieri* in Italy. This force is organized, recruited, paid, and partly controlled by the Army. Second, there is the state police properly so-called, with general responsibilities for public order, the investigation of crime, the compilation of records, and assisting the judicial authorities in all enquiries; it normally also includes special sections for police intelligence work and for counter-espionage. It has a general competence throughout the country. It is organized on a pyramidical basis, with contingents in each province, stationed in the main towns, and with special investigation squads attached to the regional judicial authorities. It is run by a central division for police affairs in the ministry of the Interior, which operates both directly through its hierarchy of officials, and indirectly in policy matters through the local governor or prefect. It is called the Sûreté Nationale in France, the Polizia Armada in Spain, the Pubblica Sicurezza in Italy.

The disadvantages of this system are obvious. The opportunities for abuse open to unscrupulous politicians or corrupt officials are very great, and difficult to detect. While financial corruption and illicit freedom from prosecution are the price of over-localized forces, corruption of power is too often the price paid for over-centralized forces, and this is much more dangerous. The extent of the police problem varies considerably from country to country in western Europe, and few foreigners appreciate the enormous difficulty of policing cities like Amsterdam, Naples or Marseilles. Many technical police matters are too often overlooked from the outside; for instance, the need for rapid reinforcement in times of crisis, and the special difficulties of dense and potentially explosive populations. It is worth remarking that whenever the English have had to deal with a volatile and vivacious population they have always adopted a Napoleonic type of police force: in Ireland, for instance, and in the colonies.

Denmark has a special problem which is unique in western

Europe, but not uncommon in other parts of the world. A widely spread agricultural population with only one important city is likely to be at a loss as to how to recruit and properly train enough efficient policemen. To leave this to local authorities produces a body of men able to cope with only the simplest and most elementary forms of disturbance and crime. For this reason the Danes have accepted the nationalization of the police service; all police recruits spend their initial two years training and probation in the Copenhagen police (thereby incidentally ensuring a regular flow of men to the city); they are there grounded in all aspects of police work, and when they are later transferred to rural or small town communities they arrive already adequately trained. This is probably the only solution to Denmark's particular problem.

(iii) In several German Länder, in most of the Swiss cantons, in Sweden, Belgium, Holland, and England, the police service is a mixture of central and local forces. England only barely comes into this category, since the one force which has a national character, the Metropolitan Police, only assists local forces, and then only by invitation. It has no direct right to operate nationally, except for its Special Branch concerned with subversive movements.

In Holland, the Swiss cantons, and some of the German Länder, urban areas above a certain size are entitled to maintain their own independent forces; rural areas, and urban communities with small populations, are policed by a state force. This force is a modified version of the gendarmerie. It may have special functions, in policing, for example, the Dutch waterways which are of vital national importance.

In Belgium local police forces are independent, but criminal investigation work, counter-espionage, and crime records are matters for the director of public security in the ministry of Justice, and he has under his control a regionally organized police force responsible for this specialized work.

Sweden has a state police, but organized it only contre-cœur. Like the British, the Swedes were hostile to a centralized police force for fear that it would degenerate into a tyranny. But grave disturbances in the 1930's, and serious and widespread unrest in the mining area of Luleå, finally forced the government to re-consider their opposition. A state police was created which is primarily designed to act as an emergency force to maintain public order, and to operate in under-policed areas where local authorities cannot properly be expected to maintain sufficient forces. The important element in the Swedish system, however, is that there is no direct recruitment to the state police and therefore no possibility of creating a para-military force with a special esprit de corps and isolated from the population among which it lives. The force is composed of men seconded from the local police forces. The state police operate partly under the control of the chief constable in whose area they are stationed, partly on the orders of a small group of full-time officers with both police and judicial functions. The force is paid and deployed by the ministry of the Interior. Sweden offers here an excellent compromise solution.

To return now to the extent to which state officials are to be found in local government. The first complication is this. In all countries of western Europe there are at least two levels of local government, the commune and the province. They are to be found in France, Belgium, Italy, Spain, Portugal, Denmark, Sweden, Norway and Holland. Italy has a third level; according to the Constitution of 1948 all the provinces of Italy should be grouped together into nineteen regions, each region having a regional council and a regional executive exercising its own powers. In fact these constitutional provisions have been applied to only four areas, those with a strong tradition of separatism, the South Tyrol, Val d'Aosta, Sardinia, and Sicily. Each of these regions has its own special constitution with its own regional authorities. Although their powers vary all have an elected regional council and a regional executive. Attached to each of them is a government high commissioner who holds a watching brief for the central government and has reserve powers over the police and other regional activities. This means that in Italy in addition to ordinary provincial and communal officials there are regional officials directly employed by the region, and some central government officials working in the region in charge of the state services which have remained under central government control.

Germany and Switzerland offer further complications. In some German Länder there are four levels of government, to which must be added the federal authorities, making five levels in all. They are the commune; the grouping of rural communes, the Kreis (larger towns are excluded from the Kreis); the Bezirk; the Land; the federation. Each commune has its Bürgermeister (in larger towns Oberbürgermeister) and communal council, each Kreis its Landrat and Kreistag, each Bezirk its Regierungspräsident, each Land its set of ministries and president; the federation the federal ministries and other federal authorities.

At all five levels there are public officials. This situation is unique in western Europe. The German definition of Beamter ('public official') is that he is a person who is in a public law service relationship with any public law corporation.[1] Each Land has its public service law based on the federal law; for example, 'This law applies to all authorities, and all established and unestablished posts in all public law corporations in the Land Hesse. Excluded are the railway, radio, posts and telegraph administrations.'[2]

Since all communes, Kreise, unions of communes (Gemeindeverbände), öffentliche Anstalten, and the Land itself, are all public law authorities, their employees are regarded in German public law as 'public officials', just as the employees of Land or federal ministries. This has important consequences, since the German public official has special rights as well as duties. The special disciplinary process and protection in office apply to all Beamten, irrespective of whether they are employed by a commune, Kreis, Bezirk, ministry or öffentliche Anstalt.[3]

To add to the confusion this special 'public-law service relationship' (which German writers admit to be an ill-defined phrase) does not necessarily imply a person nominated to office by the state or other public law body. The quality adheres to the office, not to the appointing body. Thus, an elected mayor, or an elected Landrat is in a public-law service relationship with his commune or Kreis, and he is therefore regarded as a Beamter; so Beamten may be elected or appointed. Furthermore, the constitutions of the Länder differ, so that in some Länder Landräte are appointed by the Land government, while

[1] *The Bundesbeamtengesetz*, 1953. Abschnitt I, § 1: defines a federal official as 'Wer zum Bund oder zu einer bundesunmittelbaren Körperschaft, Anstalt oder Stiftung des öffentlichen Rechts in einem öffentlich-rechtlichen Dienst- und Treuverhältnis (Beamtenverhältnis) steht.'

[2] Littman and Wolf: *Hessisches beamtenrecht*. Wiesbaden, 1952.

[3] See below, p. 161.

in Bavaria or Württemberg Baden they are elected by the people. Both, fortunately for our purpose, have the same legal status once in office.

This means, however, that in dealing with 'the civil service' in Germany, one is dealing with a concept which is vastly wider than that used by most countries.

In Switzerland there are in principle three levels of government, the commune, the canton, and the federation. Certain cantons, however, for instance Canton Bern, have intermediate groupings of communes within the canton, and administration of cantonal services in this area is the duty of a cantonal official, the prefect. In Bern the prefect is an elected official, who once elected becomes a cantonal official. In Vaud, on the other hand, more closely affected by its neighbour France, the prefect is appointed directly by the cantonal government. The real basis of government in Switzerland is, however, still the commune and much communal administration is performed not by officials but by the citizens themselves in an unpaid capacity or as councillors. There are, of course, full-time communal officials in the large towns. Several cantons have regulations governing the employment of both communal and cantonal officials; these cantonal regulations vary from canton to canton, and differ in some important respects from the regulations governing federal officials. In Switzerland, which has by far the most democratic form of public administration in western Europe, to concentrate entirely on federal officials would give a misleading impression. Yet short of regarding Switzerland as a number of different countries (which in some respects it is) federal officials form the only manageable and coherent group for study.

Germany and Switzerland are the most complicated examples. All other countries have two levels of local government, with at each level a council and an executive. In all countries except Spain and Portugal the councils are elected, and even in those two countries they are in a sense elected though by special procedures not recognized as elections elsewhere.

The common pattern is that the communal council elects its own executive, the mayor, and the mayor then assumes some of the police powers of the state, becoming for these functions a subordinate state official, while remaining for all communal functions responsible solely to the council. The position is by no means as simple as this in Sweden where local administration is to a large extent in the hands of committees, each of which has certain powers of administration in its own right, but in other respects is responsible to the council. In Scandinavian countries in general it would be regarded as eccentric to consider any local elected representative as in any way an official, even when, as sometimes happens, powers of administration are devolved to persons or committees by the state.

In Spain and Italy, for various social and political reasons, the senior officials in communes are state officials who form a national corps with its own internal system of appointment and promotion.[1] These communal officials are recruited and trained under the auspices of the national ministry of the Interior, and they always remain subject to ministerial control even though they are appointed to office and paid by the communes. This system has much to commend it in countries with a large and uneducated rural population and with some municipal corruption in larger towns. It ensures a general standard of competence and efficiency which might otherwise be lacking.

Finally, the extreme form of central nomination in local government is to be found in Belgium and Holland where the mayors themselves are appointed by the Crown. In Belgium the bourgmestre is nominated and dismissed by the Crown; in principle he is chosen from the members of the communal council, but with the approval of the députation permanente of the province he may be chosen from outside the council. Together with from two to six échevins (seven for Brussels) he acts as the permanent executive of the commune; some of his powers come from his position as a state official, particularly in the fields of law enforcement, general security and public health. The échevins in the larger cities are more or less full time, are salaried, and are each in charge of a division of communal administration.

Normally it is the provincial governor who recommends a person for bourgmestre to the Minister of the Interior; in the small communes, however, this duty is frequently devolved to the governor's subordinate, the commissaire d'arrondissement.

[1] Ministerio de la Gobernación: *Reglamento de Funcionarios de Administración Local.* Madrid, 1952, and A. Lentini: *L'amministrazione locale.* Como, 1953.

The bourgmestre is always chosen from the political majority, if there is a political majority, and from the senior members of that majority if one of them is clearly indicated. Not infrequently the position is more complicated, and the governor then has to use his discretion to find the bourgmestre who will arouse the least hostility, and at the same time be efficient enough for the job.

In Holland the office of burgermeester is to some extent professionalized. He is appointed to office by the Crown for six years, and may be removed at the end of his period of office, or, under special circumstances, suspended by the commissioner of the Queen for a short time while still in office. The procedure for appointment is that the commissioner of the Queen proposes three names to the Minister of the Interior, who chooses one of them. The commissioner is not required to consult local or national party machines, though the Minister may be asked to justify his choice in parliament. It is fairly common for the Minister not to choose the person at the head of the Commissioner's list; it is suggested that the latter tends to put forward three names chosen from different parties, and the Minister makes the political choice where that is necessary. It is clear that in most cases the local political situation is taken into account. A socialist would hardly be appointed to a municipality with a strong conservative majority, or a catholic to a predominantly protestant area, and in certain provinces such as Limburg the burgermeester is normally chosen from within the province. But there are exceptions to this. For instance, the burgermeester of Arnhem was a catholic for several years after the war even though it is a protestant area.

Vacancies have to be advertised by the ministry. In the smallest communes the man chosen is frequently a person in his early thirties who has been serving in municipal or provincial administration for several years. Sometimes he comes from within the central ministry, but this is unusual in the smallest communes. Medium-sized communes find their mayors from two principal sources: either from the ranks of the fairly senior officials in local and provincial administration, or from the burgermeestern of the small communes. The five largest cities in Holland are in practice treated differently and attract high administrators; for instance, the burgermeester of Amsterdam was previously the director of the State Bank, and the Burgermeester of Eindhoven an ex-Minister of Justice.

Anyone can apply for a post of burgermeester if he is over twenty-five. There may be from twenty to sixty candidates, of whom four or five are serious competitors. The important qualifications are to have had experience of provincial or communal government, to be experienced in local politics, to have the right kind of religious and political background, and to know the commissioner of the Queen. For a young man who starts in a very small commune there is a sort of career which is unofficially recognized in the cabinets of the Commissioners of the Queen; he can reasonably hope for a move to a more populous commune after ten to fifteen years. But the really big posts are likely to be taken by distinguished outsiders who have made their mark in another field of public life.

The interesting point about the Dutch mayoral system is that in some cases it gets close to the city-manager concept; but a city manager recruited and chosen by the central government. He has no dictatorial power since the executive organ of the municipality is the mayor plus the aldermen, and the latter are elected by and from the communal council. It is a form of local administration which seems satisfactorily to combine efficiency, democracy, and the minimum of direct state control. It is, however, unique in western Europe.

In every country there is always a senior state official at the level of the province. He represents the government, and is the chief state official in the area, appointed, paid by and responsible to the central government, normally through the Minister of the Interior. The title of this office varies; governor, civil governor, commissioner of the Queen, provincial governor, prefect. All are based on the same principle: that the government needs its own representatives in the provinces to coordinate the national services operating there, to ensure that local authorities act within the law and use their discretion reasonably, to act as the ultimate authority for maintaining public order, and to act as a focal point for common local interests between different authorities.

The law in every case makes these officials more closely dependent on the government than any other kind of official. The freedom to nominate normally entails a freedom to dismiss without notice or cause. In no country is this power used indiscriminately, and in some countries, for instance Belgium or Sweden, there are very few recent examples of a governor, once appointed, being removed from office before the normal age of retirement. But they are protected by convention rather than by law.

These prefect-governors are not everywhere regarded as state officials. In France, Holland, Italy, Spain, the Scandinavian countries and the German Länder the prefect-governor is a state official, even though of a special kind. But in Belgium the civil service law explicitly excludes the gouverneurs de province; the preliminary clause is quite explicit: 'Ne sont pas agents de l'Etat . . . c) les Gouverneurs de province, les Commissaires d'Arrondissement.' They may therefore either be provincial officials, or, more likely, officials with a special status outside the national civil administration, as are, for instance, army officers or judges.

The prefect-governor has a dual rôle; he is head of the provincial administration, with under him a staff of provincial officials; he is also the representative of the state supervising the exercise of local authorities' discretion; he deals with administrative appeals from local authorities, and he has control powers of varying importance in the fields of public order, public health, education, highways, and town planning.

In Holland and Belgium the executive of the province is a corporate body elected by and from the provincial council; the governor is president of this provincial executive, but the elected members direct and control the different branches of provincial administration. This provincial executive council is a type of local cabinet with a permanent chairman appointed by the government. The principal task of the governors in Holland and Belgium is therefore to keep in touch with local affairs generally and to ensure that the interests of the state and of the province as a whole are duly protected and fostered. In both countries the provincial governors are highly honoured and very distinguished gentlemen drawn from elder statesmen, high administrators and notable figures in law, education or industry. Their primordial rôle of keeping public order has largely disappeared, and they have become focal points for decentralization of state services.

The status of the provincial staff other than the prefect-governors presents some problems. Normally the prefect-governor has, as his immediate collaborators in charge of the principal sections of administration, two or three state officials, nominated, like himself, by the government; for instance, the greffier provincial in Belgium, the secrétaire général in France, or the landssekreteraren and the landskamreren in charge respectively of general administration and of financial administration in the Swedish län. All these immediate assistants to the prefect-governor appointed by the ministry rank as state officials and not as provincial officials.

The remainder of the people employed directly in the provincial offices normally have the status of provincial officials; usually they do not have the same rights, the same pay, pensions or conditions of service as state officials. They are in many cases nominated to their posts by the prefect-governor and strictly speaking are more comparable to ordinary communal officials than to state officials. On the other hand, the personnel employed in French prefectures form a national corps of provincial employees, administered by the ministry of the Interior. This is a relatively new departure, and seems already to have given good results in ensuring better career prospects and a higher standard of recruitment.

Co-ordination at a provincial level of the growing services of central ministries is one of the major justifications for the prefect-governor system at the present day. There are clearly many matters which require close and frequent contact between different departments of government, and the formation of a common policy. The general feeling on the continent is that unless there is a single state authority on the spot with a general responsibility and a recognized superiority over other state officials, this co-operation must either consist in informal arrangements between the local heads of services, or be imposed by decisions taken at the centre by ministries. The first alternative is unlikely to result in effective co-operation, while the second is contrary to the principle of divesting central administration of as much detailed administration as possible.

The second justification for the prefect-governor is that decisions and activities of local authorities can be controlled locally, and not by remote control by central officials unaware of local circumstances and sentiments. It may be that Britain has developed into such a highly centralized state through lack of such an office. In the absence of a local organ of tested competence in which the government has full confidence, control is inevitably concentrated in the ministries. It is impossible to estimate the actual cost in time and efficiency that this may mean, nor is there any way of measuring the compensating elements of democracy and self-government. But anyone who has examined the work of the Swedish governors or the Dutch commissioners is unlikely to be greatly impressed by the view that these offices are harmful to local self government.

This short survey shows how impossible it is to find a generally accepted definition for the term public official. Some jurists have analysed the concept in very refined terms.[1] Public officials can be classified from different points of view: (i) according to the public body which they serve, e.g. state, province, municipality; (ii) according to the way they perform their duties, individually or in corporation; (iii) according to whether they were elected or nominated to office; (iv) according to whether they are invested with powers of full decision, that is, whether they are agents or authorities; (v) according to whether their service is compulsory (e.g. military service) or voluntary (e.g. ordinary professional public service).

Each country has different arrangements, and regards a different range of officials as 'state' or 'public' officials. It seems best to recognize the fluidity of the term. In this book the title 'civil servant' will be restricted to the permanent official directly engaged in central administration, normally employed in a ministry, but sometimes in the field service of a central government department. 'Public official' will be used as a generic term meaning all the people who are covered by the general statutes or regulations which apply to 'civil servants'. 'State official' will refer to public officials whose salaries are paid directly or indirectly from funds controlled by the state; this will cover people employed in autonomous state institutions.

[1] e.g. Gabriel de Usera: *Legislación de Hacienda*. 3rd. ed. Madrid, 1948. p. 56, and H. Peters: *Lehrbuch der Verwaltung*. Berlin, 1949. pp. 248–53.

CHAPTER 2

Recruitment

In the last hundred years European countries, at varying rates of progress, have attempted to standardize and formalize methods of entry to their public services. Pressure to do so came from two sources. First, the public officials themselves; second, enlightened political and academic opinion. Apart from Prussia and the German states which followed the Prussian tradition, the traditional view of public office was that it was the gift of government. In both monarchical and republican countries this meant in practice the political leaders of the day. There is little point here in elaborating the doctrine of patronage and the spoils system; they are well known. Experience showed this system had two defects: favouritism and inefficiency. The worst effects of favouritism could be offset by tacitly accepting the principle of security of tenure; but efficiency could only be obtained by prescribing some fairly objective tests of merit before appointment.

Some countries were always in advance of others in this field. By 1794 Prussia had developed a highly trained and homogeneous body of public officials as an essential element in creating a strong state. Long and gruelling training prior to acceptance in office, fixed rules of entry and conditions of service encouraged the emergence of a social-bureaucratic élite, but avoided personal favouritism and inefficiency. In France, some of Napoleon's reforms tended in the direction of a state machine based on merit, but he left little behind him in the way of an impartially controlled system of entry to civil office. However, the great technical schools—the Ecole Polytechnique, the Ecole des Mines, and the Ecole des Ponts et Chaussées, which expanded during his time, did provide a route to some of the highest posts of state, entry to which was determined solely by intellectual capacity; if a young man could enter these schools he would not fail for lack of financial backing. The technocratic administrator who emerged from these schools has been an important social and administrative factor in France.

Otherwise France, like other European countries, recruited public officials by political favouritism, exercised generally by ministers. The favour of the minister or of the head of a department acting for the minister was essential both for appointment and promotion. If liberal public opinion reacted to the waste and corruption of such appointments, the officials themselves objected to the system of promotion. This double pressure gradually brought change; basic qualifications for different types of post were specified by law or regulation; appointment and promotion boards were set up within ministries to prevent arbitrary personal choices; advancement not entailing an advance in post but simply an increase of salary was accepted as a means of providing officials with a proper career.

But even today there are great differences in the way European countries organize entry to the civil service. In some countries recruitment is still the concern of individual ministries and services; in others recruitment has been centralized in one organization on a general service basis. In some countries entry can only be obtained after open competitive examination; in others by a comparison of candidates' paper qualifications and recommendations. In some countries there are special requirements for specialized services; for instance the diplomatic corps or the technical corps of the state. This chapter will deal with all these aspects of recruitment.

One preliminary point should be borne in mind. Recruitment is to some extent affected by the general organization of the civil service in a country. Where there are general classes of officials common to the whole service it is a great deal easier to have centralized recruitment. Where the ministries remain strong and independent they are each likely to insist on their own requirements, specify their own ranking system, and refuse to collaborate in attempts to classify their specialists together with the specialists of other ministries.

One can distinguish two patterns in European civil service organization: one in those countries with general classes common to the whole service, the other in those countries which simply list the titles of posts to be found in various ministries. In the latter case it is normal to find that these posts have been roughly formalized into a recognized hierarchy by linking posts to a specific salary scale. Sweden, for instance, classifies its posts according to a recognized pay scale; Holland lists 108 posts classified into a salary scale from 1 to 153. To each number in the scale there is a corresponding income and on this basis officials can be divided into more or less coherent groups and then arranged in broad classes.

Britain, France, Germany, Italy, Austria and Belgium have general classes common to the whole civil service. Generally there are four classes. This is partly due to the common educational pattern in European countries; it is clearly wise to link entry to government service with the various school-leaving ages; for the highest class, entry after graduation at a university; for the intermediate class entry for school leavers at the age of university entry; for the clerical class entry at the point where the first major school examinations are held, age about sixteen. The fourth class are normally drawn from those who have only primary school education, but they may well not enter government service until they are mature men and women, to serve as messengers, porters, chauffeurs, and so on. In all countries ex-servicemen and the partially disabled are given some preference for these posts.

These four classes correspond to the tasks performed by modern public administration. The fourth class of messengers and porters needs no explanation. The third class comprises the staff responsible for mechanical and routine jobs; typists, secretaries, computers, counter clerks. The second class comprises the staff responsible for the detailed management of blocks of routine business, for supervising the work of the third class, for the day to day operation of the more complicated branches of administration, for taking decisions which do not involve questions of administrative principle or the policy of the ministry, and for assisting and preparing work for members of the first class. The first class is responsible for the general supervision of the work of the entire ministry or public service, for preparing and advising on major questions which require ministerial decision, and for dealing with the whole broad field of government policy as it affects and is affected by the work of a ministry or other major public service.

The titles given to these four classes differ from country to country. France has the simplest nomenclature: A, B, C and D. Germany divides the classes into the höherer Dienst, the gehobener Dienst, the mittlerer Dienst and the einfacher Dienst. Italy uses the terms carriere direttive, carriere di concetto, carriere esecutive, and carriere del personale ausiliario. In all these cases the classes coincide with the British division into the administrative class, executive class, clerical class, and the messengerial class.

Standing outside these four general classes, but normally linked to them by comparable wage structures, are the specialists nowadays widely employed in public administration: doctors, scientists, architects, economists, statisticians, draughtsmen, naval constructors, and so on. It is also usual to treat the foreign service and the consular corps as a separate branch of the civil service.

CENTRALIZED RECRUITMENT

Britain, France, Belgium and Holland have central recruiting agencies with some responsibility for the entire civil service. Germany really does not come in this category. In Germany a special office of the federal ministry of the Interior has some responsibility for centralizing recruitment to the federal civil service; but only as regards the appointment of persons who are not already established public officials from Länder governments. The general rule in Germany is for Beamten to be trained and recruited by Länder ministries; recruitment is intimately linked with training as will be seen in a later chapter. Training is invariably the responsibility of either the ministry of Justice or the ministry of the Interior; but there is no single organization for selecting candidates for established posts in ministries; this is done by each individual ministry. Thus, in principle, the recruitment of civil servants in Germany is the work of the personnel departments of individual ministries.

The Dutch and Belgian central personnel organizations are weak compared with those of France and Britain. In Belgium, recruitment always used to be the responsibility of the different ministries. Staff was recruited without any competitive examination or other tests of ability. The directors of the ministry and the minister himself had almost unfettered powers of appointment, and political favouritism was common. Only a long and reasonably honourable bureaucratic tradition (combined with purely departmental rules) prevented Belgian administration from degenerating into a spoils system.[1]

In the 1930s agitation in well-connected circles resulted in the appointment of a commissaire royal, M. Camu. His report recommended the establishment of a permanent and full-time body solely concerned with recruitment; it further proposed that rigorous conditions of entry should be formulated, and that only under very exceptional circumstances should there be any direct entry by persons not satisfying the requirements laid down.

These proposals were accepted, but for various reasons, which included the personality of M. Camu, two bodies were set up instead of the single body he proposed. The first was the secrétariat permanent de recrutement, responsible for the examination and acceptance of new entrants to the civil service. The other was a new directorate, the service d'administration générale, attached to the Prime Minister's office, which should act as the research and advisory body for all matters affecting the reform and working of the civil service.

This was in many ways a sensible and practical arrangement, and if it left unsettled certain border-line matters between the two services, they could have been cleared up with some good will. Instead, the war came, and neither body could undertake its proper tasks. Mass recruitment to undertake the work of newly formed ministries and to cope with the mass of wartime controls left no room for anything but the most cursory examination of individual qualifications. After the war considerable pressure was exercised through the civil service trade unions to transfer these war-time entrants to the permanent staff. The pressure was largely successful, and a series of royal ordinances put whole classes of these officials on a permanent footing. Not for about ten years were properly formalized methods of recruitment re-established under the direction of the secrétariat permanent. Furthermore, ministries are loath to give up their freedom, and they do not always co-operate wholeheartedly

[1] T. H. Reed: *Government and Politics of Belgium*. New York, 1924. p. 95.

with the secrétariat permanent. Indeed the secrétariat permanent finds it difficult, even for the most general classes such as typists or clerical officers, to obtain sufficient co-operation from the ministries to arrange for a single annual examination to meet all requirements; it has been beset with erratic and trivial demands simply to suit the convenience of individual ministries. It will therefore be some time before the secrétariat permanent can set its mark on the quality of the Belgian civil service.

The service d'administration générale was set up with the intention of making it the permanent instrument for administrative reform. In fact, its first rôle was to deal with the complicated and rather chaotic affairs of the civil service during the war. After the war it had to cope with the problems presented by the very great number of temporary civil servants taken on during and after the war, and try to disperse them back to the private sector in face of considerable resistance from the staff and their trade unions. It arranged a series of examinations to weed out those temporary officials who were clearly below standard; but the government was too seriously threatened by the unions and insisted on a lowering of standards despite these examinations, a concession which will have awkward results for a long time.

The service d'administration générale has therefore only recently been able to turn its attention to its principal task of administrative reform. Both it and the secrétariat permanent de recrutement have yet to show what contribution they can make.

In Holland the Central Personnel Service (Centralpersoneeldienst) was created in 1946 to assist the government in general personnel questions, and to act as the focal point for recruitment to all the ministries. It is attached to the ministry of the Interior, the ministry which had in the past been generally responsible for civil service questions. The Central Personnel Service is subdivided into four departments. The first deals with recruitment, and advises the government on promotion policy, salary questions, transfer of personnel and internal reorganization. The second deals with questions of administrative reform and basic questions affecting the civil service as a whole. The third department is responsible for working out training schemes and trying to get ministries to treat these matters seriously. And the fourth department acts for the government in discussions with outside bodies such as trade unions on questions which affect civil servants as a body.

The Central Personnel Service does not touch large sections of the public service: police, judges, teachers, railwaymen, mines, KLM, provincial and municipal officials, and certain higher posts in central ministries are excluded. It does not have the powers over normal recruitment possessed by comparable bodies in other countries. When a vacancy occurs in a ministry there are four possibilities. Ministries can ignore its existence and some do so, making their own appointments as they think fit. The ministry may fill the vacancy by promoting an official already serving in that department. If no one is suitable it should inform the Central Personnel Service. The Central Personnel Service issues a weekly bulletin of vacancies to the personnel directors of all the ministries. If a director considers he has an official suitable for a vacancy, and that official is ready to go, and the ministry is prepared to release him, the director informs the Central Personnel Service. In this way it is hoped to overcome some of the worst promotion blocks in certain ministries, and to provide possibilities of promotion between departments.

It functions very much like a labour exchange registering applications for posts, and sifting demands for personnel. Some of its members complain that it is too dependent on the goodwill of the ministries which are neither required to inform them of vacancies nor to accept the persons suggested by the Central Personnel Service. At the moment the Central Personnel Service has a long list of applicants, many of them qualified for higher posts; these are mainly people repatriated from the East Indies who are not properly settled in private business. Each candidate is expected to write once every two months if he wishes to keep his name on the register.

The Central Personnel Service is undoubtedly the weakest of all the central recruiting agencies. It may well do useful work in the broader field of personnel training and management, but it will never fulfil its recruiting rôle satisfactorily until it is given more comprehensive powers.

Until 1945 France had no central body responsible for recruitment to the civil service. Recruitment was left to the individual ministries; the method used was open competitive examination, and candidates would frequently find themselves forced to sit for several examinations to ensure a reasonable chance of success. In 1935 it was estimated that over two hundred separate examinations were held each year, and even by 1945 there must still have been well over seventy. To complicate the picture further the grands corps—the Cour des Comptes, the Conseil d'Etat, and the Inspection Générale des Finances—recruited their own people separately from the ministries, the Prefectoral Corps had its own rules of selection and entry, and the technical grands corps—the Inspection Générale des Ponts et Chaussées, and the Inspection Générale des Mines—had their own methods of recruitment and training.

There was one common factor in recruitment to the grands corps (not the technical corps): entry to them was very largely dependent on possessing the diploma of the Ecole Libre des Sciences Politiques, a private institution which gave first-class training, but which was more or less reserved to the wealthy. The grands corps have always enjoyed a special status in the French administration and the most important posts at the head of ministries and public services were the preserve of their members. This meant that the ordinary university candidate who entered a ministry by open competitive examination could not reasonably aspire to the highest posts in his department. This was a vicious circle. Unable to aspire to the highest posts, the best young university graduates without means would not enter public service if they could avoid doing so. The intellectual level of entrants by ordinary ministry examinations declined. Ministries rarely had people of sufficient calibre in the middle ranks to fill posts of director and so they were forced to seek members of the grands corps for the highest posts.

During the war several prominent French jurists, politicians and administrators served with de Gaulle in England. In the war-time mood for reform they considered methods for reforming the French civil service. As soon as Paris was liberated a committee of three was set up to draft proposals. Its guiding principles were to raise the standard of the higher ranks of the ministries, to unify methods of entry and standardize classes within the civil service, to break down the barriers between the grands corps and the higher class of the civil service, and to democratize recruitment, which essentially meant democratizing the grands corps.

The proposals of this committee were wide-ranging and well conceived. They included the preparation of a comprehensive statute for all civil servants to unify conditions of service, the creation of a special direction de la fonction publique attached to the Prime Minister's office and therefore independent of the ministries, and the creation of an Ecole Nationale d'Administration to be responsible for the recruitment and training of all higher personnel. These reforms were put into effect during 1946–7; they revolutionized the system of recruitment and training in the French higher civil service.[1]

The detailed preparation of these reforms was largely the work of the direction de la fonction publique. It had a statutory duty to deal with all general matters concerning the organization of the civil service, and with research in the field of organization and methods.

Its work in these fields has been extensive and in the main fruitful. If several of the aims of the 1945–6 reforms have not been entirely met (they will be discussed below) this has been mainly due to the strength of the grands corps, which was underestimated, and to a waning of the reforming spirit of the immediate post-war period.

The Ecole Nationale d'Administration was concerned with the selection and training of higher civil servants. It was to produce a body of civil servants of the highest quality who could be transferred easily from ministry to ministry (an idea borrowed from the administrative class in England). This reform was co-ordinated with further educational reforms which set up twelve Instituts d'Etudes Politiques in different universities in France (one in Algiers) which prepare students in modern studies, particularly economics, politics, and the social sciences; these subjects form the basis of the entry examination to the highest ranks in the service. The ENA was to select by open written competitive examination sufficient candidates each year to fill the foreseeable vacancies in the highest class of the service, some eighty to ninety posts each year. The directors of the ENA are responsible for organizing these annual examinations (dealt with more fully below), but the examiners are appointed by decree from amongst senior civil servants and

[1] French ministries continue to recruit their own personnel for Cadres B, C, D and specialized corps.

university professors. The ENA course of training lasts three years: and the directorate of the ENA is responsible for its general administration. Instruction is given by eminent public men, university professors, and senior civil servants nominated by the directors. One of the directors is responsible for placing students in outside public authorities for a period of practical administrative experience.

ENTRANCE REQUIREMENTS

European countries fall neatly into two categories; those which recruit personnel by competitive written examinations, and those which recruit them by a comparison of the paper qualifications already possessed by the candidate. Britain, France, Belgium and Italy are in the first category; Sweden, Finland, Switzerland, Holland, Portugal, Denmark, the German Länder and Norway in the second category. In all the countries in the second category the procedure for entry to the civil service is for the candidate to apply to an individual ministry or public service in writing, stating his qualifications. Normally, ministries are required by law to announce publicly when a vacancy occurs, but in Holland and the German Länder applications can be sent in without formal notice of a vacancy. The qualifications and references of the candidates are examined, and the most eligible may be interviewed. Responsibility for examining and recommending a candidate for a post lies with the personnel department of the ministry or public service concerned. In the higher service the successful candidate is appointed to office by the minister; the middle and lower staff are appointed to office by the director general of the service concerned or the head of the personnel department of the ministry.

It is fairly clear that this system offers fewer guarantees of impartiality than does a system of open competitive examination. But only in Spain does the observer have the impression that undesirable pressure is seriously exerted. Normally the chief concern of personnel directors and directors general is to obtain the best available material, for the really promising candidate today finds the public service less attractive than in the past. It must also be remembered that under this system no candidate is dependent on one ministry or one board of examiners. He is free—if he can—to play off one ministry against another; a candidate with good qualifications should have little difficulty in finding a post suitable to his talents. But he may have to wait longer than he would if there were a single organization responsible for recruitment, and he will certainly be involved in a good deal more correspondence; and from the public service point of view the best man may not go to the most important post.

In order to diminish the chances of undue favour and influence most appointments—or recommendations for appointment—are made not by a single official, but by a small board of heads of departments. Given this guarantee there are some advantages in this method of recruitment for a small country where the annual intake is small and rather uneven. It nevertheless is a reminder of the great independence possessed by most ministries in Europe today; central government not infrequently looks more like a loose confederation of ministries than a unified central administration. There are, of course, constitutional reasons for this in most cases, for each minister is supposed to be in absolute charge of his own ministry and to accept responsibility in his national parliament for all it does.

Two special cases must be mentioned. Sweden has a constitutional provision that all public documents are to be available for public inspection, unless clearly certified as involving national security or foreign affairs. This excellent doctrine provides additional guarantees against arbitrary appointment. In Sweden not only does each ministry make its own appointments but so does each royal board. The boards and the ministries determine the qualifications required for a post, and are legally compelled to advertise each vacancy with the appropriate details. When the name of the successful candidate is announced, an unsuccessful competitor has the right of appeal and can inspect the documents on the strength of which the appointing authority came to its decision. Appeal lies to the ministry from the boards. In the great majority of cases the appeal is unsuccessful, but this is largely because the knowledge that publication and appeal is possible means that there are very few indefensible decisions.

The second special case is that of the federal countries, Germany and Switzerland. In both countries entry to the federal civil service is to some extent dependent upon the preservation of a correct balance between the constituent states. In Switzerland further factors are taken into account. The federal authorities try to keep a balance not only between the cantons, so that each is properly represented, but also between the political parties, the religions, and the languages. There are no formal rules laid down, but informal agreements are normally made. To the knowledgeable, therefore, an advertised post may be destined from the start to go to a French-speaking Roman Catholic Social Democrat from Canton Basle. Sometimes, for certain posts, particularly in the higher service, there can be no more than one or two serious candidates. These precautions may at first sight seem a little exaggerated, but the sustained and deliberate effort to maintain unity is an integral part of Swiss life. Switzerland is an artificial creation in which the gulfs that divide are at least as numerous as the bridges which link. The national populations are touchy about their rights. The French-speaking population is particularly sensitive to the gradual extension of the German-speaking population into positions of influence in the federal service. The figures issued by the chancellery to show that the French-speaking population has exactly proportional representation in the federal service for its size have been openly challenged as disguising a very real lack of influence. A French analysis shows that in the top four classes there are only nine French-speaking officials as compared with sixty-seven German-speaking officials. Only if all the subaltern officials are counted is the French-speaking proportion of 20% valid. This is also true in the department of Posts and Telegraphs. It seems that the qualifications required for senior posts are sometimes changed to fit particular people. For instance, in 1948 the vacant post of personnel director in the Posts and Telegraphs was advertised as requiring a man between thirty-five and forty, a strong personality, with a good knowledge of English, a good administrator with experience of personnel questions in a large undertaking. When the post fell vacant again in 1953 it was advertised as simply requiring long experience in a leading position in the administration, and there was no mention of age, languages or experience in a large undertaking. It was thus possible to appoint to the post a fifty-nine-year-old official without secondary education, who had formerly been assistant in the Posts and Telegraphs personnel division.[1] It is clearly difficult to please everyone by a system of appointment by permutation.

Of the five countries which recruit by competitive written examination, Britain and France do so on a general service basis, Spain, Belgium and Italy do so by ministry. In all four cases in order to be eligible candidates must either hold the educational qualifications appropriate to the class they apply to enter, or have served in the class immediately below for a certain period of time. In Italy candidates for the carriere direttive must either possess a university degree, or have reached the rank of assistant secretary in the carriere di concetto and have the certificate of secondary education. Similarly candidates for the carriere di concetto must possess the certificate of secondary education, or have attained the rank of archivist in the carriere esecutive and possess the intermediate certificate of secondary education.[2]

Each ministry in Italy announces and holds its own examinations. An examination commission must be formally appointed for each examination, and the syllabus announced. In the two higher classes there must be at least two written tests, and there are also oral examinations on related subjects. Attempts are being made to limit the very frequent reservation of a percentage of posts to certain categories of citizen. But the examination commission, when drawing up its final examination lists, gives priority in the list (when the marks are equal) to candidates who fall into one of the categories mentioned in the Decree Law of 5th July 1934: these range from those decorated for valour, through war widows and war orphans, to those with exceptionally large families. This system of priorities is not unique in western Europe, and it reflects a social conscience not always noticeable elsewhere in Italian administration.

In Belgium examinations are held under the auspices of the secrétariat permanent de recrutement;[3] a ministry which

[1] *Curieux*. Berne, Feb. 3, Feb. 17, and March 10, 1955.

[2] A. Bennati and E. di Giambattista: *Il nouvo statuto e la carriera degli impiegati civili dello Stato*. Naples, 1956.

[3] *Le recrutement du personnel de l'Etat*: published by the secrétariat permanent de recrutement, Brussels.

wishes to recruit personnel must do so through its offices. The 1938 statute lays down that entry to the civil service is to be by examination. Article 18 of the Belgian statute allows direct entry to the civil service without examination to people with high administrative, scientific, technical or artistic qualifications. This possibility was greatly abused after the war for political purposes. But entry by this means was tightened up by the ordinance of 12 March, 1948, which required that: (*a*) there should be no competent candidate for the post already in the administration, (*b*) the secrétariat permanent de recrutement be consulted, (*c*) notification of intention be published in the official gazette, (*d*) the conseil de direction of the ministry should give its opinion of the candidate proposed, (*e*) the council of ministers should make the final decision. However, there seem to have been some dubious nominations even since then.[1]

In principle there are three stages before final acceptance as an established civil servant: the competitive entrance examination; a probationary period of three years for the first class, two for the second class, and one year for the other two classes; and a final examination at the end of the probationary period. The entrance examination for people in the first and second classes has one written paper which is peculiar to Belgium. Candidates attend a 'conference' on a certain subject at which they are not allowed to take notes. At the end of the 'conference' they are required to give a résumé of it in their own words and to criticise its content. Those who successfully pass this test are called to a personal interview at which they may be faced with questions on any subject designed to test their general knowledge, general culture and ability to hold their own with the examination commission.

After their probationary period they take their final examination. Officials in the first class are given two tests; the first a written examination on subjects relating to the branch of the administration in which they have served, and an oral examination in the same field. Officials in the second class are required to draft a report on an administrative question relating to their branch of the administration, and given an oral examination in the same field. Officials in the two lower categories simply have written tests to show that they have a working

[1] See J. Verspecht: *Des agents de l'Etat: leur statut administratif.* Brussels, 1951.

knowledge of their current duties. All these examinations are held under the auspices of the secrétariat permanent de recrutement.

Some of the difficulties encountered during the reform of the Belgian civil service have already been mentioned. There are several loopholes in the above scheme, the most serious being that ministries recruit some people on a temporary basis without having to pass through this examination network. Some officials have made a career up through the hierarchy by jumping from one temporary post to another. In the end most of them managed to get themselves established in one way or another. But there is a strong desire to return to the original conception of the statute, to hold annual entrance examinations for combined ministries, and exclude temporaries, and this will no doubt gradually be done.[1]

The French Ecole Nationale d'Administration recruits the higher ranks of the entire civil service. Entry to it is by written competitive examination. There is one examination for people with university qualifications and another reserved to men and women under the age of thirty who have already served for five years in some part of the administration; for the latter competition it is not necessary to hold any particular educational qualification or have served in any particular class of the service. No proportion of places is reserved for either of the two categories: the final list is in joint order of merit for both categories.

Some of the candidates who are already serving officials are unlikely to be found taking this sort of examination in other countries. In the first place the second class in the French civil service, Category B, although designed for people who have completed their higher school studies but not gone to universities, nevertheless attracts university graduates in some numbers. This is a common phenomenon in French administrative history: the standards set at each level become progressively higher, so that the people for whom the examinations were originally designed are eventually ousted in favour of those with qualifications for higher posts. This is particularly true at the present time, for the standards of the ENA are so high that many university graduates who would have little

[1] See: *La Réforme du Statut des Agents de l'Etat.* 2 vols., edited by Institut Belge des Sciences Administratives, 1954.

difficulty in entering the higher class in other countries have no chance of succeeding. Competition is so keen that the entry standard to the ENA is tending to become advanced degree level, and few can compete with any chance of success without at least a year's further study after graduation.

This means that the ordinary graduate is forced back on the examinations for category B, with the hope of competing for entry to the ENA in future years as an 'official' candidate.[1] French administrations are very generous in allowing leave and study time to anyone who wishes to compete for the ENA.

This has, however, unfortunate repercussions throughout the service. Those university graduates who enter category B but do not succeed in entering the ENA later on, are faced with a lifetime of work in jobs which are below their mental capacity. Those people who in the ordinary way would be holding their posts are pushed back to the examinations for category C, and they in their turn are likely to become restless and embittered by doing work below their natural capacities. This is perhaps one of the pressing dangers for the French administration which will have to be faced up to one day.

Candidates for the 'official' competition to the ENA also include elementary school teachers. The instituteurs are a force of much greater importance and prestige than are British elementary school teachers; they are entitled to enter the 'official' competition since they are members of the state educational service, and therefore are recognized as having the status of public official. They have provided some of the best candidates to the ENA.

The entry examination for both the 'official' and the 'student' categories is in two parts, a preliminary part and a classifying part. Only those who reach a certain standard in the preliminary are allowed to sit for the classifying part.

The preliminary examination for the 'student' category is in four parts: three are essay papers each lasting six hours. The first is on a subject concerning the general development of political, social and economic history since the middle of the eighteenth century. The type of question set is to discuss the respective rôles of the town and of the country in France since

[1] See D. Mallet: 'Pour une vraie réforme des administrations centrales.' *Revue Administrative,* 1954. pp. 611–25.

1800, or to consider whether a country that is economically weak can exert cultural and spiritual influence. The subjects chosen are designed to disclose the general knowledge, the analytical and synthetic capacities of the candidates, and not to test detailed knowledge.

The second essay paper taken by the 'student' category deals with the political institutions of the major states or with French administrative law. And the third is on a subject concerned with political economy, for instance, on the monetary policy of the principal European states since 1945. In all three essay papers only one subject is set, and candidates have no option. The last paper is a three-hour test in a foreign language: German, English, Spanish, Italian, Russian, or modern Arabic.

The preliminary paper for the 'official' category is similar to the 'students' examination. There are three essay papers, of which the first is frequently the same as for the 'students'. The other two essays are on political economy and on political institutions and administrative law, but the questions set are designed to give weight to the more practical experience of the candidates. Instead of the foreign-language paper the 'official' candidates have to make two résumés in the space of four hours of a document or group of documents, the first résumé of the order of a thousand words, the second of fifty words. The type of test given is to tell the candidate to assume that his minister has been absent from, for instance, the budget debate; and to ask him to make the résumé for the minister's information; the relevant copies of the Journal Officiel will be used.

For those 'student' candidates who pass the preliminary examination, the classifying examination is designed to test their more specialized knowledge. When entering for the examination candidates are asked to state a preference for one of four groups of careers; General Administration, Financial Administration, Social Administration, and Foreign Affairs. The teaching inside the ENA is based on these divisions. In the classifying examination this choice is important, for three of the four tests require answers in the chosen field. In the first 'student' examination there is a question on either administrative law, financial law, social economics, or international relations since 1815; this is a four-hour paper and the candidate is expected to do the question appropriate to his section.

The remaining three 'student' tests are oral examinations; in the first the candidate is given the title of a general subject half an hour before he appears before the examining board. Before the board he is required to give a ten-minute commentary on the subject, and is then interrogated by the board on what he has said. In each of the second and third oral tests the candidate is interrogated for fifteen minutes on a specialized field of knowledge within the section for which he has opted; General Administration candidates are interrogated on social questions and on financial legislation; Financial Administration candidates on social questions and economic and human geography; Social Administration candidates on sociology and demography and on financial legislation; and Foreign Affairs candidates on international public law and on economic and human geography.

The classifying examination for the 'official' candidates is in only three parts, but together they account for the same total number of marks as the four tests for the 'student' category. The 'official' candidates have only one oral test of fifteen minutes instead of two but the subjects they are expected to deal with are more or less the same as for the 'student' category.

All candidates from both categories must attain certain standards in running, jumping, climbing, swimming and putting the weight. If a candidate is physically handicapped he is exempted, and is awarded the average figure obtained by all the other candidates.

Additional marks can be obtained by all candidates in three different ways: if they show evidence of audacity, in being pilots or parachute jumpers; if they reach a good standard in a second foreign language; if they show proper knowledge during an oral interview of scientific subjects. The list for the last group comprises astronomy, biology, chemistry, ethnography, geology, the history of science, social medicine, mathematics, general human physiology, applied psychology, agricultural economy, and industrial techniques. These three additional tests are optional, and are common to both groups of candidates.

The number of places to be filled is announced by the direction de la fonction publique before the examinations are held, and the examining commission compiles a list in order of merit. Should two candidates at the margin have the same marks, the examining board can call them for a further interview, and decide definitively between them.

There are three points worth making about the French system of recruitment through the Ecole Nationale d'Administration. In the first place they have gone a long way past both the German and the British traditions of recruitment. The French are no longer satisfied with candidates narrowly specialized in the field of law, which was for a long time the normal European tradition and is still very strong in Germany. This tradition has often been misunderstood in Britain, since continental university degrees in law have always been much broader than comparable English degrees; a continental university degree in law frequently covered economics, political science, political and legal philosophy, and sociology, and never had the narrowness ascribed to it by the British. Although many of the French papers have a basis of law, this has more to do with the logical framework within which subjects are set than with their subject matter. For instance, what the French call financial law and legislation often means no more than what British economists teach as public finance.

On the other hand the French have also rejected the British belief that any discipline can be used to test a man's capacity to make a good civil servant. This is partly because the French have no cult of the amateur in government and also because they believe that certain subjects are essential to a good administrator, and that without them a civil servant will be handicapped in the course of his work. They are not simply interested in a man having a good mind, but in his having a mind trained in the affairs with which his government has to deal. There is no conclusive end to the argument between the British and French points of view. One general comment is perhaps in place here. The British administrative class is underpinned by the executive class in a way the French is not. The impression an observer obtains is that the highest branches of the French civil service have an intellectual capacity, an independence of judgement, a talent for leadership, and a willingness to accept personal responsibility, which their British counterparts do not have. The French high administrator is 'the State' in a way his British colleague is certainly not 'the Crown', and this clearly affects the qualities sought in recruitment.

But it is due to the lack of a strong, knowledgeable executive class, some of whose personnel reach the highest administrative posts, that the high French administrator has to be more genuinely polyvalent and informed in detail than his British counterpart. The difference in quality between the top administrators of the two countries is counterbalanced by the difference in quality at the middle level. It is highly improbable that any senior French administrator could rely on his assistants in the way a senior British official can rely on his senior executive officer, and it is certain that posts which in Britain are held by members or ex-members of the executive class would never be entrusted to their French equivalents.

In France the great gulf between the highest and the middle ranks of the service is likely to be a self-perpetuating phenomenon. There are no places in the highest class reserved to the middle grade, nor is there any closed competition they can enter; they must compete with outsiders as candidates for the ENA. In this way the French certainly ensure the very highest intellectual qualifications for their administrative class. Executive class officials in all countries tend to be narrow in outlook and pedestrian in character, and to have too many of them in the highest posts undoubtedly lowers the general vitality and authority of the civil service; it may well be that there are too many ex-executive class officials at the top of British administration. Yet there are posts in the higher administration which do not require brilliance but merely detailed knowledge, administrative expertise, and patient intelligence, and the French have no way of filling these posts economically. It is just as stupid to make a racehorse pull a plough as it is to expect a carthorse to win the Derby.

The difference of outlook is reflected in attitudes towards the tests appropriate to recruitment. The French civil service tests take very little account of 'character'. This is a peculiarly Nordic preoccupation, and probably has something to do with monarchical traditions and the belief that government was the business of an aristocracy. There are two objections to making 'character' an important element in selection. The first is that consciously and unconsciously it is likely to favour candidates cast in the social and intellectual patterns of the existing administrative leaders. It is very frequently a test of conformity to a social and administrative ethos rather than a test of character in the broader sense. The French take out guarantees against even this kind of bias by weighting their examining commissions against the official element, and in favour of the academic and outside element. It is inevitable that the senior civil servants should deplore and react against the introduction of elements they consider likely to disturb the harmony to which they are accustomed; unless of course those administrators have had wide experience of the outside world, and standards of judgement formed outside the civil service. They are clearly likely to prefer candidates formed in their own image.

The second objection to stressing 'character' is simply that with the present size of public administration there should be ample room for all the talents and all types of personality. The shrewd cynic at the minister's elbow is as necessary as the intellectual with a passion for expertise in a special field, or the brash and forthright manager. The harmony of the team may be very pleasant for those who belong to it, but friction may be a function of efficiency.

SPECIAL REQUIREMENTS

Every public service has to recruit a number of specialists as well as general administrators: architects, doctors, engineers, statisticians, and so on. It is also customary to regard the foreign service as separate from the ordinary home civil service with special methods of entry. Finally, those few countries which still possess colonial territories tend to recruit their colonial services separately from every other branch of the administration. Colonial services are a rapidly declining part of public administration, and it seems safe to omit them here. Something must, however, be said of the other groups.

No country imposes further tests before entry to the public service on people with professional qualifications. Doctors, lawyers, architects, and so on, are normally recruited after advertisement and interview. Not infrequently specialists are recruited on contract for a specified time, and even when they are made established civil servants they remain within a specialist career, with little or no chance of transferring to the administrative career. Naturally, these careers often carry high prestige of their own: the head of a government's architectural service or its chief medical adviser at the head of the state medical service, has an authority and prestige quite comparable to that of the head of a ministry, or senior specialists in their own professions.

Most types of professional specialist civil servant are of little interest in the context of this book. But one group of specialists raise rather wider issues, and ought to be considered here. They are the technocrats, the engineers and scientists in government employment.

This group is especially important in modern administration because so many modern public services such as railways, electricity and gas undertakings, transport, trade, nuclear research, the fuel industry, clearly need a type of high administrator who is at home not only with the normal administrative techniques, but also with the language and practice of specialists. In addition, many of the traditional aspects of government can now be properly handled only with some knowledge of advanced engineering and scientific thought.

Perhaps one of the most important tasks of modern administration is to create a new group of administrative technocrats at home in both fields. Certain European countries have always been in advance of others in this. Germany and Switzerland have long traditions of scientific education which have always enabled them to draw into government service some of the best scientists and engineers of their day. The technical universities in Germany and the Federal Polytechnic in Switzerland have produced an abundance of first-class material. The Italians too have an honourable tradition of recruiting some of the best of their engineering students into public service, and their hydraulic, transport and highway engineers bear comparison with those of any other country. In a smaller way the agricultural engineers in Spain form a corps of quite high standing, though their highway and transport engineers are not of really international stature despite their local prestige. The Dutch Waterstaat engineers are a corps with a strong family tradition but they work in a very small professional field.

France has the longest history of any country of deliberately producing engineers specifically trained for state service. The three major institutions responsible for this are the Ecole

Nationale des Ponts et Chaussées, the Ecole Nationale Supérieure des Mines, both founded in 1747, and the Ecole Polytechnique founded in 1794.[1] The first two draw many of their students from the Ecole Polytechnique. This institution retains some of the military flavour of its origins; it is commanded by a general, and its pupils rank as army cadets. They wear eighteenth-century uniform on formal occasions and live under a modified form of military discipline. Entry is fiercely competitive amongst young men between the ages of eighteen and twenty who possess their advanced secondary school leaving certificate. Entry is conditional on accepting to serve the state for a period of ten years after completing the course. Uniform, messing and instruction are provided free, and there is an allowance.

This institution has always been a favourite of the French; from its earliest days it was thoroughly democratic, and its students enjoyed some of the sympathy the French have for students, plus some of the affection they had for the army. The courses of study are primarily scientific, mathematics, chemistry, physics; and its principal aim is to lay the intellectual foundations for advanced specialization in scientific and engineering subjects. At the end of two years there are examinations after which students are classified in order of merit. The students choose in order their future career. They go out into either the great civil technical corps, or into the army technical corps of artillery and engineers.

Those who choose the civil technical corps now enter either the Ecole des Mines or the Ecole des Ponts et Chaussées. On entry they are given official status and are paid accordingly; they follow courses of instruction both in the school and in the field for three years. At the end of this time they go out to their respective corps.

The training they receive in these institutions will be discussed later; it is designed to fit them to be not only qualified engineers, but also competent administrators. Their future careers in their corps also alternate between specialization and administration, and those who reach the top of their profession form a unique corps of technocratic administrators which has left a profound mark on French administration. For a century

[1] *Livre du Centenaire*, 1794–1894: Ecole Polytechnique. 3 vols. Paris, 1895.

and a half these corps have provided a means whereby a young man of talent but no means could reach the highest posts in the state. These corps meant that the French had ready to hand a body of people able to run their nationalized industries without having to resort to generals, private businessmen and ordinary civil servants. The high quality of the French public services is primarily due to the existence of these corps.

France is faced with the same unusual situation in her technical corps as in the rest of her civil service. She has little worry as to where she will find top-flight technocratic administrators: there has been a steady supply for many years. A recent estimate was that as far as can be seen France will be able to provide 90% of all her requirements for first-class engineers with administrative experience. On the other hand, before the recent reforms in technical training her requirements for ordinary engineers were only being half met, and only about a third of the necessary number of skilled tradesmen were being trained.

In most countries, including Britain, the problem is reversed. The usual difficulty is that of finding adequate numbers of civil servants with sufficient specialized training to enable them to control modern government services. In Europe Britain has had a unique disadvantage in this field. No other country has emphasized to the same extent the strange division between science and the humanities; a system based on the temporary nineteenth-century need to produce proconsuls, from which she has never recovered. This educational pattern has led to a division between 'practical' men and civil servants. This has never arisen in France, for the simple reason that many of the French state engineers are better engineers than their counterparts in private industry; furthermore, there is a constant flow from the public to the private sector with consequent personal ties and mutual respect.

Finally there is the question of special recruitment to the foreign service. Every country considers that it has to pay rather special attention to recruitment to this branch of the civil service. Even in France there is a special division for Foreign Affairs inside the ENA, although all candidates must take the common entry examination. Yet the time may have come to question whether it is still necessary to recruit a foreign service according to special criteria.

The argument in favour of a specially recruited foreign service is straightforward. Service abroad as diplomatic representative of the home country calls for special qualities of tact, social aplomb and self-possession which must be specially tested on entry. Most of these requirements are designed to exclude those candidates who do not give the necessary guarantees that they will mix easily in the diplomatic world. But the diplomatic world is no longer the world in which government is carried on. In no European government is the civil service or the majority of political leaders drawn from the same social class as the diplomatic corps accredited to their head of state. What is true is that the various national diplomatic representatives come from similar social groups, so that special recruitment requirements for foreign service allows for close contact between the diplomats themselves; but it isolates the diplomatic corps as a whole from the important affairs and personages of the country. This probably explains the unreality of most of their activities. It is perhaps significant that the special entry requirements deliberately favour a particular social class.

In fact, the purpose of the foreign service has changed substantially since its great days in the nineteenth century. The important aspects of international relations today are those concerned with finance, military affairs, trade, scientific research, labour and commerce. No country allows its foreign service officials to deal with these affairs, but instead appoints special representatives from home ministries to act as specialist attachés and counsellors. The more one examines embassies, the more one becomes aware that the vital aspects of international relations are nowadays handled by home civil servants serving abroad rather than by members of the foreign service. When important international business has to be transacted delegations from the home country are sent to deal with it.

In these circumstances the strongest case that can be made in favour of a separate foreign service is that embassies, which are a necessary focal point for a country's business in a foreign country, require a small administrative service staff, and there is no reason why this should not be recruited by the normal home civil service entry programme.

CHAPTER 3

Training

There has been more discussion about the training of civil servants in the last twenty years than ever before. This has been due partly to the greater attention being paid to the rôle and influence of public officials in the process of government; partly to administrative and psychological studies emphasizing adjustment and integration as prerequisites for administrative and personal efficiency.

This recent concentration on training should not, however, obscure the fact that for generations many types of public official have been instructed in their jobs in specially organized institutions. All European countries can show examples of schools for training policemen, customs officers, revenue inspectors, technical experts such as agricultural engineers, highway engineers, post office engineers, and so on. Many of these schools, within the narrow limits of their courses, are of high standard, and have been so for many years. France is the country which has embraced the principle of specialized schools almost with passion. There are advanced schools for archivists and paleographers, for the colonial magistracy, for road, rail, hydraulic and atomic engineers, for communications engineers, forestry experts, agricultural engineers, customs officers, public works construction engineers, and so on.

France has consistently held that the state should itself assume the responsibility for training its own specialists, and that specialized institutions under its own control will produce the type of person needed by the state rather than those needed by private enterprise.

No other country possesses France's wealth of first-class specialist training schools. Nevertheless, it is commonly accepted throughout Europe that training schools are necessary for preparing public officials engaged in specialized technical fields. Most of the training schools run by the state are, however, for officials of relatively minor rank.

Discussion in the last twenty years has centred on whether training under state auspices should be extended to the general administrative branches of the public service, and, even more precisely, whether the senior branch of the public service would be improved by systematic training in affairs of state. No one would dream of questioning the desirability of schools for specialists; but there is room for discussion whether training is desirable for administrators.

Different countries hold divergent views on this subject. They range from the complete rejection of all training for administrators in Switzerland to the complex arrangements in France; from the marked suspicion in Scandinavia that administration has to be assimilated and cannot be taught, to the growing pressure in Spain for a properly organized administrative college. Three different types of training can be distinguished. First, a person can be trained under state auspices before he is allowed to enter the public service at all; the successful completion of this training may not necessarily guarantee entry to public service. Second, candidates may be accepted as public servants by means of open or closed competitive examination, by co-optation or by nomination; once accepted they may be trained full time or part time in a state institution. Third, training may take the form of refresher courses, given to already established civil servants of some seniority, to bring them into touch with other fields of government or public activities and to give them the opportunity of re-examining themselves and their own work in a dispassionate atmosphere.

PRE-ENTRY TRAINING

The classic example of intensive and exhaustive pre-entry training is the German system. In Germany, as in the Scandinavian countries, the public official has traditionally been regarded as in a position similar to that of a judge. His primary task is the application of the law, dealing objectively with those matters which arise in the course of administration, finding the law appropriate to the particular case, and making a decision entirely within the terms of that law. The principle difference between the administrator and the judge is simply that the judge deals with litigious affairs, and the administrator with administrative affairs: legal knowledge and the qualities of impartiality and disinterestedness are clearly needed for both.

In the Scandinavian countries, and in particular Sweden and Denmark, although a law degree is widely regarded as the most necessary qualification for higher administration, there is no formalised pre-entry or post-entry training of officials for administrative duties.[1] Instead, in both these countries it is very common for the young law graduate wishing to enter public service to attach himself to a provincial court for two or three years, and this experience undoubtedly improves his chances of successfully applying for a senior administrative post. Transfer between the administrative career and the judicial career is common in these countries, but it is informal, difficult to document from outside, and only thoroughly understood by the people involved.

The informal arrangements whereby future administrators serve for some time in courts cannot legitimately be regarded as pre-entry training in the accepted sense of the word. However, the Scandinavian attitude reflects the strong Germanic tradition of government.

Entry to the German civil service has for two centuries been conditional on some form of pre-entry training. The rules have varied at different periods, and different states have adopted different procedures; but the basic conception has remained constant. Before being appointed to an established post in the public service the candidate should have shown, under conditions laid down by the state and subject to state supervision, that he possesses the practical experience and theoretical knowledge of law and public affairs which will enable him to give the state the highest standard of service. The conditions under which the aspirant public servant serves this pre-entry training period are, subject to the general provisions of the federal civil service law, laid down by the individual Länder. There is little practical difference between these Länder laws,

[1] N. Herlitz: 'Die gegenwärtige Lage der Verwaltung und der Stand der Verwaltungswissenschaftlichen Forschung in den Scandinavischen Ländern.' In *Verwaltungsarchiv*, October, 1957.

and each Land must accord full recognition to the provisions of other Länder. This is of some importance, since the pre-entry training of administrators in the senior branch of the public service is closely linked to the training of people wishing to enter the state magistracy or set up in private legal practice. In some Länder a fairly clear line used to be drawn between candidates for administrative office and candidates for legal office: in Bavaria, for instance, from the ordinance of 1899 until 1934, the first group spent much longer during their practical pre-entry training in different administrative offices of Land and provincial government, while the latter group spent most of their time in the courts. The Reich law of 1934 on training universalized the Prussian system throughout Germany, and this amalgamated the administrative and the judicial streams. In April 1946 a return was made to a very simplified version of the pre-1934 system, and in 1949 the Bavarian Landtag asked the Bavarian government fully to reform the system along the traditional lines. A Land personnel office was set up by the Landtag to study the problem, and discussions took place with ministerial representatives, law professors, and civil service associations.

The result of these deliberations was a new ordinance on training and examinations promulgated in 1952, in force from June 1953.[1] Agreement had been reached during the discussions that it was in the best interest of both the administration of justice and the administrative services in general that candidates for both branches should have common training. The ordinance held that 'The judge who has a basic knowledge of administrative law, and the senior administrator who has undergone a basic training in civil law, are widely interchangeable. Their common training makes for a greater breadth of vision and a better mutual understanding of each others problems.'

The general pattern of training is the same for all the Länder; there are minor variations in the exact choice of subjects and in the period of practical training spent in the various branches of public administration.

There are three stages in this training programme: first, the

[1] K. Raumer: *Ausbildungs- und Prüfungsordmung für den höheren Justiz- und Verwaltungsdienst vom 12 März,* 1952. Text and commentary.

final university examination in law; second, a lengthy period of service in various parts of public administration; third, a final state examination.

In Bavaria, the first state examination, held at the end of the course for a university law degree, is under the control of an examination committee composed of a judge, senior civil servants and law professors; examiners in particular subjects include university law and economics professors, a judge, senior civil servants and a state notary. The examination consists of six written papers of five hours each, and they may be followed by oral examinations. The oral examination covers all the written papers and is chiefly concerned with factual questions of current law.

A student who passes this first state examination and wishes to continue to the second state examination has the right to the title Referendar. He submits a written request to the Oberlandsgerichtspräsident in the administrative region (Bezirk) in which he wishes to serve. His request can only be refused if he has not complied with a certain number of enumerated conditions. An appeal against refusal lies to the Minister of Justice.

The purpose of the training to which the candidate will now be subjected is to encourage him to understand the practical realities of administration and legal practice, and also to test his abilities and assiduity. This period of service is under the general control of the Oberlandsgerichtspräsident, but a full-time senior member of the middle class of the civil service is responsible for detailed arrangements. Each official under whom the Referendar serves reports on the quality, reliability and competence of his work and on his personal character. The Referendar has to spend nineteen months in the courts; ten months in an Amtsgericht, five months in the Land civil court and four months with the public prosecutor's department in the Land criminal courts. The next fourteen months are spent in public administration under the supervision of a Regierungspräsident; two of these months must be spent in financial administration and four in a Kreis administration. Two months may be spent in a social security administration or any other public law body approved by the Minister of the Interior.

The Referendar spends six months with an administrative

court, two months of which may be in a labour court. He spends five months with a lawyer or state notary.

Until recently each Land was entirely responsible for the training of its own Referendaren, but since 1950 an increasing number of Länder have been sending their Referendaren to an administrative college, the Hochschule für Verwaltungswissenschaften at Speyer. This college was originally set up in Land Rheinland-Pfalz in 1947 under French inspiration, and in 1950 it was given the status of a public law body. Its purpose was to act as an administrators' training school for Rheinland-Pfalz, Baden and Württemberg-Hohenzollern. One by one the other Länder joined in the scheme until, with the entry of Hesse and the Saar in 1956–7, all Länder belong with the exception of West Berlin.

Speyer was originally designed only for Referendaren intending to enter the administrative branch of the higher civil service, but because various Länder refused to distinguish between the training of administrators and judges, the programme had to be readjusted. Its future programme will clearly depend on the result of the discussions which are always going on as to the need for common training for both the administrative and judicial careers. The broad purpose of the school is to give its students the opportunity for supplementary studies in administration, by dealing with details of general administrative law which have to be omitted from university programmes. The courses are designed to give the students an insight into the more intimate political, social and economic aspects of government.

The course lasts about three months, and the student only has to meet a small weekly charge for his room. He has some freedom to choose which courses he attends, but he must belong to a study syndicate on public law appropriate to his Land of origin, and he must also attend for a minimum of twenty-four hours a week.

The teaching staff consists of six established professors with chairs in the fields of public law, sociology, psychology and economics; there are four part-time professors teaching comparative government, constitutional and administrative law (a judge), local government law, labour law, and constitutional law. A supernumerary full-time professor teaches modern political history, and there are ten part-time teachers who are senior administrators.

The courses offered therefore cover a wide range of subjects, and the administrative law courses deal with not only ordinary administrative law, but also police administration, social insurance, financial law, and taxation law. There are some rather wider cultural courses given, on modern social history or on capitalism and socialism, for instance. Each of the established professors holds a regular seminar on his own subject.

The Hochschule für Verwaltungswissenschaften at Speyer is a valuable innovation in traditional German training practice, and should in the course of time have some effect in broadening the Referendaren. At the moment it is still too narrowly specialist, but this is mainly because the course is so short. At which stage in their career the Referendaren attend the school is a matter for the Land authorities to decide. It seems fairly certain, however, that the school's authorities would like to see a complete separation of the administrative and the judicial careers. This would certainly simplify the task of instruction.

At the end of his three and a half years' period of training, the Referendar in Bavaria sits for the final state examination, not unjustifiably called the Grosse Staatsprüfung. The written examination is in two parts, one law, one administration; there are seven papers in each part, six of five hours each, and one double exam of eight hours. In the law part five papers are on the field of private law, including commercial and company law, and two on criminal law; the double paper is on private law and civil law procedure. In the administrative part there are questions on constitutional law, administrative law, canon law, and there may be questions on taxation law, labour law, and social insurance law; one paper must be taken in either economics or public finance or political science. Oral examinations are also held in these subjects by the examining committee.

In some Länder the first state examination is less legalistic than in Bavaria. In Hesse, for instance, stress is laid on the philosophy and history of law, and on knowledge of sociology and economics;[1] in Rheinland-Pfalz the candidate is expected

[1] G. Littmann and K. Wolf: *Hessisches Beamtenrecht.* Text and commentary. Wiesbaden, 1952.

to show general education in art, philosophy, history or languages.[1] In Rheinland-Pfalz also the period of practical training is three years rather than the three and a half years normally found elsewhere. The proportion of practical training spent in various parts of the administration and the courts also varies. In the Grosse Staatsprufüng some Länder emphasize the need for practical application of theoretical knowledge acquired during practical training; candidates have to show how they would deal with a complicated piece of real business. They may be given this work to prepare at home within a specified time before the examination proper.

This extensive pre-entry training is not restricted to the highest administrative class of the civil service. Entry to the gehobener Dienst is also meticulously organized along the lines of a period of study followed by a period of practical experience and ending with a qualifying examination. The longest period is six years for the gehobener Dienst in Nord Rhein-Westfalen; in other Länder, for instance Schleswig-Holstein and Rheinland-Pfalz, it is five years. Entry is normally conditional on possessing the higher school leaving certificate; but this may be waived for established officials in the class below. The candidate who is accepted for training spends the first three years in further academic study normally in a professional school. This is followed by two or three years practical experience in administration under the direction of an official on the staff of either the local Regierungspräsident, or the Land ministry of the Interior. During this period the official has the rank of Regierungsinspektoranwärter and works in different branches of state and local administration, with at least six months in communal administration. Each Land also organizes, either at the beginning or the end of this practical training, a period of service in the Land ministry of the Interior. At the end of these two periods of training there are written and oral examinations consisting of five or six papers lasting in all between seventeen and twenty-four hours.[2]

There is no doubt that German opinion is strongly attached to this system of pre-entry training. It provides a common background for all the high officials in federal, Land, regional and

[1] *Justizausbildungsordnung*. Coblenz, 1948.
[2] W. Bohr: *Die Ausbildung für den gehobenen Verwaltungsdienst.* Mimeo, 1954.

communal government, in public law bodies, in the magistracy, and in the private legal profession. Furthermore, successful Referendaren not infrequently go into private industry. This common background, combined as it frequently is with common membership of students' clubs while at university, produces a closely knit and cohesive governing cadre with ramifications in all fields of public life. This has always been an important factor in German affairs, and has ensured a high level of competence in the management and administration of public bodies. In most other countries it would be unbelievable to find people capable of going through this training process working in local government. It sometimes increases the tension normally found between the full-time officials and elected representatives, but in the ordinary run of things the gulf between administrator and elected representative is emphasized in a way which can leave no doubt on either side about the relative positions. People who have successfully completed such an exacting training are unlikely to suffer fools gladly; on the other hand in Germany administrative superiority has for so long been recognized and admired that it seems common for even elected representatives to acknowledge that their own administrators have a leading rôle to play in the determination and execution of policy.

A notable advantage of this common pre-entry training is an absence of tension between judiciary and administration, of the mutual incomprehension between judge and civil servant which is sometimes found in Britain, for example. An instinctive appreciation of the needs of 'the office' colours the relations between the magistracy and public officials, and between public officials serving in different organizations. These ingrained instinctive reactions are an important factor in the smooth running and solidity of the German administrative apparatus.

On the other hand, foreign observers have for some time been preoccupied by the total effect of this system of intensive pre-entry training. Political scientists question whether the rôles of administrator and judge are so similar as this system assumes. The emphasis on legal training is only reasonable if it is true that the administrator simply applies the law as he finds it, and the judge simply judges infractions of the law. There is of course no need to exaggerate. By the time the Referendar reaches the Grosse Staatsprüfung he has quite enough experience of practical administration to have no illusions about the complexity and tortuousness of human affairs; under a good supervisor he learns to apply the law with charity and humanity. It is also as well to remember that a German law degree is more broadly based than its equivalent in Anglo-Saxon countries.

The whole system is, however, open to two important criticisms. The first is that by strictly enforcing this pattern of pre-entry training as a prerequisite for entry to the higher civil service, the administration of public affairs loses the flexibility and variety of experience that would be gained by accepting entrants from different disciplines and different backgrounds. One does not have to go so far as the British and argue that all subjects furnish equally valid proof of capacity to deal with public affairs, but there is some evidence to show that a properly trained graduate in history or in economics has a qualification for the profession of government as important as that of a law graduate.

The second major criticism refers to the length of the training. It must be very rare for a person to become a full-time Beamter of the highest administrative class before he is 27 years old. Behind him will stretch a concentrated course of unremitting intellectual work. It may be argued that survival proves fitness, and that successful completion of the course guarantees thoroughly robust and well-tempered faculties. But it may also mean a thoroughly tired person, prematurely formed in an orthodox pattern of thought and character; competent in law, deficient in imagination, just but aloof, responsible but contemptuous of human weakness, the precise and learned bureaucrat.

This has indeed been the traditional type of German civil servant. After 1945 Allied occupation authorities considered that the success of the Nazi régime was largely attributable to the civil service. When the time came to re-form a German civil service the Allied Control Commission drafted a letter to the German authorities stating their views on the form the new civil service should take. This curious letter is a hotchpotch of British and American ideas concerning the rôle of a civil servant in democratic society. It abounds in glaring inconsistencies. But the letter called particular attention to the two major criticisms mentioned above. It stated that 'any personnel system for a democratic state ought to include the following features. . . . (*d*) Any educational requirements for the higher grades of the public service should recognize the importance in modern government of economics and political and social sciences. A degree in law ought to be merely one of several fields among which the candidate may choose'. The Military Government Law of February 2nd, 1949, attempted to put this into practice, and laid down that legal training was no longer required except for posts of strictly legal character. Promotion examinations were not to have the purely academic basis which had characterized them in the past. The French in their zone positively encouraged the introduction into the higher civil service of fresh blood drawn from fields other than law. For a time the Allied High Commissioners insisted that they reserved the right to examine and if necessary reject the new German government's draft law on the civil service unless it conformed to the principles they had enunciated.[1] The new German government solemnly agreed that it accepted these principles as the basis for its new legislation on the subject, and would draft its texts accordingly. On this basis the High Commissioners accepted the new German government's preliminary draft subject to amendment.

Despite this solemn undertaking, however, the German government managed to avoid committing itself until after the High Commissioners had ceased to exercise control powers. The new German civil service law, drafted very much under the influence of the senior civil servants' association, rejected out of hand several of the basic principles previously accepted by the government, and in particular left the way open to the re-establishment of the traditional 'Juristenmonopol'. It is perhaps charitable to regard this breach of good faith as evidence of the very strong attachment Germans have for their traditional system.

[1] See background letters June, 1948 and December, 1949, from the High Commissioners, Allied Control Commission.

POST-ENTRY TRAINING

Specialized training for officials in some public services has been common for many years. If an official is required to show special skills in fields reserved to government action, it is only natural that the state should train him. Certain types of inspectors have to possess an appropriate technical qualification before being eligible to enter their particular public service; the state has no responsibility for this training, and generally it is not specialized in a way entirely suitable for the needs of the public service. Not infrequently additional courses for these people are provided by non-governmental institutions; for instance, medical faculties arrange special courses in public health for public health inspectors and medical officers of health.

Only France has a lengthy history of specialized post-entry training, in particular in its great technical schools, the Ecole des Mines and the Ecole des Ponts et Chaussées.

Both these schools accept students from several sources, and train them for both public and private service. The cream, however, are destined for public service, not for private enterprise. These students will already have spent two years at the Ecole Polytechnique[1]. They already have the status of public official, and are full-time, salaried, and committed to serve the state for a period of ten years. They spend three years in the Ecole des Mines or the Ecole des Ponts et Chaussées.

The courses followed by the ingénieurs-élèves in these schools are remarkable for two reasons. In the first place, one of the three years is spent in the field practising their own professional techniques under the general supervision of senior members of the Inspection des Ponts et Chaussées or the Inspection des Mines. In the second place, they are deliberately instructed in fields of studies which will later fit them for posts of higher management and administration.

In their first year at the Ecole des Mines, for instance, the ingénieurs-élèves study general metallurgy, geology, resistance of materials, mining technique, iron and steel smelting, industrial heating, mineralogy, crystallography, petrology;

[1] See above, p. 96.

these scientific subjects are studied at an advanced level based on the theoretical scientific and mathematical studies completed at the Ecole Polytechnique. In addition they must in their first year study English and German, and take a course in general economics.

The second year the ingénieur-élève spends in a major industrial undertaking under public control. Account is taken of the field in which the student will later specialize as a full-time engineer: the normal choices are between mines of different kinds, petrol refineries or oil wells, atomic energy, iron and steel smelting plants. During this year each ingénieur-élève is given specific responsibilities within the organization. His superiors report to the Ecole at the end of the year on his capacities, and this report will later count for future promotion.

In the final year there are courses in advanced technology, electrical engineering, industrial chemistry, applied geology, metallurgy and mineralogy, and map-making, with, in addition, special courses on law, economics, social and financial administration, and statistics. This last group of courses is deliberately inserted in order to prepare the ingénieurs-élèves for their future careers, when they will be called on to assume wider administrative responsibilities. They are designed to show the primacy of social studies over technological studies, and to humanize the extreme scientific outlook which is the normal result of intensive theoretical and practical training.[1] The ideal aimed at is the formation of the technocratic administrator, the person eminent in his own field of specialization yet not bound by its frontiers; an engineer trained to think and organize as an administrator, and an administrator capable of directing with complete mastery the work of scientists and engineers. These two Ecoles are perhaps the greatest specialized technical training establishments in Europe. In some ways the élites which they have produced are likely to be more important in the future than the purely administrative leaders formed in the Ecole Nationale d'Administration, but perhaps because they are such a long-established feature in France foreign observers have paid much less attention to them than to the ENA.

[1] Notice sur l'organization de l'école et programme des cours. Ministère de l'Industrie, 1956, and Note sur la formation complémentaire spéciale donnée aux jeunes ingénieurs des mines. Mimeo, Paris, 1957.

Most discussion in the post-war era has concerned post-entry training for general administrators.

The traditional view is that administration is learnt, like any other craft, by practice. The best training for an administrator, therefore, is for him to be immersed in the day to day work of his administration, to deal with current business as it comes to the office, to learn step by step under the watchful guidance of his superiors the appropriate method for dealing with the affairs which come to hand, and in the course of time to build up a profound and comprehensive knowledge of his own field. As his experience broadens, so the field for which he is responsible will be extended. The greater his powers of assimilation and his understanding of detailed matters, the greater his competence for assuming wider responsibilities: by coping with a multitude of detailed affairs, he will learn, instinctively, the essence of administration itself; he will grasp the common nature of complex administrative problems, and will be able to apply to the problems of other fields the lessons learnt from his experience of many detailed matters in one special field.

This view commands some respect, particularly where it is held by those countries which make no pretence of having general administrative classes. It is advanced persuasively by the head of the Swiss federal personnel office.[1] He stresses the importance of keeping the civil service in close touch with the population, and considers that the continual injection of fresh blood from outside the service at all levels is essential to the democratic health of the system. He holds that since the pay of the Swiss civil service is comparable to salary scales of private industry, public administration gets its fair share of the best brains. In Switzerland, as in most small countries, the official is hired for a specific job. It is very rare for people to go straight into the administration from school or university, and candidates with business experience are preferred. In private business or commercial schools candidates obtain a grounding in bookkeeping and commercial subjects, and become proficient in the second and third language which they will need in public service. In the Swiss tradition a good proportion of the highest

[1] E. Lobsiger: *Die berufliche Ausbildung des Staatsbeamten in der Schweiz.* Paper read at a conference of the Institut International des Sciences Administratives, 1951.

posts in public service are filled by those who have progressed up the ladder from the lower and middle ranks, or have come in at a mature age from outside. University qualifications in law and economics can be helpful provided they are reinforced by good general experience, but the academically qualified person has to forget his qualifications and adapt himself to ordinary administrative work, and in this he is at a disadvantage compared with the man of humbler intellectual origins who has worked his way up through the administration. The former tends to rely too much on his subordinates, because he is not thoroughly familiar with the necessary detail, and it it has frequently been found that the simple non-academic administrator with his personal experience and knowledge of lower-grade personnel has far greater capacity for management than his academic colleague. Although the business-training school at St. Gall has training schemes for people who wish to enter the public service, its graduates are given no preference when competing for posts, and certainly have no reason to suppose they have any right to the highest posts. The Swiss firmly reject the view that special schools for post-entry training are either desirable or necessary. Indeed, the state arranges for private institutions to instruct customs officers and postal and telegraphic staff.

The Belgian administration also uses private establishments for post-entry training.[1] For example, the training of entrants in the ministry of Communications is done by correspondence courses run by a private establishment, the Ecole de préparation aux carrières administratives. But in Belgium there is a growing feeling that a properly organized system of post-entry training is becoming necessary. The ministry of Finance has for some time organized correspondence courses for its officials, some for new entrants, others for officials seeking promotion to higher grades. But this is not regarded as very satisfactory. The customs administration has also relied upon handbooks as a means of training its officers, supplemented by attendance at special courses held in Brussels and Antwerp. But the administration regards this system as inadequate for higher grades, and hopes to be able to set up a proper school for customs

[1] L. Talloen: 'Notes sur la formation professionnelle en Belgique.' Mimeo. *IISA*, 1955.

officers along the lines of the recently inaugurated French Ecole Nationale des Douanes. There is no move in Belgium towards full-time post-entry training for the general administrative classes. This question has received little attention.

Denmark, like Switzerland, considers that the best post-entry training is day to day work under supervision. In Sweden the issue is complicated by the fact that all posts are advertised individually, and the candidate is not supposed to belong to a general administrative grade common to the whole civil service. In practice, as has already been mentioned, there is a reasonable amount of movement in the Swedish civil service, both between departments and between the civil service and the outside world.

After the war there was in most countries renewed interest in the training of public servants. It was increasingly felt that training by doing was no longer adequate to meet the demands of modern public administration. It creates a very narrow type of public servant, at a time when the state particularly needs more open-minded, all-round administrators. It is almost certainly true that a great deal of detailed administrative work is best learnt by practice under supervision, and that training by doing may easily be unchallengeable as the best method for clerical and executive staff. But whether this system of training is proper for the highest grades of the civil service is open to question. To push the new entrant to the highest class into detailed administrative work under supervision is likely to narrow his horizons to his own ministry, if not to his own division or office; it is likely to restrict his technical competence to dealing with the specific matters for which his department and office are responsible, and his administrative culture will to a great extent depend on the luck he has with his supervisor. Underlying this criticism is the view that to cope with the complex problems of modern government, a senior civil servant must have a general knowledge of, for example, economics or the way his country is governed; and underlying this again is the belief that the modern administrator is engaged in a profession of government, and that a profession has no place for the gifted amateur. There would be no objection to training by doing, provided a man came to his task properly prepared beforehand. There are some successful bone-setters, but most people prefer to be looked after by doctors. That this type of criticism became general after the war was partly due to the emphasis laid on management and training in American books on administrative science; it is, however, mainly due to the great success and high prestige of the French Ecole Nationale d'Administration, and the attraction it has had for those countries in the early stages of building up a modern civil service. The ENA is not, of course, a new experiment, though it has often appeared to be so to the outside observer. It is based partly on the experience of the Ecole libre des Sciences Politiques which before the war trained most of the members of the grands corps. It has also drawn on the experience of the great technical schools mentioned above, the Ecole des Mines and the Ecole des Ponts et Chaussées. The most striking departure of the ENA, of sending its students for *stages* in the provinces under a senior administrator, closely resembles the practice of the two technical schools.

This *stage* in the ENA is during the first year.[1] Successful candidates in the entry examinations, if they are not already established civil servants, are given the status of official under instruction, and receive a salary with marriage and children's allowances. They are covered by the General Statute for public officials.

Shortly after joining the ENA each student is sent for the whole of his first year to serve under a senior administrator in the provinces, in North Africa, or, until recently, in Germany. They are not sent abroad, since the ENA considers that lack of experience would prevent them from deriving the maximum benefit from travel and foreign countries. It is also held that all senior officials of the future, whether serving in the foreign or the home civil service, should have a deep personal knowledge of France, have mixed with all classes and types of men, and have first-hand experience of rural, industrial and workers' circles.

But the ENA hardly disguises the psychological motives for this period of exile; it is to give the student a complete break from all past associations and ideas, to force the metropolitan man to live in the provinces, and to bring him into contact

[1] The ENA publishes each year details of its examinations, its courses, and statistics concerning its candidates.

with those parts of French society which, once started on his career, he will have no further chance to contact or explore.

During this period in the provinces or in North Africa students are under the direct supervision of either the Prefect or the Civil Governor. The ENA deliberately sends its pupils to work with officials whom they feel to be responsible and sensible instructors: one of the three directors of the ENA is personally responsible for supervising the students *en stage*, and he travels widely throughout the year keeping in touch both with the students and with the officials in charge of them. This minimises the chances of a serious error.

The supervising official is asked to regard the student attached to him as his personal assistant: to bring him into the closest touch with his own day to day work, to show him all but secret correspondence, to take him to official meetings and formal social occasions.

He is also asked to introduce him to the detail of administrative work, progressively making him responsible for the preparation of official business in his private office. When the prefect or civil governor's personal assistant goes on leave the student normally deputises for him. At the end of the student's *stage* the supervising official is asked to fill in a very detailed questionnaire compiled by the ENA, concerning the student's activities, capacities, competence and bearing. After appropriate weighting according to the known characteristics of the supervising official, the report is given a formal mark.

While serving his *stage* the student is required to choose a subject of local interest, and to prepare a twenty-five to thirty page thesis on it. The standard of this written work seems to be quite high and covers a wide range of subjects from rural housing projects to local irrigation schemes, social welfare programmes, and so on. This is also given a mark.

Finally, each student is required to send the ENA periodical reports of his past, present, and future activity during his *stage*. These reports do not receive any marks, but they must be forwarded through the supervising official, and no doubt their quality influences both the supervising official and the ENA's estimate of the student's capacities.

The second year in the ENA is spent in study in the ENA

itself in Paris. When he passes the entrance examination each student is assigned to one of four major divisions: General Administration, Financial and Economic, Social Administration or Foreign Affairs. Each division prepares the student for entry to a group of specified ministries: the General Administration division prepares students for careers in administrative courts, the ministries of the Interior, Defence and Education, the Cabinet Office, the central administration of Radiodiffusion et Télévision Française, and the Inspectorate General of Administration; the Foreign Affairs division for consular and diplomatic service; the Social Affairs division for the ministries of Ex-servicemen, the Interior, the Merchant Marine, Public Health, Labour and the Social Security administration; the Financial and Economic division for the ministries of Agriculture, Finance, Economic Affairs, Industry and Commerce, Interior, Merchant Marine, Public Works, Transport, and commercial attachés abroad. It will be seen that some ministries appear twice—for instance, the Merchant Marine; and the ministry of the Interior appears for all divisions except Foreign Affairs. Normally, the students in the principal division responsible for the ministry (e.g. the General Affairs division for the ministry of the Interior) have priority. Appointments may be either in the central administration in Paris, or the central administration in Algiers. During this second year instruction falls into two categories; courses of general instruction common to all or to several divisions, and courses specially designed for the needs of individual divisions. The ENA tries to be both a source of higher administrative culture and education and a professional body.

The courses common to all or several divisions are of various kinds. There are general courses on national questions of vital concern, and as far as possible these are treated in the context of relevant foreign experience in the same fields. In 1955, for instance, general courses were given on the technical problems of industrial economics, the question of under-developed countries with special reference to South American experience, co-partnership in industry, the bases of French agriculture, and judicial control over public authorities and the protection of the individual. Others are more specialized: for instance, the development of French territories in the south Sahara;

the administration's use of statistical techniques, demographic research, or the present problems of national defence.

A set of general courses common to the students of all divisions is devoted to North African problems: in 1955 they covered elements of Muslim history and sociology, the Franco-Tunisian conventions of 1955, and the problem of employment in Algeria, Tunisia and Morocco.

There are also general lectures given by distinguished specialists; these may either be a formal hour's lecture on a particular subject, or a set of three to five hour's lectures followed by a general discussion between the lecturer and the students. The principal purpose of these lectures, apart from their general educative value, is to introduce students to distinguished men in public affairs with whom they will later come into contact in the course of their administrative careers.

Another set of courses, still general in character but more specialized than the previous groups, is attended by the students of several divisions, and is designed to broaden the horizons of the students by bringing them into touch with the problems of their colleagues in fields other than their own. The students of the relevant division do not attend these courses, but the students of the other three divisions do. Thus, for instance, under Social Affairs, courses are held on social class, the social security system and its problems, the French trade union movement, collective bargaining in industry and labour conflicts, and the housing problem in France. These courses are not attended by the students in the Social Affairs division, who clearly ought already to have a specialized knowledge of these subjects.

The courses specially designed for the needs of individual divisions are much more intensively specialized. In the Financial and Economic Affairs division, to take an example, there are three courses in the year: public finance and accounting, economic programming, and the problems of international finance and the balance of payments. In addition there is a programme of seminars on economic and financial affairs, and on industrial administration. The first covers international economic problems, particular aspects of financial and economic questions in France, the problems of financial management, and the economic and financial problems of overseas territories.

Where two or more divisions are interested in the same specialized subject common seminars are arranged.

It should perhaps be noted that teaching in the ENA is not undertaken by any member of the staff. The director of the ENA determines which courses shall be given and proposes the names of people to give them. The ENA draws on outside experience; its annual list of lecturers includes senior civil servants, university teachers, directors of nationalized industries, people with special competence or particular experience likely to be of value to the students. This would seem to be an excellent system. It brings the students into close contact with specialists and experts in their own field, and ensures that the ENA should not fall back in time on stock courses and generally become too rigid. It allows a wide field of experiment and continual intellectual rejuvenation. Moreover, the benefits are not confined to the ENA. It is undoubtedly an excellent thing for senior officials to force themselves to understand and synthesise their own knowledge and experience; for them it is a valuable form of refresher course. But it does presuppose a group of senior civil servants with the intellectual energy and capacity for putting their own minds in order, a gift for clear thinking and presentation of ideas, and a desire for self expression. Given the material, there is a great deal to be said for this method of advanced instruction.

At the end of the second year in the ENA, when the various courses, lectures, seminars, and written work performed during the seminars, have been completed, the final classifying examination is held. This examination is conducted by a commission, members of which must not have had any teaching responsibilities in the ENA during the current session. This is to ensure, as far as humanly possible, the strictest impartiality.

The examination consists of written and oral parts. The first written paper is divided into two four-hour papers and it is common to the students of all four divisions. Eight questions have to be answered; two on constitutional and administrative matters, two on economic and financial affairs, two on social and health administration, and two on international affairs and international public law.

The second and third papers are highly specialized. One is a six-hour paper with a general question on the field covered by the division; the other the drafting, within six hours, of an administrative report on a specified subject.

For the first oral examination each student draws by lot the title of a subject within the general field of his division; he has an hour to prepare a statement on this subject, which he makes to the examining board for fifteen minutes, after which the board questions him on the content of his statement.

The second oral examination is a half hour's interrogation and discussion with the examining board on any subject, and in any way, the board chooses. Finally all students have an oral examination in a foreign language; the students in the Foreign Affairs division, and those in the Financial and Economic division who wish to be considered for posts abroad, must take two languages.

The weighting in these examinations is heavily in favour of intellectual ability rather than 'character'. The marks allotted to the half hour's interview with the board, which is the only occasion when personal prejudice might affect standards, are no more than can be obtained from the language tests; they amount to about one seventh of the total marks awarded. This is a reasonable proportion.

The marks obtained during the examination are added to the marks obtained for written work during the year, and the marks from the first year. The total of these marks determines the place obtained by each student in the final classifying list.

Before the final examination begins the government fixes by decree the number of vacant places in each ministry or administration. The students, in order of merit, choose their posts from this list, subject to two reservations. First, the post must be within the group of ministries covered by their division. Second, posts in the Conseil d'Etat, the civil administration in North Africa, and the Prefectoral Corps are open to students from any division, and posts in the Cour des Comptes and the Inspection Générale des Finances to all except the Foreign Affairs division. These posts in the grands corps are highly prized and are filled by students at the top of the list; normally the top fifteen or twenty students can reasonably hope to enter one or other of them.

At the beginning of his final year in the ENA the student is once again sent *en stage*. Each student now knows his future post, and the third year is primarily concerned with broadening his horizons as well as with work particularly relevant to his future career. The aim of the ENA is as much to produce humanists as to produce experts. This second *stage*, then, which lasts for between two and three months, is spent in a large industrial, commercial or agricultural undertaking. The student should aim at finding out how such organizations actually work, understanding the relations between the various sectors of the undertaking to see how, in practice, administrative regulations work at the receiving end, and finally entering as fully as he can into the spirit and preoccupations of the trade unions and the workers' world. Students who are to enter the civil administration in North Africa spend this *stage* in agricultural and rural engineering schools; future commercial attachés go to import-export agencies, merchant banks, and commercial houses; and those entering the ministry of Merchant Marine gain experience of big shipping lines, dock organization, and seamen's organizations.

At the end of their respective *stages* the students return to the ENA, and receive instruction specifically related to their future tasks. They are initiated into the work of their departments by lectures given by senior administrators, and they take part in departmental and inter-departmental committees. The student is expected to deal with complicated pieces of business as they present themselves to the administrator in the course of his ordinary working life, and as far as possible, he is expected to examine in depth the work of all the different divisions of the ministry or administration to which he has been appointed.

After a period of leave at the end of this third year, the student takes up his post.

The system of the ENA has been treated at some length since it is by far the most famous experiment in training civil servants. After a decade of experiment and experience it has become an established part of French public life, and its products show a breadth, intelligence, competence, and administrative and humanistic culture rarely to be found in administrators of comparable age in other countries. Most observers seem to agree that the greatly improved quality of the younger members of the administration is well worth the extra period of training and the additional expense involved. Assuming that most administrators who join the civil service have forty years service ahead of them, two and a half of them may justifiably be spent in training if this significantly increases their maturity and competence. It seems fair to say that the ENA does manage to do this. Nor would most observers deny the very positive value of the system of *stages*. In the course of time it will eradicate from the senior civil service that administrative oddity, the senior official who has no conception of life in the provinces, of the work of local government, of the spirit and outlook of trade unionists, or of business and commercial practice.

Some of the praise bestowed on the ENA by foreigners has been extravagant and uncritical. To put it in perspective some of the shortcomings which the French have found in their own system should be mentioned.

Certain basic aims of the ENA system have only been partly met. Despite the creation of Instituts d'Etudes Politiques attached to universities throughout France with the principal purpose of preparing students for entrance to the ENA, the pre-war dominance of Paris over the provinces still continues. The Institut d'Etudes Politiques of Paris produces an overwhelming majority of the successful candidates for the ENA. This is, of course, partly a reflexion of the fact that Paris attracts the brilliant and the ambitious among both teachers and students. It may also be related to the entry standards of the ENA itself. These are of doctoral standard, and at such a level many potential candidates are frightened off by the prospect of long and arduous preparation to enter the ENA with very uncertain prospects of success. This may also account for the only relative success the French have had in democratizing their higher civil service. So far the ENA has been unsuccessful in recruiting people from the skilled worker level of society; the majority of the successful candidates from other than middle class families have entered through the 'officials' examination. It may be that the length of training combined with the very high standard of entry examination effectively eliminates candidates entirely dependent on their own resources.

Another factor which has been noted by French critics is that no candidate can be sure of choosing his career. Before the war a graduate who wanted to enter an administrative court could do so by passing the appropriate competitive examination. With the ENA system a candidate might enter hoping to become an auditeur of the Conseil d'Etat and end up as an administrator in the French Radio. This is not in itself particularly important, but it has two significant results. The first is that this career gamble might well scare off some good potential candidates who would in principle be prepared to take the initial risks of studying for the entrance examination, but not to spend a further two years before taking the final examination which will determine their future careers. At the end of his second year he must take one of the posts open to his place on the list, and since he is required to sign a document committing himself to serve the state for ten years it is then too late to change his mind: alternatively, he must reimburse the costs of his training in the ENA and the salary paid to him as apprentice official. Only wealthy dilettantes can afford this kind of gesture.

The second result of the allocation of posts is to exacerbate relations between the various services of the administration. Traditionally, all the top posts in the ministry of Finance went to members of the Inspection Générale des Finances. The ordinary administrators in the ministry could only rarely hope to contest them on grounds of merit. But the ENA graduates tend to be unwilling to accept this situation; by the luck of the draw in any particular year the twentieth in the ENA classification examination may go to the Inspection des Finances and the twenty-first to the ministry of Finance as an administrateur civil. It is hardly likely that the latter will acknowledge without demur that the former should have automatic priority for the highest posts. The ENA, for all that it has done, has certainly not so far been able to abolish the esprit de corps of the grands corps, and this may have serious effects later on the general morale of the higher service.[1]

Finally, there is the question whether the ENA may not be casting its net too wide. It seems possible that it should cut down the number of administrations it caters for. There have been complaints that some ENA products who have been posted to the field services of the ministry of Finance have been of

[1] J. Sabatier: 'L'avenir de l'ENA.' *Promotions.* January, 1952.

much worse quality than the pre-war entrants. Before the war a competitive examination was held amongst the contrôleurs des finances already in service in the provinces, and the successful candidates were taken into the central ministry of Finance for ten years and were then sent back to the provinces as percepteurs généraux. This provided a solid corps of very able men, although they were, of course, normally ten years older than the people appointed now after graduating from the ENA. But since these field services are amongst the least attractive to the students in the ENA it follows that most of those who now enter them do so because they are the ENA's mistakes, and have no option.

All told the balance of the ENA's achievement seems to be this. It has not, according to the best informed opinion, raised the standard of people in the grands corps, which was already very high before the war. It has if anything lowered the quality of those entering the least attractive parts of the administration, and there seems to be a case for forming these posts into a group comparable to the departmental classes of the British civil service with separate entry. But it seems substantially to have raised the level of the higher civil service employed in central administration; there is general agreement that the post-war administrateurs civils in the ministries are of higher quality than the pre-war rédacteurs. If this is true, as it almost certainly is, the French administration during the next few years will be an interesting case study of the conflict between promotion by seniority and promotion by merit.

ADVANCED COURSES

It is now widely accepted in Europe that advanced refresher courses for officials are desirable. They seem to be so for three reasons. First, specialized officials need to be brought up to date in their own fields in order simply to maintain their current efficiency. Second, proper instruction in the principles of management and training for supervisory work is coming to be regarded as an essential preliminary for promotion from the lower and middle ranks to senior posts. Finally, there seems to be a good case for relieving high-ranking officials of their current responsibilities for a short time in order that they can refresh themselves intellectually, renew contacts with other groups and other professions, and have a brief opportunity to put themselves and their work into perspective. This is particularly important for those officials between the ages of thirty-five and forty-five who are clearly destined to become administrative leaders.

All three forms of advanced course have been common practice in the armed forces of every country for many years: the artillery schools' refresher courses for gunners, training courses for NCO's, staff colleges for officers. But only in recent years has it been appreciated that expertise, leadership and management, strategy and planning, are as essential to civil government as to military affairs.

But if all countries recognize the desirability of one or more of these types of courses the pace at which they advance is very uneven. Denmark, for instance, only has refresher courses for specialists. Spain has gone furthest in the field of local government; the Instituto de Estudios de Administración Local provides not only the original entry training for people wishing to enter the national corps of communal secretaries, but also advanced courses for established staff seeking promotion.

Most countries, when they have attempted to organize refresher courses for the normal administrative services encounter the difficulties experienced in Italy.

Italy had practically no experience of refresher courses until 1949, apart from narrowly specialized courses given to tax officials before the war and an experimental course run by the local tax office in Naples during 1947–8. Those started in 1949 were restricted to the ministry of Finance and were for a long time the only examples of their kind. In 1949 a two-month course was attended by officials from the direct and indirect tax administrations and the Guardia di Finanza (frontier and customs guards). Lectures were given by university teachers on aspects of financial administration such as budgetary control, statistics, credit houses, as well as on technical subjects connected with industry and commerce. The results were promising and the following year a specialized course was begun for accountants, to expand their knowledge of recent techniques and to give further instruction in business accounting. This course was also given by university teachers. Since then the

Italian financial administration has gradually expanded its courses, some for new entrants, some refresher courses in very specialized fields, and some broadly based refresher courses bringing together officials from various services.[1]

In Italy the ministry of Finance is clearly the only ministry which as yet takes training seriously, but it has fought an up-hill battle against difficulties which are not confined to Italy.

In the first place it is very difficult to persuade the heads of divisions to release their officials to attend refresher courses. This is partly no doubt the usual conservative reaction of older officials in face of new ideas; it is also partly due to the pressure of work in all European ministries, which is much greater than the layman realizes. The head of an office is naturally loath to release his best men for even short periods, when this inevitably increases the backlog of matters awaiting attention.

Experience shows that it is also difficult to get the officials themselves to take these courses seriously. For some it is simply a release from the routine of the office, and if the courses are voluntary but with full-time attendance this is the class of official which will principally be attracted. If, on the other hand, officials are nominated to take part in the course, psychological difficulties are encountered. Officials in the middle and lower grades with some experience tend to regard themselves as experts, and are, therefore, unwilling to co-operate in the courses even when it is clear to the teaching staff that the officials were wrong in believing themselves expert. There is the additional difficulty of persuading mature men who are settled in their ways to begin to study again. This attitude can be modified, if not broken down, by good teachers, and by providing an incentive to the official who assiduously and conscientiously follows the course.

For this reason the Italian ministry of Finance relied to a considerable extent on university teachers, even for narrow specialist courses. Their outlook and attitudes of mind proved stimulating and captured attention. Although senior officials were used for some lecture courses they were not uniformly successful, although their rank commanded dutiful attention.

[1] G. Stammati: 'Corsi de perfezionamento tecnico per i funzionari dell' amministrazione finanziaria.' *Rivista Amministrativa*, 1953. pp. 232–40.

The ministry is also trying to establish an unofficial order of merit with the hope that it may come to be used informally by promotion boards; it does not in fact matter whether it is so used provided the officials themselves believe it is. One important departure is gradually to make the university teachers who conduct the courses responsible for evaluating the officials who attend the courses, and not to leave this to the senior organizing officials or the officials who lecture. This would add weight to the 'chit', since the Italian authorities believe that the marks obtained in examinations are an independent and objective estimate of an official's worth, and it could usefully supplement the reports of the official's hierarchic superiors whose views are always likely to be biased by 'the practical exigencies of the service'.

In Holland efforts, of very recent date, in the field of advanced training have been directed at creating a properly trained body of organization and methods experts. These experts now being trained are to be available both as experts in their own right, and also as instructors of other higher personnel. In 1954 the government set up a special advisory committee to plan a programme of courses on the basis that 'the leading officers of all grades must be better trained for management and for the critical assessment and reform or construction of their own organization, with or without the assistance of organization experts'.[1] An organization development adviser was appointed, and after consultation with the permanent heads of ministries he laid down the types of organization and methods specialists needed in the civil service and arranged a programme of courses for them. These courses cover the principles and methods of administrative organization, some administrative law and the structure of government, and a number of special courses in economics, psychology, sociology and statistics. The course is divided into three parts. Each part is based on private reading and study, and on periods of lecturing in small groups where case studies and group discussion methods are used. After he has completed the course, the organization expert serves in

[1] G. van Poelje: 'Complementary training for higher grade officials in the Netherlands,' and J. Smit: 'Training in the field of organization and its influence on the training of leading officers in the Netherlands.' In *Actas*, Xth. International Congress of Administrative Sciences, Madrid, 1956. p. 639 seq.

various departments learning his new expertise under supervision.

At the moment the major part of the course is given, under the general supervision of the organization development advisor, by a private agency with experience in catering for large-scale industry.

This system seems to have had a fairly promising start; an encouraging point is that some ministries are beginning to request that their senior officials attend these courses, not in order to become organization experts, but simply to increase their capacity and competence as administrators. It is also planned that the civil servants trained as organization experts will, after serving in that capacity for several years, return to their original administrations. In due course it is hoped that all higher officials will have undergone this organizational training at some point in their careers.

Probably only Britain, with the Administrative Staff College at Henley, and France, with its Centre des Hautes Etudes Administratives, have institutions specially designed to prepare senior administrators for posts of the highest responsibility. In the future the German administrative school at Speyer may develop further along these lines, but at the moment it is not equipped for work of this kind: the most it can do is hold weekend conferences during the breaks in the normal training year, and invite senior officials and distinguished foreigners to attend. This is better than nothing.

The French Centre des Hautes Etudes Administratives has not established itself as firmly in the French administrative structure as it might have done. It remains an adjunct to the ENA, partly because its director is the director of the ENA, partly because it is dependent on the ENA for accommodation, but mainly because the ENA is taken seriously whereas the CHEA is not.

The CHEA is required, first, to perfect the culture of officials who have already had considerable experience of administrative life, to keep them up to date with national problems, and to give them the opportunity of broadening their horizons by meeting and working together with officials from other branches of the administration. Second, to give people with experience in private business an opportunity to obtain an administrative training to prepare them for posts in the civil service which they might be offered. In practice, the second objective has been quietly ignored.

Between 1947 and 1956, 385 officials attended the courses given by the CHEA. Of these the great majority were senior administrators in ministries, but there were also members of the judiciary and the Prefectoral Corps, and some state engineers and officers in the Armed Forces. In addition there were 45 people from outside, the majority from the nationalized industries, and a few from private industry. To enter, a civil servant may himself apply with ministerial approval, or the minister can put forward the official's name. In both cases the official's administrative superior has to be consulted. The choice is made by a special council attached to the CHEA.[1]

Each course lasts four months, and is devoted to a single topic. These have included the reform of the state, central-local government relations, the co-ordination of transport, civil defence, the state's rôle in scientific research, the economic development of Brittany, Lorraine and Languedoc, the administration of conurbations, France's rôle in the United Nations' technical assistance programme. Each course is under the supervision of a person specially appointed by the government; they have included conseillers d'Etat, prefects, professors, members of the Institut, senior technical officials, and directors of ministries or major public institutions. Specialists are invited in from outside to lecture on their particular field. The work of the course is divided between work syndicates, each member being liable to serve either as chairman or as rapporteur for the detailed examination of a specific aspect of the subject.

A major difficulty is that, because of financial difficulties and the reluctance of central administrations to release their officials for a long period, the courses are part time. Members attend for two or three days a week, spending the rest of their time on their own job. During several of the courses arrangements have been made for the members to travel in order to examine their problem at close quarters. Some of the reports prepared by courses have been of very high standard, and this

[1] F. Méjan: 'Le perfectionnement des cadres supérieurs de l'Administration en France.' In *Actas*, Xth. International Congress of Administrative Sciences. Madrid, 1956. p. 684 seq.

is only to be expected given the quality of the people selected for attendance. But the principle object of the course is not so much to provide the government with authoritative reports on subjects which should interest the state, as to rejuvenate and re-humanize the officials who attend the course, and to prepare them while still in early middle age for the mental adjustments which will be necessary when they are called on to fill the highest posts. It has not even begun to achieve this objective. In comparison with the ENA, the experiment of the Centre des Hautes Etudes Administratives has not been a success. There is, however, both room and need for further initiative on these lines. Most countries are beginning to realize that if senior officials are not to arrive at the highest posts jaded, harassed and narrow, they must be given a breather in the middle of their career when they can benefit from intellectual stimulation and a rest from current business. Also, even when different groups have mixed together in the course of their training, there is a great need for people from different branches of the public service and from private industry to associate together consistently over a period after they have had experience of the burdens of authority. Mutual comprehension and mutual instruction is extremely valuable, and is perhaps the best way to ensure that senior administrators grow in stature as they assume greater responsibilities.

PART TWO

CONDITIONS OF SERVICE

CHAPTER 4

Rights and Duties

In most countries at the present day the conditions of service of public officials employed by the state are regulated by public law. In France, it is the statut général de la fonction publique of 1946; in Germany, the Bundesbeamtengesetz of 1953 (which was closely modelled on earlier statutes); in Italy, it is a group of executive decrees authorized and delimited in scope by the law of December 20, 1954. A consolidated text was promulgated in January, 1957. Previously the Italian public service had been regulated by a consolidated text of 1918, which had been modified and amended out of recognition by later provisions promulgated by different governments and different ministries. Belgium has a general statute comparable to the French and Italian statutes, but unlike either of these the Belgian statute was issued as a royal ordinance under the prerogative. In Switzerland, federal officials come under the federal statute of public officials of 1927, amended in 1949. Finally in Sweden, the civil service is to some extent covered by constitutional provisions, supplemented by individual instructions of particular ministries and royal boards.[1]

The legal position, therefore, varies widely; from constitutional clauses to legislative enactments to executive ordinances. But despite the differences in the formal nature of the instruments governing state officials in different countries, there is a notable degree of uniformity in the provisions themselves, and in the problems each country is attempting to solve. Moreover, closer analysis reveals the extent to which nowadays civil services

[1] The factual information used in this Part is drawn from the civil service statutes and regulations of the individual countries. To avoid undue proliferation of footnotes these will not be referred to in detail, but the reader should refer to the bibliography.

in all countries have become self-governing, self-administering groups, insulated from outside interference, whether social, political or judicial. This is by far the most significant event in this field during the last fifty years.

GOVERNING BODIES

Before considering conditions of service in detail the governing bodies of civil services should be mentioned; these are the bodies which have the daily responsibility for administering the public service as a profession.

The most striking point is the extent to which political and legislative influence has been eliminated. In the fields of discipline, promotion, rating, and recruitment a group of officials is generally responsible, not an outside body.

In France responsibility for the civil service is divided between the direction de la fonction publique, the personnel officers of the different ministries, and commissions administratives paritaires, joint bodies with advisory powers and the right to be consulted on questions of training, promotion, discipline, and so on.

In Belgium general responsibility for the civil service is divided between two bodies; the secrétariat permanent de recrutement responsible for organizing entry into the civil service, and the service d'administration générale attached to the Prime Minister's office for general questions of civil service policy. Each ministry has a conseil de direction comprising the heads of the divisions within the ministry, assisted in disciplinary and rating matters by a departmental chambre de recours; for the discipline of the highest officials there is an interdepartmental chambre de recours. Half the members of these chambres are nominated by the civil service trade unions, and half by the minister.

In Italy hierarchy has been the dominant traditional characteristic and until recently the few representative councils which existed were very weak. The new statute however makes a determined effort to set up organs comparable to those of other countries. A consiglio superiore della pubblica amministrazione has been formed, entirely composed of officials, some sitting ex officio and others as representatives of various categories of public officials. In addition in each ministry the directors general at the head of each division form a consiglio di amministrazione with extensive powers over pay, promotion, discipline and rating. Finally, the new statute creates in each ministry a commissione di disciplina of three high officials to act as the ministry's disciplinary court. What distinguishes the Italian from the French or Belgian statutes is that the middle and lower ranking officials have no place in these various bodies; they are staffed entirely by the senior civil service.

In the Scandinavian countries there are no central governing bodies, though special arbitration courts, and in Sweden a special ministry, deal with questions of pay. Individual ministries and boards are responsible for negotiating conditions of service and for disciplinary matters, subject to special procedures laid down by law.

The German civil service has always been largely self-administered, but it has in some ways become petrified. Like the new Italian civil service it is self-administered by senior civil servants; there are advisory and disciplinary committees, but it is basically a professional autocracy from which are excluded the representatives of the middle and lower categories of public officials.

The Germans may be partly right. An observer sometimes feels in every country that it is a handful of conscientious, imaginative and intelligent civil servants who have prevented the public service from becoming a closed, rigid, and mechanical organization administering according to strict rules of procedure and precedent. There are few members of the lower and middle ranks of the public service who understand the fluidity, flexibility, and informal aspects of higher administration. They transfer their own sectional approach and detailed knowledge of restricted fields of administration to the highest level, and fail to recognize the fragility and subtlety of the most essential parts of administrative technique.

This fundamental difference of approach between high-ranking civil servants and the lowest and middle ranks comes out clearly during discussions of conditions of service. Lower and middle grades want to have as far as possible precise rigid and detailed provisions, preferably laid down by legislative enactment. The highest civil servants, on the other hand, always favour executive responsibility with a considerable degree of latitude and discretion to meet the changing needs of the service. This conflict of opinion is well instanced in the discussions which took place before the Belgian, the French, and the Italian public service statutes were passed. Similar psychological differences can be noted in Great Britain if the works of Gladden and Dale are compared.

Clearly, in a book such as this it is quite impossible to enter into the finer details of administrative law in a discussion of conditions of service. Every country has a body of case law determining, for instance, under what conditions an official has a right to a pension, or the circumstances under which a particular offence should be punished by down-grading rather than by dismissal. But minute description of this kind would be out of place here. It seems far better to concentrate on questions which all countries have to deal with, and to bring out the points of similarity and dissimilarity in the way they tackle them.

RIGHTS AND DUTIES

Certain rights are closely associated with the status of public official, and they are in particular the official's right to security of tenure, his right to be paid,[1] his right to a pension, his right to a special disciplinary process, and his right to some sort of career within the service. Although these rights are not always classified or even formally recognized, in every country both the official and the public regard them as essential to the office. They are all sufficiently important to demand separate sections; and some of them raise difficult problems which can only be touched on in passing.

There are in addition two basic questions which could be dealt with here, but which seem to fit better into a later chapter. First there is the right which officials have now come to

[1] Normally he will only receive the salary and emoluments appropriate to his grade in the service. He may also receive additional fees for service as a nominated director in a private company in which the state holds shares. In many countries he only receives a proportion of these directors' fees. In Italy and Spain certain financial departments levy a charge for administrative services, the proceeds of which are distributed to the staff of the department. See Enterria: *Los Funcionarios y el futuro de Nuestra Economia*. 'Arriba', April 1, 1955. (' . . . un sistema de exaciones proprias sobre el publico . . .'), and for Italy, see President Einaudi's denunciation of the system of 'casuali' in a message to parliament, November 21, 1953.

share with other citizens, the right to organize and form civil service unions and associations. Until relatively recently officials were forbidden to do this in nearly all countries. Then gradually the right was extended from the industrial employees of the state to the lower and middle ranking officials, until after the war it was recognized as desirable to allow civil servants the same rights in this field as any other worker. Partly this was due to the great political influence of trade unions immediately after the war, partly the result of the de-mystification of the state started by French jurists like Duguit. Normally even today the highest branch of a civil service is subject to special conditions. The logical complement to organization in unions—the right to strike—has not been widely accepted, and in several countries a strike of civil servants is forbidden by law.

The second question is the extent of a civil servant's political rights. In some countries there is no restriction at all on a public official's right to engage in political activities, and no restriction on his right to enter an elected political assembly, even including the national parliament. In other countries some classes of officials are allowed full political rights, while other classes are restricted. As with the first question this raises problems affecting the whole field of relations between politics and administration, and it seems best to postpone discussion until a later chapter.

A civil servant's liberties are curtailed more than those of other citizens by the special duties imposed on him, and the special responsibilities he bears by virtue of his office. Every country requires its officials to be true to their oath of office, to obey their superiors, and to keep inviolate the secrets they learn in the course of their work. Indeed, some countries go so far as to claim they should not disclose anything they learn in the course of their work. But probably the British Official Secrets Act is unique in its severity and rigidity.

A very delicate point is the extent to which an official's private life is the concern of his service, and under what circumstances his private behaviour could lead to suspension or dismissal from office.

It is, of course, obvious that certain officials such as policemen have to be extremely circumspect even when not on duty, since indiscreet or irresponsible behaviour can lessen both their own personal authority and that of their service. In the past this private responsibility of the official was held to imply that he could only marry with the consent of his superiors. Traces of this are still to be found today in the requirement that policemen, diplomats and soldiers must obtain their superior's consent before marriage. It is based on the grounds that an unsuitable marriage could affect the efficiency and moral authority of an official; it is also held that an eccentric wife might be a security risk.

Certain restrictions are also placed on an official's right to take part in private business. It is everywhere regarded as reprehensible, and in most cases positively forbidden, for an official to have any business dealings in fields with which he will come into contact in the ordinary course of his duties. The reasons for this are obvious: the temptations which might arise could place an unreasonable strain on a man's integrity, particularly if his official duties require him to control certain branches of business, or if he is responsible for business dealings on behalf of his administration. A moderate statement of the formal limitations on a full-time official having outside interests is contained in the Swiss civil service regulations.[1] It effectively summarises the general rules in force in other countries: 'The public official must obtain official permission before he may: (*a*) pursue activities outside the scope of his official duties, if they bring him financial gain or consistently take up much of his time; (*b*) be a member of the board of any organization working for financial gain, or of any association or institution which seeks, through mutual assistance, economic advantages for its members.' Moreover this ordonnance positively forbids the exercise of a profession which '(*a*) may lead to a breach of the official secrets acts; (*b*) may involve unfair competition with craftsmen, industry, commerce, or any other economic activity; (*c*) may seriously endanger the life or health of an official.' The authority which can give the authorization is in principal the Conseil Fédéral as head of the entire federal civil service, but the ministerial departments and the directorates general of Customs and Posts and Telegraphs have delegated authority, which they may in turn delegate to subordinate offices.

[1] Ordonnance sur les rapports de service des fonctionnaires de l'administration générale, art. 13.

Two questions however which are not easy to dispose of are these. Should the same restrictions also apply to an official's wife, and should the term 'economic activity' also cover cases in which officials hold shares or otherwise indirectly participate in a business with which they might be required to have official dealings.

In general there are some restrictions on a wife's right to engage in business. The limits are generally a function of the official's own position and seniority. The more senior he is, the less likely is it that his wife's activity in a closely parallel field would be regarded with favour. In some countries it is probable that for the wife of a senior official to engage in any form of commercial activity, even unconnected with his work, would seriously prejudice his future. There is a snob element in this, but the danger of financial difficulties must also be taken into account. Such a ban is more rigidly enforced in the area where the official is serving.

The second question is not dealt with in any legal code governing an official's behaviour. His, or his wife's, participation through share-holding or other means in business is nowhere forbidden. This is partly due to the impossibility of detection; it is also due to the feeling that the mere possession of a few shares is not likely to exercise any preponderant influence on the integrity or fair-mindedness of a normally balanced official. Yet the remote possibility does exist, and in several countries the internal code of administrative ethics would demand that in certain circumstances an official should declare his personal interest to his superior, or refuse to handle a particular piece of business. This seems a highly desirable precaution, and rightly treats the official as a moral adult with his own responsibility. Nor can he ignore the possibility that if for any reason there was a scandal or an enquiry his silence would give rise to the worst interpretations.

The business dealings of officials involves a further difficulty. In all administrations today there are a certain number of officials who are in close contact with industry or commerce, either acting on behalf of the administration in business dealings with outside bodies, or, by the nature of their duties, required to exercise control functions over them.

The danger is that an official may be exposed to indirect

corruption. He may favour a firm in one way or another, by, for instance, awarding contracts, or by being less than rigorous in demanding compliance with the law. There may be no question of money changing hands or any other form of punishable corruption. But he may be given to understand that when he leaves his service a post of responsibility, or a directorship on a board will be waiting for him. It is even possible to put this in terms in which there is no open element of pressure or inducement.

To avoid this possibility several countries, amongst them France, Germany and Great Britain, have a rule that a civil servant may not accept a post with a firm with which he has had official dealings for a specific period (generally two years) after the time he leaves the service. This is almost certainly a wise precaution; it affects very few officials, and the possibility of occasional unfairness is very slight.

The limitations on an official's rights and liberties may probably be regarded as duties of a negative kind, but in addition he has positive duties, which, if he fails to perform them, make him liable to disciplinary action.

The positive duties enjoined on an official are the same in every country. He has a duty to obey his superiors, though this raises complicated issues which will have to be mentioned; he is required to work to the best of his ability in the post to which he is appointed, and to obey the regulations governing the operation of that office. Like any ordinary employee he must attend at a regular hour in a proper condition to perform his functions satisfactorily. An official is normally expected to work reasonable overtime if his services are essential, and in the higher branches of administration to do so without being paid for it. He is expected to regard information he obtains in the course of his duties as being secret.[1] He is normally required to reside near his place of work; in certain cases, for instance prefects, governors and other officials in comparable posts, he may only leave his place of residence with express permission. He may not hold more than one official post at any one time. Certain officials must wear uniform when on duty, and others must do so on ceremonial occasions.

[1] This is not as simple as it sounds. For some of the difficulties see R. Tunc: 'Le secret professionnel.' *Revue Administrative*. May, 1948.

There are a few exceptions to these rules. Members of some of the grands corps in France, for instance the Conseil d'Etat and the Inspection des Finances, are expected to work at home and only attend on formal business occasions. In all countries university teachers are required only to attend to give their courses of instruction, and otherwise have no fixed hours. In Spain the rates of pay in many branches of the administration are so low that officials are forced (contrary to the rules) to take other part-time jobs in order to live, or alternatively to have several official jobs each with its own salary. The authorities tacitly accept this, and no effort is made to enforce the rules[1]

The German code formalises what are elsewhere regarded as implicit duties.[2] An official must co-operate to the best of his ability with his colleagues. He must be polite with the public and honest and conscientious in his dealings with them. He must devote his attention to the training and formation of staff put under him; and this implies not only that he must guide, advise and discipline subordinate staff, but that he has a responsibility as a member of an administration to train the younger men who will later accede to his own or comparable posts. This duty, of course, is particularly important for senior officials. Elderly members of the middle and lower ranks of public offices frequently neglect this important part of their duties: indeed they give the impression of being unaware of it. Two reasons are normally advanced for this state of affairs, both psychological. The first is that the work of the middle and lower grades is often monotonous, and that since promotion is largely a matter of seniority only tired and relatively elderly men hold the highest posts. The second is that people recruited to these grades have little conception of the need for a continual recreation of cadres to replace themselves when they retire. Whereas in all countries the large majority of officials faithfully fulfil their normal duties (though not always with enthusiasm) this particularly vital duty of securing the succession is often ignored except by a handful of the highest officials.

To return to the duty of obedience to a superior. In certain countries such as Spain, Portugal and probably Germany, this is still regarded as an absolute duty. Thirty years ago it would

[1] E. García de Enterría: op. cit. 'Arriba'. April 1, 1955.

[2] H. Peters: *Lehrbuch der Verwaltung*. Berlin, 1949. p. 266 seq.

have been surprising even to hear the question raised. The new awareness of the problem is a direct result of the extremely difficult moral problems which during the war faced officials of occupied and of occupying powers.

There are in fact two problems. The first is how far an official can go in calling his superior's attention to the fact that a proposed measure is apparently in conflict with the law. The second is more difficult: it is how far an official may be expected to carry out an order which is undoubtedly legal but which is morally repugnant or even blatantly outrageous.

No country has in fact discovered any satisfactory answer to the second question.

The first question presents little difficulty. At its simplest the accepted practice is this. When an official has reason to suppose that a measure contemplated is in conflict with the law, he has the right—and in some countries the duty—to inform his superior. If he is overriden the responsibility rests entirely with his superior who will be held liable if in the event the subordinate official was proved right. No other method could in fact be devised which both ensures the frank exchange of opinion within an administration and the effective execution of administrative decisions. It is clear that no administration can tolerate the continual submission of decisions to subordinate officials' views of the law. It is for the superior official to decide how far he will go to insure himself against mistake. And it is common, whenever an important matter is involved, for expert legal advice to be taken.

In the past the main trouble has been to know exactly what course of action the subordinate official should take. If he regards an order as illegal the doctrine in most countries has been that he should refuse to obey. If on the other hand he considers simply that it *may* be illegal he should obey once he has drawn his superior's attention to the question and been overruled. But this puts the official himself in the position of having to decide between manifest and possible illegality; to introduce an entirely subjective element of this kind is bad for administration. The most recent attempt to decide this problem in formal terms is in the Italian civil service statute. This lays on the individual official the personal responsibility for informing his superior whenever he considers the execution of an order would break the law. If the order is then repeated, this time in writing, the official is required to obey. But, no order is legitimate which would involve the official in a breach of the provisions of the Penal Code; it is then his duty to refuse to obey the order.

The jurisprudence of the French Conseil d'Etat is similar. 'The official who receives an illegal order can inform his superior of his view; but if his superior continues to insist he must be obeyed. . . . But there is no longer a duty to obey when the execution of an order would involve a flagrant and serious breach of the law and raises the serious possibility of gravely compromising the public interest. When the official can have no doubt that to obey an order involves a serious breach of the law he will commit no disciplinary fault in refusing to carry it out. Indeed, there are cases where obedience to an order will render the official liable to disciplinary action.'[1]

The second case poses difficult political and moral problems. What does an official do if he is given an order which is legal but is morally or politically repugnant? At what stage should the moral responsibility of the citizen override the official irresponsibility of the civil servant?

The answer normally given to this problem is that the official concerned should resign rather than obey. But there are substantial difficulties in the way of this. First, there is the official's own point of view. He is put in a position without parallel in any other profession: to obey his conscience means the destruction of his career. An official prepared to do this deserves the highest praise, and there are a few cases to show it can happen: for instance, General Paris de Bolladière who resigned his appointment in Algeria in 1957 in protest against the policy of the French government. There were a certain number of cases in the early days of the Hitler régime in Germany where officials managed to obtain transfers from police administration to posts in, for instance, the hospital service in order to escape the intolerable demands made on their consciences. This course is always advocated in Britain but there are virtually no examples to prove it happens in practice.

Second, governments in fact dislike such resignations; they are a public disavowal of a policy and may well have more political repercussions than any parliamentary debate.

[1] A. Plantey: *Traité pratique de la fonction publique.* Paris, 1956. p. 178.

Third, it is sometimes held that public confidence in the impartiality of the civil service would be shaken if there were any serious number of resignations on questions of policy.

Finally, there are some countries in which an official's resignation because of disagreement on moral or political grounds would involve him in some personal danger.

The first and most important step is to recognize the existence of the problem. Once this is done steps can be taken to reduce the number of officials likely to be placed in such a situation, and to meet the public's desire for a firm government entitled to pursue its own policy, and officials of strong and honourable character. Most European countries have taken steps to do this. They involve, however, important questions regarding the organization of ministries and the relations between the political and the administrative worlds. It would be more convenient to examine this question in a later chapter devoted to these problems.

CHAPTER 5

Security of Tenure

In all countries civil servants have great security of tenure, a security sometimes sanctioned by the law, sometimes by convention. In the extreme case, Sweden, this security is sanctioned by the constitution itself. Indeed, in all Scandinavian countries except Finland the civil servant's right to his post is almost a vested right. In Sweden the constitution not only guarantees the official against removal except after trial, but also protects him from any transfer except with his own consent. The Norwegian constitution follows this very closely. It protects the official from dismissal unless judgement has gone against him in the proper tribunal; nor may he be transferred against his will. The Danish civil service law also protects officials from arbitrary dismissal or transfer. Only in Finland, among the Scandinavian countries, is this extreme protection modified. Before 1926 Finnish officials had the same security as is still to be found today in Sweden.[1] But since the law of 1926 on public functions this right has been substantially modified, and only judges are protected in their posts to anything like the same degree. The other three groups of officials are all liable to dismissal or enforced retirement; the most senior after a special administrative process; the other two grades, contractual employees and simple employees, can be dismissed by ordinary administrative action.[2]

Although other countries do not go so far as the Swedish or Norwegian constitutional safeguards, all offer very substantial protection to permanent civil servants. Even in the nineteenth

[1] It should be remembered, however, that in Sweden this constitutional protection only applies to a relatively small group of public servants. Those who are appointed by warrant or on contract are not covered by these provisions. Heckscher: op cit. p. 340.

[2] V. Merikoski: *Précis du Droit Public de la Finlande*. Helsinki, 1954. p. 110.

century when promotions and appointments were frequently subject to influence, favouritism and nepotism, a civil servant once appointed had very considerable personal security. In France, for instance, by the middle of the nineteenth century judges and officers were entirely protected, and members of the technical corps hardly less so. Officials in several of the central administrations could be dismissed only after due administrative process, and although other officials were not strictly covered by any legal protection they were very rarely badly used in this respect. The Diplomatic and Prefectoral Corps were entirely without protection, but even there drastic purges occurred only at changes of régime.[1] Only in Italy, Spain and Belgium were there no legal or conventional safeguards against summary dismissal, and even in those countries certain administrations—for instance the various cuerpos tecnicos in Spain—had substantial security of tenure.

In practice today the only class of permanent official liable to dismissal without an elaborate disciplinary process are the probationers, and it is by no means certain that they can properly be regarded as permanent officials.

On the other hand every country distinguishes between permanent full-time officials and others who, although employed full-time in the public service, are regarded as being in contractual relation with the state, and therefore not covered by the normal right to security of tenure. This is the German distinction between Beamten and Angestellten, the Spanish tecnicos and ausiliarios, and so on. In addition the industrial workers employed by the state are in most countries regarded as a separate group altogether, are normally paid at standard industrial rates, and are subject to dismissal as they would be in private enterprise. Finally, every administration employs a certain number of specialists—lawyers, doctors, veterinary surgeons, and so on—normally on contract. The difference between this group and the unestablished Angestellten type of official is that the latter may pass his entire career in state service; it is much rarer for the technical expert employed on contract to do this.

Indeed the status of unestablished staff has considerably altered since 1939, and they are no longer deprived of all the

[1] Vivien: *Etudes Administratives*. 3rd. ed. Paris, 1859.

rights of the permanent official. In many countries they have achieved almost equal security of tenure. In Belgium for instance several ministries are staffed largely by unestablished personnel who originally entered during the war and have ever since through their unions made strenuous efforts to avoid any dismissals.

What in fact distinguishes the permanent established official from the unestablished official is that the latter will not get a pension when he leaves state service (though he may receive a gratuity according to the length of service), and he has no right to demand the protection of the elaborate disciplinary procedures if he commits an offence while in office.

Although permanent officials have everywhere a legal or a conventional security of tenure, the extent of their protection varies. Two types of security can be distinguished: (i) the right to serve in a particular post, with a particular rank, and (ii) the more general right to remain a civil servant with a particular rank. In the first instance, removal from a specific post can only be obtained after a special procedure. In the second case transfer from one post to another is perfectly permissible and gives rise to no legal proceedings.

(i) Certain posts regarded on the continent as civil service appointments are traditionally protected from outside interference, and their holders have an absolute right to one particular post. Foremost among these are judges and university professors. The appointment of university professors in every country is peculiar, and quite different from normal recruitment. Provided they give the courses required of them by law they are not subject to direction as to the content of what they teach, or the opinions they express, nor can they be removed except by a very special procedure in which their own colleagues are closely associated. In practice they enjoy conditions of service much the same as their colleagues in countries where the universities are independent; the only important difference is that they spend much less time on administration.

Judges are carefully protected in every country, and ostentatious efforts are made to show their independence from the executive. It is of course as well to remember that in several countries 'the magistracy' includes the public prosecutor's department (the parquet) as well as the judges, and there is transfer between the two. The special protection afforded to judges does not apply to members of the parquet.

The right to security in one post is never absolute. A judge who was guilty, for example, of a criminal offence, or who went certifiably insane, or who left the country and refused to return, would in any country be relieved of his office. The important point about judges and professors is that the procedure for dismissing or enforcing resignation normally requires the participation of the highest members of their own profession, and very rarely the direct intervention of the highest legislative body in the land. In Germany federal judges accused of unconstitutional behaviour can only be compelled to retire after a motion in the Bundestag, followed by a two-thirds majority in favour of compulsory retirement in the Federal Constitutional Court. In France judges may be removed only after an affirmative vote of the Conseil Supérieur de la Magistrature on which judges themselves are in a majority.

The protection accorded to ordinary judges is extended to judges of the supreme administrative courts in the countries where they exist. The one curious exception are the judges of the French Conseil d'Etat who, unlike virtually every other civil servant in France, have practically no formal protection in office. However, the tradition of independence and the high prestige of the court are so strong that it would be as unlikely for a French government to interfere with the councillors of the Conseil d'Etat as it would be for the British parliament actually to vote a judge out of office.

In Italy and Germany no distinction is made between the security of tenure of the judges of the supreme administrative and the supreme civil courts. In Italy the councillors of the Consiglio di Stato cannot be removed from office without their consent unless they are manifestly incapable of performing their duties. They cannot even be suspended for misconduct or neglect of duty, and may only be removed from office or compulsorily retired if they refuse to perform a duty required of them by law. They may not be dismissed for inefficiency, in the interests of the service, or for redundancy. A case involving the status of a councillor of the Consiglio di Stato can only be decided by the Prime Minister on the advice of the cabinet after formal consultation with the Consiglio di Stato meeting in plenary session. These somewhat excessive precautions must be seen against the special Italian preoccupation to avoid the pressure and abuse of the Fascist period. The Consiglio di Stato is still not wholly trusted by the public or civil service who suspect it of excessive partiality towards the government.

The independence of the magistracy and of the university are accepted elements in the system of government in all countries in western Europe, and security of tenure is an indispensable part of this. A price of course has to be paid. Every country knows the problem of the elderly irremovable judge who is a positive obstacle to the liberal and efficient working of the judicial system. The price of judicial independence is sometimes judicial obstruction and malice, but countries are rightly prepared to pay it.

It is impossible in the modern world to extend such an absolute right to a particular post, in a particular place, in a particular rank, to other types of public servant. Even Sweden has been forced to modify the constitutional right of all established civil servants to this kind of protection. It was found extremely difficult to persuade officials of the right calibre to transfer to the barren northern zones and when this became serious an escape clause was made. Provisions were written into a new salary agreement specifying that civil servants covered by its terms must accept transfer to another post at the same rate of pay if the reorganization of the service made it necessary. The courts held that civil servants employed before the provision was written into the agreements were also liable to transfer if they had accepted the new pay scales.[1]

(ii) Security of tenure, as enjoyed by judges and university professors, is for many civil service trade unions an ideal which they would like to see extended to as many branches as possible. But it is probably unattainable in the immediate future. What the great majority of civil servants have obtained instead is security of tenure in a particular rank within the civil service. Normally civil servants are not even liable to transfer between different branches of the administration. There is very little movement in any country between different ministries or services for lower and middle rank officials. Only at the highest

[1] G. Hesslén: *Public administration in Sweden.* Swedish Institute, Stockholm, 1954. Also Heckscher. op. cit.

levels does one ever find any considerable number of officials with experience of more than one branch of administration. The two countries where movement even on this scale is noticeable are Britain and France; in Britain the whole concept of 'general' services is based on the belief that interchange between ministries is desirable; in France movement between ministries is almost entirely confined to the members of the grands corps which furnish a mobile reserve force of administrative direction. But both in France and Britain the number of people actually transferred in this way is very small indeed; very many members of even the small administrative class in Britain are never likely to leave the ministry to which they were first appointed on joining the service. In Germany there is some movement between federation and Länder and Länder and local government.

At the opposite extreme is Spain, where the cuerpos especiales have obtained such a dominant position that they have come each to control a special branch of the administration and effectively exclude all outsiders, sometimes to the point of excluding from the higher posts of particular ministries even the general service officials of those ministries. For instance the ministry of Public Works is completely dominated by the state corps of civil engineers, the ministry of Industry by the civil corps of mining engineers and the ministry of Agriculture by the civil corps of agrarian engineers. Virtually the only interdepartmental movement is confined to the small groups of Abogados del Estado, Letrados del Estado and Letrados del Tribunal de Cuentas.

The security of tenure possessed by the vast majority of officials is substantially greater than that of any comparable group outside the service. Transfers on any scale are to be found only in those countries with large ministries with extensive field services, such as the Board of Inland Revenue in Britain, the ministry of Finance in France, or the ministry of the Interior in Italy. In these administrations transfer is a known and accepted condition of service.

Security of tenure in a particular rank is the most obvious feature of all civil services. This is recognized by the civil servants themselves, by politicians, and by the general public. It is in some ways the hall-mark of the career. A rank once obtained can only be lost as the result of disciplinary action. There are very few officials who would accept that the collateral for promotion by merit is demotion for lack of merit. Almost vested right to a personal rank is probably the basic target of public criticism (not always unjustified at the lower levels) of casual negligence, lack of concentration and carelessness of public officials.

In certain countries however there are special provisions to ensure that no-one whose conduct or opinions endanger the régime shall continue in public service. This is, of course, particularly true in the case of Spain and Portugal, where loyalty to the party is required from all civil servants. If an official is found wanting in this he may be dismissed without the ordinary disciplinary procedures, and indeed without having committed any disciplinary fault in the normal sense of the word. In most other countries a person suspected of active hostility to the existing form of government will if possible be removed from office, but this is normally extremely difficult unless associated with a particular disciplinary fault. In France it is legally impossible since the constitution specifically protects a civil servant from dismissal on political or racial or religious grounds, and it is certain that any dismissal motivated on these grounds would be quashed by the Conseil d'Etat. The British security regulations are probably the only regulations which can reasonably be compared with those of Spain and Portugal.

In most countries certain posts are held to be outside the normal terms of employment and security of tenure. These are the strategic policy-making posts in the public service, and their holders are expected to be particularly sensitive to government direction. Such direct responsibility, it is held, can only be ensured if the government itself has the power freely to nominate and dismiss people from these posts; consequently every country has a list of posts which the government fills at its discretion.

The political questions this raises will be dealt with below.[1] Here it is sufficient to point out one of the practical consequences of this position. In theory, governments can call on virtually anyone they wish when filling these posts. (There are of course special cases in which their choice must be within

[1] See p. 276.

some broad category of persons.) The government can therefore go outside the public service if it wishes. Clearly, if it does so, a change of government will probably lead to the prompt dismissal of the person appointed.

In these circumstances it is sometimes held that the best men will not accept posts from which they can be summarily ejected, and that the ministries will eventually come to be headed by adventurers and place-men. It is in fact truer to say that with the decline in the number of people of independent means trained to consider themselves as having a particular responsibility to serve the state, the number of potential applicants from outside the service for these posts has been rapidly declining during this century.

The practice is therefore to call on civil servants to staff the highest posts in public service, although some countries still regard it as desirable occasionally to infuse new blood with men drawn from outside the service.

Although these civil servants appointed to the highest posts are liable to dismissal at the will of the government, they are dismissed only from that particular post, and not from the civil service as such. They retain their own personal rank and have a right to an appropriate post elsewhere in the service. In the Swedish, French or German administrative lists of personnel it is not unusual to find senior civil servants with two posts, or two ranks. The first is his actual post and rank which falls in the unprotected category of posts; the second his personal rank (and sometimes post) to which he will return if and when he ceases to hold his temporary (and generally higher) office. The advantages and disadvantages of this system will be discussed later.[1]

[1] See p. 278.

CHAPTER 6

Pensions

All countries have a special pension system for permanent civil servants, often of long-standing: Spain 1835, Belgium 1844, France 1853, Germany 1873. They cover schemes for ordinary retirement pension at the end of service, for various special disability pensions, and for pensions for widows and orphans. Some countries have an organized system for appeals.

The categories of officials covered by the special pension schemes vary. In some countries they cover all officials paid from state funds: Finland 'drawing an official salary', Belgium 'être nommé à un fonction' and paid from public funds. The French pension scheme covers all the personnel of the central state administration and external services, and the non-industrial public enterprises. The German system covers anyone holding a Beamtenpost or occupying a post requiring the qualifications of a Beamter. Some countries, for instance Spain, have a joint system for civil and military personnel.

In Germany the pension fund is entirely financed by the state. In Belgium and Finland the state finances ordinary retirement pensions but disability and family pensions are on a contributory basis. In France, Italy and Switzerland a fixed contribution is deducted from salaries (France and Italy 6%, Switzerland 7%) and the rest made up by the state.

To qualify for a retirement pension an official generally has to reach the age limit for his service, or to have completed a certain number of years' service, or to be disabled either in the course of his work or independently, or to give evidence of what in Germany is called 'Dienstunfähigkeit' and in France 'preuve d'insuffisance professionelle'. The most common age limit is 65, although in France it is 60, in Finland 63 (judges 67), and in Switzerland 70. Nearly all countries provide for special dispensation to allow extra years' service where it is in the public interest, and most countries have a lower age limit for police, prison staff, etc. In Switzerland an official must complete 50 years' service before he qualifies for a full pension, in Italy it is 40 years, in France and Finland 30. A full pension, however, does not signify a particular figure, but the maximum percentage of a given salary, and this latter may continue to increase after the official has qualified for full pension. In some cases the pension rate is calculated on the basis of full pension after full years of service with a percentage deducted for each year short of this number. In others there is a minimum period of service before which the official is not eligible for an ordinary pension at all (Germany and Finland 10 years, Italy 20 years, Belgium 35 years), and a percentage is added for each additional year up to the maximum percentage of a full pension. There is always a minimum age from which effective service counts towards pension rights; Spain 16, Germany 17, France 18, Finland 21 years of age. In Germany war-service counts towards pension seniority, and time spent in certain types of training counts as half; in France certain types of war-service count as half or a third.

The level of ordinary pensions is generally calculated according to two principles: years of service and salary just before retirement. Usually the pension is a multiple of the years of service and a percentage of the final salary. In France an official receives 2% of his last salary for every year's service, counting promotion of at least 6 months' standing (with the proviso that all earnings exceeding six times the official minimum vital count for half; there is also a minimum based on the minimum vital, and allowances for children under 16). It is common to take as a pension basis the average salary over the last few years in service; Germany the last 6 years counting promotion of at least 1 year's standing, Belgium 5, Spain 3. Germany is the most generous: her officials are entitled to a retirement pension of 50% of their pension basis after 10 years service, plus 2% for every additional year up to the 25th; the maximum is 75%. The Belgian figure is $\frac{1}{60}$ of the pension basis for each year of service (or just over 58% after 35 years' service, Belgium's qualifying period). In Spain the pensions range from 20% after 20 years to 40% after 35 years. In Switzerland the full pension at 70 or after 50 years' service is 60% and deductions are made for each year short of these figures. In Finland there is a full pension of 64–66% after 30 years; after the first ten years an official qualifies for $\frac{10}{30}$ of this pension and for an additional $\frac{1}{30}$ for each additional year up to 30; there are minimum and maximum figures for all pensions. In Italy the pension basis is 80% of the last salary; the pension is equal to 50% of this basis after 20 years, plus an extra 2% for every additional year with a maximum of 90% after 40 years' service; for posts where there is a lower compulsory retiring age (police, carabinieri, prison staff) the extra percentage after 20 years is raised to 3·1% for those retired at 45 and to 2·15% for those retired at 51. In Great Britain the pension is a minimum of $\frac{10}{80}$ ($12\frac{1}{2}$%) after 10 years' service rising by $\frac{1}{80}$ each year to a maximum of $\frac{40}{80}$ (50%) after 40 years, and in addition there is a down capital payment of three times the pension basis. Usually non-permanent officials retiring after a certain number of years' service, 10 to 15 generally, receive a lump sum bearing some relation to their salary and years of service.

All countries make provision for extra benefits to officials disabled (by injury or ill-health) in the course of their work. In Finland they simply receive a full pension (64–66% basis) regardless of their age or years of service. In Belgium and France they enjoy a long period of disponibilité with full pay (France 12–70 months); in Belgium there is a minimum of 5 years' service in the case of illness and higher pension rates. In France the ordinary pension is supplemented by an allowance calculated according to the degree of disability, with a maximum of the combined pensions at the figure of the pension basis. Officials disabled outside the course of their duties qualify for an ordinary pension irrespective of age or years of service. Germany also has a scale of extra allowances according to the degree of disability, and the minimum pension for a disabled official is $66\frac{2}{3}$ of his pension basis. In Spain an official (or serviceman) who is 100% disabled receives 80% of his salary if it is below a certain low figure and 60% if it is above that figure, with an absolute minimum. Italy recognizes simply two categories of disabled; those resident in communes of over 100,000 receive considerably more than those in communes of under 100,000. In most cases the state pays for all treatment and there is usually a special body inside the administration (for instance in Belgium the pensions commission in the ministry of Public Health) which determines on the degree of disability subject to appeal.

In the event of death family pensions are paid to widows and orphans (and in the case of Spain to certain other dependents). But while in Germany family pensions are automatically paid by the state, in some other countries they are on a contributory basis, compulsory in the case of Finland and Belgium. The relative generosity of these pensions generally corresponds to the levels of the retirement pensions in different countries. In Germany, for instance, a widow receives three months' full salary at the time of her husband's death and a pension of 60% of the pension he would have received had he retired the day he died, together with 60% of his disability allowance had he qualified for one; she receives an extra 12% for each child, and if she dies each orphan receives 20% of the father's pension. In France a widow receives 50% of her husband's pension and 10% for each child under 21; there if the mother dies the orphan takes over the widow's pension too. Both widow and orphan receive an extra disability allowance if the father qualified for one, and there is no age limit for an orphan's pension if he is crippled or in any way unable to earn his living. In Finland a widow's pension is 20% of the official's last salary, not of his pension; she receives an extra 8% for the first child, 4% for the second and 2% for any further children under 18; if the mother dies the widow's pension is transferred to the first child; in the first year the widow or orphan receives 1½ times the usual pension. In Belgium a widow receives 30% of the basis for her husband's pension after the first 20 years' service, which is the same as he would himself be entitled to if he retired at the end of those 20 years; she then receives 1% extra for each additional year with a maximum of 50% of his last salary. There is a proviso that a widow's pension must never be less than the maximum pension allowed under the social security to a worker in similar circumstances; she receives 5% extra for the first child, 3% for the second and 2% for any further children under 18, and if she dies, the first orphan receives 60% of the widow's pension, two orphans receive 80%, three 100%, and so on. In Spain a family pension is paid first to widows and orphans, second to widows and needy mothers, and in exceptional circumstances to mothers and fathers; the official must have a minimum of ten years' service, after which his dependents receive a pension equal to 15% of his pension basis (last 3 years pay) for a period of years equal to his years of service with a maximum of 15 years and a minimum payment of 1,500 pesetas; this pension may be increased by voluntary contributions on the part of the official while in service: the maximum for a widow's and orphans' pension combined is 25% of the official's salary.

In several countries it is not possible to receive more than one pension from the state. In France and Spain it is expressly forbidden, and in Italy the only exception is permission to draw an ordinary pension at the same time as a widow's or orphan's pension. In Germany it is allowed subject to a maximum for the combined pensions received. The acquisition of a foreign nationality generally automatically suspends the right to a pension (Germany, Finland, Spain, Italy only if voluntary), and in Finland and Germany this is also true of prolonged residence abroad. In Italy and Germany a pensioner must not re-enter state service, and it is always possible to lose pension rights through certain disciplinary measures or by being specifically deprived in the courts.

CHAPTER 7

Discipline

An official charged with an offence in the course of his duties has the right to be dealt with according to a special disciplinary procedure. This is perhaps the most striking—and is certainly the most important right he possesses. This right originated in the attempts of public servants to escape from complete dependence on their superiors and to provide themselves with guarantees against arbitrary action.

Even when abuses were rare there was strong reaction against complete dependence on the authority of the immediate superior, and against the atmosphere this created. In Germany, to take a case of rigorous hierarchy combined with a high ethical standard, 'secret reports constituted a vital element in the complete domination of the superior. Until 1919 they could not be inspected by the person reported on, and although between 1845 and 1919 a disciplinary procedure was established to abolish arbitrary action, the officials could never know what storm was brewing'.[1]

Nowadays all countries have elaborated very careful disciplinary procedures, and even where, as in Britain, they are not strictly formalized and minutely defined, substantial safeguards exist in practice against any form of partiality or discrimination.

A distinction must be made between disciplinary procedure and civil or criminal procedure. The latter is concerned with breaches of the law and in all countries they are dealt with by the normal civil and criminal courts.[2] That is, if an official steals public funds he will be tried in a criminal court as

[1] H. Finer: *Theory and Practice of Modern Government*. London, 1949. p. 739.

[2] If an official is found guilty he will in every country be dismissed from his service, quite apart from the legal penalties imposed.

would anyone else. The distinguishing feature of the disciplinary fault is that it is a fault committed in office, which is condemned not because the law is broken, but because it offends against the internal regulations or rules of the administration. The difference, as Turegg points out, is a difference between legality and expediency.

It is, of course, possible that the same offence, or set of offences, raises questions both of law and of discipline. For instance, an official may be unable to account for public funds for which he was responsible in circumstances which give rise to a prima facie suspicion that he has committed a theft. At his trial in the criminal court he may be found innocent of the charge of theft; but his innocence on that charge does not prevent him from being charged under the disciplinary procedure for gross negligence. In Sweden this double jurisdiction has caused some difficulties. But the distinction is everywhere recognized.

In the past officials in some countries were protected from any action being brought against them in ordinary courts, on the grounds that they were particularly exposed to vexatious and malicious prosecution. This protection nowadays only exists in Italy where, before a prefect or a mayor may be charged in a civil or criminal court, permission to proceed must first be obtained from the Consiglio di Stato to ensure there is a prima facie case. This protection does not apply to electoral offences. Some countries possess a properly organized administrative jurisdiction which may be competent in cases which elsewhere would fall under the civil courts: for instance, the question of obtaining damages from an official in Britain still frequently involves the official himself appearing before the ordinary civil court, while in France it will probably (but not certainly) be dealt with by the administrative courts. But these questions will be dealt with in a later chapter.

The point to stress here is that the disciplinary process deals in principle with matters in which no civil law offence has been committed. Disciplinary courts, where they exist, can only properly be compared to domestic tribunals set up in other professions.

Disciplinary faults are connected with the improper or negligent performance of official duties. They may sometimes be concerned with the official's private life, for instance in bringing discredit on his service, or failure to observe the accepted limitations, as for example in writing to newspapers criticising his minister in violent terms.

In some countries a body of case law has developed from which it would be possible to draw up a list of punishable offences. The Swedish view is that offences should be described in general terms and not detailed, since general phrasing allows an administration to protect itself against new and ingenious forms of abuse, and also allows an official greater liberty to manœuvre should his case come before a disciplinary tribunal. The regulations of different Swedish administrations allow disciplinary measures to be taken against officials for 'negligence, unskilfulness or censurable conduct'; for 'faults or negligence in the performance of his duties or failure to observe proper forms, or for disobedience'; for 'conspicuous ignorance of the regulations which he is called upon to observe or administer'.[1] Phrases similar to these are to be found in all countries, and they adequately summarise the normal limits of disciplinary action. Various disciplinary codes insist that a specific and precise offence must have been committed, and that disciplinary procedures may not be set in motion in order to get rid of an official who merely shows a general lack of ability for his work, or is physically incapacitated, or is 'not showing the right sort of spirit'. It is widely felt that disciplinary action should be firmly restricted to disciplinary cases, and that other methods should be devised if it appears desirable to dispense with a man's services on other grounds.

Different countries have different scales of penalties, some preferring an elaborate and extended list while others restrict themselves to three or four simple penalties. In Sweden, for example, the scale of penalties goes (i) an official warning which can affect promotion or pay increases; (ii) cuts in pay or a fine calculated in relation to salary, usually for a maximum of three months; (iii) suspension from service and pay usually for three months; (iv) dismissal from the service. Heavier fines than those mentioned above may be inflicted on certain officials: for instance pilots and lighthouse keepers may be

[1] G. Heckscher: op. cit. pp. 344–6.

fined up to three months' salary for negligence in their duties.[1]

In Italy there are five penalties: (i) censure; (ii) reduction of salary; (iii) suspension without salary; (iv) revocation, that is dismissal from the service with a loss of some pension rights; and (v) destitution, that is dismissal from the service with loss of all pension rights.[2]

France has the most extensive and subtly distinguished scale of penalties: (i) warning; (ii) censure; (iii) removal from the list of candidates for promotion; (iv) disciplinary posting; (v) loss of seniority in grade; (vi) demotion to a lower grade; and (vii) and (viii) dismissal from the service with or without loss of pension rights. The only instance where an official has no knowledge in advance of the case being prepared, no right to examine the relevant documents, no right to question witnesses, no right to rebut specific charges because the charges may not be specific, no right to legal representation, and no right of effective appeal, is contained in the British security programme. This is now unique in western Europe.

The disciplinary authority varies greatly, and depends on the gravity of the offence. For minor offences it is always the official's immediate superior who is originally responsible for considering the offence, and in most countries he has power to impose the minor penalties of warning or censure on his own authority subject to an appeal.

More elaborate procedures are used where serious penalties may be imposed. The most elaborate procedures are to be found in Germany.[3] There a properly organized system of disciplinary courts has been created, complete with a full-time prosecutor. The federal disciplinary courts of first instance, the Bundesdisziplinarkammern, are set up by the federal Minister of the Interior by ordinance in which their seat and area of jurisdiction are defined.[4] The members of the disciplinary courts are appointed by the minister. There is a full-time legally qualified chairman, who may be chairman of a maximum of three such courts; a vice-chairman; and assessors,

[1] G. Heckscher: op. cit. p. 345 seq.

[2] A. Sandulli: *Manuale di Diritto Amministrativo*. Naples, 1954. p. 138.

[3] K. E. von Turegg: *Lehrbuch des Verwaltungsrechts*. Berlin, 1954. p. 339 seq.

[4] It must be remembered that Beamten are to be found in federal, land, communal and public law authorities, and they are all covered by similar provisions.

half of whom must have proper legal qualifications and the other half are appointed mainly on the recommendation of the public service unions, the Spitzenorganisation of the Gewerkschaften und Berufsverbände der Beamten.

The court of second instance is the Bundesdisziplinarhof attached to the Bundesverwaltungsgericht. It has a president, and is divided into senates, each of which has its own president, who is appointed from federal judges. The assessors of the court must be full-time career Beamten.

In addition there is a full-time Bundesdisziplinar Anwalt, who acts as permanent prosecuting attorney in disciplinary cases. When an offence is committed involving an official the highest authorities of his administration can send the case directly to the prosecuting attorney if the evidence is clear and requires no further investigation. If the case involves further enquiries an independent official of the same administration is appointed to act as investigator with powers to interrogate, take evidence on oath, and search. The prosecuting attorney can direct the general lines of the investigation, and his permission is needed before the enquiry can extend to cover new fields or enquire into possible new offences.

At each stage the accused official must be given the right to know what evidence there is against him, to examine it, and to rebut or refute it.

When the enquiry is complete the case as prepared must be sent to the administration's highest authorities, who inform the prosecuting attorney of what steps they propose to take. If they consider that the evidence shows that disciplinary action must be taken the case is forwarded to the local Bundesdisziplinarkammer. The case is presented there in an act of accusation by the prosecuting attorney. The accused may be represented by defending counsel, and the case is held in private. All the evidence must be presented, and the accused has the chance to attack or question any of the items, witnesses and documents. A properly authorized senior official must attend as delegate of the highest authorities of the administration, and shall speak on their behalf. The verdict must be signed by the members of the court and reasons must be given for the decision.

Appeal lies with the Bundesdisziplinarhof, which can either

reject the appeal as unacceptable on legal grounds, or return the case to the original disciplinary court for further instruction, or hear the case again itself, when the same trial procedure is followed.[1]

No other country has a system as elaborate, as formal, or as watertight as this. What is even more important (and found nowhere else) is that the penalty to be imposed is not decided by the official's superior or by any higher authority; it is decided by the disciplinary courts.

In other countries, the case against an official is prepared either by the establishments officer, as in Britain or Switzerland, or by the immediate superior as in France, Italy and Belgium. The case is heard in all cases by a special administrative disciplinary committee, in Italy by a body composed of a director general and two inspectors general, in France and Belgium by specially constituted boards of the joint staff-official organization—the commissions administratives paritaires in France, and the chambre de recours in Belgium.[2] In Switzerland the Conseil Fédéral is in principle the highest disciplinary body, but it delegates its powers to the ministerial departments, which set up their own disciplinary commissions. In none of these cases can the disciplinary courts actually impose any penalties; they simply recommend a suitable penalty to the minister or head of department (in Switzerland the Conseil Fédéral) who decides. In Italy the minister is bound not to inflict a heavier penalty than that proposed by the disciplinary commission, though he may impose a lighter punishment. In France the head of a department may impose a heavier penalty than that proposed by the commission administrative paritaire, but if he does so the case can be taken on appeal to the conseil supérieur de la fonction publique.

Most countries have a system of appeal on points of law. In France and Italy an appeal lies to the supreme administrative courts if there is any violation of procedure or abuse of power, and in Switzerland an appeal lies under certain conditions to the Tribunal Fédéral.

[1] *Bundesdisziplinarordnung*. November 28, 1952.

[2] A. Plantey: op. cit. p. 216.

CHAPTER 8

Promotion

During the nineteenth century in most countries the minister was master in his house, and promotions were decided by him. In some countries the highest posts were closed to promotion since their holders were directly appointed by the minister who only rarely chose properly established people from inside the administration.

This meant that for the vast majority of officials there was no hope of promotion to the highest levels, and therefore no reason to overwork. This led to the general feeling that promotion should be taken out of the hands of the minister, and organized in a way which eliminated favouritism or politics. The only known way in which absolute objectivity can be ensured is for all promotions to be made entirely on grounds of seniority. If a post falls vacant it is filled by the person who has served longest in the post immediately below.

The trouble with the seniority system is that it is so objective that it fails to take any account of personal merit. As a system it is fair to every official except the best ones; an official has nothing to win or lose provided he does not actually become so inefficient that disciplinary action has to be taken against him. Thus, although it is fair after a fashion to the officials themselves, it is a heavy burden on the public and a great strain on the efficient handling of public business.

To introduce the idea of merit into promotion procedure introduces an element of personal evaluation, and personal evaluation opens the door to the abuses of nepotism and favouritism against which the officials (and liberal thinkers, too) originally reacted.

There is, in fact, a genuine dilemma in promotion which has caused all countries concern over the last twenty or thirty years. How to ensure reasonable prospects of advancement to all officials and at the same time protect the public's interest in having posts filled by the most able men?

Over the course of time every country has come to more or less the same conclusion. In simple terms it amounts to this. An administration has several points of entry, and qualifications to enter at each of these points are normally linked to the various school-leaving certificates. Stemming from each of these points of entry is a coherent and self-contained career within which there are promotion steps leading to the top of that particular class. In the normal structure the top of each class overlaps, from the pay point of view, the bottom of the next higher class.

Three methods of advancement are now possible.

First, an official can be awarded more or less automatic pay increases (provided his work is satisfactory) while he retains his present rank in his present grade of the administration. Thus, a clerical assistant can have periodic pay increases while still remaining a clerical assistant. In Sweden an Amanuensaspiranter begins his service at the salary group 17; after eight and a half years he rises to salary group 20; after another two years to salary group 22; after another two years to salary group 23, and after a further two years to salary group 24.[1] That is, without changing his grade, this official will reach the maximum salary for his grade within fourteen years of joining the service.

Second, an official may obtain advancement by being promoted to the next higher post while still remaining within the same general class. That is, he goes from being clerical assistant grade three, to clerical assistant grade two, to clerical assistant grade one, and so on. He remains throughout a member of the clerical assistants' class, but he assumes greater responsibility within that class.

Third, an official may obtain advancement by promotion out of his original class into the class above. For instance, in Great Britain by obtaining promotion from the executive class to the administrative class. In this case he completely leaves his original class of entry, and joins a class whose original entry qualifications were academically higher than those he originally possessed.

[1] G. Heckscher: op. cit. p. 349 seq.

By a judicious mixture of these three types of promotion, countries attempt to find the proper balance between promotion by seniority and promotion by merit. The methods they use have much in common.

(i) In the first case all public services nowadays accept the need to give some sort of financial increment at periodic intervals to every official whether or not he is promoted to the next higher grade or class. In this way every official has some financial inducement to work moderately efficiently, since the pay increase, although in most cases virtually automatic, may be refused as a disciplinary measure. Some countries require the superior positively to state that the official concerned has performed his duties efficiently; other countries make the increment dependent on the official obtaining a certain average competence tested by the annual reports made on him by his superiors. This method of advancement is firmly embedded in civil service practice and gives rise to few complications. It does not involve the creation of new posts, it arms the administration with both a whip and a carrot, and it affords a career, even if a narrow one, to every official. Statistically it seems that most countries favour a system which ensures the normally competent official under this scheme reaching his maximum in his early thirties. This seems to be socially and psychologically correct. It is at this age that family responsibilities are likely to be at their heaviest, and the official arrives at his maximum at an age when he is still fresh and ambitious enough not to be content to remain at the same salary for the rest of his career. This gives him an incentive to push higher.

(ii) Advancement by promotion to the next higher grade while remaining in the same class is the first stage at which complications set in. In the first place the number of posts in each grade is normally fixed. Promotion from below cannot therefore be automatic, since a vacancy must occur before any advancement is possible for officials in the lower rank. This means that promotion must be competitive, since there will always be more posts in the lower ranks than in the higher.

This involves an appreciation of respective merit, and the question is how to find the correct balance between seniority and merit. Some countries still continue to put the major emphasis throughout the service on seniority. Only a few political appointments at the heads of ministries are excepted; there is fear amongst public service personnel—reinforced by long memories—that any substantial breach in the seniority rule will open the door to widespread promotion on political and personal grounds. In Germany the justification for seniority is not political. It is justified on the grounds that seniority is the only safe guide for ensuring that the best men are chosen; those with the longest service are likely, all things being equal, to have wider experience and greater administrative culture. It is felt that rapid promotion of young men may saddle the service with an official who may, in the end, prove to have been the wrong choice. This is by no means an absolute rule in Germany, but the clear impression is given that the only real choice should be between men of roughly comparable seniority. Underlying this approach to the problem is a whole philosophy of administration: that the state needs from its civil servants the greatest possible guarantees of 'character suitability',[1] and these guarantees are best given by placing the greatest reliance on the official's general record over a long period of time.

Other countries accept seniority as the principal factor for promotion in the lower classes of the service, and restrict the merit factor to promotions in the highest class. A good case can be made out for this. At the level of ushers or clerks the work is essentially automatic and it is extremely difficult to distinguish between two men doing the same standard job with reasonable efficiency. This will always mean that for most vacancies to the grade above there will be several equally qualified people. Under these circumstances seniority is the socially accepted element in deciding promotion. It is regarded by the officials themselves as equitable; it closes no doors to the average official in the grade, and it frees the superior from charges of favouritism, nepotism and susceptibility to pressure. From the public point of view it has some drawbacks, the most important being that it gives the person appointed no extra prestige. Age and seniority are accidents, and are accepted as such by the personnel involved. There is no distinction in obtaining a post on grounds of seniority. It is for this reason that in every civil service the lower supervisory grades have

[1] For an excellent example of this thinking, see H. Peters, op. cit. p. 241.

the least control over their subordinates. Sometimes they lack proper disciplinary powers, but more frequently they have no recognized moral or professional superiority; realizing this, their main object is not to cause unpleasantness; they lack the natural authority of a person appointed by merit who is aware of his own distinction compared with his immediate fellows.

Discipline is always likely to be weakest in the lower ranks for this reason, and the only possible remedy is an active policy of supervising the supervisors. This is rarely done, both because it is time-consuming, and because, all too frequently, senior officials themselves lack personal authority. They therefore evade the issue.

But if seniority is a pis aller as far as lower staff is concerned, most countries do not regard it as sufficient for promotion between grades or between classes. The simplest case is that of Switzerland's federal service. Promotion there can only occur if a post becomes vacant or if the work being done by an official is clearly of a higher grade. In the first case the vacant post is advertised, and naturally officials of lower grades are as entitled to apply as anyone outside the service or in another ministry. Promotion in this case is competitive, decided for senior officials by the Conseil Fédéral, and for minor posts by the heads or directors of ministries. It is for the Conseil Fédéral or the appointing authority to decide whether or not an official is in fact performing work of a higher grade; if they decide he is, he is then raised to the appropriate rank.

In Sweden, too, vacant posts are normally advertised, and as in Switzerland there is no guarantee that the successful candidate will come from the lower grades in that administration, nor even that he will already be a civil servant. There is keen competition for entry into the state civil service from local government officers, and in some ministries the latter are very strong candidates.

A rather special case arises in Holland where an official figure is that only about 50% of the posts in the higher civil service are in fact filled by promotion from within the administration concerned. About 5% are filled by officials from other services, and the remainder are brought in from outside. But this seems to be exceptional in western Europe as a whole.

In each country there has grown up unofficially, and often without any obvious premeditation, a 'standard' expectation of career; that is, that any person joining a particular class has a normal assurance that he will reach a given rank before he retires. For example, a person joining the administrative class in Great Britain has to do something very foolish indeed not to reach the rank of assistant secretary; in Germany the entrant to the highest service cannot very well avoid becoming Oberregierungsrat.

To achieve this type of 'standard' career, which is normal to the middle and higher ranks of public service, the question of promotion does not pose very great problems. There is normally an age span within which a man has a general probability of promotion. In these branches of administration the promising young man is likely to be marked out at an early stage for a good career and the 'standard' man put into the 'standard' career. It is therefore reasonable to count promotion by grade in the context of a 'standard' career as being essentially promotion by seniority. In most cases this type of official appears to reach his maximum by his middle forties, generally a matter of three (sometimes four) grades above his point of entry.

The question of testing merit arises in the case of the young men who show promise, and who give some token that with proper care they will one day be fit to occupy the highest posts. It is they who in fact are in conflict in the earlier years of their career with the 'standard' career man, for in the nature of administration they must arrive at a comparatively early age at the point where the standard career ends. It is usual in all countries to specify a minimum time to be served in each grade; no man is eligible for promotion until he has served this period. Sometimes a man must also be a minimum age before he can be considered for promotion to certain posts; for instance, in Germany an official must be at least 35 before he is eligible to be promoted to Ministerialrat.

There are four principal methods of assessing merit. The first, and obviously most objective, is to hold a competitive examination for the eligible candidates. Although the most objective, few countries in fact use this system. The competitive examination may be for a limited number of places to which the successful candidates are appointed. It may be to test whether or not an official is eligible to be considered for promotion. This is the second method. In this case the examination is more a test of competence than one of comparative merit; unless the test is passed the official cannot be promoted, but the mere passing of the test does not give a right to immediate promotion.

Italy has carried the use of these two methods of competitive examinations and tests of competence further than any other country. At the strategic points of the careers in the two senior classes promotions are made by a mixture of examination results and seniority. For instance, the posts of primo segretario in the carriere di concetto (executive class) are filled for a quarter by competitive examination amongst those eligible in the class below, and for three-quarters by idoneità: that is, promotion by seniority amongst those who have satisfactorily passed a test of competence.

Italy, unlike any other country, also uses the system of competitive examination for promotion in the highest class (carriere direttive). The two crucial stages in this career are promotion from consigliere to direttore di sezione, and from direttore di sezione to direttore di divisione. One quarter of the posts of direttore di sezione are reserved to the successful candidates in a competitive examination; the remaining three-quarters to those selected by idoneità. In the higher-ranking promotion from direttore di sezione to direttore di divisione four-fifths are decided by comparative merit amongst the officials with the requisite seniority; but the remaining fifth is filled by special written competitive examination plus an interview. In this way the Italians try to ensure a balance between age and merit, and between promotion on the basis of subjective judgements of character and ability on the one hand, and impartial, objective tests of ability and intelligence on the other. This should ensure a satisfactory 'standard' career for the normal run of officials, while at the same time leaving the door open to young men of the highest technical ability to forge ahead with some speed. The only other country with actual examinations for promotion in the highest ranks is Spain. In principle all promotion in that country is strictly according to seniority. But the law of 1918 provided that for promotion to jefe de negociado there should be alternate lists: the first on grounds of seniority, the second by competitive oposiciones between the eligible candidates.[1]

The Belgians also have a system not unlike the idoneità of the Italians. In several cases promotion is dependent on satisfactorily passing a test of competence. It is, for instance, impossible for a rédacteur to be promoted to sous chef or chef de bureau unless he has passed a qualifying examination held under the auspices of the secrétariat permanent de recrutement. Normally the French only go in for promotion examinations when it is a matter of promotion from one class into another. (See below.)

The other two methods of determining merit are subjective tests, and they tend to be favoured in northern countries.

The first is the traditional method of relying on the opinion and judgement of the immediate superior of the official concerned, or of allowing the head of the ministry (either the administrative or the political head) to make his own choice freely. This system was normal in the nineteenth century, and the abuses to which it gave rise were one of the reasons for more elaborate procedures being devised.

It is very rare nowadays for one man to have the right to decide promotions. There are traces of the old system in the powers possessed by ministerial directors in Germany with regard to promotion. In virtually all countries there are special provisions regarding nomination (which is generally also a promotion) to the highest posts of, for instance, ministerial directors, police chiefs, governors, and so on. The common practice is for nominations to these posts to be made by a minister but for the appointment to be made by the cabinet, or even the head of the state. In Spain, however, promotion to jefe de administración alternates between promotion strictly according to seniority, and promotion at the free discretion of the minister himself.

In general, however, the power to promote, or alternatively power to recommend names for promotion, has been put into commission. Promotion boards are now a common feature. They are normally composed of the heads of the different divisions of a ministry meeting under the presidency of the administrative or political head of the ministry (or their

[1] Gabriel de Usera: *Legislacion de Hacienda Española*. p. 57.

deputies). They not infrequently also act as advisory bodies to the minister in other fields such as discipline. Their recommendations for promotions are based on the annual reports on the officials concerned plus an interview of the most eligible candidates. Their effective powers vary. In Belgium the recommendations of the conseil de direction appear to be followed in nearly all cases concerning promotions in the executive class; but it has been suggested that they are not infrequently overruled by the minister in the case of promotions in the highest class. There are criticisms that too often ministers are still preoccupied with favouring their political friends.

These committees of heads of divisions are also sometimes assisted by the joint civil service boards set up within the ministries. In France the old commissions d'avancement have in several cases actually been replaced as advisory bodies on promotions by the commissions administratives paritaires.

This last method of promotion is a striking example of the gradual and general tendency towards the syndicalisation of public service. It says much for the corporate spirit of modern public services that there has been practically no public discussion as to whether it was wise to have no outside representation on promotion boards. It is not always certain that the interests of a particular ministry are the interests of the service as a whole; nor is it always necessarily true that the interests of the service are the interests of the government or the public. The most extreme conquest obtained by civil service personnel in this field is to be found in Belgium, where names proposed for promotion by the conseil de direction must be made known to the staff, and appeals and remonstrances may be made by the personnel against these proposals during a period of ten days. The right to appeal against being passed over, which is also generally possessed by officials, is another instance of the quite exceptional rights possessed by civil servants as compared with ordinary employees.

(iii) Advancement by promotion to a higher class is rarer for obvious reasons. Entry to a class is a function of particular educational qualifications, and there is some danger in drawing up into that class people of lower intellectual standing. This view is unpopular with the numerically influential groups in all civil services, since it is the lower classes who in the nature of things are most numerous. They hold strongly that administration is essentially a subject which is learnt by practice, and that the best administrator is the one who has practised longest. Underlying it there is often a genuine belief that organization and behaviour according to known rules are the essence of good administration. The middle-ranking civil servant, meticulously observing rule and precedent and exercising discretion within precisely limited fields, often seems to be profoundly ignorant of the fact that higher administration is a very different matter; that a good senior administrator requires more sophisticated qualities to deal with the economic or political aspects of his work, with inter-ministerial conflicts, and so on. And, of course, there is always the purely human element, that it is in some ways humiliating to accept the seniority of a younger man who apparently is not as well informed on routine matters as his more elderly subordinate.

It may be that the proportion of ex-executive class officials now serving in the British administrative class has weakened its intellectual calibre and collective imagination. No other country has anything like the same proportion of ex-middle-ranking officials in the highest class, nor such elaborate methods for ensuring a continual flow of such people.

On the other hand there is something to be said for keeping open a fairly well-defined route from one class to another, if for no other reason than that it acts as a continual spur to younger men. There is a great psychological value in promoting a number of people each year into a higher class by merit shown under competitive conditions. There is little doubt that this is preferable to promotions of this kind being a matter of co-optation based on record and personal judgement. The first breeds concentration, private study, and application; the second sycophancy.

In some countries, such as Spain, Italy and Denmark, it is virtually impossible to pass from the middle class into the upper class, and quite difficult to pass from the lower clerical class into the middle class. This is principally due to the rigidity of the educational requirements in Italy and Spain, and to the overproduction of university law graduates. In Germany it is possible, subject to certain conditions regarding length of service and age, to move from one class into another, from the gehobener Dienst into the höherer Dienst, but statistics indicate that this is rare. The normal requirements for entry into the höherer Dienst are so severe that it is clearly unreasonable to have too large a back-door entry. For promotion from the gehobener Dienst to the höherer Dienst an official must be at least forty years old, and have served a minimum of twenty years in either federal, Land, or communal administration. But one important factor must be mentioned in this context. The Germans have a long and firmly held preference for qualified administrators as Bürgermeister and Landräte, and it is very common in small and medium-sized communes to find the communal authority electing an already qualified Beamter as Bürgermeister. In the ordinary course of events, these Beamten come from the gehobener Dienst, and it is normal in some Länder, for example Württemberg-Baden, to find that election to mayor is regarded as a perfectly normal and greatly sought after method of promotion for members of the gehobener Dienst.

In Belgium there is some movement between the middle and higher classes; direct entrants from the university join the higher class as secrétaires d'administration, parallel to the post of chef de bureau, which is filled by promotion from rédacteur in the middle class. The secrétaires d'administration and the chefs de bureaux are then in competition for promotion to the higher posts of the higher class. There is no formal examination for promotion from rédacteur to chef de bureau, but a rédacteur is not eligible unless he has already passed a test of competence. (See above, p. 171.)

Only Great Britain and France have a regular and properly organized method for allowing access to the highest class to relatively young men by means of objective and impartial tests the French special internal examination for the ENA, the British closed examination to the administrative class for executive class officials.

RATING

But the problem of objective judgements by superiors on subordinates remains. The unions and associations of civil servants have made strenuous efforts to exclude as far as possible arbitrary discretion at any stage. The first victory was won when most countries accepted the principle that the annual report on an official should be communicated to him; if not as a matter of course as in some countries, at least whenever the report was likely to damage his chances of promotion or when his rating was below average.

Undoubtedly the most elaborate procedure is to be found in France, not Germany. In France, as in all countries, the reports are annual, and they are made for all officials below director general. There are different report forms for different categories of officials. The questions to be answered by the superior official concern, for officials in cadre A, knowledge of job, general education in relation to job, efficiency, and public service acumen; for cadre D officials, their suitability, attentiveness, punctuality and behaviour on duty. In all the three lower classes an official's ability and attitude when dealing with the public must be mentioned whenever it is appropriate. Each factor is marked on a scale 0–5, and the final rating is out of 20. A system of weighting is used to equalize the personal idiosyncrasies of individual supervisory officials. The appropriate authority for reporting is the head of the service, but in fact the immediate supervisor normally makes the first draft and submits it to the head of the service who approves it. There is also a general appraisal of an official's work, which is essentially a qualitative judgement and is not reduced to numerical form.

In addition to these safeguards, the annual reports of officials must be presented to the commission administrative paritaire, which examines both the rating marks and general appraisal and may request the head of a service to review a particular official's rating; the head of the service must then reply; he may refuse to allow an alteration to be made, but if he refuses he is expected to give his reasons.

A rather less elaborate method is used in Holland where the psychological make-up of an official is emphasized. The rating form asks for numerical appreciations of the subordinate official's knowledge for the performance of his duties; of his independence of mind, understanding and resourcefulness; of his initiative in organizing his own work and that of others; of his ability to express himself in writing and speaking; of his efficiency, and especially his speed and accuracy; his job performance, its quality and quantity; his personal relations with his equals, subordinates, and the public; and his behaviour in relation to the means, both human and material, placed at his disposal for the performance of his duties. When these reports are to be used for promotion purposes they are supplemented by considering the special requirements of the new job, and by a general qualitative assessment by superiors of the official's potential ability to hold the higher post.

As in France precautions are taken to eliminate the personal bias of individual superiors. But instead of a system of weighting, the rating reports are made by two superiors who together compile a single annual report. There is also an appraisal expert whose task is to see that only objective evaluations are made, and he, as expert, advises the rating authorities on the appropriate mark to be awarded to the opinions expressed on an official. He is entirely advisory and cannot take any decision in the matter; but he acts as a co-ordinating element throughout a particular ministry and when efficient undoubtedly helps to ensure common standards of judgement throughout the department.

France and Holland furnish perhaps the best examples of the more elaborate methods of ensuring equitable and objective rating of officials. In Belgium, the proposed mark (exceptional, very good, good, fair and unsatisfactory) must be shown to the official concerned. If the official thinks he has been badly treated he can appeal in writing to the chambre de recours, or, for the officials in the higher class, to a chambre de recours interdépartementale. One special feature of the Belgian system is that the mark 'exceptional' can only be given to an official with at least eight years' seniority in the service and at least two years' seniority in his present grade; it has to be supported by a special written report. The right to appeal and the limitations on awarding the highest marks seem to guarantee for virtually all officials a mark of 'very good' or 'good'. This diminishes the value of the annual report.

There has been little attempt to develop rating schemes in Germany and Scandinavian countries. In Germany there is no systematic rating, and although promotion in principle is by merit there is no objective and uniform standard of appraisal.

The official's merit is judged by personal reports by his superiors and these are expected to take into account his intellectual qualities, his character, his education and his state of health. The appraisals are not made known to the official, but he has the right to see his personal file at any time.

In Sweden and Finland there is no formalized system of rating or appraisal, and where an official is in line for promotion special reports are made by superiors on his suitability for the job. This is the opposite extreme to the French system. It is effectively the nineteenth-century German system without modification; except, of course, for an utterly different atmosphere within the administration.

Switzerland has no uniform system of rating. Of the federal departments only the political department, the customs department and the tax department have worked out any formal system of performance reports. But certain cantonal and communal authorities have done so, amongst them Neuchâtel and Biel. The most highly developed formal system of rating is undoubtedly in the political department (that is, the foreign office) where the superior officer makes annual reports based on replies to specific questions. But in general in Switzerland there is little attempt at formalized objective reports.

There is a great deal to be said for lessening an official's dependence on the opinion of one man as was too frequently the case in the past. But public officials may be going too far. It is important to remember that these methods of rating are only a means to an end, and that too much concentration on them may well have the effect of diminishing the superior's day-to-day responsibility for controlling, advising and ordering his subordinates. A right balance must be kept. The complete absence of objective terms of reference in annual reporting leads, as in Germany, to excellent discipline, but also a tendency to authoritarianism on the part of the superior and of hesitancy and sometimes cowardice on the part of the subordinate official. In the highest ranks this is least noticeable, and in the best ministries, for instance some of the federal ministries at Bonn, the atmosphere is one of poise, consideration, and frankness between all ranks in the höherer Dienst. It is in the gehobener and mittlerer Dienst that the greatest danger of uncontrolled authority arises. Probably the Germans would argue that it is in the mittlerer Dienst that discipline is most needed, and that the unfettered judgement of senior officials is the most satisfactory way of ensuring this.

These chapters show the growing tendency for public officials to demand and eventually to obtain better conditions, more safeguards, and an increasing measure of self-government. There is no obvious reason why public officials should, as a matter of course, have conditions of service markedly better than those in comparable positions outside the public sector. That they have obtained them throughout Europe shows how far they have managed to make public service into a self-governing profession, insulated from outside pressures and outside influence.

PART THREE

CONTROL

CHAPTER 9

The History of Control

The need to control public services grows as their scale increases. Different countries have become aware of this need at different times; at the present day in western Europe it is a universal preoccupation.

Basically there are two types of control. There is a control of legality, and there is a control of policy and expediency. The first is to ensure that actions of private citizens or public authorities conform to the law of the land; any act which does not do so may be declared null and void, and may result either in the payment of compensation or in punitive or disciplinary action.

The second is to ensure that the public authorities act in accordance with the declared policy of the government or of the legislature. The first is in principle a task for judges, the second for legislatures.

In practice the situation is much more complicated than this. One view, for instance, is that to be legal a measure must also be just and reasonable; control of the legality of an act may then involve judgement as to its conformity with some general principles of law which are regarded as inviolable, even though they may not be made explicit. Again, vast masses of current business in public administration may involve points of principle which in theory should be decided by the government or by the legislature. In practice, they have to be decided by permanent officials, in some countries acting ostensibly in the name of the minister, in others acting in their own names. Some of their acts and decisions may well involve not only questions of legality, but also of policy.

Furthermore, discretionary powers are frequently vested in officials. By definition the exercise of such powers can never be properly controlled without having a duplicate administrative apparatus to deal with every question a second time ab initio. Logically, this would entail a further para-bureaucracy to control the controllers, and so on ad absurdum. A more practical possibility is to select a number of key points in the administrative apparatus at which random sample checks may be made. An alternative possibility is to control only after the event those decisions which provoke some complaint from an affected person.

This however raises two further questions: first, who should set the machinery of control in motion? Logically there are three candidates: the administration itself, or politicians, or private citizens, or agents acting on behalf of any of these. Second, who should be responsible for exercising control? The administration itself, the ordinary courts, special administrative courts, or the legislature.

In some countries parliamentary control of public services is still regarded as efficacious, and methods have been devised to maximize legislative control. But legislative control is virtually never concerned with assessing the legality of administrative actions, but with raising questions of policy, expediency, and abuse of power. In some countries the ordinary courts remain competent for issues of pure legality arising out of administrative action, but they have no control over questions of policy and expediency, and only rarely are they able to deal with abuses of power.

This part is concerned with the formal methods which have been devised for controlling public administration, excluding legislative control. It is obviously not possible in this book to deal fully with the constitutional relations of legislature and executive, nor with ministers' political and personal relations with parliaments. The next Part will however attempt to fit the civil service into its political environment.

The way the question of controlling public administration is approached reflects both a philosophy of the state and a national social psychology. There have been times when no control at all was regarded as necessary because the philosophy of the state denied the subject any rights as against the state (or Crown). On the other hand, there have been countries which insisted that the administration, and officials acting on its behalf, were no different from other citizens and were equally liable with them before the ordinary courts of law. There have been countries in which the officials were regarded as being on the same footing before the law as ordinary citizens, but in which the administration possessed powers and rights which could not be challenged before the courts. Finally, the most common European tradition of the last hundred years has been to concentrate on the fact that in practice the state and other forms of public administration possess extraordinary powers compared with the private citizen, and that therefore special precautions are necessary in order to prevent illegality, abuse of power, and administrative immorality.

These views of the state are reflected in the famous German distinction between the Justizstaat, the Polizeistaat, and the Rechtstaat.

In the Polizeistaat, the state is all-powerful, and its interests override any private interests of individuals. In its extreme form this philosophy of the state denies that private interests can ever, as a matter of principle, be in contradiction with the real interests of the state. In these circumstances there is no way at all for the private citizen to protect his interests against the state. Any appeal or request for change in a decision can only be granted as a matter of grace, and only if the interests of the state allow it. In the Polizeistaat the citizen is utterly dependent on the will of the state; he has no rights in face of the state. The Polizeistaat existed in Prussia under Frederick-William I, and was gradually extended in varying degrees to other parts of Germany. It is not unreasonable to regard the Hitler régime as the most modern example of this philosophy of government.

The Justizstaat is a state in which conflicts between public authorities and the ordinary citizen are judged by the ordinary courts of law; there is a basic assumption that the citizen has rights which may have to be defended against the state, and the state has much the same status before the court as any other citizen or corporate body. It is in fact rare to find this pure form of Justizstaat. States which have adopted this philosophy of government frequently accept that all public authorities—other than the state itself and its immediate emanations—should be on an equal footing with the ordinary citizen before the courts. But the state is given a different status with special powers to withhold information, documents, or witnesses; sometimes with a special privilege of denying the jurisdiction of the court, and even of having some of its actions, when in certain legal forms, altogether immune from control of any sort.

The Rechtstaat has often been regarded on the continent as the most advanced form of the state, and the most socially conscious method of state organization. It has two distinguishing features: the state itself imposes a regularly formulated body of rules which it regards as binding on itself and as a point of reference for the conduct of all administrative action. At the same time it creates an independent authority to ensure that administrative actions do in practice conform to the established principles. A Rechtstaat must have a constitution which lays down the supreme laws of the land, the respective competences of the various state organs, and the powers of the state itself vis-à-vis the citizens of the state.

From this follows a dual principle: the executive power is limited on the one hand by the sphere of autonomy allowed by the legislator, and on the other hand by the fact that the decisions of each organ of the executive are subordinated to the control of the next highest executive organ.

In order to maintain and assert the superiority of the law, some independent body must have the power to annul any decision of an administrative body which violates the law. If this independent body is an ordinary court of the land, we soon revert to the Justizstaat; if the only check is afforded by bodies composed of state officials still subject to the administrative hierarchy we tend towards the Polizeistaat. The third possibility is the creation of special administrative courts whose members have the same status and independence as the judges of ordinary courts. This is the case of the Rechtstaat properly so-called.

These definitions are useful up to a point, but at the present time in Europe there are no pure instances of either the Rechtstaat or the Justizstaat. All countries have elements of both systems. A state such as Sweden which is basically a Justizstaat has a Supreme Administrative Tribunal with certain special powers over administrative actions to the exclusion of the ordinary courts. In a Rechtstaat such as Italy the ordinary courts have some powers over the administration whenever the administration acts in the same legal capacity as a private citizen or causes him damage.

But the point of departure is generally clear, and the basic conception of the structure of the state is reflected in the institutions which predominate in the control of the administration.

It may be as well at this stage to dispose of one of the most confusing factors in this entire problem, a confusion which is particularly prevalent in common-law countries. It arises partly out of linguistic usage. There is a basic difference between administrative tribunals and administrative courts. What are generally termed administrative tribunals in common-law countries are institutions set up within the administration itself to decide questions which come within the statutory competence of a particular branch of the administration. A typical instance of an institution of this kind is the National Insurance Tribunals in Britain.

Similar tribunals are to be found in all countries, for instance in France the commissions pour la fixation des indemnités dues aux communes pour occupation de leurs cimetières par des tombes militaires in France. These administrative tribunals are essentially instruments of the administration, used by it to exercise some of the discretionary powers vested in it by law.

Administrative courts on the other hand are quite different in scope and powers. They are concerned with litigation arising between the private citizen and public authorities, with administrative actions in so far as they have affected a citizen's private rights. Their task is to see that public bodies have observed the law, and they have come to assume the rôle of protector of the citizen against the administration. Whereas administrative tribunals are part of the administration itself (even when staffed by laymen), administrative courts are essentially judicial bodies with a special competence. Their function is to dispense justice, not to administer.

It is extremely important to keep this distinction clear. In these chapters we are concerned (amongst other things) with administrative courts and not with administrative tribunals, and we shall take the definition of an administrative court formulated in a famous judgement of the French Conseil d'État; that it is a body which deals with 'all litigation between public authorities and third parties, or between public authorities themselves, concerning the execution, non-execution, or bad execution of public services'.[1]

By the end of the eighteenth century states in Europe were either Justizstaaten or Polizeistaaten. Even in Justizstaaten the medieval powers of the Crown continued to exist, and some of the most important powers exercised by the public administration were regarded as prerogative powers and by that fact excluded from the control of the courts. In addition the civil servants employed in the services which were direct emanations of the Crown were regarded as servants of the Crown, and although they were liable to the courts for civil or criminal offences while in office, their exercise of administrative powers was often subtracted from the review of the courts, being regarded as activities of the Crown itself.

Parliaments in western and northern Europe have continuously striven to limit the discretionary powers of the Crown by bringing the King's ministers under political control exercised in parliament. Once achieved, it was believed that the dual control by the courts for legality and by parliament for discretion and policy was sufficient to ensure the subjection of the executive branch.

This was the first of the major traditions. A second development arose from the adaptation of monarchical institutions to the new philosophy and conditions of the French Revolution, which replaced the myth of the Crown with the myth of the Nation, or alternatively, of the People. A myth persisted but it was a healthier myth in that it presupposed that civil servants were servants of the state, and that they were the aides or advisers of the head of the state rather than his servants. This was a vital change of emphasis.

One of Napoleon's greatest reforms was to revive, under the title of the Conseil d'Etat, the institution used by the Crown under the ancien régime, the Conseil du Roi. The rôle assigned to the new Conseil d'Etat differed from that of its predecessor.

[1] From the judgement in the case of Terrier, 6 February, 1903. Quoted in Rolland: *Précis de Droit Administratif.* 9th ed. Paris, 1947. p. 293.

It was above all an advisory body to the head of the state, his general staff for civil administration. It was also the forcing ground for producing an élite of young men capable of filling at an early age the highest administrative posts.

Napoleon accepted without hesitation the rigid separation of the executive from the judiciary. Underlying this doctrine were the arguments of Montesquieu and the theorists of the Enlightenment as well as the well-grounded belief that the judiciary was a conservative body which would deliberately hamper the élan of the revolutionary spirit.

This however left outside judicial control a large and active administration responsible for operating an unprecedented range of public services. It was obvious that even if the administration acted with the most scrupulous honesty and fairness it must give rise to protests and attempts to reverse decisions which adversely affected private citizens. One course was to appeal to the administrative superior of the person or office responsible for the decision, and if necessary on up through the administrative hierarchy eventually to the head of the state himself. For since neither the legislature nor the judiciary could interfere with the executive, the head of the state was ultimately responsible for the fair and efficient operation of all the public services. His decisions would be given in conformity with the law and with the needs of the service.

One of the principal functions of the newly formed Conseil d'Etat was to advise the head of the state in dealing with these appeals. It is important to realize that originally continental administrative courts only had power to advise and no power to decide. The Conseil d'Etat simply suggested—and even drafted—a decision in a particular case for the consideration of the head of the state. It had no right to give a decision of its own. At any time the head of the state could ignore its recommendations if he considered the interests of the state demanded it. In French terms, the original Conseil d'Etat exercised a justice retenue not a justice déléguée.

This system was introduced by Napoleon into the countries conquered by France. Councils of state were created in the Low Countries, in the various states of Italy, in Spain, and in some German states. In many cases existing institutions, such as the Raad van Staate in the Low Countries, were adapted to the new system. Within France itself Napoleon created a lower level of administrative courts, the conseils de préfecture. These were advisory bodies in each Department with the prefect as chairman, and they dealt with appeals against local administrative decisions. Appeals from the conseils de préfecture could be made to the Conseil d'Etat. A general rule in all these courts was that existing remedies available through the normal administrative channels must first be exhausted before bringing an action to the administrative courts. Inside France, legislation was introduced to allow appeals directly to the conseils de préfecture in certain fields: for instance, appeals by communes against the division of the rate levied within the Department.

After Napoleon's fall the whole concept of the Conseil d'Etat and specialized administrative courts fell into disrepute. They were widely regarded by liberal thinkers and politicians as instruments of authoritarian government, which was not incorrect: special provisions were made to ensure that only safe and respectable members of the establishment were appointed as councillors, and councils of state were extremely prudent when handling government business. The French Conseil d'Etat never had an advisory opinion rejected by the King in administrative cases, but on certain occasions it was clear that the threat of rejection made the Conseil change its mind and conform with the government's wishes in order to avoid creating a precedent.[1]

The belief that councils of state were instruments of authoritarian government had important repercussions. When, in 1830, the Belgians gained their freedom from the Dutch, the question arose as to whether or not an institution similar to the Raad van Staate should be created. The idea was rejected in view of the unanimous hostility of liberal Belgian thinkers and politicians who had little confidence in an institution which, like the Raad van Staate, offered so few guarantees of impartiality.

The Belgians decided instead to follow the British example. The result was that the constitution forbade the creation of special courts, and laid down that all appeals against administrative acts of the executive on grounds of illegality should go to the ordinary courts.

[1] A. Batbie: *Traité théorique et pratique de Droit Public et Administratif.* 2nd ed. Paris, 1885. Vol. III, p. 252.

In Italy there was a similar hostility to administrative justice. The courts left behind by Napoleon were rarely impartial. After 1814 the council in Piedmont reverted to the form it had originally had before 1790; it was reformed by Charles Albert along the lines of the contemporary French Conseil d'Etat in 1831.

When Italy was unified between 1859 and 1861 under Piedmontese leadership, Piedmontese institutions were extended throughout the new country. Amongst them was the Piedmontese Consiglio di Stato, with its advisory, legislative and administrative powers, and its powers of justice retenue. When, during the following years, the leaders of the new Italy—particularly those of the moderate Left—began to discuss institutions which would be genuinely Italian and not mere extensions of Piedmontese institutions, the Consiglio di Stato was one of the first to be attacked. The Liberals saw the Consiglio di Stato as an instrument of the absolute monarchs, and in particular doubted whether any such instrument could impartially dispense administrative justice. They found a more acceptable model in Belgium which was, like Italy, an 'Orleanist' state, yet had avoided the dangers of administrative courts.

In 1865, in the first major reform of Italian administrative institutions, the Consiglio di Stato almost entirely lost its powers of administrative justice. As in Belgium the ordinary courts became competent to deal with any case in which the civil or political rights of a citizen were affected by an action of the administration. The Consiglio di Stato retained its jurisdiction in very exceptional cases, which had to be specifically mentioned in the law.

The Consiglio di Stato was further weakened by the attitude of the left-wing governments and successive parliaments which became progressively less tolerant of its advisory rôle in legislation.

But by 1870 opinion was changing all over Europe. The rapid increase in the scale and scope of public services was bringing the administration and the citizens into much closer contact. A fatal weakness in the Belgian and Italian arrangements was that the civil courts could only deal with matters involving illegality and not with matters involving the exercise of administrative discretion where the private interests of individuals might be affected even though no law was broken. In Italy the problem was enhanced by the increase in the number of officials with no protection from the authoritarianism of their hierarchic superiors; in other countries the encroachment of the central government on local liberties and some notorious administrative scandals where the ordinary courts proved powerless made for a gradual change of atmosphere.

In the 1870's the three administrative leaders of Europe, Austria, Germany and France, gave a lead in the same direction. In France, in 1872, at the beginning of the Third Republic, the Conseil d'Etat was reorganized, with powers of justice déléguée; that is, it now had a statutory competence to issue final judgements in administrative litigation and no longer simply to submit proposed decisions for ratification to the head of the state. The Tribunal des Conflits was created, composed of equal numbers of members of the Conseil d'Etat and of the Cour de Cassation (the supreme civil court), to decide conflicts of competence between administrative and civil courts.

In the new German Empire legal theorists were also beginning to be preoccupied by the need to subordinate the administration to the law, and to limit some of the more excessive powers of sovereignty possessed by the princes and by the Emperor. Like all other liberals in Europe during the nineteenth century, the German liberals had been resolutely hostile to the creation of special administrative courts. Article 182 of the abortive Frankfurt Constitution of 1848 abolished all administrative jurisdictions, and gave the ordinary courts the power to annul administrative acts which violated the law. But by the 1870's the atmosphere had changed. In 1872, the year of the reformation of the French Conseil d'Etat, Rudolf von Gneist's famous book *Verwaltung, Justiz, Rechtsweg* appeared, in which he proposed the creation of administrative courts as an indispensable step towards the formation of the Rechtstaat. Already in 1863 the state of Baden—under French influence—had set up its own administrative jurisdiction. In the years following Gneist's book others were created in different states of the Empire, of which the most important was that introduced in Prussia by the laws of 30 July and 1 August, 1883. But no general imperial administrative jurisdiction was ever created, since it was held that this would trespass upon the autonomy of the individual states. In the German Empire, therefore, each state had its own system of administrative justice, its own form of organization, its own principles for determining the competence of these courts, and its own hierarchy of courts. The two courts of lower instance in Prussia, for example (the Kreisausschuss and the Bezirksausschuss), were staffed by members of the administration still in full-time employment; similarly in Bavaria and Saxony. In Thuringia and the two Mecklenburgs, on the other hand, a rigorous distinction was made between the personnel of the administrative courts and of the active administration. In all the important states, however, the administrative courts of appeal were staffed by special independent judges with the same status and protection as the judges of the ordinary courts: for instance, the Oberverwaltungsgerichte and the Verwaltungsgerichtshöfe of Prussia, Saxony, Bavaria, Baden, Hesse and Württemberg.

The German administrative courts, however, differed from the French Conseil d'Etat and parallel institutions in other countries in that they had exclusively judicial functions, and no administrative or legislative duties.

Under the double impetus of the new prestige of the French Conseil d'Etat and the influence of the German and Austrian theorists of the Rechtstaat, the Italians, though not the Belgians, reformed their Consiglio di Stato in 1889 to make it once again competent to deal with administrative litigation. It maintained a distinction between matters of law and matters of interests; in matters involving the violation of the law by the administration the ordinary courts remained competent. But in all cases where a private interest was affected by administrative action, and in any other case specified by law, the section of administrative litigation of the Consiglio di Stato was competent. The Italian Consiglio di Stato was further strengthened by a law of 1907 giving it powers to decide questions of *merito*.

There is an important difference between the French system and the nineteenth-century German system, which has some significance at the present day. In the French system the Conseil d'Etat was, in the French sense, the juge de droit commun: that is, it had jurisdiction in all litigation between public authorities and private citizens and between two or more public authorities, unless a law specifically provided otherwise.

The German system was for a court's jurisdiction to be limited to those specific matters where a law gave it explicit authority; all other cases automatically went to another court or had no legal redress at all.

By 1900 other countries had become preoccupied with the problem of administrative justice. In Britain the question was posed, and the wrong answer given, by Dicey in his famous work *The Law of the Constitution*. He managed both to define the 'Rule of Law' in a way which meant that virtually no other country in Europe possessed it; and also so to misinterpret the powers and responsibility of the Conseil d'Etat as to mislead whole generations of British lawyers as to what administrative justice was about.

In fact, Dicey's views were in full accord with the particular spirit of the English law. The administration of the law and the practice of the law in England retained much more of the medieval spirit than in other European countries. It was a small closed profession and judges in the courts were drawn from the most successful practitioners of the art. The complications of common law made its full understanding much more of a mystery (in the medieval sense) than that of the more coherent written law on the Continent. Furthermore, the social composition of the English judiciary and legal profession was far narrower than on the Continent, so that lawyers and judges drawn from the wealthier classes were almost unanimously hostile to the extension of public services, to any form of state intervention, and to interference with property rights and the relations between master and servant.

A contrary process was occurring in other European countries. Law was the subject recommended for any poor student who wished to make his way in the world. University education was far more widespread, and law could be read as a mental discipline rather than as a feat of memory. It was the discipline which opened all doors except those of literary salons. Law was not a mystery, but a widely studied subject in which journalists, publicists, businessmen, and civil servants had graduated.

This had important repercussions. Continental countries had state magistracies; that is, candidates entered the judicial career by examination, and worked their way through courts as judges or through departments of the State Attorney as prosecutors and examining magistrates; if they were successful they might reach the highest ranks of the judiciary. This meant able young men without resources could enter the judiciary as they might the civil service, and many posts in the judiciary were filled by men of humble, or at least unostentatious origins. The social weighting of the judiciaries in European countries is quite different to that in England.

By the end of the nineteenth century countries other than Britain which had started from the principle that the ordinary courts should deal with the control of the administration, had seriously revised their views.

In Sweden the constitution of 1809 was based on a strict division of powers, under which the courts controlled the legality of administrative measures, and the government itself acted as the court of appeal from administrative decisions when no point of law was involved. On several occasions during the nineteenth century the question was raised of setting up a body more impartial than the government, and in 1853 parliament proposed to create a supreme administrative tribunal. This project involved an alteration in the constitution, and when it was re-presented to parliament in 1856 it was rejected.

By 1900 the government was in danger of being overwhelmed by the number of administrative appeals it had to deal with, and various solutions to the problem were mooted. One suggestion was that some of these matters should be decided by the Supreme Civil Court, another was that a special section of the Supreme Court should be created to deal with administrative appeals; and yet another was that a number of ministers without portfolio should be appointed to examine the cases and prepare decisions.

In a message to the King in 1903, parliament asked for a special administrative court to be created on the grounds that it would save the government much time and energy, it would ensure that administrative appeals were dealt with in a judicial spirit and with proper procedural safeguards, and would afford greater guarantees of fairness for the private citizen. An enquiry was started under M. Hj. L. Hammarskjöld who, in 1907, reported in favour of the proposal and presented a draft law.

In 1909 the government put before parliament a law based on M. Hammarskjöld's draft and this was approved by parliament later in the year. This created a Supreme Administrative Court which has now a constitutional status.[1]

The Swiss were preoccupied by a similar problem. The original constitution of the confederation had made the Tribunal Fédéral the least important of the confederal institutions. The judges were unpaid, elected by the political authority for a short period of office, and the court itself had no permanent seat. Its powers were mainly restricted to questions of public law regarding the respective spheres of competence of the confederation and the cantons. When the constitution was revised in 1874 the Tribunal Fédéral was strengthened; it was given a permanent seat, and its judges were forbidden to hold any other office or exercise any profession. They became judges in the full sense of the word, and their powers were reinforced.

By the end of the century, however, there was considerable feeling that the Conseil Fédéral possessed too great an authority in deciding administrative appeals. In 1892 a first project to create an administrative court came before the Conseil National. This was followed by pressure from jurists and some politicians,[2] and finally in 1911 a project came before parliament which, after some modifications, was adopted on December 20 of that year. It was put to a referendum a few weeks after the 1914 war started (October 25, 1914) and accepted on a low poll. It was written into the constitution as article 114. This law created a special cour administrative within the Tribunal Fédéral to deal with administrative appeals brought before it either from the federal or the highest cantonal authorities. The new administrative jurisdiction of the Tribunal Fédéral was put on an equal footing with its civil and criminal jurisdiction.

During the inter-war period there was little change in the general outline of administrative justice in Europe.

In Germany under the Weimar Republic there was a general development of the administrative courts.[3] Their jurisdiction was extended, and several Länder courts which had previously

[1] Bo Lagergren: 'Le Conseil d'Etat en Suède.' *RISA*, 1949. pp. 22–30.

[2] See H. Ott: *La justice administrative*. University of Lausanne, 1904.

[3] F. Fleiner: *Institutionen des Deutschen Verwaltungsrechts*. Tübingen, 1928. p. 236 seq.

only had enumerated powers were now given general competence in all administrative matters (Generalklaus). The constitution itself made provision for the creation of a federal supreme administrative court, but in face of the continued hostility of the Länder and the lack of enthusiasm of politicians and jurists for an institution which might seriously threaten local liberties, nothing was done about it.

When Hitler came to power Germany became once again a Polizeistaat in the traditional sense of the word. The courts were forbidden to deal with any case involving the security or interests of the state, and the state itself was sole judge of which acts could be examined. The decrees of August 28, 1939 and November 6, 1939 virtually abolished the jurisdiction of the administrative courts. It was not until after 1945 that Germany again became preoccupied with the forms of law and control.

In Britain the inter-war period saw increased interest in the problem of administration and justice. The most famous broadside came from Lord Hewart in his book *The New Despotism* published in 1929. He discovered a plot of the civil service to take over the powers of government by eliminating the control of the courts, and by annexing the powers of parliament. This gross parody was taken seriously by some people. The judicial attack on the civil service was principally directed against the increasing number of administrative tribunals on the grounds that these tribunals were ousting the courts from their traditional jurisdiction. But administrative tribunals were set up as part of the administration, to assist the administration in exercising the discretionary powers granted by parliament. The judiciary's case would have been a great deal stronger had they consistently adopted the contemporary attitude of the French Conseil d'Etat which subjected the exercise of all administrative discretion to rigorous scrutiny, not only for compliance with the law, but also for compliance with an as yet vague doctrine of reasonable use of power. Traditionally the British judiciary had allowed an extensive field of administrative discretion to, for instance, the Home Office, the Foreign Office, the Armed Forces and the Colonial Office, while at the same time inveighing against the discretionary powers vested in administrative tribunals acting as agents and advisors of the administration.

This schizophrenic approach to different types of administrative discretion seriously weakened the force of the judiciary's argument. It was not surprising that critics should see in the attack on administrative tribunals and the civil service a veiled attack on the new social services which had made increased administrative discretion necessary. The effect of the lawyers' attacks over the years was to convince the Left that the judiciary was not a fit institution for controlling the executive.

The problem of controlling the administration was aggravated in the post-1945 years by the growth of new public services: but the judiciary had itself made a solution more difficult. During the war a series of judgements had extended the unfettered discretion of ministers to a point which foreign observers found intolerable. A doctrine of 'actes de gouvernement' more comprehensive than had been known in European countries since the turn of the century seemed to have been accepted.[1] A series of cases involving property rights was used to bring the problem to public notice. In 1955 the Franks Committee was appointed to enquire into administrative tribunals, their powers and procedure. Its report supported the lawyers' contention that they were not parts of the administration, but performing judicial or quasi-judicial functions. It is too soon to know what practical results the report will have, but the problem of the control of the public administration remains untouched. If all the report's recommendations were followed parts of the new public services would fall under the control of the legal profession; but the vastly more important traditional powers of discretion exercised by the civil service and the ministers would still remain subject only to the rather ineffective political control of parliament.

Belgium, after deliberately adopting British methods of control, also had to face the implications of the development of public services, their increasing contacts with the public, the cost and slowness of the ordinary courts, and the complexity of administrative questions which frequently went beyond the comprehension of the judge. But whereas in Britain the assault was directed by the judiciary against the civil service, in Belgium the government took the initiative. Proposals for a

[1] C. J. Hamson: *Executive Discretion and Judicial Control: an aspect of the French Conseil d'Etat*. London, 1954.

supreme administrative court were put forward in 1930, 1934, and 1936.[1] In a letter to the Prime Minister in January 1934, King Albert stated that 'We have no administrative courts and no administrative court of appeal: it is a gap in our institutions'. A committee was set up and reported in 1938, and the chamber accepted the proposal on April 12, 1938. This draft was far less adventurous than that originally proposed, since although it created a new Conseil d'Etat it gave it only justice retenue and not justice déléguée. The senate suggested in 1939 that the Conseil d'Etat should have powers of justice déléguée in certain fields. The war intervened.

After the war the government still considered that a Conseil d'Etat should be created. In 1946, after hard bargaining between government and opposition and between the chamber and the senate, a mixed committee managed to agree on a series of compromises and the law instituting a Conseil d'Etat was passed in December 1946. The first point of controversy was whether or not the constitution allowed the creation of a Conseil d'Etat with administrative powers; the constitution clearly allowed the executive to create a purely consultative body, but it was arguable that a Conseil d'Etat with administrative jurisdiction would constitute a juridiction exceptionelle which was expressly forbidden by Article 94 of the constitution. There were, however, precedents in some minor administrative tribunals, and opposition ceased once it was accepted that the new Conseil d'Etat would in no way impinge on the powers of the ordinary courts as defined in the constitution, but would simply have a residual power.

The second point of controversy was whether or not the Conseil d'Etat could have the power to annul royal ordinances (arrêtés royaux). It was held that in a parliamentary system these ordinances were subject only to parliamentary control. But other countries had found that this form of control was all too frequently illusory, and furthermore the constitution allowed the ordinary courts to annul royal ordinances *inter partes* during litigation. It was consequently held that the new Conseil d'Etat should have full power to annul royal ordinances and decrees for violation of the law.

The third major controversy was whether or not the Conseil

[1] H. Velge: *Le Conseil d'Etat.* Brussels, 1947. p. 18 seq.

d'Etat should have powers of justice retenue or justice déléguée; that is, if it should have original powers of jurisdiction or simply power to advise or make recommendations to the Crown. This was the most heated controversy of all, and fears were expressed that if a new and untried Conseil d'Etat were given original jurisdiction it would annul royal decrees, award damages indiscriminately and affect the proper functioning of the public services. There was strong pressure to make the Conseil d'Etat a simple adjunct to the executive so that it could be quietly controlled from behind the scenes and not embarrass the government. Eventually a sensible compromise was arrived at. The Conseil d'Etat should have original jurisdiction in all matters concerning the legality of administrative measures; in this field, justice déléguée. On the other hand, in litigation claiming damages from the administration, the Conseil d'Etat was simply to give an opinion and make a recommendation to the Crown. Theoretically the Crown could refuse to pay, but since the Conseil's opinion had to be communicated to the plaintiff, there was strong pressure on the executive to conform to the Conseil's recommendation.

This summary of the gradual emergence of administrative jurisdictions shows how closely it is related to the growth of public services. All countries have had experience of controlling the administration through the judiciary or through parliament, and all have concluded that the judiciary is only effective for enforcing compliance with the letter of the law. The whole question of administrative policy, of administrative discretion, of the exercise of prerogative powers, of the executive's claim to possess a reserve of authority beyond the reach of any control, is a challenge which no judiciary in Europe has met.

Similarly, every country has had a chance to assess the effectiveness of parliamentary control. It varies with the relative constitutional positions of executive and legislature, and a coalition parliament with an uncertain majority exercises more effective control than one dominated by a single party. But in general political control, adequate in the nineteenth century, is no longer considered capable of controlling an administration in modern conditions.

CHAPTER 10

The Structure and Personnel of Administrative Courts

In the major European countries there are two or more levels of administrative jurisdiction. In France there is the Conseil d'Etat at the national level, and in the provinces there are twenty-two subordinate administrative courts, the tribunaux administratifs. The French overseas territories have their own administrative courts, the Conseil d'Etat acting as the court of appeal.

The tribunaux administratifs are the descendants of the departmental conseils de préfecture created by Napoleon to advise and assist the prefect in the same way as the Conseil d'Etat advised and assisted the head of the state. In 1926, as a measure of economy and rationalisation, the conseils de préfecture were amalgamated at a regional level, each covering four or five departments, except for the Conseil de Préfecture of the Seine which remained unchanged. Until 1953 the Conseil d'Etat had original jurisdiction in all administrative litigation; the conseils de préfecture interdépartementaux were competent only when the law specifically said so. This meant that in many cases of relatively minor importance the Conseil d'Etat was acting as court of first as well as last instance. By 1953, it had accumulated a serious backlog of affairs it had been unable to deal with. The traditional jurisdiction was therefore reversed, the tribunaux administratifs being given original jurisdiction, and the Conseil d'Etat only when specified by law. This relieved the Conseil d'Etat of many minor matters, but it retained its rôle of court of appeal from the tribunaux administratifs.[1]

[1] A. De Laubadère: *Les réformes administratives de* 1953. Paris, 1954.

Italy adheres to the original Napoleonic pattern, in that each province has its own local administrative court over which the prefect still presides. In the law on provincial and communal administration of 1865, the Consiglio di Prefettura was made responsible for the tutelage of the provincial administration, while a provincial body, the deputazione provinciale, was responsible for the tutelage of the communes and of opere pie. The consiglio di prefettura was composed entirely of officials. It was regarded as strange that an entirely official body should exercise control over the province and the decisions of its assembly, while the control of local authorities, which were more likely to be weak and irresponsible bodies, should be confided to a partly elected body. In 1888 a new body was therefore created, the giunta provinciale amministrativa, with four members elected from outside the public administration by the provincial council, two nominated from amongst prefectoral councillors by the prefect, and the prefect as president.

In the course of time the elective element in the giunta was gradually reduced, and in Mussolini's time it was composed entirely of officials and Fascist party nominees.[1] It is now composed of five senior officials in the province and four elected members presided over by the prefect. It has certain consultative powers, the controllo di merito, and deals with litigation involving interessi legittimi.[2] When sitting as a judicial body it is composed of five members; the prefect, two members of the consiglio di prefettura, and the two most senior members elected by the provincial council. The giunta is normally regarded as the administrative court of first instance, but because of the powers of the consiglio di prefettura in financial and budgetary control Italian jurists regard the consiglio also in some respects as a court of first instance.[3]

The most extensive and widespread system of administrative courts is to be found in Germany. This is a direct result of its federal nature. In Switzerland only the Tribunal Fédéral is in the judicial sense of the word a properly constituted independent administrative court.

[1] A. Lentini: *L'Amministrazione Locale.* Como, 1953. p. 94 seq.

[2] A. M. Sandulli: op. cit. pp. 506 and 169. For details, see p. 217.

[3] Loci. citi.

In Germany each Land has its own hierarchy of administrative courts and its own supreme administrative court.

The first post-war experiment in administrative courts was made in Berlin itself where in 1946 each of the western occupying powers set up an administrative court in its own sector. In the American Sector there were two, the Stadtverwaltungsgericht and the Bezirksverwaltungsgericht; in the British Sector a single body, the Bezirksverwaltungsgericht. In July 1946 the French re-introduced in their zone of Germany the system of administrative jurisdiction which had existed in Land Württemberg-Baden up till 1935. Unable to put into effect 'revolutionary' changes without the agreement of the other occupying powers, the French authorities contented themselves with reverting to the past. The Länder concerned (which included Baden) have since, unlike the rest of Germany, merely revised and modernized the texts existing in the past. But since this corner of Germany had one of the longest and most deeply entrenched attachments to democratic government the old texts needed little modification to bring them into line with modern needs. Württemberg-Baden is the only western Land which now has a single degree of jurisdiction, the Verwaltungsgerichtshof in Stuttgart, originally based on the Austrian model.

In the other Länder there are two degrees of jurisdiction: a first instance, called the Landesverwaltungsgericht or Bezirksverwaltungsgericht, and a second instance, the Land administrative court of appeal, also known by different titles. In Hamburg, which has the status of an independent Land, there are also two degrees of jurisdiction, the appeal court being the civil court of appeal in special session.

In 1952 the hierarchy of administrative courts in Germany was further complicated by the institution of a Federal Administrative Court with its seat in Berlin.[1] The powers of this court are dealt with below. Its constitution means that in certain cases there are three degrees of jurisdiction, since in some circumstances an appeal lies to the Federal Administrative Court from Land supreme administrative courts.

In all other European countries there are central supreme administrative courts, the Conseil d'Etat in Belgium, the Regeringsrätten in Sweden, the Raad van Staate in Holland,

[1] *Bundesverwaltungsgericht*; law of September 23, 1952.

the Tribunal Suprema in Spain. In the case of Spain the administrative jurisdiction is exercised through a special formation of the supreme civil court, the Consejo de Estado being restricted to its original Spanish form of direct and confidential adviser to the government. It does, however, act in certain cases, for instance appeals in disciplinary cases from officials, pensions to be paid from public funds, and other matters specified by law.

PERSONNEL

The composition of administrative courts is of paramount importance. It varies considerably from country to country. In Italy the local administrative courts—the consiglio di prefettura and the giunta provinciale amministrativa—are both partly composed of full-time officials serving on these courts as an additional duty. Nearly everywhere else nowadays this is regarded as undesirable. In the nineteenth century several countries allowed administrative litigation to be handled by active administrators, sometimes not even taking the precaution of ensuring that a case was not handled on appeal by the administrator whose action had given rise to the appeal.[1] In Germany, under the Weimar Republic, it was not uncommon for the courts of first instance in the Kreis or the Bezirk to be partly or mainly composed of administrators. Every Land now has permanent full-time magistrates for all levels of administrative jurisdiction, and not only, as used to be the case, for the courts of appeal and of second instance. The members of these courts, and the presidents and vice-presidents, are appointed for life, as are also a certain number of the judges who sit as assessors. In certain administrative courts (as in the ordinary courts) a number of lay assessors (nebenamtliche Richter or Hilfsrichter) are appointed from judges of the ordinary courts, from university teachers of law, or from the higher ranks of the civil service. The courts are so constituted, however, that the permanent judges are nearly always in the

[1] This may be responsible for the bad standing of both consiglii di prefettura and the giunta provinciale amministrative. A circular of the ministry of the Interior (August 29, 1953) analyses in detail the faults of these two bodies; excessive delays and excessive partiality to the administration (including use of unfair legal devices) are admitted.

majority. The constitution lays down that the judges of the administrative courts are 'independent and subject solely to the law'.[1] There are additional guarantees of impartiality in some of the northern Länder where, originally under British influence, judges are forbidden to engage in any political activity.

Members of the federal administrative court must have closely defined qualifications. Federal judges are all appointed for life and there is a minimum age of thirty-five. They must either have passed all the necessary examinations for appointment as titular judge of the ordinary judiciary, or have served as a judge in a lower administrative court, or be a teacher of law in a higher educational institution. In addition to these paper qualifications, a judge must have at least three years experience in a federal, Land, communal or public law authority, or as a professional man of law in practice, or as a member of an ordinary court, or as a university teacher of law.

Although in Germany the profession of judge is an administrative career, the administrative courts do not constitute a single closed career. Interchange between various kinds of courts is always possible. In France and Italy, on the other hand, one can reasonably speak of a career of administrative judge. The French Conseil d'Etat is composed of conseillers, maîtres des requêtes and auditeurs. The career within the Conseil d'Etat begins with the auditeur, who in the ordinary way should obtain promotion to maître des requêtes within six or seven years, and, according to the number of vacancies and his reputation, to conseiller by the middle forties. A maximum of one-third of the conseillers can be appointed from outside, normally from distinguished figures in other walks of public life. But the predominant element are the members of the Conseil recruited at an early age, nowadays through the ENA, pre-war by open competitive examination. There is, however, little movement between the tribunaux administratifs and the Conseil d'Etat. The reform of 1945 reserved two posts of conseiller d'Etat to councillors of the lower courts, but in the ordinary way the career in the lower courts is an independent one, the apex of which is the presidency of the Conseil de Préfecture of the Seine.

[1] *Grundgesetz*, art. 97.

There are also two methods of entry to the Italian Consiglio di Stato, by examination and by promotion. But the examination for entry—which is certainly one of the most testing in Europe—is restricted to people already members of the higher civil service, who have attained the rank of at least consigliere in the central administration. The successful competitors are appointed as referendari, and may hope for promotion to consiglieri di Stato after six to eight years.

The remaining consiglieri are appointed by the government from high-ranking officials, jurists, and so on.

The Consiglio di Stato has a president, six presidents of administrative sections, and thirty-eight consiglieri. In addition there is a large number of referendari and vice-referendari, all of whom have been recruited by special examination. The referendari prepare the cases for decision and act as rapporteurs to the sections of the court. One consigliere and several referendari supervise the acts of each individual ministry. Most of this work is done within the court, but there are some offices outside, and a special sezione di controllo in Sicily.

In Belgium all members of the Conseil d'Etat are appointed by the government, and although there is no examination for entry all members must be doctors of law. The question of appointment caused ten months delay in setting up the Conseil in 1947, because the senate wished to avoid the first nominations being made by a left-wing government. The conseillers were eventually chosen from distinguished administrators, jurists, and ministerial directors. They have a small group of auditeurs who must have law doctorates. The Belgian court is much smaller than either the French Conseil d'Etat or the Italian Consiglio di Stato, and this makes it more comparable to the Dutch Raad van Staate and the Swedish Regeringsrätten.

Probably the Dutch Raad van Staate has the most distinguished membership of any administrative court in Europe. It is recruited from ambassadors, ex-ministers, admirals, secretaries general of ministries, eminent professors of law, colonial governors. The number of professional jurists is very small. A small number of assistants is attached to the court, but they have no status comparable to the maîtres des requêtes, for instance, in France.

This examination of the structure and personnel of administrative courts brings out one striking feature which they have in common. In no country except Spain and Switzerland is the supreme administrative court regarded as part of the judiciary. Whatever its relationship with the ordinary courts of the land its independence from judicial control is never questioned.

CHAPTER 11

The Powers of Administrative Courts

There are four major aspects of controlling public administration. First, to ensure that public administration always operates within the letter of the law. This is by no means as easy as it once was. There has been a growing tendency for parliaments to entrust the administration with powers to make regulations having the force of law. Control of legality, therefore, involves both ensuring that the administration acted within the terms of a law or regulation, and, in the case of a regulation, that it was originally empowered to make such a regulation.

Second, there is the question of discretion. The administration has to decide whether X is entitled to a pension, to a road licence; whether a public works' contract should go to A or B; whether C's land should be compulsorily purchased for building a road, and whether with limited funds it is better to build a bridge in this province rather than that province. In the course of time a body of precedents grows up which can be applied by rule of thumb methods. This applies to a great deal of administrative work in, for example, post offices, labour exchanges, pension administrations, health services, educational administration.

But even with the most generous allowance for mechanical administration of this kind, a small but politically vital group of decisions stands outside any category. While there were very few of these key decisions it did not seem unreasonable to suppose that parliament could exercise effective control through pressure on the minister concerned. But it is no longer realistic to suppose that any minister can know a tithe of what goes on under his ministry's roof, or that parliamentary procedure leaves much room for control by parliamentary questions.

Third, the public service must be made to accept responsibility for any damage it causes in the performance of its normal operations. There are several aspects of this. For instance, damage may be caused without any culpable negligence; an arsenal might blow up through a fractured electricity cable without negligence on anyone's part. Or the damage may be caused by a public servant in the ordinary course of his duties, but under circumstances which show that he was personally guilty of gross negligence. Or again, the administration may be working perfectly properly, perfectly reasonably, and with due regard for the public interest, but yet cause an individual loss which is exceptional when compared to that borne by other people.

Finally there is the question of abuse of power. Officials may use their legal powers for ends unacknowledged and unapproved by the law; they may take decisions on the basis of personal enmity or political favour. In extreme cases they may be corrupted financially into using their official powers in one way rather than another.

Complete control of public administration would cover these four aspects. And it would have to be universal, and cover all public services, whether national or local, economic or social, at home or abroad. Control of legality would have to include methods of ensuring that proper procedure had been observed, that the rules ensured an adequate presentation of the case, that all the evidence was equally available to both sides, that no documents were withheld from the controlling body on a pretext of the public interest, and so on.

Complete control would also imply control of the equity of decisions, and of their reasonableness and impartiality. It would therefore involve inquiring into the actual process of decision-making to ensure that the decision was one which a reasonable administrator would have made on the basis of the evidence he possessed. Only in this way can there be any chance of detecting abuse of power by administrators, for this is a field halfway between legality and discretion, and simply to control the legality of an act will never disclose bad faith, détournement de pouvoir, or other manifestations of abuse of power.

Finally, complete control would require adequate compensation to individuals damaged by the actions of the public administration; the assessment and payment of money from public funds; and also an assessment of the extent to which the damage can reasonably be regarded as a normal operational hazard, and how far it has been the personal fault of a negligent official.

This problem of bringing home responsibility to the particular individual official is fundamental to the control of the public administration.

The British, insisting as they do on ministerial responsibility, go to the greatest lengths to protect the individual official. This attitude is based on the constitutional contention that civil servants are servants of the Crown and the minister and not of the state, and that adequate control over a department can be exercised through parliamentary control over the minister. Less obvious but equally important are the conviction of the irreproachability of senior civil servants and of the need for strong government, the belief that strong government must mean uncontrolled government, and not least the passionate anonymity of the civil servants themselves.

No other country goes as far as this. Holland perhaps comes nearest, and it is significant that after Britain the weakest control of the administration is in Holland. Belgium and Italy also have weak systems of control. Denmark used to be the only country other than Britain with no formalised control of the central administration, but she has since adopted the Ombudsman system, and no longer really comes in this category.

Sweden, France, Switzerland, Germany (both the federation and the Länder) and Finland, on the other hand, all subject their public services to strong control, both through parliament and through special institutions.

HOLLAND

The executive was made independent of the judiciary in 1798 under French influence. The doctrine of the separation of powers was based on Montesquieu's interpretation of the British constitution. Less rigorous than the French, the Dutch never accepted the doctrine in all its aspects, and no clear division was in fact made. Nor has it been since. New problems were dealt with as they arose with compromise and adjustments.

The judiciary continued to deal with much administrative litigation, while ad hoc administrative bodies were created to deal with appeals, claims for damages, and control of decisions of the expanding social services. Finally, the Crown retained ultimate responsibility (subject to the political control of parliament) for all administrative matters not expressly assigned either to the ordinary courts or to specially created administrative tribunals. Until 1887 there was an article in the Constitution which appeared to forbid the creation of administrative tribunals, but after this had been amended the number of administrative tribunals with special powers in limited fields increased at a progressive rate. By 1932 a report estimated that there were already thirty of them; but they lacked an organized basis, their powers were drawn from different laws, there was no general court of appeal, and no unified administrative jurisprudence. The only body which could remedy these shortcomings is the Raad van Staate, but it has no status as an administrative appeal court.

The Raad van Staate is divided into fourteen administrative sections and one section for administrative litigation. Each administrative section deals with the affairs of one of the ministries. Since there are only ten councillors, and each section must have three councillors, this means that there is considerable overlapping, and each councillor is a member of three or four administrative sections. The section for administrative litigation has five councillors, with the vice-president—the effective head—of the Raad van Staate, as president. The administrative sections have no powers in their own right, they simply prepare decisions and make reports for consideration by the Raad van Staate meeting in full assembly. The section for administrative litigation, on the other hand, acts on its own authority, and does not report to the full assembly.

The Raad van Staate is a consultative body, and in principle it can examine a matter only when the government or the Crown asks its advice. In practice, the government is required by law to consult it on many matters; for instance all legislation, whether proposed by the government or as private bills by members of parliament. Government bills must be laid before the Raad van Staate for its opinion before being presented to parliament, private members' bills between the final vote in parliament and the royal signature. But in neither case is the Raad's opinion binding either on the government or on parliament. Indeed, since 1848, there has always been a current of political opinion hostile to the intervention of the Raad van Staate in legislative and political matters. That this feeling persists was made clear by an incident in 1949. It became known that the Raad had on its own initiative discussed the problem of the Netherlands East Indies, and had made proposals for the settlement of this dispute. This was widely interpreted in political circles as an unwarranted interference in a major political question, and the Raad van Staate came in for some outspoken criticism. A penetrating French critic, himself a conseiller d'Etat in France, has drawn attention to the close similarities between the position of the Raad van Staate today and that of the French Conseil d'Etat of the Restoration period.[1]

The powers of the Raad van Staate in the field of administrative litigation are not clear. They are shared with the ordinary courts. The ordinary courts have both a general power stemming from the constitution of 1815, and special powers in particular fields assigned them by individual laws. Article 165 of the constitution of 1815 states that 'disputes concerning property or property rights, debts, or civil rights, are exclusively the province of the ordinary courts'. A law of 1817 added to this litigation arising out of illegal administrative actions. The ordinary courts cannot, however, annul an administrative act, even if illegal. They can only award damages against the administration for the harm done.

The Raad van Staate is the principal channel for appeals to the Crown. Its jurisdiction is complicated by the extreme diversity of the laws. There can be no appeal to the Crown through the Raad van Staate unless it is expressly provided for by law. Sometimes the law provides for appeal to the ordinary courts; sometimes to the special administrative tribunals mentioned above, from which there is no further appeal except to the ordinary courts for ultra vires. If the law makes no provision the only recourse is through the administrative hierarchy to the minister who then acts in a judicial capacity; that is, he sends the appeal to the appropriate department in his ministry, or

[1] H. Puget: 'Le Conseil d'Etat Néerlandais.' In *Etudes et Documents.* Conseil d'Etat, Paris, 1949. p. 159.

very occasionally to a specially formed committee. In a few rare cases it is possible to appeal to the Crown against a decision of a minister when acting in a judicial capacity, against a decision of an administrative tribunal, and even against a decision of an ordinary court when dealing with administrative litigation.

When there is an appeal to the Crown, the latter decides after hearing the opinion of the Raad van Staate. This is the extent of the power of administrative litigation possessed by the Raad. The plaintiff does not have to be represented by counsel, and the costs and complications of procedure have been reduced to a minimum.

Many of the appeals to the Crown are against the actions or decisions of town and provincial authorities, with a not insignificant proportion against the actions of Crown officials. Since the appeal is in principle to the Crown, it must be sent to the royal cabinet which transmits it for comment to the ministry concerned. The appeal, together with the ministry's comments, is then transmitted to the Raad van Staate. There is no time limit within which the ministry is required to transmit the complaint, and it has been suggested that ministries have sometimes deliberately taken no action in order to prevent the appeal going any further.

When the appeal arrives at the Raad van Staate the vice-president arranges for the parties to present memoranda and supporting evidence, and he appoints a rapporteur from the section for administrative litigation. The rapporteur examines the entire case and can call for any further evidence he wishes. He presents the case to the council, and the parties have the right to make final oral statements. The section for administrative litigation then decides what recommendation shall be made to the Crown, and drafts the text of a final decision. This is communicated to the appropriate ministry. If the ministry objects to or has reservations about the decision proposed, an exchange of views between the Raad van Staate and the ministry begins, and this can last for some time. If neither side is prepared to alter its view the minister can in the end ignore the decision proposed by the Raad van Staate and substitute his own. That is, the Crown through the minister has the final word.

But when the Crown acts contrary to the advice of the Raad van Staate the text of the minister's decision, when printed in the official gazette, must be followed by the full text of the decision proposed by the Raad van Staate together with the minister's report to the Crown explaining his reasons for overriding the Raad's decision. The requirement of public justification is designed to bring pressure to bear on the minister to agree to the Raad van Staate's decision except where he has substantial grounds for not doing so. In recent times the number of cases in which the minister has refused to follow the Raad's advice has tended to increase, particularly in the fields of education, town-planning, and transport.

Some critics have blamed this on the attitude of the Raad van Staate, and hold that the policy of recruiting it only from distinguished men inevitably makes it over-conservative and inadequate for dealing with the problems posed by modern public services.

The Raad van Staate is not a very adequate protection against administrative abuse, although it does provide a check on ministerial discretion not to be found in Britain. It is inadequate not so much because its decisions can be overridden and its recommendations ignored, but because wide fields of central administrative activity are excluded from its control, and because, even when it has appellate jurisdiction, it does not possess the type of inquisitorial powers which can bring out cases of administrative immorality, abuse of power, or plain administrative negligence. It relies to a considerable extent on the ministries for the information on which it has to work. But it can force ministries ultimately to justify some of their decisions in public. This is at least more satisfactory than the casual evasion and refusal to answer questions not infrequently associated with parliamentary control of ministers.

BELGIUM

Until 1946, control of the public administration in Belgium was very weak; it relied entirely on the ordinary judiciary and on parliamentary control of the minister. The ordinary courts always took a restrictive view of their own competence, limiting themselves to appreciating the purely formal aspects of the legality of administrative actions. They had virtually no possibility of entering into the details of decision-making, and therefore little chance of exposing administrative immorality or gross negligence. They were for a long time confused by the central administration's claims of royal and ministerial immunity based on the concept of acts in the public interest, 'actes de gouvernement'. The central administration maintained that these powers were by definition sovereign powers not subject to control. It gradually adopted the French Conseil d'Etat's distinction between actes d'autorité and actes de gestion, and accepted responsibility for the latter group on the grounds that they implied liability on the part of the administration.

It became clear that this distinction gave rise to as many injustices as it cured. To obtain damages a plaintiff had to prove that the administration had broken the law, and not simply caused him damage; he also had to prove that the administration had caused damage through a fault. There was no remedy in cases where the administration had caused damage by doing nothing, or when it had taken a blatantly wrong decision, or acted in a clearly partial way.

In addition to this the rapid growth of new types of public services threw up many new problems. An administrative appeal to the Crown, that is to the minister, was only possible against communal or provincial orders, and even then there were many complaints that political sympathies affected the result of these appeals. Furthermore new special administrative tribunals sprang up, each with its own small field of operations, and with no possibility of appeal.

This was the situation in Belgium before the creation of the supreme administrative court, when it is probably true to say that control of the administration was weaker than in Holland, and even Britain.

The creation of the Conseil d'Etat did not eliminate all the original difficulties.[1] The ordinary judiciary retained its constitutional powers, and the Conseil was regarded primarily as a means of plugging the gaps. But in fact its powers exceeded this original purpose, and it does exercise a real control over the central administration.

[1] H. Puget: 'Le Conseil d'Etat Belge.' In *Etudes et Documents*. Conseil d'Etat, Paris, 1948.

The Belgian Conseil d'Etat is divided into two sections, one for legislation, the other for administration.[1] The latter is the chamber for administrative litigation. The section for legislation deals with the advisory and consultative work assigned to the Conseil. The Conseil must be consulted by the government on all proposed legislation; in particular all proposed delegated legislation, decrees, orders in council, and regulations other than purely administrative rules of internal application within the administration, must be sent to it for comment. These comments are in principle made public, though ministers try to evade this when possible, by registering a bill as 'urgent'. Like its counterparts in other countries, the Belgian Conseil d'Etat also assists the government and the ministries in drafting intelligible and internally coherent laws and regulations. The fact that the opinions and views of the Conseil d'Etat legislative section are sometimes made public, is in advance of the French Conseil d'Etat which has always been the pacemaker in administrative courts; in France the opinions of the Conseil d'Etat in legislative matters are always confidential.

The section for administration deals both with administrative litigation and with those administrative problems on which a minister may ask it for advice. The latter are not very common.

In administrative litigation the Conseil d'Etat is peculiar in that it has powers both of justice déléguée and of justice retenue. The reasons have been explained. In questions of damages it can only give an opinion and make a recommendation to the Crown, and theoretically the Crown can refuse to accept its recommendation. But since these opinions are published it has been found that the public services are not anxious to challenge them. In its first five years of existence it made twenty or so recommendations in favour of the plaintiff and only two were refused by the minister. Appeals against local authorities are simpler to handle since the minister can write the charge into the local authority's budget. As in all countries the central administrations are the worst problem, and here the Belgian Conseil d'Etat has certainly not yet found an entirely satisfactory solution.

The Conseil d'Etat is competent to deal with claims for damages against public authorities whenever there is no

[1] Conseil d'Etat: 'Loi et Arrêtés essentiels.' *Moniteur Belge*, January 9, 1947.

alternative jurisdiction open to receive the case, whenever damage is exceptional, and whenever damage has been caused through the activity or refusal to act of the public authorities. In formulating its proposals it has to bear in mind the public and private interests involved, and has an equitable jurisdiction. So far in Belgian law there is no list of actes de gouvernement, though in the past the central administration has not infrequently claimed privilege on this score. One of the major tasks of the Belgian Conseil d'Etat in its first twenty or thirty years will undoubtedly be to determine the limits of the royal prerogative and to restrict claims for exemption from jurisdiction to a clearly defined group of subjects.[1]

The original jurisdiction of the Conseil d'Etat is defined by law. It has the power to annul any administrative measure, regulation, order in council or decision which is contrary to the law. It may annul on grounds of failure to observe prescribed norms, ultra vires, and détournement de pouvoir. It therefore has authority to examine administrative decisions much more closely than has the Dutch Raad van Staate, and can call for witnesses and papers.

ITALY

As will later be explained, some of the powers regarding the promulgation of regulations, decrees, and orders in council belong, in Italy, to the Corte dei Conti. The Consiglio di Stato has six sections. Three sections are concerned with administrative affairs, three others with administrative litigation. The latter three were created as the Consiglio's powers were extended. By custom section IV, the first of the sections for administrative litigation, and section VI, the most recently created, deal with actions against the administration, and section V with appeals from the lower bodies dealing with administrative litigation, principally the giunta provinciale amministrative. The public does not have much confidence in the impartiality and judicial competence of these giunta. They

[1] For instance, in 1953 the Conseil d'Etat held that the Crown possessed no inherent power to insist that members of the foreign service obtain official permission before marrying. It held that marriage was a civil right which could only be suspended by law. 'In Rapport sur l'activité de la section de législation.' 1952–3.

have been due for reform ever since the end of the war, but since their reform has generally been linked with the creation of a regional system of government as prescribed by the constitution, it has been repeatedly delayed.

Each administrative section of the Consiglio di Stato deals with the administrative affairs of a group of ministries. Their powers are comparable to those of the administrative sections of other councils of state.[1] The drafts of bills and decrees have to be presented to them for an opinion, which is, however, not binding on the government. The main purpose of this is to ensure elegant and consistent draftsmanship, to make laws internally coherent, and to prevent conflicts between two sets of laws. Sometimes the government is required by law to consult the Consiglio di Stato, sometimes it may do so if it wishes. In emergencies, or when specifically and conditionally authorized to do so by parliament, the government can issue decrees having the force of law, and there is no constitutional provision which requires the government to present these proposals to the Consiglio di Stato. In practice, however, it does so, unless parliament deliberately provided otherwise when it authorized the government to make the decrees.

The law has required the prior opinion of the Consiglio di Stato on all ordinances of a general nature, on all administrative decisions that public works are 'of public interest', and on ordinances recognizing charitable institutions. All these matters are dealt with by an administrative section. Its permission is also required before a private person can proceed in court against a prefect or a mayor for actions performed in the course of his duties. This 'administrative guarantee' was a famous institution of the nineteenth century, but has disappeared elsewhere.

As in all countries the government can ask the Consiglio di Stato for advice on any matter of administrative or legal importance, but in practice no government since 1947 seems to have availed itself of its services in this field. This may have been a result of the sometimes indiscreet way the Consiglio di Stato reinstated officials who had been expelled from the administration for their sympathy with the Fascist party.

[1] The powers of the Consiglio di Stato are based on the royal decree of June 26, 1924, modified by several later amendments. A consolidated text is in No. 897 of the Leggi Amministrativi. Pirola, Milan, 1951.

Italy has retained from the nineteenth century a special form of appeal against administrative actions, the ricorso straordinario to the President of the Republic. Relief from a decision may be accorded as a matter of grace after all the normal appeals through the administrative hierarchy have been tried and failed. This has several advantages for the private individual in that it costs very little, no lawyer is required, and it is not subject, as administrative litigation is, to definite time limits. A major disadvantage is that use of the ricorso straordinario is a tacit admission that the action cannot be challenged on grounds of legality. It is therefore an alternative to an appeal to the administrative courts. The ricorso straordinario can be approved or rejected by the President of the Republic on the advice of the Consiglio di Stato meeting in full assembly. The government may ignore the Consiglio's opinion, but only by a decree of the council of ministers.

The jurisdiction of the Consiglio di Stato in administrative litigation is of two kinds.[1]

First it controls the legality of administrative acts. This 'competenza generale di legittimità' is the earliest of the powers of the Consiglio di Stato in this field, dating back to 1889. This type of action is based on the argument that an administrative decision which is not in accordance with the law should have no legal effect. It may be illegal because the administrative authority is not legally competent to take decisions in that particular field; and here the law may be understood in its broadest sense of laws, regulations, decree laws, ordinances, and so on. Or the case may be based on the argument that the provision involves an excess of power.[2] Originally this excess of power was barely distinguished from 'incompetence', but gradually French influence has led to a refinement of the concept (sviamento di potere, l'errore di fatto ed il travisamento dei fatti, i vizi logici, la ingiustizia manifesta). These points will be dealt with later as being typical marks of the jurisprudence of the French Conseil d'Etat.[3]

In fact the Italian Consiglio di Stato uses its powers very

[1] S. Lessona: *La Giustizia Amministrativa*. Bologna, 1953. p. 74 seq.

[2] V. E. Orlando: *Principi di Diritto Amministrativo*. Florence, 1952. p. 425 seq.

[3] A French view of the Italian court is: H. Puget: *Le Conseil d'Etat Italienne*. *RISA*, 1952.

discreetly, and is very loath, even on good grounds, to interfere with the active administration. This is partly due to the historical accident that has denied the Consiglio the steady public support enjoyed by its French counterpart. The Left has generally shown a marked antipathy to the Consiglio, which it considers too tender with the interests of property, respect- ability and political stability, and too ready to suppor authoritarian measures by the government. The Right, on the other hand, with a constitutional background which favours a strong executive ultimately drawing its powers from the monarch rather than from the people, tolerates the Consiglio di Stato only on the understanding that it will conform to this view.

Although Italian administrative lawyers have adopted French terminology, an action to control the legality of an adminis- trative act before the Consiglio di Stato is but a pale reflection of what actually occurs in France. All alternative methods of redress, administrative, hierarchic, or appellate, must have been tried and failed. This is already a major obstacle when one considers that excessive speed of decision is not a characteristic of the Italian civil service. Attempts to obtain administrative redress can therefore go on for an unconscionable time.[1]

Since the Consiglio di Stato will not accept an action based on the inherent illegality of a general regulation or decision, the action must be brought against a particular act which has caused specific damage to a particular individual. The plaintiff must therefore prove his locus standi in a way long since abandoned in France. There is a further restriction. The Consiglio di Stato has that excessive respect for the executive which characterized the French Conseil d'Etat of the Restora- tion. The Consiglio di Stato has accepted a wide definition of 'actes de gouvernement' as being all acts concerning the superior interests of the state or the superior direction of the life of the state.[2] This type of definition, like all those based on 'royal prerogative' or 'public interest', can only too easily be

[1] Cases cited in Conferenza del Prof. C. Vitta, tenuta nell'Università di Padova, April 26, 1952.

[2] E. Bonaudi: 'L'evoluzione del potere esecutivo e gli atti di potere politico del Governo.' *Rivista Amministrativa*, 1949. pp. 523–9.

used to prevent the examination of precisely those questions where abuse of power and victimization is most probable. It may even be true to say that no country's administration is under adequate control unless these terms are very closely defined and unless that definition is the work of an independent authority.

The second action which may be brought before the Consiglio di Stato is the giurisdizione di merito. This is a restricted competence which the Consiglio di Stato only has in certain fields defined by law: mainly in article 27 of the testo unico for the Consiglio di Stato of 1924. There is little in common between the various fields: actions to compel the administration to implement judgements of the civil courts, actions by legal corporations under administrative tutelage against the administration for refusing to begin legal proceedings on their behalf, actions arising out of public examinations, appeals against decisions of the giunta provinciale amministrative, and so on. An action for the control of merito differs from one for the control of legittimità in that the latter is concerned with the juridical faults of an act, whereas the former may also take account of the administrative errors and shortcomings.[1] If an action concerning legittimità succeeds on grounds of legal incompetence the court can only refer the case back to the competent administrative authority, or if it succeeds on other grounds, it can annul the act purely and simply. Occasionally this entails consequential adjustments, for instance the reintegration of an official whose dismissal the Consiglio di Stato has annulled.

In an action concerning merito the court can go further and redraft the actual decision. For instance, in disciplinary cases it can modify the punishment imposed on an official.

SWITZERLAND

Switzerland is a special case in Europe. It is a country which combines much of the best of the eighteenth-century ideal of revolutionary democracy with many of the traditions of an exceedingly conservative and ponderous nineteenth-century bourgeoisie. It has firm principles regarding the need for

[1] V. E. Orlando. op. cit. p. 426.

authority in social and family life, combined with an extreme distrust of those who exercise authority in public life.

In addition to this it has stood at the crossroads of French and German legal thinking, and several cantons bear marks of one or other influence. In the confederation as a whole the problem of control was for some time not so acute as in other countries. In the first place wide sections of public life were the responsibility of the cantons and not the confederation, and a sizeable federal civil service is a fairly recent phenomenon. In the second place public democratic control of government is jealously maintained both in the cantons and in the confederation.

In view of this the Swiss contented themselves for a long time with administrative control of the federal services by the Conseil Fédéral, the federal cabinet. In 1914, however, the Tribunal Fédéral was reformed and later further modified in 1928 and 1943, and responsibility for controlling the administration was divided between the Conseil Fédéral and the Tribunal Fédéral. When the law does not explicitly assign to the Tribunal Fédéral the responsibility for dealing with a branch of administrative litigation, the matter automatically goes to the Conseil Fédéral. The Swiss system is based on the enumerative rather than the general clause principle of dividing jurisdiction. In this can be detected the great influence exercised by German jurists on Swiss legal thinking in the late nineteenth and early twentieth centuries.[1]

The Tribunal Fédéral is perhaps the supreme court with the most complicated structure in the world; certainly in Europe. It has jurisdiction in public, civil, criminal, and administrative law, and its internal organization reflects this diversity of subjects.[2]

The Tribunal is divided into eight sections. There is a cour de droit public et administratif of nine judges; two cours civils each of six judges. For criminal law there is a chambre d'accusation, a chambre criminelle and the cour d'assises assisted by federal juries; a cour pénale fédérale with five judges, and a cour de cassation pénale also with five judges.

[1] E. Ruck: *Schweizerisches Verwaltungsrecht*: 2 vols. Zürich, 1934. vol. I. p. 154 seq.

[2] Procédure fédérale: *Organisation judiciaire, procédure civile, procédure pénale.* Published by Chancellerie fédérale, Berne, 1949.

There is a cour de cassation extraordinaire which hears appeals on points of law from the cour d'assises, and finally a chambre des poursuites et des faillites concerned with cases of debt and bankruptcy.

The Tribunal Fédéral has no power to declare a federal law unconstitutional. It must apply all the laws and decrees voted by the Assemblée Fédérale. On the other hand, it may examine the constitutionality of the acts of the cantons, to ensure conformity both with the federal constitution and with the constitution of that particular canton.

In the field of public law the cour de droit public deals with cases involving conflicts of competence between the federal and cantonal authorities, differences between two or more cantons, actions based on the violation of intercantonal agreements or violation of the constitutional rights of citizens. This cour then deals with the Parteistreitigkeit, which is one of the principal actions in German administrative law, with the additional responsibility of protecting the constitution against the illegal activities of the cantonal executives, and of protecting the cantonal executives against the encroachment of the federal administration in the fields reserved to them.

The civil court of the Tribunal Fédéral deals in first and last instance with some civil actions which in other countries are dealt with by the administrative courts; in particular civil cases between the confederation and the cantons, or between two or more cantons, and actions involving more than 4,000 francs brought by a private person against the confederation, or against a canton. It also has appellate jurisdiction from cantonal courts sitting as courts of last instance on points involving the misapplication of federal laws, and can quash judgements of cantonal courts where they have applied cantonal laws which are in conflict with federal laws.[1]

The administrative section of the Tribunal Fédéral is first an appeal court for cases from administrative tribunals exercising a judicial function, and second, a court of first and last instance in a wide variety of matters specified in the law of 1943. Appeals from administrative tribunals cover minor matters like tax assessments or the amount of caution money

[1] W. Geering: *Das Verfahren vor Bundesgericht in Verwaltungsrechtlichen Streitigkeiten.* Geneva, 1945.

demanded by the federal administration for the exercise of certain professions.

The matters specified in the law of 1943 for which the administrative court sits as court of first and last instance include litigation involving some of the operations of the railways, the electricity authorities, the patent office, the department of Police and Justice when supervising monopolies, casinos, and insurance companies, the military administration in its dealings with explosives monopolies, certain decisions of the federal office of social insurance, and many of the activities of the post office when there is no appeal to the department of Posts and Railways.

There is little difficulty in proving capacity to plead, since anyone who is a party to the decision or anyone whose rights are affected by the decision can begin an action. In addition, the Conseil Fédéral itself can bring a case before the court from the decisions of cantonal authorities acting in last instance. For this purpose it can require cantons to forward decisions to the Conseil Fédéral as soon as they are taken.

Administrative appeals to the Tribunal Fédéral can only be based on alleged infractions of federal law. But the term federal law is understood in a wide sense: 'the federal law is violated when a principle expressly laid down by a federal act or implicit in its dispositions has not been applied or has been wrongly applied'.[1] Furthermore, if a fact has been wrongly interpreted this may be regarded as a violation of the law itself.

In the case of tax assessments the federal judge has the power to alter the administration's decision for manifest inexactitude. The judge has in all cases the right to examine whether or not the factual basis of the decision is correct; that is, he has the right to enquire into the decision itself to control the material exactitude of the facts on which the administration bases its decisions.

Where the administrative section of the Tribunal Fédéral has authority to hear appeals, that authority is effective; its weakness lies in the fact that it only has enumerative jurisdiction, and a large proportion of appeals against administrative authorities go instead to the Conseil Fédéral. The Conseil Fédéral has a very special place in Swiss life as compared with

[1] Article 104 of the law of 1943.

other 'governments'. It is a type of directorate, and gives far greater grounds for public confidence in its authority and impartiality than any other executive in Europe. Its traditions, its approach to public life, its relations with the elected assembly, its attitude to the public, all mark it off from any other 'government' studied in this book. There are, therefore, far fewer reasons for objecting to it as a final court of appeal in administrative matters than would be true anywhere else.

GERMANY

The federal structure is more marked in the field of administrative law in Germany than it is in Switzerland. But there are discernible general rules governing the constitution and operation of administrative courts, and it is certainly simpler nowadays to generalize than it was during the period of the Weimar Republic.

Two persistent sources of difficulty are the constitutional relationship between the Länder and the federation, and the multiplicity of public bodies at all levels of administration in Germany.

Furthermore certain matters which in other countries are the province of the administrative courts are throughout Germany excluded from their jurisdiction and handled either by special administrative tribunals, or by the ordinary civil courts. For instance, the Gerichtsverfassungsgesetz gives the civil courts jurisdiction in cases involving appeals against the assessment of the value of expropriated property (art. 14), and in claims against a public authority for damages arising out of an action by one or more of its officials acting in their official capacity (art. 34). The last provision was also in article 131 of the Weimar constitution.

This clearly lessens the general influence of the administrative courts. An additional complication is the existence of a constitutional court with jurisdiction over all acts which affect the constitutional rights of the citizen. In Switzerland, it will be remembered, where the same problem arises, the application of public constitutional and administrative law was handled not only by the same tribunal, but within the tribunal, by the same section. In Germany there is no such clear-cut solution.

In some Länder the administrative and constitutional courts have parallel jurisdiction. Article 120 of the Bavarian constitution, for instance, provides that any citizen who has had his constitutional rights violated by a public authority may appeal to the constitutional court. An administrative order or regulation can therefore be contested either in the administrative courts for violation of the law, or in the constitutional court for violation of constitutional rights.

Formerly, administrative justice in Germany was additionally complicated by the fact that in some Länder the administrative courts—or at least the supreme Land administrative court—had general jurisdiction over all administrative acts, decisions, and activities; while in others even the supreme Land administrative court had jurisdiction only in matters enumerated in a law or laws. Undoubtedly the origin of this principle of enumeration was a distrust of administrative courts and fear that they would assert their powers in the face of the executive, and wittingly or unwittingly hamper effective government. Also, since the system of administrative justice grew up piecemeal the list could be extended as the legislator needed to find a solution to a particular problem. The general rule, now universal in actions for annulment for illegality, is the 'general clause'.

Since actions for damages against an administration or an official are dealt with by the ordinary civil courts in Germany, actions before the administrative courts are principally of two kinds, 'Parteistreitigkeiten' and 'Anfechtungsklage', though in some Länder they have additional powers as well.[1]

The Parteistreitigkeit is an action to settle a conflict of competence between public authorities. It covers all litigation between public law authorities, Länder, communes, unions of communes (Gemeindeverbände), public assistance institutions, public credit and banking institutions, and so on. The actions are brought in the name of the corporations themselves. A corporation may begin such an action in order to establish its existence as a public body, or to determine the legal extent of its powers. Or a subordinate corporation, on which a higher state authority has laid a burden or imposed a duty, may contest it as illegal or excessive. Actions to determine the

[1] E. Forsthoff: *Lehrbuch des Verwaltungsrechts*. Berlin, 1951. p. 434.

degree of autonomy of a corporation, for example its degree of autonomy in internal management, or claims against a Land for the cost of certain branches of administration, come under this type of action.[1]

The Anfechtungsklage is an action to annul an administrative act. Its equivalent is found in several other countries. Most of the administrative courts have powers to examine not only the formal observance of the law by the administration, but also that it conforms with detailed legal requirements. It is not enough that an administrative body has jurisdiction in a particular field; it must, for instance, observe the correct procedure. Since the war the jurisdiction of several Land administrative courts has been phrased in a way which allows them to deal with cases of abuse of power, or détournement de pouvoir by the administration. The Bavarian ordinance of March 30, 1947, for instance, states that: 'The administrative courts judge cases claiming the annulment of an administrative act of any kind whether general or individual in so far as it has prejudiced the interests of the plaintiff by a violation of the law, or if they are based on an abuse or an excess of power.'

This would seem to be leading towards administrative courts controlling the exercise of administrative discretion, a development at variance with the German tradition. Where administrative authorities refused to act in the past, G. Meyer's classic statement of the position was that redress could only be obtained 'where the withholding of the rights concerned results not from the discretion of the administrative authorities, but only from grounds specified by law'. This could easily result in a denial of justice, as it was relatively rare for the discretion of an administration to be defined by the law in a way which would allow an appeal to succeed.

Since the war, originating in the Länder of the British and American zones, there has been an extension of the Anfechtungsklage known as 'Untätigkeitsklage', an action to compel an administration to perform an administrative act.[2] This is somewhat similar to a writ of mandamus in common-law countries; it allows a plaintiff to require an administration to act. The administration concerned is assumed to have refused

[1] In Baden and others this action is still subject to the 'enumeration' principle.
[2] E. Forsthoff: op. cit. pp. 435, 439.

if it has not acted within two months of receiving the request. Normally the judge has the power simply to order the administration to perform the act required; but in certain fields of labour law the administrative judge can take the necessary steps himself.

It would be unrealistic to suppose that greater liberality in this field is likely to lead to an increase in the powers of the administrative judge to control the exercise of administrative discretion. The German tradition is strongly against this, and in the past the judge has refused to control administrative discretion except in cases where there may have been abuse of power or an excess of power. Administrative authorities have power to withhold documents even from the Federal Administrative Court (Bundesverwaltungsgericht), if their disclosure would be contrary to the public interest, or if they would be regarded as confidential in private law. It may, however, be said that administrative courts in Germany are gradually moving towards a position where it will be possible to bring an action against a discretionary administrative decision which is not in accordance with the ultimate objects of the enabling law, or which goes beyond the strict limits of what is absolutely necessary in the public interest.[1]

Most Länder have two levels of administrative jurisdiction, the ordinary Land administrative court and a Land supreme administrative court. These handle the administrative acts of Land and federal authorities. In some cases appeals may be taken up to the Federal Administrative Court.

In principle the administrative acts of federal authorities, public corporations and offices are subject to appeal in the administrative courts of the Land where the office is situated or occasionally where the act has taken effect. Certain of the highest federal authorities are exempt from these courts, however, and appear only before the Federal Administrative Court.[2]

The Federal Administrative Court has jurisdiction both as an appeal court from the Land supreme administrative courts for certain clearly defined cases, and as a court of first and last instance in a few other cases.

The Federal Administrative Court accepts appeals from

[1] For instance, the law of April 14, 1950, article 23, of Land Rheinland-Pfalz.

[2] Gesetz über das Bundesverwaltungsgericht: September 23, 1952.

Land supreme administrative courts when there has been a manifest defect in the procedure of the court; for example, if one of the parties was not given a proper hearing, or evidence was wrongly allowed, or one of the judges had been concerned with the case at an earlier stage (art. 54, BVG). A new trial may be held (art. 53, BVG) if an important point of law is involved, or if the Land court has dissented from a decision of the Federal Administrative Court or of another Land supreme administrative court. It is also necessary for a federal authority to be directly involved.

Three examples of where the Federal Administrative Court acts as court of first and last instance illustrate the complications inherent in the federal system. It hears appeals against administrative decisions of federal authorities in the following matters: consular affairs, currency and exchange control, insurance and building societies, the regulation of food products, forests and timber products, labour and business management, and traffic and water concerns. But it is only the court of first instance for these matters when the case covers several Länder, when it is particularly significant or likely to have widespread effects, or when it is in the public interest that it should be decided immediately. Otherwise the case is referred to a Land supreme administrative court. The Federal Administrative Court itself decides whether or not it has jurisdiction, but the federal attorney general has the right to appear and to be heard while the case is under discussion.

The Federal Administrative Court is also court of first instance in cases between federation and Land or between two Länder when the point of law at issue is not of constitutional importance. If it decides that the case involves constitutional law it transmits it to the federal constitutional court (art. 9).

The Federal Administrative Court is court of first and last instance in those cases brought against a federal decision banning movements under article 9, para. 2, of the constitution or under para. 129 of the penal code. Art. 9, para. 2, of the constitution forbids movements whose objects are contrary to the law, which threaten to overturn the constitutional order, or harm the concept of international brotherhood. It is also competent in those cases in which federal authorities are excluded from the jurisdiction of the Land administrative courts.

The jurisdiction of the Federal Administrative Court is important but not extensive, but over the course of time it should be able to build up some common principles of administrative jurisprudence and a body of nationally accepted case law. This intention is evident in the provisions which allow appeals from Länder on important points of law, or when the Land court has dissented from a judgement of the Federal Administrative Court or of another Land supreme administrative court. The same purpose lies behind art. 47 of the constituent act of the Federal Administrative Court. This article provides that when a section (Senat) of the court wishes to depart from a previous judgement or disagree on the law as stated by another section, the Grosser Senat shall be convened, shall hear the arguments, and give a ruling which will be binding on all the sections of the court. The Grosser Senat is composed of the president of the court and six other judges appointed by the presidium for two years. Here, too, the federal attorney general has the right to attend and to be heard.

The administrative courts in Germany exercise stronger control than those in Holland, Belgium, or Italy. The common social and academic origins of judges and civil servants in Germany breeds a mutual confidence which is reinforced by the inclusion of experienced administrators with judges in the administrative courts. But there are inherent dangers in this coincidence of view point between the administrative judge and the administrator. There would be much to be said for the introduction of non-jurists into the administrative courts, and indeed into the civil service proper. All too often the common academic origins of administrative judge and administrator mean an excessive preoccupation with the formalism of the legal administrative process. The result is that both administrator and administrative judge may allow the use of administrative powers by politicians for blatantly personal or political ends, provided the formal embodiment of these decisions is in due and proper form. It may not be unfair to say that the German administrative courts are excessively preoccupied with the demands of public order while they overlook the need to avoid administrative abuse of power.[1]

[1] A similar impression is given by M. Martin: 'Les juridictions administratives en Allemagne.' In *Etudes et Documents*, Conseil d'Etat, Paris, 1952. pp. 166–78.

FRANCE

The French Conseil d'Etat is by far the most highly developed and most powerful administrative court in Europe, and both by its success, and by its technical jurisprudence, it has been the pace-maker for other courts and for foreign jurists for several generations.

The present organization and powers of the Conseil d'Etat are based on an ordonnance of 1945, promulgated by the Provisional Government of General de Gaulle. It is perhaps legitimate to wonder whether the Conseil would have received such extensive powers and have such formalised authority had its constituent text been discussed, analysed and voted by parliament.

The Conseil has two types of powers, both of which stem from its origins under Napoleon. It is the government's advisory body on legislation and law, and also the supreme administrative court of the country.

Under the 1945 ordonnance, the government is required to obtain the Conseil's opinion on any bill it proposes to introduce in parliament. In addition, a minister could ask the Conseil to draft a bill for him according to his specifications. There are no post-war examples of the Conseil d'Etat drafting a bill on its own account. On the other hand, a minister quite often asks for the vice-president of the Conseil to nominate a councillor to assist his ministry in preparing a bill; particularly where the bill involves considerable legal technicalities.

The Conseil d'Etat also has the right to call the government's attention to a field where legislation appears to be desirable. The government does not, however, have to prepare a bill, nor does it have to submit the Conseil d'Etat's proposal to parliament. In fact this quasi-legislative power is unused. Intervention by the Conseil in the field of legislation would undoubtedly be resented by parliament, and for this reason the Conseil has prudently decided not to exercise its legal faculty. There is no constitutional safeguard for the powers of the Conseil d'Etat, and if parliament wished to trim its sails it could do so by simple act of parliament.

The Conseil d'Etat must be consulted on all decrees or

ordinances of general application, and on decrees particularly important in the field of local government known as décrets en Conseil d'Etat. In this field of administrative regulation the government or minister must always consult the Conseil d'Etat, but only very rarely are they bound to obtain its positive approval; they need only prove that the text of the bill or regulation has been submitted. But there are good reasons why the government and ministers cannot be too casual with the Conseil d'Etat. In certain cases the Conseil d'Etat does not simply suggest amendments to the text of a regulation, but in fact drafts a completely new proposal. The government cannot then pick and choose between its own and the Conseil's version, for the resulting compilation would not, as an entity, have ever been formally presented to the Conseil. The government therefore either has to take its own proposal as it stands, or adopt the Conseil's version as it stands, or, finally, re-draft its original proposals, and present the new draft again to the Conseil.

As far as proposed legislation is concerned the government can without difficulty disregard the Conseil's advice. Once parliament has adopted the text of a bill, and it has become law, every court in the country must apply it. But in the case of decrees, ordinances and regulations, the Conseil's opinion, although (in most cases) only advisory, has considerable force. For one of the sections of the Conseil d'Etat may later have to deal with litigation arising out of these ordinances, regulations and decrees. If the government or a minister refuses to accept the Conseil's view that a clause is illegal or ultra vires or a violation of the law, he is fully entitled to issue the regulation in its original form; but a few months later people affected by the measures taken under that regulation or decree may well begin litigation before the administrative courts for the annulment of the act on grounds of illegality. The Conseil d'Etat will then be called upon to judge, and the minister may find that his regulation or decree is formally held to be illegal, and null and void. It will be so not because the minister refused to take notice of the Conseil d'Etat's opinion, but because of the inherent illegality of the measure—as defined by the Conseil.[1]

[1] M. Letourneur and J. Méric: *Conseil d'Etat et juridictions administratives*. Paris, 1955. pp. 58, 138.

The importance of the consultative rôle of the Conseil d'Etat depends to a large extent on parliament. If parliament passes bills in strict detail, the amount of discretion allowed to the Conseil d'Etat, as to the executive as a whole, is considerably reduced. But in no other country is delegated and subordinate legislation so closely controlled as it is in France by the Conseil d'Etat. Not only is it controlled from the point of view of legality, but also from the point of view of material content, since the Conseil d'Etat can contest the utility or desirability of measures proposed. Moreover, the Conseil d'Etat has, over the course of time, narrowed its definition of actes de gouvernement, that is, acts which cannot come within the jurisdiction of any court but for which the government (executive) claims arbitrary powers.

This necessary work has been carried out by the Conseil d'Etat in its second capacity of court of administrative justice.

The Conseil d'Etat acts on certain occasions as court of first and last instance; on other occasions as a court of appeal from the decisions of the tribunaux administratifs, and their counterpart in French overseas territories; and as final appeal court, but only on points of law, from other bodies judging in the last instance. The principle bodies of this kind are the Cour des Comptes, the conseil supérieur de l'éducation nationale, the commission centrale d'aide sociale, and the professional associations and domestic tribunals of doctors, architects, pharmacists, and so on, and the Conseil d'Etat is primarily concerned with the sentences of these bodies sitting as disciplinary courts. In fact it has full authority to receive appeals from any body which has a public law status.

The Conseil d'Etat is court of first and last instance for a list of matters involving the public services contained in the decree of September 1953: actions alleging excess of power or ultra vires, cases concerning the personal situation of officials appointed to office by decree (that is, the highest officials), cases which cover the territorial jurisdiction of several tribunaux administratifs, matters beyond the competence of the administrative courts in French overseas possessions, and litigation which arises from activities in non-French territory. All other cases involving the public services go to the tribunaux administratifs in the first instance, with appeal to the Conseil d'Etat.

In general the ordinary civil courts have no jurisdiction in cases involving public authorities, or between public authorities and private citizens when the operation of the public service is involved. This covers all matters regarding the operation of these services, their functioning and any consequences arising out of it, their contracts, and any other acts of public authority. There are, however, certain exceptions.

In the first place the operations of the ordinary judiciary, including the work of the parquet, the examining magistrates, and the operational activity of the judicial police, are excluded from the jurisdiction of the Conseil d'Etat even though they are obviously part of the public service. But there are some borderline cases, in that, for instance, the Conseil d'Etat has jurisdiction in matters involving the statute of members of the judiciary since they are state officials, and it may have some jurisdiction where the creation or suppression of courts is concerned.

Secondly, for historical reasons the ordinary courts have always been regarded as the appropriate body for dealing with cases involving the liberties of the subject. Thus repressive jurisdiction is a matter for the ordinary courts. The ordinary judge can decide whether or not an administrative police regulation is in fact legal, and if not can refuse to obey it. But since it is a measure of an administrative authority, he cannot annul the measure, but simply refuse to apply it. It is for the Conseil d'Etat to decide whether or not the decision or regulation is illegal and to be annulled.

The ordinary courts are also responsible for dealing with cases which arise out of administrative activity which is so gross an abuse of power—particularly in the use of physical force—that 'it is manifestly impossible to regard it as the application of a law or a regulation' or 'of a power normally regarded as inherent in the administration'.[1] It is held that on these occasions the responsible official or administration has in fact left the field of public law altogether and has committed an offence of an ordinary civil or criminal nature.

The same rule applies when an official in his official capacity commits an act which shows such gross negligence and so little concern for the interests of his service, that he ceases to be protected by the general responsibility of a public authority

[1] M. Letourneur and J. Méric: op. cit. p. 72.

to compensate third parties for the damage caused through the action of their agents. On these occasions[1] the action for damages goes not to the administrative courts but to the ordinary courts, and the official is personally liable for any damages awarded.

Another important field excluded from the jurisdiction of the Conseil d'Etat is the nationalized industries, even though they are regarded as in many ways public services. It is held that their operations have more in common with those of private industries and enterprises than with ordinary parts of the administration, and for this reason they should operate according to civil and commercial law. The argument is historically supported by the fact that it has always been possible for an administration to enter into private law contracts which came under the jurisdiction of the ordinary courts. It is also true that it would cause some inconvenience (especially politically) if all the workers of the nationalized industries became legally officials, although some of the senior appointments in the nationalized industries do carry a personal status which comes under the control of the Conseil d'Etat. Major nationalized enterprises such as the Electricité de France have powers of compulsory purchase, a feature which might well be regarded as being the peculiar mark of a public as distinct from a private corporation.

Where it is not clear whether the administrative or the ordinary courts have jurisdiction the matter is decided by a special court, the tribunal des conflits, composed of an equal number of judges from the supreme civil court and councillors from the Conseil d'Etat. Should there be a stalemate, which is very rare, the Minister of Justice takes the chair and has a casting vote, the only occasion on which he does so.

The Conseil d'Etat has created two types of administrative suit. The first is an action for the annulment of an administrative act or decision on grounds of illegality; the second is an action inviting the court to recognize the existence of a subjective right which the administration has damaged, and to obtain redress.[2] In a sense both these actions are the creation of the Conseil d'Etat.

[1] They are becoming increasingly rare, see p. 239.

[2] There are two other actions, for interpretation and repression, which are unimportant here.

Until 1945, indeed, there was virtually no statutory basis for the action for the annulment of an administrative act; it was based entirely on a law of October 7–14, 1790, which said, 'No claim that an administrative act is ultra vires is to be dealt with by the ordinary courts; they are to be referred to the King as head of the administration.' That is, this action was based on a law of the monarchy passed nearly fifteen years before the Conseil d'Etat came into existence.

Similarly with the action for damages; administrative law is uncodified; it is simply a collection of important and unimportant laws on specific subjects. Where there are gaps in the law, or when the laws are couched in general terms, the Conseil d'Etat has made the law by its own jurisprudence. This, of course, seems less surprising to people accustomed to the common law than to those brought up in the Roman law tradition. The Conseil has in fact built up a whole concept of the liability of public authorities for damage almost entirely on 'the general principles of law'. And the general principles of law are what the Conseil d'Etat says they are.

The action for the annulment of an administrative act can be brought against decree laws, regulations and ordinances of general application, as well as against individual orders and decisions taken by administrative authorities—ministers, prefects, mayors. The action is not possible against laws, the judgements of ordinary civil and criminal courts, actes de gouvernement, and contractual acts which may be attacked by way of an action for damages. The only serious loophole in its jurisdiction in the past was the acte de gouvernement. The French administration, like any other administration, was ready to use the argument of 'public policy' or 'the public interest' to escape from the control of the Conseil d'Etat. It has already been explained how the Conseil d'Etat persistently reduced the number of matters which are immune from jurisdiction on this ground, so that today the argument is only very rarely advanced.

The Conseil d'Etat requires that for an act to be challenged it must have positive legal effects upon one or several individuals or corporations. It is not possible to start an action on the ground of purely preliminary steps, like the opening of an enquiry, or internal circulars and instructions within an administration, or warning notices issued by an administration. In such cases an action is only possible when an effective measure is taken; for instance, when a decision is based on an incorrect internal circular.

The Conseil d'Etat takes a very liberal view of the persons who are entitled to begin an action. It is, for instance, possible for a member of a profession to begin an action against a measure which adversely affects his profession and not just himself personally. It is also more liberal than any other country in its interpretation of its own rule that no action shall be received if there is an alternative method of redress available. For it accepts that the alternative method of redress must be able to give as complete satisfaction as would a successful appeal before itself. For instance, the financial administration may excuse a tax-payer from paying according to an illegal assessment, but unless he receives a judgement in the administrative court the assessment will legally stand, and he will in future years have to make the same appeal to the financial administration.

The Conseil d'Etat has recently tightened its requirements as regards the delay between notification of a decision and the time an action must be started.[1] In principle the delay is two months, but the court is generous about accepting legitimate reasons for extra delay, for instance because the plaintiff had within that space of time started an action in the wrong court, or had appealed to the minister through the administrative hierarchy.

The method for beginning an action for annulment is very simple. It requires no more than two copies of the complaint, a copy of the contested decision, and an abstract of the legal arguments or factual details in support of the case. The plaintiff may use the services of one of the lawyers inscribed at the bar of the Conseil d'Etat, but he need not do so. The cost of the case is therefore very small, and even when a lawyer's services are used, his fees are fixed by a scale of charges authorized by the Conseil d'Etat itself, and subject to its examination.

The reasons which may be invoked in support of an action for annulment are similar to those mentioned in connection with other administrative courts. First, on grounds of ultra

[1] For details of change in policy, see M. Letourneur and J. Méric: op. cit. pp. 124–7.

vires. The authority which made the decision may not be legally empowered to do so. A mayor may not take a decision reserved by law to his municipal council, a prefect may not issue an ordinance which legally requires the minister's signature, the minister may not promulgate a regulation without authorization from parliament.

Second, the administration may have failed to follow the prescribed procedure, ignored substantive requirements concerning the form the decision should take, or neglected necessary prior consultations. But the Conseil d'Etat insists that the preparatory fault be one of substance, and not merely a frivolous or unimportant oversight. The failure to observe the regulations must be such as to have seriously affected the interests of the plaintiff or the fairness or objectivity of the final decision.

The third major reason for annulment of an administrative act for illegality is that the law has actually been broken. This includes not only those cases in which there is a contradiction between a law and the decision attacked. The Conseil d'Etat also considers illegal any decision which violates the letter of the law, or a decree or regulation of general application which is in contradiction with the res judicata of an administrative or civil court.

The most interesting examples show how the Conseil d'Etat, while regarding its jurisdiction as being limited to ensuring the observance of the law, nevertheless imposes rules of conduct on the administration. Furthermore, it has frequently ruled that when the administration is legally entitled to exercise discretionary powers, the Conseil d'Etat has no powers to overturn that decision or substitute its own views. But through its own jurisprudence it has evolved methods of enquiring into the details of decision-making.

One of the ways in which it has achieved this position is by insisting that administrative decisions do not conflict with 'the general principles of law', as it defines them. It holds, for instance, that the right of equality contained in the Declaration of 1789 means that it is illegal to impose heavier duties or burdens on one citizen than on another; or to discriminate between applicants for public office on grounds of political affiliation, colour, or religion.

By the same token it insists that even discretionary decisions must conform to the facts of the case. If a minister were to refuse a building licence on the grounds that building would spoil the particularly beautiful countryside in a protected area, it would be sufficient for the plaintiff to show that the area concerned was full of industrial properties successfully to contest the minister's decision before the Conseil d'Etat. Or an official may be reduced in rank if his professional work is at fault; but the Conseil d'Etat would not allow a minister to adduce from the fact the official was a communist the fact that his professional work was at fault. Decisions which are based on facts or reasoning must be in conformity with the facts or the reasons advanced.

Clearly there are circumstances where the administration can be under no obligation to justify its use of discretionary power, and then a plaintiff's success will partly depend on his ability to attack the decision from its weakest point.

There is then one final course open to a plaintiff, which the Conseil d'Etat has developed to a point where not even when the administration is allowed the widest discretion can its acts go unchallenged and unexamined.[1] He can base his case on the charge that there was détournement de pouvoir. This is the use of legal powers in proper form for purposes or for reasons contrary to the spirit of the law or to the general principles of law. It can never be easy to provide documentary proof that this offence has been committed, but the Conseil d'Etat is prepared to deduce consequences from the facts of the case. For instance, the Conseil d'Etat has deduced détournement de pouvoir where a musical society was refused permission to give a concert on public property when in exactly similar circumstances the municipal police band was given permission. Another case concerned a mayor who refused a merchant permission to have a stall in the municipal market; the Conseil d'Etat held that there was détournement de pouvoir since the mayor had furnished no proof that the merchant was likely to break the market regulations (that would have been a satisfactory reason), and the merchant had shown that he had some time previously refused the mayor's request to apologize to a municipal councillor after a local incident. The Conseil

[1] M. Waline: *Traité de Droit Administratif*. 6th. ed. Paris, 1956. p. 145.

d'Etat deduced a connection between these two incidents, and annulled the mayor's refusal. There are many similar cases. The interesting development is that the Conseil d'Etat enquires into the reasons behind an essentially discretionary decision. It is coming close to the view that every administrative decision must be based on reasons, and that these reasons should be explicable to a body of highly trained men experienced in the practice of administration. Such a body is likely to give the fullest credit to a decision honestly arrived at, and to appreciate the margin of guesswork implicit in many of the most important administrative decisions.

The second major action before the Conseil d'Etat is that to obtain recognition of a subjective right, and to obtain redress for the damage caused by administrative action. Here the Conseil d'Etat acts like an ordinary civil court when judging actions for, for instance, breach of contract or damages. The Conseil d'Etat has gradually evolved its own doctrine of the responsibility and liability of the public services. The legislative basis of the Conseil d'Etat's action for excès de pouvoir was, until 1945, very slender. But its doctrine of the responsibility of public authorities still has no legislative basis even to this day. It is entirely a creation of the Conseil d'Etat itself.

The point of departure was the famous decision by the Tribunal des Conflits in the case of Blanco in 1873; this held that: 'the responsibility of the state for damage caused to private persons by an action of persons employed in the public service cannot be determined by the principles laid down in the civil code for the responsibility of one private person to another; this responsibility is neither general nor absolute; it is subject to special rules which vary according to the needs of the service and the need to reconcile the rights of the state and those of private persons'.

The importance of this decision was, first, that actions for damages against the state became the responsibility of the Conseil d'Etat and not the civil courts; second, that although designed to protect the state from liability for damages, it clearly stated the need to find a way of reconciling the needs of the state with the rights of the citizen. It recognized that the state may need extraordinary powers in order to perform its duties in the general public interest, but at the same time recognized that the citizen might reasonably demand redress for any special damages caused him which were not imposed on other private persons.

By 1938 the Conseil d'Etat had so developed these two points that it abandoned its original position that only administrative acts were liable to cause damage, and maintained that even legislative acts, when they caused damage to one or a small selected group of citizens, could justify the award of damages. Nevertheless, the Conseil d'Etat recognized certain limits to the responsibility of public authorities. It accepted, for example, that certain services were by their nature peculiarly susceptible to minor risks, which were inherent in the provisions of the particular service. The Conseil always required a plaintiff to show that the administration had been guilty of a fault, but in the case of services such as the police, emergency medical services, or administrative services in isolated parts of French overseas territories, it required a plaintiff to prove that the fault was of exceptional proportions. It recognized that some public services, if they are to operate at all, must entail a certain unavoidable risk to others.

Even here, however, the Conseil d'Etat has gradually shifted its position in favour of the private citizen. Formerly it always required proof of a fault on the part of the service concerned. Later it accepted that in certain cases, for instance in certain traffic accidents, there could be a presumption of fault, and then the administration concerned should pay the damages.

It also elaborated a distinction between faute personnelle and faute de service; only in the second case would it award damages against the public service. If it found that the accident could not reasonably be imputed to the charge of the service, the plaintiff had to go to the civil courts and sue the official for damages as a private individual. It often happened of course that no damages could be extracted from the official who was simply not in a position to pay them. Whenever possible therefore a person damaged would sue the administration.

In view of the frequent injustice this caused, the Conseil d'Etat accepted after 1919 that a public service could also be held liable for damage caused by a personal fault of its agent when in its service. This gave the plaintiff the alternative of suing the agent personally through the civil courts, or the administration through the administrative courts. In 1949 the Conseil d'Etat went a step further, and accepted that it was possible to sue the public service whenever it could reasonably be held that its agent was on duty.

This change in jurisprudence, while it afforded every protection to the interests of the public, left the interests of the public service inadequately protected. A public service was not allowed to recoup the damages it had to pay from the official who had caused them. In 1949 this was partly remedied by the provision that where there is both a fault by the public service and a personal fault by its agent, the courts can divide the responsibility between them proportionately. They assess the extent to which the fault was the fault of the agent, and he has to pay that proportion of the damages finally awarded.

Finally, the Conseil d'Etat has recognized that the liability of a public service can be engaged even when there is no fault either on the part of the service or on the part of the agent. Formerly it would accept an action without proof of fault only in cases involving the construction or operation of public works. This was later extended to cover those fields, such as munitions works, where the state was directly engaged in a highly dangerous trade. The question assumed particular importance as the result of the use of firearms by the police. In circumstances where the use of firearms was fully authorized, innocent bystanders might be killed or seriously injured; should the public service be held responsible for damages even though no fault was imputed to the police themselves? The Conseil d'Etat decided that persons who, through an administrative activity, suffered particular damage, which was not shared by any other significant group of people, could reasonably seek recompense for the damage suffered from the public authority concerned.[1]

It is hardly necessary to insist on the distinctive character of the French Conseil d'Etat. It has a unique record in European administrative law, and a unique reputation amongst administrative courts. For impartiality, intellectual brilliance, common sense, administrative wisdom and experience, and ability to

[1] For the reasoning used by the Conseil d'Etat, see the full report of the government commissioner before the Conseil, in Letourneur and Méric. op. cit. p. 127 seq.

reconcile the interests of efficient administration with the rights of the citizen, it has no equal.

SCANDINAVIA

The Scandinavian countries have a method of controlling the public administration not to be found anywhere else. This is the Swedish institution of the Ombudsman, copies of which are found in Finland, Denmark and Germany. An account of the work of the Ombudsmanner will be given in the next chapter. This section is concerned only with administrative courts in Scandinavia.

The Swedish administrative court (Regeringsrätten) always sits as a single body. It is recruited from officials in various branches of the administrative services, many of whom have at one time been connected with the ordinary courts. At least half the members must have the qualifications necessary for holding judicial office. It contains a provincial tax expert, a university lawyer, a railway engineer, a member of the attorney general's department, a high court judge, and officials from ministries. Members rank as under-secretaries.

There is no hierarchy within the court. All members are appointed by the government as regeringsräter. The detailed work of preparation, however, is done by specially appointed ministerial secretaries, one for each ministry. These secretaries remain employed by the ministry, but they act as the court's agents in the preparation and examination of cases prior to judgement. This has led to some questions regarding the real independence of the Supreme Administrative Court. It has been held that although members are protected by constitutional safeguards they are too closely linked with ministries by their personal origins, and by their reliance on these secretaries selected by and in some ways responsible to the ministries.

The jurisdiction of the Supreme Administrative Court is restricted to those fields specifically designated by law. This method was chosen in order that the jurisdiction of the administrative court could be distinguished from that of the ordinary tribunals, and from that of the Crown meeting in council of state. The Supreme Administrative Court has no powers beyond the immediate control of the legality of the act contested. It cannot award damages, which is entirely within the jurisdiction of the ordinary courts. It can take no cognisance of the utility or desirability of the act, and appeals against the use of discretionary powers must go in the last resort to the council of ministers, as must all appeals on points other than law (provided they do not come within the province of the Ombudsman).

When, therefore, the Supreme Administrative Court is faced with a case which involves a question of utility or desirability, it examines it, finds on any question of law, and then transmits it to the council of ministers.

A further serious restriction on the jurisdiction of the Supreme Administrative Court is that a minister's decision is final.[1] Constitutionally, it is held that when the minister acts, the Crown acts. This virtually restricts the Supreme Administrative Court's jurisdiction to government agencies and the activities of provincial and local administrations. This is less serious than it might be elsewhere, since the administrative boards frequently cover whole blocks of administrative activity which in other countries would come under a ministry. There is a school of thought which holds that it would be possible for the court to rule that a minister's decision was illegal, and certain councillors maintain that the court could annul a minister's act for unconstitutionality, but both these points are undecided and controversial.

The bulk of the work of the Supreme Administrative Court is undoubtedly fiscal and taxation cases. Sweden has a highly developed and very complex system of fiscal legislation, and this gives rise each year to much litigation. In 1954 there were 2,170 fiscal and taxation appeals to the Supreme Administrative Court as compared with 1,568 appeals of all other kinds. The most serious figures however are those showing that at the end of the year, although there were only 579 appeal cases outstanding in non-fiscal affairs, there was a backlog of nearly ten times that number of fiscal and taxation cases waiting to be dealt with. These financial cases are appeals from the central fiscal court, which receives an annual total of well over 10,000 appeals.

[1] Bo Lagergren. op. cit.

Most of the other cases dealt with by the Supreme Administrative Court arise out of the operations of the welfare state: appeals against compulsory treatment for alcoholism, probation and detention orders against children and young people, transfer of children in need of care and protection to the local authorities, and a significant number of appeals against the withdrawal of driving licences for traffic offences.

In many of these cases the original decisions are not taken by the administrative services of the state, but by committees of local authorities or justices of the peace. From these committees and authorities there is an appeal to the provincial governor, and from him to the Supreme Administrative Court. To an outsider it seems that in certain cases the Supreme Administrative Court goes rather beyond a purely formal examination of the legality of the proceedings, and examines whether or not the facts of the case justify the penalties imposed. Furthermore in several cases it is concerned with assessing whether the local authority is right, or whether the provincial governor is right. If the local authority is overridden by the provincial governor on appeal, the local authority itself can appeal against his decision to the Supreme Administrative Court through (generally) the ministry of Social Welfare.

The first stage in an appeal to the Supreme Administrative Court is to send a formal written complaint to the appropriate ministry. This is sent by the secretariat to the ministerial secretary responsible for preparing the case for presentation to the Supreme Administrative Court. He sends the complaint back to the competent authorities for information or comment. When the authorities against whom the appeal is made receive the papers, they get in touch with the plaintiff to obtain from him a more detailed expression of his views. It is possible for either side to produce new evidence, begin a new enquiry or develop fresh arguments.

When this process is completed the dossier is returned to the responsible ministry, where the specially appointed ministerial secretary prepares his report on the case, basing it on the papers contained in the dossier. In his report he is expected to give not only a summary of the facts of the case, the arguments used, and the proofs available, but also, where necessary, to summarise the law and the precedents applicable to the case. His report is completed by a draft proposal for a decision.

Each ministerial secretary attends the Supreme Administrative Court one day in every two to three weeks, when the court deals, during that day, with all the matters he has prepared. The report and draft verdict are discussed by the court, and the dossier is then handed over to one of the councillors of the court, who is responsible for ensuring that the judgement conforms to the views expressed in the court, for checking the reasoning and evidence used in the report by the ministerial secretary, and for drafting the verdict in accordance with his views and those expressed during the hearing. Each councillor studies each report sufficiently to know the general terms of the problem. The following week the final decision of the court is voted by the court when it assembles.

The Swedish administrative court is only beginning to tackle the real problems of administrative jurisprudence.

The new Finnish system of government of 1919 was based to a considerable extent on the Swedish model, and included a similar type of supreme administrative court. In Finland, however, there is an additional court, the Supreme Public Service Court, to deal with litigation involving the status, rights, discipline, and so on, of officials.

The members of the Finnish Supreme Administrative Court are appointed to office by the President of the Republic; as in Sweden, at least half the members must have the qualifications necessary for judicial office. It, too, deals only with questions of law, and questions of utility and discretion are the concern of the council of ministers. If a case before the court raises both issues the Supreme Administrative Court decides the point of law, and then transmits the matter to the council of ministers for it to decide on the other issues. In one field the Finnish Supreme Administrative Court is in advance of its Swedish parent; since 1950 an appeal to the court is possible on points of law against a decision of the council of ministers.

CHAPTER 12

The Ombudsman

Although the Supreme Administrative Courts in Sweden and Finland are weak in themselves, they, combined with the Ombudsman, with his special kind of jurisdiction, make these two countries, with France, the best protected in Europe. Denmark also has an Ombudsman since the constitutional changes of 1954; it is early to judge whether or not he is likely to be as effective as his opposite numbers elsewhere[1]

The Swedish Ombudsman for civil affairs dates back to the eighteenth century. Before then an official now known as the Justitiekansler had investigated offences in the public administration on behalf of the Crown. This latter office had been created in the seventeenth century when an official was appointed by the Crown to control the administration of justice and act as public prosecutor. In 1713 a Kansliordnung created a new office of Högste Ombudsmannen. This official was responsible for seeing that the laws and the constitution were observed and that official duties were properly performed. He acted personally in important cases, otherwise through a directorate.[2]

In 1719 the name of the office was changed to Justitiekansler, and the following year his competence was extended to cover the operations of courts of appeal and the activities of local police commissioners (Fiskalerna); he had authority to examine their police ordinances and regulations, and could report

[1] A somewhat similar post, though much more restricted in scope, has recently been created in Germany. A special commissioner for the armed forces, the Wehrbeauftragter, is to be appointed, and any soldier who considers himself ill-used may appeal to him. He is to be a civilian, appointed by the Bundestag, with full access to military files when investigating complaints.

[2] Ministry of Justice: 'Betänkande angående Justitiekanslerns'; *Justitieombudsmannens och Militieombudsmannens allmänna Ambetsställning*. Stockholm, 1939.

to the Riksdag. He remained, however, a Crown appointment. For a short time in the 1760's he was appointed by the Riksdag, but he reverted to his previous position in 1772 and remained there until the present constitution of 1809.

The 1809 constitution, which is still in force, formally recognized the office of Justitiekansler and gave him a certain independence within the structure of Crown offices. It also created the post of Justitieombudsman, an official elected by parliament to control the activities of, and prevent abuses by, public officials, and in particular to prevent the Crown from exercising undue influence over the judiciary.

In the present system there is both a Justitiekansler and a Justitieombudsman, with very similar fields of jurisdiction. The Justitiekansler, however, has remained a Crown official; the constitution said he was to be 'an able and impartial man with knowledge of law who would be useful in legal matters'. He was prosecuting officer for the Crown, and the Crown's chief agent for ensuring the fair and impartial operation of the public services including the courts. He also had powers as Crown officer over the minutes of the cabinet council.

The Justitiekansler's current instructions (June 18, 1937) are still in two sections; one covering his duties as senior Crown public prosecutor, and the other as controller of the public services in the interests of the Crown. He is instructed to conduct civil cases on behalf of the Crown and to see that official duties are properly performed. He has to decide which cases to prosecute, and when the Crown shall pursue a claim. Also the measures to be taken concerning applications for retrial when the decision lies with the Crown.

It has been suggested that his duty to investigate the actions of officials accused of dereliction of duty or abuse of power should be entirely transferred to the Justitieombudsman. Although the Justitiekansler remains the chief officer of control for the Crown, his rôle has been declining in favour of the Justitieombudsman.

In Finland the Justitiekansler (JK) has remained a more powerful figure, closer to the Swedish official of the 1809 constitution. He is head of the public prosecutor's department. He is also a member of the council of ministers, and in addition to the attributes of the old Swedish JK, he has a constitutional duty to control the legality of all decisions of the council of ministers and the President. The Finnish JK reports both to the President and to parliament. Besides having the right to attend cabinet meetings, he also has the right to inspect their minutes; and he can demand to see all the proceedings of courts, and papers from the ministries and other government departments.

The Swedish Justitieombudsman (JO) could be regarded as the Riksdag's counterblast to the Justitiekansler (JK). The 1809 constitution gave the JO no royal powers such as were devolved to the JK. His position was, nevertheless, potentially more important, because with the assertion of democratic government towards the end of the nineteenth century it was to him that eyes turned as a means of protecting the public against abuse of power by the administrative agencies. The 1809 constitution rested on the doctrine of the separation of powers, with the executive—the Crown—and the legislature—the Riksdag—independent of each other; each was provided with some instruments of control over the other. The JO was the most important instrument of control possessed by the Riksdag.

The new office was not readily accepted, and a strong body of opinion in the constitutional committee held that he should be an officer of the Crown without independent status. The office was still a bone of contention as late as 1834, when it was nearly abolished. Probably both the supporters and the opponents of the office felt that his powers had been drafted too widely and that if it was not impracticable, it was at least undesirable, for them to be exercised by one man.

Public opinion, however, came to regard the JO almost as the Tribune of the People, a protector against the abuses of those in authority, and although questions were raised from time to time throughout the nineteenth century, his existence was never seriously threatened again after 1834.

The army reforms of 1901 and of 1914 threw a whole extra burden of work on the JO. If soldiers in a conscript army were to have rights like other citizens, they too should have the right to protection against the abuse of authority. Either the JO's organization had to be substantially reinforced to cope with the extra work, or a specialized Ombudsman had to be appointed with jurisdiction in the military field. The Riksdag adopted the second alternative and in 1915 a law was passed creating the post of Militieombudsman (MO), with a jurisdiction in the military field parallel to the JO's in the civil field.

According to the current instructions, the JO is to exercise general supervision over courts and civil servants to ensure observance of the law, the constitution, and letters of instruction; he is to investigate charges of illegality, negligence, or gross disregard of the interests of their service in the performance of official duties. He can institute proceedings against officials in the courts on any of these grounds. He is to pay particular attention to those offences which involve fraud or abuse of power or which impede the course of justice. If he finds, however, that an administrative or judicial fault has been committed without any unlawful intention he need do no more than ask that the offending decision be corrected.

If a case involves a member of the supreme court, or a cabinet minister, it has to be referred to the Court of Impeachment. The JO acts as prosecutor in the proceedings before the Court of Impeachment. If the Riksdag orders proceedings to be taken against one of its own members, the JO is again responsible for the prosecution. If the Riksdag committee of finance or Revisoren should decide to prosecute the Riksbank or a central administrative agency, this is also undertaken by the JO.

The JO has the right to be present when decisions are taken by courts and administrative agencies, but he has no right to express his opinion on the matter under discussion.

The JO is also required to undertake tours of inspection throughout the country and to examine the operations of administrative agencies both in the provinces and in the capital. He can delegate his investigating authority to a subordinate if he considers this will help his work.

On the basis of these inspections and the complaints his office receives from the public, the JO makes an annual report to the Riksdag. In his instructions he is particularly asked to call attention to any serious shortcomings in the work of courts or administrative bodies, or to any loopholes in the law which appear to require legislation or amendment.

The JO has a special responsibility for all questions concerning the liberty of the citizen, particularly the arrest and detention of persons, and any other cases involving the deprivation of liberty. He has powers to demand all prison returns and can without notice examine the management of prisons and detention establishments. These include asylums, mental institutions, remand homes and treatment centres for alcoholics.

The MO's letter of instruction contains similar provisions. He has a general responsibility for supervising the activities of judges and officials employed by the Defence Department, and for ensuring the observance of the law, the constitution and letters of instruction in military courts, military prisons and military establishments. He is especially concerned with the administration of military justice and other legal proceedings before military courts, with questions involving military service laws, the appointment and dismissal of regular members of the armed forces, the management and care of servicemen, the property and funds administered by the Defence Department, and the operations of state enterprises and arsenals working under the direction of the Defence Department.

The MO has powers to proceed against officials in any of these categories equivalent to those of the JO in the civil field. He has the same powers of enquiry, and the right to call for papers and witnesses, and to institute proceedings against officials in the courts.

Both the JO and the MO are elected to office for four years by the Riksdag from persons of 'outstanding integrity'. They can delegate their powers of enquiry to a deputy, for example when they are absent on tour, but they cannot delegate their powers of decision. In addition both have a small administrative staff. The MO and JO appoint their own staff, who are permanent officials. They need not, however, necessarily have already been officials before their appointment, and in the JO's department there is usually at least one member of staff who has come from the judiciary. A recent chief of staff in the JO's department had served there for over thirty years after originally coming from the ministry of Justice.

The staffs of the JO's and MO's departments do not change when a new JO or MO is appointed. Both staffs have the same status. It is, however, always customary for the MO to have on his staff a military officer of the rank of colonel or lieutenant-colonel as well as at least one official from the judiciary.

In addition, when on tours of inspection the MO normally takes with him a senior naval officer to act as expert advisor on naval matters.

Both the JO and the MO work in two ways: they investigate complaints by the public sent to their office in writing, and they make tours of inspection and enquiry into the working of state offices.[1]

Any citizen can bring a complaint before the Ombudsman; he does not require the services of a lawyer, although it is not unusual to have one. The complaint has simply to be sent in writing with any documents or evidence in support of the complaint. A prisoner is entitled to forward his complaints directly through the prison governor's office in a sealed envelope, not subject to censorship. Military personnel are also entitled to send their complaints to the MO without the permission of their commanding officer.

When the complaint arrives in the office it may be written off as clearly the work of a crank, or prima facie unjustifiable and unverifiable; otherwise it is forwarded to the office or official whose actions are challenged. The JO asks the office concerned for further information or for comments. It is not unusual for the original complaint to be based on a newspaper cutting supported by a more elaborate version from the individual concerned. The office concerned returns its comments, together with any statements or documents demanded, to the JO. The JO's office then forwards this explanation to the person making the complaint. Many cases go no further than this, the office concerned either having given the affected person satisfaction or justified its action to the JO.

Some more complicated cases may involve several authorities. A complaint against the Gothenburg police over their handling of an alcoholic's case, for instance, went from the JO's office to the police headquarters, was returned to the JO and forwarded to the person responsible for the complaint; he in turn added further comments denying the police version of the case, and returned this to the JO; the JO's office sent the dossier to the chief public prosecutor in Gothenburg for his comments and explanation; he returned it to the JO, who forwarded it to the

[1] *Justitieombudsmannens Ambetsberättelse*, 1955, and *Militieombudsmannens Ambetsberättelse*, 1955. Reports to Riksdag. Stockholm, 1955.

police commissioner of Gothenburg. The latter made further enquiries and returned the file to the JO who forwarded it to the person concerned for his further comments. On the basis of this dossier the JO decided no further action was necessary. No action is taken in about a third of the complaints received in an average year because they are clearly unjustified. In 1955, 160 complaints were written off in this way. The complaints cover the whole range of administration. From 1950 to 1955, between a third and a half of all complaints were against the courts, the police, and the public prosecutor's officials, in roughly equal proportions. Another third of the complaints were against central ministries and government departments. The next largest category—though declining in relative importance—was against prisons, mental institutions and other places of detention. Finally, an insignificant number of complaints were against the managerial staffs of nationalized industries and against pastors of the state Lutheran Church.

A substantial proportion of offences dealt with by the JO and MO are discovered in the course of tours of inspection. The administration or service receives only a day's notice of an inspection visit. The inspections are made at random, and they may concentrate on financial affairs; sometimes they are set off by public complaints or newspaper reports, more rarely by confidential rumours of abuses. The JO or his deputy make between three and five tours of inspection a year. The MO averages six. Each inspection takes about a week. This means that the JO covers the country every eight years or so, while the MO, with a more specialized field of investigation, covers the country every five years.

The proportion of cases discovered by investigation on the spot is much greater for the MO than for the JO. Of an annual average of about 700 cases dealt with by the MO, about 600 arise out of tours of inspection. One point about cases uncovered in this way is that few of them are found to be unsubstantiated, whereas one in three of the complaints from the public are eventually rejected.

The JO also has a significant proportion of cases which are discovered as a result of his tours of inspection. Of the JO's cases, in 1947, 260 out of a total of 774 came to light as the result of investigations; in 1952, 167 out of 685; and in 1955, 246 out of 779.

In addition to complaints and tours of inspection the MO looks through between 200 and 300 cases a month involving military arrests and detentions. These are checked for irregularities and may be investigated further. Some 100 each year require further enquiry.

Out of an average of about 700 cases which come to the notice of the JO each year, about 100 are dropped as not warranting attention, another 100 are rapidly rejected as being unfounded or inaccurate. This leaves some 500 cases a year which are pursued. In 1952 and in 1955, 150 of these cases, when investigated, showed administrative errors, fault, negligence or bad faith.

An Ombudsman has considerable discretion as to how far he takes a case against an official. He has not ultimate powers except to prosecute the official concerned before the ordinary courts, and he is normally loath to do this unless the offence is serious or he is left no alternative. In most cases an Ombudsman simply points out the official's error and suggests that he puts it right; if he agrees to do so the Ombudsman notifies the person who made the original complaint and advises him how he should now approach the office.

In other cases the Ombudsman may be prepared to allow the official to settle matters informally. For instance, military commanders who use their cars for private purposes will usually be asked to pay an amount assessed by the Ombudsman.

Only an average of ten cases a year involve prosecution. The figures of these cases suggest that the Ombudsman has little interest in victimising minor officials, for they appear rarely and only in cases where there was clearly no alternative to prosecution. It is more common to find senior officials being publicly faced with their responsibilities. In 1955 the police chief and the public prosecutor in a county area were prosecuted for illegally confiscating a fisherman's boat. A county governor was prosecuted for the wrongful detention of a chronic alcoholic. There was one odd case in which a pastor of the state Lutheran Church was prosecuted for threatening one of his erring parishioners with police action.

Since the office of JO was created, five cabinet ministers have been prosecuted as well as several very senior officials including the administrative heads of ministries and royal boards. The

JO requires the permission of the Riksdag before proceeding against a minister.

The JO's powers extend over the judiciary as well. This used to be his major field of operations but it has declined in importance. The JO can point out to a court that it has applied the wrong law or incorrectly applied the right law. He cannot reverse the judgement; only a superior court can do this. The MO has similar powers over the courts when they deal with military personnel, but the non-military business of the court is outside his jurisdiction. The JO and the MO are mainly concerned with cases where a judge or magistrate has been guilty of negligence or has abused his position or the trust placed in him. For instance, a woman magistrate who disclosed the secret deliberations of a court was prosecuted and fined for breach of her oath of secrecy.

In the majority of cases brought before them by an Ombudsman the courts impose light penalties. The official is usually fined; in 1950 the maximum fine was £50. But in serious cases the courts have power to dismiss the official from office, or to send him to prison.

An Ombudsman has great responsibilities. He is the tribune of the people and principal protector against abuse of power by the administration or the magistracy. At the same time his powers are designed to protect the citizen from abuse and must not themselves be abused. The Ombudsman has the right to examine any document, question any person, and demand every assistance. The only field he cannot touch is city government, which is under the general supervision of the county governor, but the county governor and his office are subject to the Ombudsman.

The age of appointment as Ombudsman tends to be in the early forties; in the nineteenth century it was older. The period of office varies, and since 1900 one Ombudsman only served for a year (during wartime), while the longest holder served for seven years. During the nineteenth century long terms of office were much more common; one Ombudsman served continuously for twenty-three years, from 1861 to 1884.

Both the JO and MO are usually lawyers; they come in particular from the ranks of the corps d'élite of Swedish lawyers, the Revisionsekreterare. Six out of the ten JO's appointed between 1900 and 1939 were Revisionsekreterare, and two of the seven MO's between 1915 and 1939. The same is true of the JK's, who generally spend much longer periods in office; there were only fifteen JK's between 1809 and 1939, and ten out of the fifteen had been Revisionsekreterare.

Although a legal background has always been considered necessary for this post, concerned as it is with appeals, investigations, and evidence, purely legal training is held to be quite insufficient, and it is general to find that a JO has had fairly wide experience in administration before being elected to the post. It is essential that the two elements, law and administration, should be combined.

There has been some criticism of the insistence on legal training. Some experts[1] consider it might be desirable to widen the field of selection, and there have been suggestions that a scientist with the appropriate technical qualifications would be suitable for the post, particularly that of MO.

There have always been some critics of the Ombudsman system as such. The original desire of the right wing to put control of the public administration under the Crown with the Ombudsman as a Crown official disappeared by the end of the nineteenth century. Since the rise of social democracy there has been no hope of abolishing parliament's most valuable instrument for controlling government business.

By 1939 the argument had swung the other way; it was claimed that the parliamentary system of government provided all the checks necessary, and the disappearance of the old dichotomy between executive and legislature had made the Ombudsman superfluous.

A Swedish parliamentary committee which examined the position in 1939 rejected the idea of abolishing the office. It believed, however, that with the greatly improved guarantees for fair and impartial justice afforded by a parliamentary state, and with a more independent ordinary judiciary, the Ombudsman should perhaps concern himself more with constitutional matters and less with detailed work of administration. The committee added, however, with great prescience, that with the obvious growth of social services and the extension of state

[1] Ministry of Justice: 'Betänkande angående Justitiekanslerns', *Justitieombudsmannens och Militieombudsmannens allmänna Ambetsställning*. Stockholm, 1939.

activity the abolition of the Ombudsmanner would only lead in the long run to the need to find some new method of controlling the public services. There was, indeed, every likelihood that the real importance of the Ombudsmanner would increase in the near future. The committee concluded by reiterating the far-sighted comment of its predecessor in the 1859–60 Riksdag: 'The less cause the JO has to intervene with his official authority the more surely is the objective of his office attained.'

Both the Finnish and the Danish Ombudsmanner were modelled on the Swedish institution. In both countries, however, the model taken was the pre-1915 Ombudsman; that is, a single office combining responsibility for both civil and military affairs.

The Finnish Ombudsman and his deputy are elected by parliament for a period of three years. He must be a well-known jurist. His powers of enquiry are similar to those of the Justitiekansler. The Ombudsman can prosecute any official guilty of a fault or negligence in the performance of his duties. Like the Finnish JK he is entitled to attend the deliberations of the council of ministers and have access to all official documents.

There are clear disadvantages in the JK and JO having exactly similar fields of competence; complaints can be addressed either to one or the other, which is inefficient, could be unfair, and might lead to conflicts. In 1933 a law relieved the JK of responsibility for controlling the military administration, penal establishments and other detention centres, but no formal change was made in the respective fields of competence of the JO and JK. The Ombudsman seems to be a firmly established institution in Finland.

Denmark, in the post-war period, was also preoccupied with the need to find some method of controlling administrative activities. As in Britain the situation was complicated by the position of the executive, some of whose authority still rests on prerogative powers, and by the strong hostility of senior civil servants and politicians in office to subjecting the inner workings of government to independent scrutiny. In addition, Denmark had a tradition of associating judicial with administrative authority in the provinces.

The new social security and other public services increased the activities of the administration in the inter-war years, but judicial control was inadequate to ensure proper safeguards. It was sufficient to prevent flagrant violations of the law, but it could afford little protection when the administration was exercising prerogative powers or discretionary powers voted it by parliament.

After 1945 the subject was discussed in parliament, and enquiries were made regarding the functioning of administrative courts abroad. In general, the Danes, like the British, were anxious to avoid creating special administrative jurisdictions outside the normal judiciary. However, matters came to a head during the drafting of the new constitution. In a famous speech in 1949 Professor Hurwitz proposed that, in view of the general hostility towards administrative courts, Denmark might be well-advised to examine an institution closer to hand, and one which would blend harmoniously with her own traditions, the Swedish Ombudsman.

This specifically Scandinavian institution not unnaturally appealed to a section of Danish opinion. There followed several years of bargaining and compromise as to whether or not such a post should be created in Denmark, and if so with what powers. At one point it was argued that the post should closely resemble the original Swedish Ombudsman and concentrate mainly on the work of the provincial judges who exercised administrative and judicial powers. This proposal was rejected in the interests of judicial independence. The proposal that it should effectively control the administration was only half-heartedly welcomed by the government, where only the Radical party supported it unreservedly. It was determinedly opposed by the civil service trade unions, who were supported in their opposition by the Socialist party, who feared that the minor officials would suffer most. Eventually the office of Ombudsman was inserted into the draft constitution of 1953 and carried by a small majority, mainly because the Radical party insisted that this post had been part of an agreement between the parties during constitutional discussions.[1]

A compromise was reached over the Ombudsman's powers.[2]

Denmark

[1] For the different points of view, see: *Betänkning afgivet af Forfatningskommissionen af* 1946. Copenhagen, 1953.

[2] His powers are contained in the Lov om Folketingets Ombudsmand, June 11, 1954.

The whole of the central administration and the parts of provincial administration under government direction were included, but judicial and municipal affairs were excluded. Religious questions were also excluded, though the activities of pastors could be controlled. It proved difficult to make the first appointment of Ombudsman, and it was not until the end of 1954 that Professor Hurwitz himself was appointed to the post. He took up his duties in April, 1955. His staff consisted of one secretary. The obvious course was to draw staff from the upper ranks of the ministry of Justice, but there was opposition to this since career civil servants might be unwilling to criticize their own services. Eventually a judge was appointed.

The Danish Ombudsman is responsible for investigating any complaint against public officials concerning abuse of power, negligence, or abuse of trust. He can inspect all state administrations, and enter all state establishments. He has access to all minutes and official documents.

Anyone who feels his personal rights have been damaged by public officials may complain to the Ombudsman. Complaints may be sent directly to his office in writing, with any supporting evidence, within a maximum delay of one year from the time of the incident. If the incident involves a matter outside the Ombudsman's jurisdiction, his office must inform the person concerned, and send the complaint to the appropriate authority. If the complaint is groundless, the Ombudsman must inform the person concerned as quickly as possible.

When the Ombudsman considers that a case requires further investigation, he can ask for further information in writing and he can collect any evidence he considers necessary for his investigation. If the evidence shows that an official has committed a fault in office, he may, if it is a civil or criminal offence, have the official prosecuted in the courts. If, on the other hand, prosecution is not justified, the Ombudsman reports the case to the official's superiors, and they apply the ordinary disciplinary procedure.

If a minister appears to have committed a civil or criminal offence in office, the Ombudsman himself takes no further action, but refers the whole case to a special committee of parliament (Folketingets Ombudsmandsudvalg). The Ombudsman is also expected to inform this committee and the minister concerned of any weaknesses he discovers in the administration of the law, or any failure to observe legal provisions.

Finally, he makes an annual report to parliament on his year's work, which is published and public.

It is clear from the first year's report (1955–6) that people did not fully appreciate the limitations placed on the Ombudsman's jurisdiction.[1] Of 565 cases reported, 250 were immediately ruled out as being concerned with the activities of the courts or of local government and therefore outside the Ombudsman's competence. Of the remaining 315 cases, 175 had been dealt with by the end of the year. One hundred and fifty-seven cases were, after investigation, returned to the person who made the complaint on the grounds that the decisions gave no cause for criticism. Half the remaining cases showed minor faults of administration which the Ombudsman did not consider serious enough tc warrant any formal proceedings against the authorities concerned. The remainder showed faults sufficiently serious for the Ombudsman to intervene and obtain a reversal of the decision by the administration concerned. In these cases it was for the authority in question to take disciplinary action against the official and to decide how far he should be held personally responsible.[2]

The report shows the same incidence of complaints as in Sweden. Three-quarters of all the complaints against central ministries were against the ministry of Social Affairs. The ministry of Justice, in particular the public prosecutor's department, and the ministry of Finance were the only other two ministries with any substantial number of complaints against them. Of the other authorities the highest number of complaints was against the Police. These are in general the fields one would expect to be most sensitive in a social democracy, both by their wide-spread influence and the number of minor officials employed.

It will be interesting to see how the Danish experiment fares. It is a deliberate attempt to graft a body on to an administration from the outside, in the face of trade union resistance. The

[1] Foreløbig beretning afgivet af Folketingets Ombudsmand til Folketingets Ombudsmandutvalg. Copenhagen, February, 1956.

[2] An official threatened with an enquiry by the Ombudsman can, as an alternative, voluntarily submit to a formal disciplinary enquiry by his own department. This has very rarely happened.

number of complaints in the first year shows that even in a well-run and peaceable country there will always be certain state activities which cause public concern. It is as much in the interest of the officials themselves as in that of the public that these complaints should be promptly aired and examined impartially by a body independent of the administration. If in a small country like Denmark eighteen cases of maladministration are found in its first year's operations, of which half were sufficiently serious to require the complete reversal of the decision, it seems obvious that the number of such cases would be proportionately higher in larger and more intensively administered countries. Indeed, in the Danish context there seems to be a case for extending rather than curtailing the Ombudsman's jurisdiction. It is disquieting that nearly half the first batch of complaints were against the courts and the magistracy, in particular for abusive prosecutions, and against local government officers. The fact that there has been a high initial proportion of fantastic and unsupported allegations forwarded to the Ombudsman is partly a matter of education. In Sweden the Ombudsman has a secular reputation which by now has earned him the fullest public confidence and respect. This will no doubt come in time in Denmark.

In any case a high proportion of vexatious complaints does not necessarily mean that they should be discouraged. The Danish Ombudsman has a tiny staff of eight including his deputy, assistants and clerks. He was able, despite staff and accommodation difficulties, thoroughly to examine over five hundred cases, and sift the genuine from the vexatious. A democracy should be ashamed of even one substantial abuse of administrative power each year. Scandinavian experience tends to show that the figure per head of population is much higher.

CHAPTER 13

Financial Control

The control of public funds and the financial operations of public authorities raise issues similar to those dealt with in the chapters on administrative courts. Financial control involves both legality and policy. It is not always easy to see where one begins and the other ends.

The general control of financial policy is usually constitutionally in the hands of the legislature, and the field of parliamentary procedure and general politics is beyond the scope of this chapter, and to some extent of this book.

The formal control of financial legality is everywhere in Europe confided to special institutions. These institutions normally have a national jurisdiction, although the German Länder each have their own bodies. They are generally on a collegial basis, and most of them control the finances not only of the central ministries and agencies but of all public authorities. These institutions can be ordinary administrative courts, or special financial courts, or bodies specially created by parliament to act as its agent in this field and report to it directly. In theory the ordinary courts could act as examiners of public accounts, but there is no case of this actually happening. The ordinary courts may sometimes be involved in a formal legal enquiry, for instance where corruption or embezzlement are alleged, but they are then acting within their normal civil or criminal jurisdiction, and not as technical administrative controlling bodies.

It does not seem necessary here to enter into details of the organization and structure of the special financial courts. The most famous are probably the French Cour des Comptes and the German Bundesrechnungshof. They work on the same lines as the ordinary administrative courts already described. The

Italian Corte dei Conti, however, should be examined in some detail, because it is in fact both a financial and an administrative court, and has greater control powers than any other comparable official body.

Sweden, working on entirely different lines, has the most advanced system of legislative control of public funds, with specially appointed parliamentary agents exercising control powers which in other countries are vested in administrative bodies. These two extreme examples are by far the most interesting in this field.

In addition, France has a body attached to the Cour des Comptes which is designed to cope with a problem of financial control not yet tackled seriously in other countries. Just as legal control of administrative acts tends gradually to extend to a control of their reasonableness and impartiality, so financial control tends to shade imperceptibly into an examination of efficiency and the rational and economic use of public resources. This becomes particularly acute where large-scale public corporations undertake public services on a national scale. There is a danger that such corporations might eventually escape from the control of the government and of parliament, and constitute a new type of administrative feudalism. The most successful attempt so far to meet this danger is the creation of the commission de la vérification des comptes, and its work will be described briefly in this chapter.

THE CORTE DEI CONTI

The Italian Corte dei Conti has far wider powers than other financial courts, for instance the French Cour des Comptes.[1] The one field in which it remains inferior is in its ability adequately to control the finances of para-state authorities in the way that the commission pour la vérification des comptes does in France.[2] But the Corte dei Conti performs several duties which in France belong to the Conseil d'Etat. In the hierarchy of Italian courts it is probably true to say that the Corte di Cassazione, the supreme civil court, takes first place, the Corte

[1] A lengthy analysis of French methods is J. Carcelle and Mas: 'Le contrôle de l'Etat sur les finances publiques.' *Revue Administrative*, 1953. p. 473 seq.

[2] O. Sepe: *Il Controllo della Corte dei Conti sugli Enti sovvenzionati.* Florence, 1955.

dei Conti second place, and the Consiglio di Stato third place. This is quite unlike other countries.

The powers of the Corte dei Conti are these.[1] Every decree, unless expressly exempted by parliament, must be examined for legality and registered by the Corte dei Conti before it is presented for signature to the President of the Republic.

A councillor of the court is attached to each ministry to ensure this control. Should he contest the legality of a decree or authorization it is returned unregistered to the ministry concerned. If the ministry insists that there is no illegality, the matter is referred to the special chamber of control (sezione di controllo) of the Corte. If the sezione di controllo also refuses registration on the grounds of illegality the matter may be referred, at the instigation of the minister, to the council of ministers. If the council of ministers supports the minister concerned the matter is referred back to the general assembly of the Corte. If the latter still maintains its reservations, it registers the decree or authorization 'con riserva'. This means that the decree is enforceable, but the political responsibility of the council of ministers is engaged. Every fortnight the Corte sends to the presidents of the Senate and of the Chamber of Deputies a list of decrees registered 'con riserva', together with the relative documents. It now becomes a matter for parliament to draw what conclusions it wishes from the case.

In certain fields the Corte's refusal to register a decree or an authorization is absolute. It is absolute if an attempt is made to exceed credits allowed in the budget, or to charge work to the wrong section of the budget; it is absolute when an attempt is made to exceed the number of officials allowed in the budget in a certain rank or office, or to authorize payments to an official in excess of what he is entitled to by law or regulation.

In the field of financial control the Corte has powers similar to comparable bodies in other countries. It audits the accounts of all officials responsible for public money, with the exception of most local authorities whose accounts are certified by the consiglî di prefettura, with the Corte dei Conti acting as court of appeal for litigation arising out of the findings or decisions of these consiglî.

[1] Raccolta di leggi e decreti sulla Corte dei Conti. Rome, 1950.

The Corte is responsible for ensuring that payments made from state funds have been properly authorized in the budget, and that authorizations apply to the appropriate section of the budget. It also has the power to check that sums owing to the state have been collected. It supervises the financial administration of state property; for instance, it examines the accounts of state factories, warehouses and arsenals. It is also required to make an annual report to parliament on the financial conduct of the public administration and on controversies arising out of registrations 'con riserva' and to propose reforms and make criticisms which should be brought to public notice.

Finally, like its counterparts in other countries, the Corte dei Conti has a judicial function, in that when it decides that the accounts of public authorities are not properly balanced, it assesses the responsibility of the various officials or offices concerned. It can require officials to repay money lost or mis-spent through their personal shortcomings. It can also authorize the cancellation of bad debts, and it deals with litigation involving certain types of state pension.[1]

The Italian Corte dei Conti is one extreme example of control exercised by a predominantly financial court. But it is by no means untypical of those countries where public services are largely controlled by the administration itself.

THE SWEDISH SYSTEM

Sweden has the most highly developed form of parliamentary control with far greater power of appointment and responsibility than in any other country.

First, the Riksdag itself appoints and directly controls the National Debt Office (Riksgäldskontoret). This office is in many ways parallel to the government accounting institutions under Crown control. The explanation of this dual control is historical. Mainly as a result of his wars with Russia and Denmark, King Gustav III contracted a heavy debt burden which in 1789 he asked the Riksdag to assume. The Riksdag agreed on condition that a special institution was created under its own control designed to prevent the Crown borrowing

[1] A detailed account of the work of the Corte dei Conti is by its then President A. Ortona: *In Rivista della Corte dei Conti*, 1949. Also G. Amatucci, Ibid, 1953.

money without Riksdag approval.[1] The existence of this office is regarded as one of the principal guarantees for maintaining parliamentary control of public finance.

In addition to controlling this strategic institution, the Riksdag also controls the Bank of Sweden, and can through this influence credit policy. The Crown, however, has some influence on the bank's board of directors as regards policy.

In 1920 a Government Accounting Office was created as an independent administrative agency to perform the normal duties of accounting for tax collection. In addition most agencies have their own auditing and accounts sections, and each one has to send monthly reports to the Government Accounting Office. It has powers of investigation and enquiry to ensure that financial operations are conducted with honesty, accuracy, and a reasonable degree of economy.

An exceptional institution is the Riksdag's own body of auditors distinct from the Government Accounting Office. Every year each house of parliament nominates six government examiners (Statsrevisorer) from among its members to inspect the management, financial activities and administrative operations of the National Debt office, the Bank of Sweden and the independent administrative agencies. These examiners for the most part investigate methods and internal arrangements and hold random snap audits. But they also make inspection visits to government offices and the administrative agencies to study on the spot the problems of the entire public administration. They are not restricted to questions of financial administration.

At the end of each year the Statsrevisorer report back to the Riksdag making criticisms or recommendations. The Riksdag can then ask any agency for an explanation of any matter which has caused concern to its examiners, and if the reply is unsatisfactory the Riksdag can request the Crown to take action. The Riksdag cannot interfere directly in the operations of any administrative agency, except for the National Debt Office and the Bank of Sweden. In addition many nationalized undertakings are beyond its control, a shortcoming by no means confined to Sweden.

[1] *The Swedish Budgetary System*. Paper produced by the Swedish Foreign Office. Stockholm, 1950.

COMMISSION DE VÉRIFICATION DES COMPTES DES ENTREPRISES PUBLIQUES

The commission de vérification des comptes des entreprises publiques was set up by the law of January 6, 1948. It is a committee, the majority of whose members are magistrates of the Cour des Comptes, and although its secretariat is provided by the Ministry of Finance it is part of the Cour des Comptes. It is required to examine and report on the financial operations of all nationalized industries or commercial undertakings, some national banks, and all public companies in which the state holds 51% or more of the shares. The list of the companies affected is laid down, and if necessary amended, by an ordinance of the ministry of Finance. There were about 110 such bodies in 1958. The commission's jurisdiction covers not only the formal accounting procedure but also the rational and economic use of resources. It reports to the ministry of Finance and to the other ministries concerned with the operation of particular undertakings. Every undertaking which falls within the jurisdiction of the commission de vérification des comptes is under the technical supervision of a tutelary ministry: for instance, the French Railways are under the ministry of Transport. The commission de vérification des comptes has no powers of decision; its reports are drafted in the form of recommendations, and it is for the ministries concerned, together with the undertakings involved, to agree as to whether these recommendations should be put into effect. It was maintained in 1948 that the operations of commercial and industrial companies needed to be very flexible, and that it would be undesirable to subject them to the traditional formal accounting procedures of the Cour des Comptes. The commission de vérification des comptes therefore has no jurisdictional authority such as is possessed by its parent body.

The task of the commission de vérification des comptes is primarily to provide an independent assessment of the general economic and financial policies of the national undertakings and their tutelary ministries, to comment on them as financial and technical experts, and to make recommendations concerning their faults and their future. The commission's reports on individual undertakings are confidential, but a general report issued on the authority of the commission sitting in full session is published each year and presented to parliament.

The commission has its own president, its own rapporteur général who drafts the general report, and it is divided into four sections. Each section comprises six members; four of these, one of whom acts as president of the section, must be conseillers of the Cour des Comptes, one a representative of the ministry of Finance, and one a representative of the ministry of Economic Affairs.

The industries subject to examination by the commission de vérification des comptes are divided into four groups: power, transport and communications, credit and insurance, engineering and chemicals, and each group is the responsibility of one of the sections. The fourth section is, in addition, responsible for undertakings which do not fall clearly within the competence of one of the other three sections. Nationalized deposit banks are subject to direct control by a special commission under the chairmanship of the President of the Bank of France. This special banking commission is independent of the Cour des Comptes. The report of the special banking commission is, however, examined and reported on by the third section of the commission de vérification des comptes. This is the only case where the commission deals with bodies indirectly.

A rapporteur is appointed to examine the work of each industry or firm subject to inspection by the commission de vérification des comptes. This rapporteur is responsible for drafting the report on that undertaking, but he is assisted in this work by a group of specialists, generally numbering seven or eight, who are appointed from members of the Cour des Comptes, from the other grands corps (in particular the technical grands corps), and from senior officials of the ministry of Finance, the ministry of Economic Affairs, and the technical ministries. These specialists remain in their normal employment, but are seconded for agreed periods to carry out the work of inspection. They receive a small indemnity fixed according to the burden of their duties by the president of the commission. They normally serve for several years at a time. Under the direction of the rapporteur they examine particular aspects of the undertaking's operations, commercial, financial and technical. The individual reports are sent to the directors of the undertakings concerned, and at a joint meeting of the section, the directors may reply to observations or criticisms. The report is then drafted by the rapporteur, presented to the section where it is discussed and a final draft agreed upon, and then it is sent to the appropriate ministers and to the undertaking concerned.

All the reports on individual undertakings are used by the rapporteur général of the commission when he drafts the annual report.

The work of the commission de vérification des comptes seems to have given general satisfaction. It has done something to prevent the nationalized industries from forming themselves into independent empires, and its reports have been notable for their clarity, independence of judgement, and honesty. Its criticism has not infrequently been directed against the ministries rather than the undertakings, when the latter have suffered from the caprices and vagaries of ministerial policy. It has some reputation. This is primarily owing to the calibre of the personnel employed in the work. The commission has pointed out however that the considerable expansion in its work was placing a strain on all concerned; it has clearly felt that there was a danger that either the quality of the work done would decline or that the appearance of the annual reports would become inordinately delayed.[1] It would be a pity if this were to happen, as the commission is an institution which might serve as a model (even if an imperfect one) for other countries with similar widespread state interests in commerce and industry.

CONCLUSION

The control of public finances is perhaps the easiest type of control to organize in a mechanical and rational way. In essence, it is, like any other form of accountancy, simply a matter of checking income against expenditure, to ensure that appropriations have been properly authorized, and that sums have been expended for their proper purpose. The ease of

[1] Introduction to the 5e. Rapport d'Ensemble de la commission de vérification des comptes des entreprises publiques, 1956. Paris, 1957.

control and the virtual certainty of discovery has always made financial control the most straightforward method of ensuring public accountability.[1]

Evidence in previous chapters shows that there is an increasing tendency to create machinery for enforcing public accountability in other fields of administrative activity. This is still a relatively new departure, except in the case of France and Sweden, but it is likely to assume greater importance in the future.

There are evident reasons for this. The scale of public enterprise has increased to a point where public services impinge on the citizen in every aspect of his life. At the same time he has become better educated, and is no longer prepared deferentially to take on trust the good faith and scrupulous honesty of ministers and public servants. As he has become more sceptical, he has become more exigent: public services should be run for the benefit of the public, and not be used as instruments of personal or political favouritism. No one expects political decisions to be impartial and rational, but administrative decisions are expected to be so. This may be naïve, and in a later chapter some of the complications of this view will be examined.[2]

But if the hallmark of an administrative decision is its impartiality and reasonableness, it follows that every administrative decision can ultimately be justified by a reasonable administrator to reasonable men. This view smacks of nineteenth-century rationalism, but it undoubtedly underlies much thinking on the subject.

Why then have the traditional instruments of control—the ordinary courts and the legislatures—not dealt with this problem? To some extent they abdicated voluntarily. The courts fell victim to their own virtues: a concern for legal form, procedure and precedent, a strict observance of the laws of property and contract, a tenderness to executive demands for preroga-

[2] The Austrian Administrative Procedure Act is the best example of the attempt to break down administration into verifiable stages comparable to financial operations. Since the United States passed a similar law in 1946 the former Anglo-Saxon tendency to snigger at these precautions has disappeared. Their utility would now probably only be questioned by the narrow, self-righteous lower-grade official.

[1] See p. 319 seq.

tive powers when public order or the national interest were invoked. Legislatures were transformed with the advent of mass parties, political programmes, organized pressure groups, and extensive social legislation. Pressure of work led to more delegated legislation, and the vastly increased public services could only be examined in broad outline, short of creating new and more efficient parliamentary methods of control.

To some extent judiciaries and legislatures were never really appropriate instruments of control. Nineteenth-century parliaments rarely made a distinction between administrative and political decisions, and the use of administrative powers for political ends was widely regarded as being a legitimate perquisite of office. But a fundamental change has occurred now that state services have become public services, and the provision of services is regarded no longer as the gift of a beneficent state, but as the organization of mutual resources by the community itself. The shortcomings of the ordinary courts might have been overcome had it been possible to elaborate new forms of legal action, had there been time to develop a new type of administrative common law, had new and cheaper procedures been devised, had a specialized branch of public law been created within the judicial system with its own expert practitioners comparable to specialists in criminal, bankruptcy, or divorce law. It is not certain that even this would have sufficed. In practice the opportunity was not grasped, partly due to the fault of the executives, partly the fault of the judiciaries themselves.

To meet the changing situation some countries adapted old instruments, as for example the French Conseil d'Etat or the Swedish Ombudsman, others have created completely new jurisdictions. But the essence of all of them is to make the use of administrative powers for personal or political ends more difficult and more dangerous. The key to control is the possibility of publicity, the chance that every decision might later be subject to rigorous scrutiny. And this helps the administration as much as the public as it encourages the official to withstand improper political pressure.

Pressure to institute proper methods of control has come therefore from two sources: representatives of the public and the administration itself. Where there has been a close identification of people and parliament as in Sweden an agent of parliament protects the public from the administration, and incidentally the administration from the politicians. Where there has been suspicion and some hostility between parliament and people as in France, the administration creates its own methods of protecting itself from the politicians, and incidentally the public from the administration.

PART FOUR

POLITICS AND PUBLIC

CHAPTER 14

Politics and Administration

The boundary line between politics and administration is not at all clearly drawn. Politicians are involved in administration as ministers, as members of legislatures, as representatives of pressure groups. Public officials are involved in politics as drafters of legislation, as individuals working with ministers, as members of civil service trade unions acting as professional pressure groups. Politicians try to use public officials to further their own plans and policies; public officials are dependent on politicians for rapid and brilliant careers, though not for ordinary ones. Public officials have social, religious, and academic attachments which may or may not be those of the politicians. The politician and the public official may have common ends or a common past. They are both engaged in the business of government, and their paths cross, and double cross. Many politicians have greater integrity than many public officials, and many public officials have more astuteness and political acumen than many politicians.

The innuendos and the discreet language used in this half-world are only imperfectly understood by the outsider. Sometimes the politicians and officials themselves are bemused by their own etiquette, and solemnly believe their own protestations of purity. This is rare in western Europe, outside Britain, but it happened in Germany under the Empire.

Many German civil servants at that time abstained from party politics, and argued that they therefore abstained from politics altogether. They did not consider that membership of any of the supra-party national organizations, such as the Protestant League, the Pan-German movement, or the Eastern Marches League, involved them in political activity. They were politically neutral provided they did not belong to any political party; the cause of national greatness (Das Nationale) was 'above politics', even though these movements discriminated against whole sections of the German nation, and fostered clearly defined internal and external policies.[1]

It is indeed noticeable that in countries with a long tradition of paternalistic government, with the ruling class also a social élite, the word 'politics' is a rather dirty word. Its connotations are of some grubby disreputable activity in which the best people do not indulge. This attitude towards 'politics' undoubtedly has many historical overtones, expressing the political resentment of a ruling class challenged by mass forces; of a social élite forced to give way to social inferiors; of conservatives, prizing above all a stable and orderly society, menaced by democrats demanding a new social pattern. Those who prefer the status quo 'administer'; those who wish to change it play politics. The first are engaged in protecting the national interest, the second in advancing sectional interests.

It is natural enough for senior civil servants to adopt the same attitude as the old governing class. They may not themselves come from the same social class, nor may they be consciously authoritarian. But in the nature of things higher civil servants rightly regard it as their principal duty to safeguard the continuity of the state. They are therefore always likely to consider that what they do is in some way on a higher plane than what politicians do; that they are the protective force of society and politicians the destructive force.

This seems to be the explanation of their wish to use the term administration for the respectable part of government business, and politics for the less respectable part. The word 'politics' then comes to be associated exclusively with the activities of political parties. Provided, therefore, public officials do not engage in party politics, they consider they do not engage in politics.

But this narrow definition of politics is both misleading and dangerous. Politics means much more than the manœuvring of parties and their relations with particular clientèles. It is not possible for ever to evade questions about 'the right kind of society', the purposes of the state, the basis and justification

[1] R. Mende: *Notes on the political activities of civil servants in Germany*. Frankfurt, 1950.

of government business. The determination of ends, the choice of means, the balance of social forces, are the stuff of politics. In these terms it is clear that some civil servants are engaged in politics. The word 'policy' is a recognition of this; it is a way of describing what civil servants do when they play a part in determining ends, choosing means and fixing priorities. It is distinguished from politics, which is limited strictly to the activities of political parties, and from administration which is the maintenance of the status quo. 'Policy' is then nothing more than the political activity of civil servants.

This disguise is useful both for civil servants and politicians. It is useful to civil servants since it protects them from outside interference and prevents awkward questions, and it helps to preserve their anonymity. It is useful to politicians in office, since it gives the impression that they are acting more objectively than is in fact the case.

On the other hand it exposes society at large to fraud; and it tends morally to corrupt the public officials themselves. The fraud is largely involuntary. Public officials may quite honestly believe that they are not engaged in politics, yet home office administrators may take decisions which affect the freedom of the press, education administrators decisions which affect the relations between church and state, and foreign office officials decisions which affect the whole balance of peace and war. One dangerous aspect of the myth that civil servants play no part in politics, is that political decisions are taken free from the awkward enquiry and demands for justification of motives to which they should be subjected by parliament, the press, and the public. No minister or potential minister is likely seriously to criticize the position, since the myth is often a godsend to the politician in office.

The other danger is more serious. Neutrality in public office tends in the end to moral corruption. If all governments are to be served with equal impartiality and loyalty there are no grounds at all for criticizing the German official who served Hitler to the best of his ability. In any profession other than government such people would be regarded as dangerous cynics or weaklings.

However, this danger is not as acute on the continent as it might be. The problems facing politicians and public officials employed in strategic posts have been modified by a long tradition of recognizing certain public offices as posts of confidence.[1] These may be regarded as the political posts in public administration. Their distinctive feature is that those officials who hold posts of confidence have neither legal nor conventional security of tenure. These posts are normally specified in the law relating to the public service. In Sweden they are actually specified in the constitution, and since this list is by far the most exhaustive in Europe it can be used as illustration.

Article 35 of the constitution reads: 'Members of the Council of State (i.e. the council of ministers), presidents of administrative boards or of agencies established in their place, the Attorney General, the directors of the prisons, the land surveying service, the state railways, the pilot, postal, telegraph, customs and forestry services; the under secretaries in the government ministries; the governor, deputy governor and chief of police of the capital; county governors, field marshals, generals and admirals of all grades, adjutants-general, adjutants-in-chief and adjutants of the staff, commanders of fortresses, colonels of regiments, colonels in command of both cavalry and infantry regiments of guards and of the household guards, as well as chiefs of other military corps and battalions separately constituted, the chiefs of the artillery, fortifications, topographical and hydrological survey; minister envoys and commercial agents in foreign countries as well as officials and employees in the King's foreign office and in missions abroad, hold positions of confidence. The Crown may remove them whenever he considers the interests of the realm demand such

[1] The problem was frequently discussed during the nineteenth century. Both Vivien (op. cit.) and Bluntschli (op. cit.) held that politics was the general overall direction of the state, while administration was the detailed subordinate activity. Posada, in Spain (*Tratado de Derecho Administrativo*, vol I. pp. 224–5), thought that administration should be regarded as a fourth power in the state, but he made no attempt to define it. Presutti (*Lo Stato Parlamentare ed i suoi impiegati amministrativi*. Naples, 1899. p. 295) suggested that the distinction lay in this: that there could be no discussion about the criteria to be used for some acts, either because they were dictated by nature or science, or because they had been provided for in detail by instructions and orders issued by the competent authority; these were administrative acts. In other cases there could be different opinions about the criteria to be used; these were political acts. He recognized that the dividing line was not clear, and depended on whether the body or person taking the decision had full freedom of choice.

action. The Crown shall, however, announce its decisions on such matters in the Council of State (i.e. council of ministers), the members of which are obliged to make humble representations against the measures if they find reason to do so.'[1] All other properly established civil servants are protected in their office.

This Swedish list illustrates the fact that posts of confidence fall into two distinct categories: those which are 'protective' in character, normally concerned with aspects of internal law and order and external defence; and second, those strategic posts through which the government of the day implements its particular programme. The task of the first group is to maintain the status quo, and to prevent any violent change not sanctioned by the government. Their primary responsibility is to the existing constitutional order, irrespective of the government of the day. 'Law and order' may be defined differently by different governments. For instance, police chiefs who have concentrated on breaking left-wing strikes or demonstrations under a right-wing government, may well have to transfer their attention to right-wing movements under a left-wing government. In Denmark, in 1954, the inspector general of infantry and the commandant of the officers' training school were found to have sanctioned instruction to cadets by the late chief of the Danish Nazi brigade which had fought in Russia during the war. They were dismissed from their posts as unsuitable for responsible posts. That is, they had raised doubts as to their complete loyalty to the existing constitutional order.[2]

In the normal way, these protective posts of confidence are filled by professionals who consider that the conservation of the present order of things is by definition a non-political activity.

The second group of political appointments are the key administrative posts for putting into effect the programme of the government of the day. While not proposing to modify the existing constitutional order, these programmes may differ considerably on quite basic matters: for instance, the relations between labour and capital, educational policy, defence, foreign affairs, electoral systems, agricultural programmes, the burdens to be assigned to each social class.

[1] Official translation by S. Thorelli.

[2] Reported in *Neue Zürcher Zeitung*. November 22, 1954.

Every European country considers that the minister has the right to be seconded by people whose political views are in harmony with his own. If he wants a policy of full employment, it is unfair to expect him to rely on officials whose predilection is a stable currency at all costs. Also, most Europeans have, for reasons stated above, some suspicion of the selfless and impartial official: if he has principles and is prepared to adapt them to keep his job he is an object of contempt; if he has no principles he is regarded as a cynical timeserver.

Furthermore, since the whole object of posts of confidence is to help the minister span the worlds of politics and administration, holders of these posts must belong to both worlds. The minister himself can generally hold his own in parliament and with the political parties, perhaps with the assistance of a junior minister; but he may well not be fully conversant with the work of the administrative machinery of which he is the head. The holder of a post of confidence needs to be integrated into the administration, for only then will he have sufficient authority to support the minister and keep the minister master in his own house.

It was indeed for these reasons that the state secretaries of ministries were added to Article 35 of the Swedish constitution after the 1918 war. The conservative and aristocratic administrations of the nineteenth century made little use of the powers of appointment to and removal from posts of confidence. The more conservative the régime, the easier it is for the minister to believe that he is simply an administrator. Hence the same permanent head might act quite satisfactorily as advisor on questions of policy to changing ministers. But increased social legislation and the rise of liberal and social democrat parties changed the position, and in 1917 a committee was set up to enquire into the question. It recommended that the functions of ministerial advisor should be taken over by a specially appointed state secretary, who should be part of the administrative hierarchy, of the same rank as the permanent administrative head. The report said that state secretaries should be persons of experience in whom the minister had complete confidence; they should have distinguished academic careers, proved capacity, and ability in political and legislative matters. They should be chosen chiefly for their non-political merits but their general political orientation should be such that they could collaborate closely with the minister.[1]

It was assumed, on the basis of past tradition, that civil servants would probably perform these functions satisfactorily, but in fact once the issues were posed clearly it was realized that they had serious shortcomings for this type of work. From 1920 to 1940 nearly 80% of the state secretaries appointed already had a civil service post to which they returned on relinquishing the state secretaryship. But since 1940 the proportion has dropped steadily; to 50% in 1949, and to about 40% five years later. The people who have come in from outside have come from senior local government service, trade union administration, industry, university staffs, and the editorial departments of major newspapers. Their age on appointment has been significantly lower than that of the administrative heads of the ministries. In general, this seems to have been a very satisfactory experiment in combining political direction with dministrative efficiency.[2]

It is important to keep the distinction between political appointments and political patronage clear. Political patronage or spoils, in the American sense, scarcely exists in Europe. But, generally speaking, posts of confidence to which governments can freely appoint are filled according to merit plus political orientation. They are not rewards for political services rendered. There are no clean sweeps with a change of government, but a few changes in those branches of the public service which the new government expects to be of particular importance to its programme. For the rest it is only when a post falls vacant through death or resignation that the political orientation of the candidates assumes importance.

MINISTERIAL CABINETS

If it is desirable for the minister to be seconded by a political administrator in the direction of his ministry, it is also widely held that he should have the right to a private secretariat

[1] Bo Lagergren: 'Les secrétaires généraux des cabinets ministériels en Suède. *RISA*, 1949. pp. 31–7.

[2] G. Heckscher: op. cit. pp. 356–8.

staffed by people of his own choice. In the northern countries the private office has remained small and amounts to one or two personal assistants and a private secretary. Even in Germany, where the appointment of outsiders is nearly as strongly opposed as in Britain, the posts of personal assistant and private secretary are recognized as incontestably the minister's personal appointments. Not infrequently the minister chooses a young official he has met in the past or who has been recommended to him. But there are many instances of personal assistants from outside. The normal German practice is for him to become eligible for establishment if he has the qualifications and remains in state service for six years.

In the past ministerial cabinets were severely criticized on several grounds. In Italy, Crispi's cabinet was widely believed to be engaged in corrupt practices. In France they were accused of interference, irresponsibility, and overstaffing. In 1912 an acute though consciously witty observer claimed that some ministerial cabinets contained anything up to 40 attachés.[1] Many of them were relations, sons, brothers, cousins, and nephews à la mode de Gascogne. Only two officials in the cabinet had definite functions, the director of the cabinet who was the link between the minister and the administrative services, and the head of the private secretariat who 'looked after the minister's personal correspondence, his relations, his electors, his suppliers, and, when, necessary, his mistresses'.[2] The rest of the cabinet consisted of a floating body of young men, the majority of whom were simply trying to enter public service without the necessary qualifications. Their only duties were to look after minor visitors and second-rate journalists. Many of them worked for nothing, simply hoping that in time the minister might find something for them.

It is not surprising that the administration proper viewed these cabinets with some hostility. But even in De Jouvenel's day there were some distinguished members of the grands corps acting as directors of ministerial cabinets.[3] After 1918, and more particularly after 1945, ministerial cabinets became

[1] R. De Jouvenel: *La République des Camarades*. 16th. ed. Paris, 1914. p. 112.
[2] R. De Jouvenel: loc. cit. p. 107.
[3] Loc. cit. p. 106.

much more a normal part of the administration, and most of their members were officials seconded temporarily from their departments at the minister's invitation. Nowadays virtually all the directors of cabinets in the major ministries, in Italy and Spain, as well as in France, are senior members of the more respected branches of the administration. Sometimes the same official stays on as director for successive ministers if they continue to be of more or less similar political colouring.[1] Gradually, the cabinets are losing their old reputation, and they have been greatly strengthened by the increasing number of technical specialists appointed for their expert knowledge to act as advisors to the minister in specialist fields.[2]

As in Britain, service in the private office is frequently a stepping stone in the career of a promising official. The observer has the impression, however, that those appointed as directors of ministries abroad are generally somewhat older than their British counterparts, and are already poised for the jump to the highest administrative posts.

THE AMBITIOUS CIVIL SERVANT

Posts of confidence serve two purposes. First, they make it possible to introduce outsiders into the administration at a high level; first-class people in outside professions will never be attracted by special entry into the middle grades of administration. Yet some infusion of new blood seems generally desirable to offset the natural conservatism and parochialism which beset those who spend all their lives in one profession.

Second, posts of confidence attract the ambitious civil servant, offering prospects of accelerated promotion. Ambition in a civil servant often coincides with the interests of good administration. Of course, it is sometimes one of the rules of the game to deny ambition; these protestations should be heard with courtesy but scepticism.

The first-class civil servant is nearly always a man of ambition; if he has ambition he will carefully cultivate his contacts

[1] Their movements can be traced through the *Annuaire des Cabinets Ministériels*, published by the Office Français d'editions documentaires, Paris.

[2] R. Catherine: 'Cabinets et Services.' *Revue Administrative*, 1953. p. 347. He discusses the present position.

and make the best use of his social, educational and religious background. Those who do not, and they are the great majority, prove by their inaction that they are not of the right timber for high office.

In all countries the best means of attaining high office is close contact with those with power of appointment and promotion. In most countries this is the minister, as well as the permanent administrative head of the service. One route to high office runs everywhere through the minister or the permanent head's private office.

At certain moments in most countries there emerges also the curious phenomenon of the administrative patron. His appearance on the scene is always unpredictable, and frequently he emerges in times of tension or when an administration is entering a new phase of its existence. His influence seems to reside in personal ability of a high order, a mastery of political techniques, and the confidence of the men engaged in public affairs. He normally has as many enemies as friends, but he manages to exploit their enmity to strengthen his personal position. Most of the known masters in this field have entered public service from outside. Their influence comes from their skill in attracting into their orbit exceptionally able young men, whose quality strengthens their patron's influence, while he uses his influence to place them in strategic posts in public service. In the course of time a small group, originally built up round one single overwhelming administrative personality, becomes a force with its own impetus, linked by a personal freemasonry of sentiment, interests and power. It normally continues to function, unknown to the outside world, long after the original patron has disappeared.

The very personal nature of the administrative patron's power makes objective identification difficult. The best British examples are Morant and Warren Fisher, and the best contemporary European examples are Monnet in France and Gunnar Myrdahl in Sweden.

The administrative patron is an unpredictable phenomenon. Normally it is better for the ambitious civil servant to attempt to enter the largest number of influential groups in his society. Because the social structure of each country is different the groups which wield power are also different, and this must be taken into account. The Frenchman destined for high office in France would use cards which would debar him in Germany.

Each government machine has its own élites. Financial administrations normally have the prestige to attract the best candidates, and also have within their sphere of influence a number of outside appointments in semi-public and public corporations. 'Pantouflage' is recognized and accepted by the French administration, where it is practised mainly by the technical grands corps and the inspection des finances. Within reasonable limits it does the service no harm. Fluidity within the public service should work both ways, and there is some value in having a flow of people from state service into private enterprise as well as vice versa. A tradition of pantouflage attracts to state service young men of talent who would hesitate to enter if they thought it would mean spending their whole career there. The young man trained at government expense in France undertakes to spend ten years in state employment, and this may be quite attractive if it means that his subsequent chance of first-class employment outside the service is correspondingly increased. Meanwhile the state has, for a minimum of ten years, an official of high capacity it would not otherwise have had. In 1956, of the 273 members of the Inspection des Finances, 119 were hors cadres in other more lucrative parts of the public service; among these were the governors of the Bank of France and the Crédit Foncier, and directors general, directors and deputy directors of several state financial agencies, corporations and banks. Sixty-three had retired from state service, and many of these were in private banks and big business.

But undoubtedly the most striking example in this respect is the Spanish corps of Abogados del Estado. In 1956, this corps, whose active strength is a little over 200, included among its members the minister and deputy minister of Finance, the minister and deputy minister of Justice, the minister of Foreign Affairs, the deputy minister of Agriculture, the ambassador to China, the directors general of Banca y Bolsa, Aduanas, Contencioso, Beneficenza y Obras Sociales, Administración Local, and the Instituto Social de Marina, the president and vice-president of the Instituto Social de Marina, the president and vice-president of the Instituto Nacional de Previsión, the Abogado Fiscal and the Fiscal General del Tribunal Supremo.[1]

Other internal administrative élites are frequently to be found in the Prime Minister's office and the ministries of the Interior, of Public Works and of the armed forces. They may be sufficient in themselves, but normally the ambitious civil servant reinforces them by other outside contacts.

Membership of a political party is a two-edged weapon, except under special circumstances such as those of the Weimar Republic or contemporary Spain and Portugal. Party membership marks an official too clearly; it may improve his chances at one time, but seriously handicap him at another. Furthermore, the official who ostentatiously wears his political colour is generally not well regarded in the higher civil service. It arouses his colleagues' distrust, since it seems to imply that he has found an alternative to relying on the good opinion of his superiors and colleagues. The administrative esprit de corps, useful in many ways, must not be flouted.

But in some countries confessional political parties complicate the situation. In countries with Christian Democrat and Catholic parties, like France, Germany, Italy, Austria, Holland and Belgium, membership of a party can be confused with membership of a church. In most countries in western Europe religious ties assume some significance for a civil servant. In Holland, for instance, there are two militant churches, each with a conservative and a more or less progressive wing. In the post-war coalition governments a succession of catholic ministers so effectively colonised the ministry of Education that when a socialist prime minister was pressed by his party to take it over he refused on the grounds that a socialist's position would be untenable. Other examples of catholic colonisation are the ministry of the Middle Class in Belgium, and the ministry of Population in France, not to mention several ministries in Germany and Austria. The classic case of catholic colonisation was in Germany under the Weimar Republic, when the Centre party was in a pivotal position and could sell its support to both left and right. In the course of five years it obtained control in Prussia of the personnel division of general administration, and its members held the posts of personnel director in the

[1] *Boletino Oficial del Estado*. March 17, 1956. p. 1862 seq.

ministry of Agriculture, dispensing substantial agricultural subsidies, personnel director of the ministry of Education, appointing school teachers, and personnel director of the ministry of Justice, controlling the appointment of public prosecutors. Catholic parties tend to concentrate on those ministries which affect family and social relations, so as to support the demands of catholic educationalists, and policies favourable to parents with large families. In these ministries the promotion of civil servants without the necessary religious qualification is likely to be slow.

Even in ministries which have not been colonized, a catholic minister or a strong catholic bloc of senior officials may easily determine appointment to influential posts according to religious affiliation. The successful attempt to pack the Bavarian State Radio with catholic elements is well known, mainly through the indiscretions of the Cardinal.

Religion is a hurdle which must be cleared in most countries; it is helpful to have the right one, and one should try to avoid departments of the wrong cloth. In Sweden, where virtually the entire population is Lutheran, church membership counts for little. Contacts, to be useful, must be fairly exclusive. To be a Jew is a handicap in all countries. Their lack of numerical representation is as much due to the prejudice on selection and promotion boards, as to the distaste for government service normally assigned them by people looking for excuses.

In Spain, another country with a single religion, colonization is carried on by secret associations within the church. Since the war in Spain members of the Opus Dei have gradually used their influence to capture strategic posts in the educational field. It is now believed to have effective control of the ministry of Education, and several university chairs are held by its members; there are signs it is extending into other fields. From the point of view of contacts in government, Opus Dei should be regarded rather as a society than as a religious movement. Its tactics are the same as those of an organization of free thinkers who infiltrated into the educational field in the 1920's in order to combat clerical influence.

Many influential societies on the continent had anti-clerical origins, and many of them began as secret societies. The free-masonry movement has been the most prominent of these, and on the continent it has the radical freethinking traditions of the Scottish lodges rather than the prim, businessman's social orthodoxy of the English lodges. It retains considerable influence in some government circles. In French public life it is associated with the socialist and radical parties and in some branches of the ministry of the Interior is still an important aid to advancement. In Italy it was important during the Depretis, Crispi and Giolitti periods of government. But the lodges were disbanded by Mussolini, and seem never to have regained their influence.

The test of a useful society is that it should be exclusive, with a limited membership; that its members should include prominent political figures, senior civil servants, and representatives of powerful outside interests; and finally that it should offer an atmosphere in which influential people unbend, so that the ambitious young civil servant can make his mark by his tact and modesty.

Educational contacts are equally important. The British tend to imagine that their public school tradition is unique. This is untrue, it is only more juvenile. The important educational contacts on the continent are made at a later stage, at the university level. The German student clubs are perhaps the most famous example, and in some university clubs a majority of the total membership are public officials. In France university contacts are relatively unimportant as compared with those made at the grandes écoles. To be a polytechnicien or normalien may be important in a career; a strong esprit de corps makes for easy informal contact between different generations and provides access to many different worlds. Only in the Scandinavian countries does educational association not seem of very great importance.

Outside contacts are not only useful to the individual civil servant, they help to facilitate the task of government: to oil the wheels. The number of people engaged in decision-making is always fairly small. Decisions are the result of the interaction of a number of groups each powerful in its own field. If these groups fail to work together the political system eventually breaks down. The function of the senior civil service is to bring about the interaction; it is the catalysing agent in government. Its members must therefore be in contact with all the groups, and move amongst them on equal terms. The better the civil servant can perform this function, the greater use he is to the government. It is far more usual nowadays in all countries for this ability to be consciously acquired. This reflects both the shift in political power within communities over the last fifty years, and the change in social structure. Modern civil servants of lower social origins have to learn what was instinct to their predecessors.

THE CIVIL SERVANT AND ELECTIONS

All public servants in western Europe have the same right as any citizen to vote in local and national elections. But their right to stand as candidates in local or national elections is in most countries subject to special conditions.

In general civil servants can be candidates in local elections without permission from any superior authority, and may hold elective office on local councils without resigning their posts. However, an official cannot stand for election in areas where he has a special responsibility: if he exercises control powers, or has to maintain public order, or dispenses state money. This means that provincial governors cannot stand for election in their own province, commissioners of police in their operational district, judges inside their circuit.

There are greater differences of practice concerning national elections. The disadvantages of allowing a full-time civil servant to sit in parliament are obvious. He could be a member of the opposition and would, as a member of parliament, criticize government policies which, as a civil servant, he would be expected to put into effect.

There are then four possibilities. Civil servants can be forbidden by law to stand for parliament at all. This is very exceptional; one marginal instance is that no French prefect can stand for parliamentary election in his department unless he has resigned from his post at least six months previously.

Second, a civil servant can have the right to stand for parliament, but before he can take his seat he must resign from the civil service. This is the position in Switzerland, Portugal, Belgium and Germany at the federal level.[1] The legal

[1] In some Länder, e.g. Bavaria, certain categories of active officials can sit in Land parliaments.

situation in Portugal is somewhat confused; the constitution says that members of parliament lose their seats if they carry out duties as civil servants during the parliamentary session. In law therefore it would seem possible for a civil servant to be a full-time parliamentarian during parliamentary sessions, and a full-time civil servant during parliamentary vacations. This can only be feasible where parliament is not taken seriously.

The constitution of federal Germany provides that anyone who wishes to stand for election to the federal parliament must be given leave of absence for his campaign, and may not be dismissed from his job because he stands for election or takes a seat in parliament. However, article 137 allows certain restrictions on Beamten, and the Bundesbeamtengesetz says that a Beamter must resign if he is elected to the Bundestag; he can apply for reinstatement should he cease to be a member of parliament, and although he has no legal right to return, he has a good chance of doing so.

Third, a civil servant elected to parliament can be granted indefinite leave of absence; if he ceases to be a member of parliament he is entitled either to return to the civil service, or, if he is now too old, to retire with the civil service pension. This is the position in France, Holland, Italy and Spain. In France and Italy no civil servant in parliament may be promoted, but he can count the time he spends there for purposes of seniority in his present grade.

Finally, in Denmark, Sweden, Austria, and Finland, a civil servant can remain in office and sit in parliament at the same time. His department must allow him sufficient time to perform his parliamentary duties. In the Scandinavian countries the question of promotion does not really arise, because an official is normally appointed to a specific post; in principle, therefore, he can only retain his right to normal seniority. In Austria, and this is exceptional in Europe, the civil servant can be promoted in his department or nominated to another civil service post while serving in parliament.

There are two general comments. First, in small countries the talent available for high public office is likely to be limited, and it is understandable that civil servants are allowed to be members of parliament at the same time; an argument frequently used in the German Länder. But this requires a considerable degree of self-discipline on the part of the civil servant, and a temperate political climate; parties must not be divided by questions of fundamental constitutional importance, nor anxious to use the public service as a spoils system.

Second, no country has such a profusion of political talent that it can afford effectively to exclude civil servants from parliament by insisting on their resignation. There seems a good deal to be said for either the German federal system of allowing a civil servant to reapply for reinstatement with a reasonable chance of success; or the French system of granting indefinite leave of absence with a right to return to the service, but no right to promotion while in parliament.

THE CIVIL SERVANT AND PARLIAMENT

All civil servants have several points of focus: the minister, several pressure groups which have received or are trying to obtain recognition by the ministry, the top of the administrative hierarchy (which may not be the minister), parliament, and political parties. In no European country is the civil servant's attention concentrated on the minister to quite the same degree as in Britain. European parliaments have greater powers of interfering in administration than the British parliament, and the civil servant's attention wanders accordingly.

Civil servants come in contact with parliament through the legislative process and through the parliamentary committee system.

The great majority of bills presented to legislatures in west European countries are the work of officials. A model of the legislative process is this. First, the origins of a bill are frequently to be found in the day to day work of administrations: in gaps which have been discovered in existing legislation or in loopholes which have been enlarged to a point which jeopardises the fair or efficient operation of a service. The responsible official seeks his superior's approval in principle for a change in the law. In other cases the minister himself may request his department to prepare a bill on a subject which he or his party considers important. In yet other cases the proposal for legislation may come from an organized interest which is likely to try to bring pressure to bear both on the minister and the officials. A pressure group recognized by a ministry or department as representing an important interest is often in a strong position to influence future legislation. For instance, the German civil service federation itself played a very important rôle in the drafting of the civil service law of 1952. Through its influence the 'Juristenmonopol' was re-introduced, and the introduction of outsiders to public service drastically curtailed.

Once the principle of a bill has been accepted it is prepared very largely by the officials concerned. The first draft is normally the work of a young, middle-ranking member of the higher civil service. He, in consultation with his immediate superior, invites other interested departments to take part in discussions, and to agree to a common draft. If there are difficulties, decision on a contentious point will be transferred to a higher level.

By the time the first draft is nearing completion it will have been discussed by a fairly wide circle of officials. It is then decided which outside bodies should be consulted: trade unions, business interests, local authorities, churches, as the case may be. Discussions with representatives of these bodies will normally be conducted by a senior official in collaboration with representatives of other departments. It is at this stage that individual politicians are most likely to be involved, called in either as party spokesmen or as representatives of outside interests; or occasionally in their private capacity as experts in the field.

The purpose of these discussions is to meet legitimate criticism in advance; all legislation is up to a point a compromise. Officials will give way where they can in order to neutralise opposition, but cannot at this stage commit themselves to any major alterations of principle. Interested parties who object to a principle must seek the ear of the minister or the cabinet. If consultation has been successful, the process of drafting begins again. If unsuccessful, the final draft of the bill is agreed to by senior officials and the minister, and presented to the cabinet by the minister. With its approval the bill is presented to parliament.[1] In Switzerland the cabinet normally

[1] This 'model' procedure was suggested by a senior German civil servant; civil servants of other countries accept it *grosso modo,* subject however to serious modification in the case of Spain and Portugal.

asks the department of Finance to prepare its own report on any important bill, not only, apparently, to consider its financial ramifications, but also as a check on the other departments.

In most European countries the work of parliamentary legislative committees brings the politician into closer contact with the official than is usual in Britain. In Holland, for instance, bills are normally discussed in committee before they are formally presented to parliament, and as far as possible controversial points are dealt with before the bill is discussed in the house. Parliamentary committees normally have the right to question the officials themselves, and not simply the minister. This is an important safeguard. It is necessary if parliament is to have full grasp of a situation. In Sweden legislation is preceded by written reports and recommendations on the subject under consideration from the heads of the administrative boards concerned, as well as an elaborate résumé of the facts of the case by the ministry. No attempt is made to hide differences of opinion between the various parts of the administration.

The view that parliament must rely for its information on the facts the minister chooses to put forward is not widely held in Europe. Knowledge of the disagreements behind the scenes is an important element in allowing parliament to take a constructive part in government. One test of a democratic government is the extent to which information on important issues is made freely available to parliament and public. Public administration in private is a remnant of more autocratic days and is gradually disappearing in western Europe.

In most European legislatures the participation of parliament in government is the business of standing committees attached to individual ministries or groups of ministries. Normally, both houses of parliament have the same number of committees, specified in standing orders. Both houses of the Belgian parliament, for instance, have seventeen standing committees, Denmark six, France nineteen, Italy eleven, Holland eight. Sweden is peculiar because all its standing committees are joint committees of both houses, and because their number and jurisdiction are specified in the constitution. The nine Swedish committees are for constitutional amendment, ways and means, banking, agriculture, foreign affairs, finance, and three committees of judicial affairs (private law, social legislation, residual matters). The committee of finance is divided into five sections, each controlling a group of ministries and the boards attached to them. In all countries experience shows that standing committees are an excellent method of strengthening parliament against the executive. After several years' service on one committee even the average member of parliament reaches a certain standard of proficiency in a special field.

From the administration's point of view standing committees have several disadvantages. First, it is easier for ministers and for their official advisors to deal with people who are not fully informed. The average senior official who is an expert in his subject has a not unnatural impatience with the amateur, and sees nothing morally wrong in his minister avoiding points which might cause serious dissension or which are based on nothing but guesswork. For him, as for the minister, the fewer amateur experts there are, the better.

A second disadvantage is that these committees tend to develop into institutionalised pressure groups; members of fishing or agricultural constituencies trying, generally successfully, to serve on the committee which deals with the affairs which matter to their constituencies.[1] This danger can probably be exaggerated. It obviously arises in the case of functional ministries. But competition is keenest for posts on the great committees—defence, foreign affairs, the interior, finance—and these committees genuinely reflect the interests and groups in parliament itself.

The two most important committees in every country are the committees of finance and foreign affairs. The first owes its importance to its ability to supervise the whole range of government operations. Although it has the right to examine government spending in detail it has little chance to do so. It intervenes when it considers it necessary. But often the opposing interests in the finance committee neutralize each other, and skilful officials know how to propose measures which will provoke a clash on unimportant (for the administration) details, to ensure that important issues will be discussed in an atmosphere of lassitude and exhaustion.

[1] P. Williams: *Politics in Postwar France*. London, 1954. p. 234 seq.

Committees of foreign affairs, although regarded as of great importance, are rarely so in practice. Governments throughout western Europe tend to think they should have complete discretion in the conduct of foreign affairs. This is partly a memory of the great days of diplomacy; it is partly the belief that successful diplomacy requires secrecy. The result is that public officials employed in foreign service are the least subject to control of any kind. It is also a field in which it is extremely rare to find a minister who can dominate his officials.

Some countries have recognized the dangers inherent in this situation. In Holland, before the war, the standing committee for foreign affairs accepted that the conduct of foreign policy was part of the prerogative. But since the war, and since the loss of Indonesia, the committee's importance has increased.

Disasters are a common cause for strengthening the legislature against the foreign office. The drafters of the Swedish constitution took particular pains to ensure legislative participation in the conduct of foreign affairs. The commission for foreign affairs has a different status and a different title (nämnd instead of utskott) from other committees of the legislature. It is regarded as an advisory committee to the government and it has no effective legislative power like the other committees. 'The members of the commission on foreign affairs . . . shall also be members of an advisory council to confer with the King concerning the relations of the realm with foreign powers. Conference with the advisory council should take place before all matters of major importance relating to foreign affairs are decided. When a matter comes up for consideration all available documents and information shall be communicated. The decisions made by the King in matters which have been the subject of a conference with the council shall be communicated to its members not later than the next meeting' (article 54).

It would be difficult to argue from Swedish experience that the conduct of foreign relations has suffered in any way from its provisions. Indeed, there have been occasions in Swedish diplomatic history when the intelligence and savoir faire of the members of the commission have prevented mistakes by the professional diplomats.

Sweden uses committees to a remarkable extent in order to bring officials, politicians and outside experts together. In 1954 there were 37 committees, set up on the initiative of parliament or the government, attached to the ministry of Justice; 5 for foreign affairs, 17 for defence, 19 for social affairs, 18 for communications and transport, and 35 for finance. Some of the subjects under discussion were methods of taxing capital gains, the reform of the alcohol licensing acts, the rôle of the Ombudsman, and juvenile delinquency. They combine the work of departmental committees, royal commissions, and outside expert committee groups in Britain.

Switzerland also tries to bring as many groups as possible into the work of government. The inner mechanism of Swiss government is highly democratic, partly because of the reduced position of the Swiss official. The formal machinery of government counts for less than the horizontal contacts between officials, parliamentary and cantonal committees, interest groups and trade unions. Much of the dullness and formality of Swiss parliamentary proceedings is the result of the large number of parliamentary committees. Professional associations of all kinds, from finance experts to police chiefs, are a feature of Swiss public life. The Swiss have humanized these contacts. Most of these associations and committees meet in the relaxed atmosphere of the Swiss resorts where the conditions are conducive to Kuhhandel.[1]

In every country there is a delicate balance between public official and politician which can easily be disturbed. It was disturbed during the German Empire by the fact that over half the imperial ministers appointed came to office after serving as civil servants in departments of the Reich. The Bundesrat itself was 'an assembly of administrators'.[2] This was a case of civil servants encroaching too far on the political field. The Weimar Republic showed the dangers of politicians encroaching too far on the public service field. There are, of course, occasions, particularly in small countries, when political crises can be overcome by the appointment of 'non-political' cabinets of senior civil servants: a device used, for instance, in Finland. But public officials may get the upper hand for less reputable

[1] G. Soloveytchik: 'Switzerland in Perspective.' *OUP*, 1954. p. 51.

[2] Maxwell E. Knight: *The German Executive 1890–1933*. Stanford, 1952. p. 16.

reasons. It was widely believed in the years after the war that the proceeds of some of the corruption in the Italian public service went into the government party funds. Certainly some of the post-war currency, licensing and demi-monde scandals have suggested that prominent politicians, as well as senior officials, were involved. In these and similar circumstances it is not really possible for the political leaders of a country to insist on the highest standards of integrity from the officials nominally under their control.

CHAPTER 15

Public Service Trade Unions

Viewed in proper perspective the problems and machinations of the individual public official are overshadowed by the mass public servant, the associations of public officials organized to protect the interests of their members. Public service unions have become part of the fabric of the state in many countries, and in no country can they any longer be ignored.

Fifty years ago in most countries public service associations were either friendly societies or banned institutions. Their power now lies in their numerical strength and its potential electoral importance to politicians. This is reinforced by the fact that they are the accepted spokesmen for those employed by the state. Their aim is to protect the interests of the state in so far as those interests coincide with the interests of their members. Indeed, some extremists have held that the body of civil servants is the state.

Civil servants represent both themselves and the state. Negotiations between civil service unions and the state are duologues between a small group of designated civil servants acting the part of employer, and another group of civil servants acting as representatives of the employees. The result has been greatly to increase the power of civil service unions within the machinery of government and to make possible the unique conditions of service enjoyed by civil servants. For a long time, for example, there has been an excellent case for restricting the right to established posts to the relatively small group of civil servants whose work is sufficiently important to the state to warrant their being given the best conditions of service. This was the original intention behind the German distinction between Beamten and Angestellten. The great majority of public servants in the manipulative, clerical and executive classes perform functions fully comparable with those to be found in private employment. There is no obvious reason why they should be given any special status. But the strength of public service trade unions is in the lower ranks, and naturally they cannot be expected to embrace measures which would adversely affect the majority of their members. Even in Germany trade unions of lower-grade civil servants have managed greatly to increase the proportion of Beamten to Angestellten, and posts which in the past would have been classified as under the second group are now classified in the first group. Demands for special conditions of service are frequently supported by the argument that the state-employer should be a model employer. But this is based on the assumption that the state is an employer in the same sense as a private, or even a public, company. The truth is that people employed in government service are tending to become not only self-governing but also self-employed. All the evidence in earlier chapters points in this direction. This drift towards the syndical state machine is one of the unnoticed oddities of the last fifty years.

Belgium is the country which has gone furthest in this direction. The Belgian state railways, for example, are the most striking example in western Europe of 'co-gestion', a system in which the unions of the employees are actively engaged in administration of the service.

The origins of the syndical movement in the Belgian public service lie in the period 1890–1920, when public servants, especially in the lower grades, were seeking the same rights of association as workers in the private sector. The law of 1898 on workers' unions did not cover the public service, and in the following years several bills were presented to parliament proposing better conditions of service, security of tenure, and the right to form unions.[1] It was not, however, until 1918, when the socialist party could lay down conditions for joining a coalition government, that public officials were given the same right to form unions as workers in private employment.

From 1920 to 1937 union activity spread to the whole public service, but at different rates of progress. The strength and militancy of the railwayworkers' union enabled it to claim a

[1] V. Crabbe: 'Syndicalisme et fonction publique en Belgique.' *RISA*, 1955.

special position in railway administration. After 1926 its influence extended when its representatives joined with the railway administration to draft a statute of employment for the workers. Personnel committees and disciplinary councils were set up, trade union representatives were granted paid leave of absence, and a joint administrative body was created between the unions and the managerial side.

In the administrative sector of public service the pace was slower. In the course of time the socialist party won the support of the neo-Thomist wing of the catholic party, who claimed that the state had a moral duty to bring workers into management, and workers had a moral right to set up unions to improve their conditions of service.

In 1937, at the time of the first general civil service reform, civil service trade unions were for the first time properly integrated into the machinery of government. Officials' associations collaborated in the organization of administrative services, and were consulted on all matters affecting careers. Half the seats on the newly created chambres de recours were reserved for union representatives, and they were given a privileged position on the personnel committees which were closely modelled on the Whitley councils.[1]

The war intervened before these reforms were fully implemented, and after the war came the era of the mammoth trade union. In 1946 a central commission de consultation syndicale was created, including representatives of the principal public service unions, the centrale générale des services publics, the confédération des syndicats chrétiens, the cartel des syndicats indépendants des services publics, and the syndicat libre du personnel de l'état. The central commission had general authority to discuss all proposals affecting public officials employed directly or indirectly by the state. Comités paritaires de consultation syndicale were attached to each ministry for the same purpose at the ministerial level. They have a statutory right to be consulted on all questions affecting personnel, organization of work, conditions of service and questions of hygiene and security.

In 1949 the joint bodies at the national and ministerial level were reinforced by sub-committees in all administrative

[1] *Arrêté royal*, October 2, 1937, and *arrêté royal*, December 14, 1937.

units with more than 1,500 employees. In addition personnel committees were set up in all local, regional or national services employing more than twenty-five people. These various committees and commissions have a statutory right to be heard, and if a minister makes an order on any of the subjects mentioned without consulting the appropriate bodies, it may be quashed by the Conseil d'Etat as ultra vires.

Only in the Belgian state railways have these joint bodies powers of decision, but there is common agreement that the trend in Belgian public administration is towards co-gestion rather than co-operation. This is seen as an inevitable result of the growth of public services, and is indeed regarded as desirable in itself on democratic grounds.[1] The director general of the ministry of Labour, in an article on the subject, wrote: 'These committees (conseils de personnel and comités paritaires de consultation syndicale) are similar to co-partnership arrangements in industry: they bring public service closer to private enterprise, and public law closer to private law. They favour the unity of all workers with all that implies. . . . By recognizing the rôle of the public officials, the trade union statutes will effect radical changes in the law relating to public office, and will progressively lead to its abolition. It will abolish hierarchical authority, that is, the superior's authority limited only by law; and bring about the active participation of the employees in the administration of the public service, that is to say, a truly democratic authority. . . . The public service will then no longer be simply an exclusive appendage of constituted authority, but the work of the entire body of people interested in the service including the people employed by that service.'

In the rest of Europe the power of public service trade unions has been limited by various factors. Some still have an uphill fight to obtain full recognition, and are regarded as irresponsible and politically unstable organizations. In some countries public service unions are divided between themselves on religious, political or social grounds. And in all countries, except Switzerland, there is a division between the unions representing the higher officials and those representing the lower officials.

[1] V. Crabbe: 'Syndicalisme et fonction publique en Belgique.' *RISA*, 1955.

The Italian public service unions are undoubtedly those regarded with most suspicion by the government. The suspicion has largely arisen from the leadership given them by the communist confederation of unions. For some time after the war, and sporadically since, public service employees have been called out for political strikes which clearly had no relation with legitimate complaints concerning conditions and pay. These strikes have been used by the right wing to justify resistance to quite legitimate demands for improvements. Union leaders are regarded as politically disreputable and irresponsible, and those unions which have acted with caution and reserve have suffered for their more volatile confrères.

Italian public service unions have also suffered from deep political divisions between them. The various professional public service associations and unions are affiliated to one of the three principal federations, the communist, catholic and socialist confederations of unions. In some ministries co-ordinating committees have been set up between these three blocs, but the political estrangement of the confederations from each other has seriously limited their smooth operation. They have had some success in improving the conditions of work inside offices, and in raising standards of hygiene and safety. But the policy of successive Italian governments has been to deal very sternly with demonstrations by public service unions. The industrial and manual public service employees in, for instance, the railways or local government have fared best. But clerical, executive and office staff in the civil service are always likely to be severely disciplined for taking part in token demonstrations.

Even when public service unions are regarded as responsible and respectable bodies, their effectiveness can be reduced by these political divisions. The most notable case of this kind is Holland, where both political and religious differences in the country are reflected in the atomisation of the public service unions.

The first Dutch trade unions were socialist, and the marxist nature of the Dutch federation of trade unions forced the religious bodies to examine their own doctrinal positions. For some time the protestant view was that unions as such were morally wrong: Collosenzen had laid it down that servants must obey their masters in all things. Talma however managed to neutralise this argument, and in 1909 a protestant group of trade unions was founded. Christianity, the family, and private ownership were the foundations of the good society, and protestant unions still reject any activity based on a doctrine of class war or a policy of nationalization. The protestant trade unions might conceivably have joined a completely neutral trade union movement, but with the marxist unions on one side and catholic unions on the other there was no chance of unity.

In 1909 the catholic hierarchy decided to forbid catholic workers to join unions which had non-catholic members. The papal encyclical De Rerum Novarum was regarded as the embodiment of progressive social doctrine, and catholic trade unions were set up under the supervision of the local bishop, who approved their statutes and appointed an advisor for ecclesiastical affairs.

During and immediately after the second world war the competition for members between the various unions abated, and genuine efforts were made to create a single unified movement.[1] But this movement was abruptly halted in 1954 when the catholic bishops issued a joint letter forbidding catholic unions to amalgamate with others. Political parties based on religious tenets are always inclined to insist on their universal nature and to condemn parties based on social or class differences. But in practice it is not surprising that some catholic workers found more in common with their socialist fellow workers than with their catholic employers.

Dutch trade unions are not formally affiliated to particular parties, though their sympathies are well known. The public service trade unions are divided into five principal federations: the Algemeen Comite van Overheidspersoneel (Socialist), the Prot.-Christelijke Centrale (protestant), the RK Centrale (catholic), the Ambtenarencentrum (neutral), and the Centrale van Hogere Rijksambtenaren (for higher civil servants). Each federation consists of a number of unions: the socialist federation comprises five organizations, the protestant six, the catholic six, the Ambtenarencentrum nine (which themselves

[1] P. van Praag: 'The rôle and function of the trade unions in and towards politics.' Mimeo, 1954.

comprise fifty-eight professional associations), and the Centrale van Hogere Rijksambtenaren forty-two. Altogether there are 117 public service associations representing some 120,000 people.[1]

This very complicated arrangement means that there are five different, and generally competing, unions for each category of personnel. For instance, the 18,000 policemen are divided between the Ned. Politiebond, the St. Michael association, the Chr. Politiebond, the Bond Hogere Politie-ambtenaren, and the Rijkspolitieverenigung.

Even when public service trade unions are not so excessively subdivided as in Holland, they nearly always tend to be handicapped by their isolation from the rest of the body of organized trade unions, and by the fact that higher civil servants have separate associations.

These two features are readily understandable. In the past trade union activity in most European countries has been regarded with some disfavour, and the idea of a general strike in which the public services as well as private industry would cease to function haunted some governments, for if it ever happened the government's authority would collapse. The temptation to join with workers in other industries has been particularly strong for the mass public service unions, like the postal, railway, clerical and school teachers' unions. But generally speaking strike action by public service unions has been potentially so serious a menace that legitimate demands have been settled more speedily than those of workers in private employment. Furthermore, the great attraction of public employment has been its security, and this has always strengthened the hand of moderate elements in public service unions. By marking themselves off from more militant trade unionism, public service unions have been able to achieve a position of respectability which has been more successful than brute force. Moderation in their demands, particularly by unions of middle and higher ranking civil servants, has encouraged the belief that they are responsible; as a result they have gradually been brought into the structure of government. They have much more to gain from this position than they have by associating with the rest of the trade union movement.

[1] Statistics published by Algemeen Comite van Overheidspersoneel. Hague, 1956.

Sweden and Switzerland are the countries in which public service employees are most closely associated with those in private employment. In Sweden the principal federation which represents public officials is the Tjänstemännens Central organisation (TCO), the central organization for salaried employees. This organization was formed in 1944 by the amalgamation of two smaller groups. The first (DACO) was formed in 1931 on the initiative of the bank employees' union, and included associations of ships' officers and engineers, and industrial foremen and supervisors. A second organization (TCO) was set up in 1937 on the initiative of the police and the elementary school teachers' unions. Eight associations joined with a membership of 40,000. They represented state and municipal employees, which DACO had wished to absorb but had been unable to do so, since it was not until 1937 that state employees had a statutory right to take part in wage negotiations, and until 1940 that municipal employees could do so.

In 1944 these two organizations amalgamated to form the present TCO, with a present membership of about 320,000. There are forty-five affiliated unions and associations, of which the largest are the union of clerical and technical employees in industry, the foremens' and supervisors' union, the union of municipal employees, the union of commercial employees, and the civil service salaried employees' union. There are other unions for journalists, midwives, non-commissioned officers in the forces, teachers, insurance agents, printers and hotel and restaurant employees. TCO is a genuine white-collar federation. It has a special civil service section to which all associations whose members' conditions of service are mainly based on state regulation must belong, and a special section to deal with municipal affairs.[1]

Two points are worth noticing however. First, although the TCO represents a mixture of private and public employees, it has no industrial workers. They belong to the Landsorganisation (LO), which is numerically more powerful than the TCO, and influential in a rather different way. The differences between the TCO and the LO are familiar differences of attitude between white collar and manual workers. The former pays considerable attention to improvements in conditions of

[1] *TCO*: 'Styrelsens och Revisorernas Berättelser.' 1954.

service, in social and pension benefits, in vacations and contracts of employment, and to reasonable differentials for skill, responsibility and length of training. The latter concentrates on wages, and uses its influence to obtain better general conditions by means of social legislation rather than by pressure on individual employers.

Second, the TCO does not, in principle, represent the higher grades of public service. The National Union of Civil Servants is mainly recruited from senior officials in transport and public works departments, and has no non-civil-servant members. The Central Organization of Graduate Workers has both public and private employees; a university degree is normally required for entry to the higher civil service, and for most senior administrative posts in private business. Despite the breadth of public and private employment covered by the TCO, therefore, the Swedish public service unions still tend to be isolated from the industrial unions, and the associations of higher public officials from the middle and lower ranks.

This internal cleavage between the different ranks of the public service is common throughout Europe with the exception of Switzerland. There are some grounds for it. Since 1945 most countries have witnessed a reduction in the differentials between the various ranks in public service. The power of the mass public service unions has been sufficient to maintain their parity with outside employment; the higher civil service has not been able to do so. Increases have been staggered in a way which has favoured the lower official, even though the cost is always considerably greater. In 1954, if the salaries of all cadre A officials in France had been doubled, it would have amounted to no more than a one per cent increase in the total civil service budget. But, as higher civil servants' unions in most countries know to their cost, the unions representing the lower and middle grade officials will never accept a policy of discriminatory rises for particular grades. Financially, there is a genuine conflict of interest between the various grades of the public service, and it is for this reason that the higher public officials insist on their own special representation.

Only in Switzerland, where the differentials between the lowest and the highest posts in public service are the lowest in Europe, are to be found unions which all ranks of the public service join, and a federation which mixes public and private employment together on an equal footing.

The Swiss Föderativverband unites industrial and administrative, technical and clerical, and communal, cantonal and federal employees. It is made up of ten different associations, most of them catering for special branches of the administration, for instance the Swiss union of postal and telegraphic officials, or the Swiss association of customs employees. Six of these constituent unions are also members of the Swiss trade union confederation thus bridging the gap between the public and private sectors.

The two most important unions in the Föderativverband are the railway union (Eisenbahnverband) and the public service employees' union (Verband des Personals Oeffentlicher Dienste). A single union for all railway employees has only existed for thirty years, but its membership represents 90% of all those employed, irrespective of religion, language, politics, or public or private employment. Senior railway officials' and engineers' associations are affiliated to it.

The public service employees' union has some 28,000 members, as against the railway union's 43,000. It was founded in 1905, and includes wage-earners of all kinds and at all levels of administration. Half its members are employed by communes in administration, transport, building, gas, electricity, and hydro-electric stations; a quarter are employed in cantonal administration, and most of the remainder by the confederation. There are some members from semi-public corporations such as Swissair, and a sprinkling of outsiders like eight hundred theatre artists.[1]

There is a separate union for the officials and employees of federal central administration. It numbers 5,600 members and genuinely seems to cover all the grades and all the departments of the federal civil service.[2] It was founded in 1912 and is not attached to any political party. It has the same type of precise aims as civil service unions in other countries. But the atmosphere in which it exists is different. The Föderativverband, in

[1] Fritz Croner: 'Tjänsteman och Tjänstemannaproblem i Schweitz.' *TCO*, Stockholm, 1954. pp. 82–88.

[2] 'Nous sommes un précieux élément de complément, parce que nos membres se recrutent parmi le personnel de toutes les classes de traitement, et de tous les départements.' *Journal des Fonctionnaires fédéraux*. January 7, 1955.

all its public statements, insists on its close contact with all other trade unions, and its desire not to be cut off from the general public. In this it is unique in western Europe. 'The federation has always tried to demonstrate its profound unity with the whole body of workers. Nothing offends the members of this association more than the unwarranted criticism levelled at it that it is seeking a special position for itself and following its own special interests. This federation knows perfectly well that a democratic state like Switzerland will not tolerate an official caste such as exists in other countries. Our members do not seek any privilege which would separate them from the rest of the people. They belong to the Swiss population and wish to continue to do so.'[1] In all its literature the Föderativverband defends itself against charges which, if true, would simply mean it was doing what other public service unions abroad have been doing with no qualm of conscience. The assertion recurs again and again, which could not honestly be reiterated outside Switzerland, 'Public service personnel do not want a civil service state.'

The essential features of a profession are that entry to it is controlled by its own members, that disciplinary action for professional faults is taken by domestic tribunals, and that promotion to the leading posts in the profession is largely determined by a man's reputation within his profession. A profession also has a special expertise and a graded set of qualifications which are widely recognized, and a monopoly of practice in its own field.

European public services have acquired most of the characteristics of a profession. The outsider has been virtually eliminated from the recruitment, the discipline, and the promotion of public servants, except for a very limited number of cases at the top. What is missing is a recognized professional qualification, and any general acceptance that the profession should have a monopoly of government. The acquisition of a recognized public status and the growth of professional training schemes in the civil service compensate in some measure for the lack of a professional qualification.

Yet according to western democratic theory government is

[1] Rapport de gestion et comptes, 1952–3. Berne.

the task of representatives of the electorate, not of a profession of government. Except in Switzerland resistance to the growth of professionalism has been largely incidental to the division between public service unions and other trade unions, and between the higher service and the rest of the public service. There is now, however, little doubt that it is the higher civil service which represents the state, round which legislatures, ministers, the public and the judiciary revolve.

CHAPTER 16

Public Officials and the Public

Heine contended that some countries are temperamentally monarchist and some republican. His examples were Germany and France, and they remain today the outstanding instances of different attitudes to authority. Monarchical populations instinctively trust their public servants, and assume, short of evidence to the contrary, that they are uncorrupt, unambitious, and worthy of some respect. In these countries there has normally been a long tradition in which public service was associated with service to the Prince or Crown, and in which there are still traces of the aristocratic conception of government as the responsibility of a small class.

Republican countries, in Heine's sense, are countries whose populations instinctively mistrust political power, and who tend to assume that in all likelihood their public servants are idle, wasteful, authoritarian bureaucrats, always prepared to abuse their position. In these countries authority is the enemy, always trying insidiously to capture new outposts.

Germany on the one hand, France and Switzerland on the other, are pure examples of these attitudes to government and officials. In between them lie the other European countries, each with its special blend of respect and distrust.

The German public official has a status unique in western Europe. His position comes partly from the German trust of the expert; the public official is the expert in government (far more so than the politician) and when he speaks or acts in his professional capacity his words carry an authority which public opinion will recognize in no one else. Opler rightly remarks, 'Skepsis gegenüber den Wissen des Fachmannes ist in Deutschland selten.'[1] This attitude is well illustrated in the electorate's

[1] K. Opler and E. Rosenthal Peldram: *Die Neugestaltung des öffentlichen Dienstes.* Frankfurt, 1950. p. 7.

tendency to prefer public officials as mayors, Landräte and Land ministers. The German public believes in the science of government; as a science it can be learnt, and public officials have mastered the subject.

Two examples will suffice to show the strength of this feeling. In 1954 a Bavarian minister broadcast a talk on the public service offering some slight criticisms. He received a voluminous correspondence on the subject. The same theme was repeated monotonously in the letters. 'The principle of equality in our democracy has cast aside the old élite based on birth, tradition and training, and it has not put anything in its place . . . People must understand that even a democracy needs an élite. It needs a "layer of leaders" who embody the culture of the day, and at the same time have the strength and will to power to grasp the reins of government.' Again, 'the growth of the bureaucracy is always a sign that parliament is not coping with its job . . . if our parliamentarians complain that they are at the mercy of the "secret knowledge" of the officials, then the parties should see that better people get into parliament who understand the working of bureaucracy'. The minister himself concluded, 'we have in our people reserves of Tradition, Order and Authority which are still recognized as virtues even by the discontented and unstable. These values are the religious needs of people, their feeling for their country, the desire for an élite and efficiency'.[1]

In fact a country's view of public administration reflects its underlying philosophy of society and the state. The German public service is still associated in people's minds with a concept of the state which found its highest expression in the days of German power and success combined with peace and respectability, the Germany of the late nineteenth century.[2] Ritter undoubtedly speaks for many educated Germans when he expressed his scepticism of western democracy and of the idea of natural law replacing the power concept of the state. He expresses in different terms the same views as the Bavarian minister's correspondents. For Ritter opposition to the state and dissatisfaction with the work of government are not

[1] R. Zorn: *Die Als-ob-Demokratie*. Munich, 1954.

[2] An interesting examination of Germans' attitude towards public service is in a series: 'Der Staat bist Du' in the *Stuttgarter Zeitung*. January, 1954.

compatible with civic virtue.[1] Parliamentary democracy leads eventually to dictatorship, and dictatorship to terror. Only the German bureaucracy embodying the 'unique character' of the German people has the strength, the spirit and the will to protect the Rechtsstaat, and in such a state to ensure some degree of freedom. In this view the German Beamtenkorps is not simply a body of people providing public services, but the living embodiment of the state.[2]

In no other country does the idealization of the public official go nearly so far. The most that could be said of Sweden, Denmark, Austria and Holland is that in these 'monarchical' countries the public official is trusted, respected, and in some ways reluctantly admired. But he is not regarded with affection, nor assumed to have a monopoly of political wisdom, nor to typify all that is best in the national character. In Sweden and Denmark the social democracy of the last decades has whittled down the aristocratic pretensions of the higher civil service; yet to some degree they remain rather aloof and self-consciously guardians of the public interest. The Austrian Beamter retains some of his past mystique.[3] His social position is good, and the security of public office attracts a people whose recent history has been unsettled and divided. The public official has greater prestige in the provinces than in the towns. The city of Vienna itself is a special case, consciously flippant in the face of pomposity, and more likely to reward public service with irony than with respect.

The Dutch public servant has the qualities of the solid and respectable burger; and he fits without difficulty into the social scene. He is the epitome of middle-class virtues in a middle-class country, and he has the common sense, stability and lack of ostentation of his countrymen. He is respected because he makes a good citizen rather than because he is a public official.

[1] G. Ritter: *Europa und die Deutsche Frage. Betrachtung über die geschichtliche Eigenart des deutschen Staatdenkens.* Munich, 1947. p. 195.

[2] It is, of course, important to realize that there are some jurists, publicists and trade unionists who are dissatisfied with the present situation. Between 1950 and 1953 there was a spate of literature on the subject, some of it very critical; e.g. the symposium: *Neues Beamtentum,* published by the Institut für Förderung öffentlicher Angelegenheiten, Frankfurt a/M. But the criticism quickly died down after the new Beamtengesetz was passed in 1953.

[3] P. Heiterer-Schaller: 'Die gegenwärtige Lage der Verwaltung, etc. in Osterreich,' *Verwaltungsarchiv.* October, 1957.

His position is somewhat different from public officials in most other countries because of religious differences. These differences are not likely to jeopardise the stability of the country, but equilibrium has been consciously achieved, and has to be consciously maintained. The Dutch public servant is therefore constantly subjected to the suspicious scrutiny of religious interests. He may be acknowledged as a serious and responsible citizen and an industrious and conscientious public servant, but he can never for long ignore the fact that decisions taken according to the light of reason or the most effective use of resources may nevertheless lay him open to attack.

Switzerland and France are the great European examples of the republican's innate distrust of authority. Their attitude to public office is totally different from the German. The German idealization of the Beamter is met with the freezing Swiss slogan, 'Der Beamte soll Bürger sein'. The official in Switzerland is an employee of the public, and the Swiss public is aware of its rights as employer. 'Beware the prosperous official,' is part of Swiss folk-lore, with the direct and literal consequence, as Professor Imboden remarks, 'that there is in the world hardly any other salary law which makes so little difference between the top and bottom grades; but a change would have to get past a popular referendum, and this would never happen'. In the canton of Zürich the ratio between the highest and lowest salaries paid in public service is 1:2·8, in the city of Basle 1:3·14, and in the federation 1:3·8.[1]

The Swiss are hard taskmasters both with themselves and their employees. As Fleiner remarked, the Swiss view is that everyone dedicates his life to the service of the community, and performs duties voluntarily which have to be paid for in other countries.[2] Many of the manifold tasks of representing Switzerland in international life are undertaken by leading businessmen, university teachers and professional men on the government's behalf, often at considerable personal inconvenience, without remuneration, and often without thanks.[3] This 'moody sovereign' has grasping habits, and high officials are pestered to

[1] M. Imboden: 'Die gegenwärtige Lage der Verwaltung, etc. in Schweiz.' *Verwaltungsarchiv*. October, 1957. See also: 'La Pénurie des fonctionnaires.' *Journal des fonctionnaires fédéraux*. February 18, 1955.

[2] F. Fleiner: *Beamtenstaat und Volksstaat*. Tübingen, 1916. p. 41.

[3] G. Soloveytchik: op. cit.

justify the minutest items of expense accounts or the cost of telephone calls. Men of talent and experience who would otherwise have been prepared to enter public service refuse to do so for these reasons. The Swiss government is to some extent to blame, as its public relations are not well conducted; better communications between the government and the electorate might help to overcome some of the instinctive antipathy and suspicion to those in public office.[1]

In France the distrust of authority is equally strong, and criticism more vociferous. From the time of Balzac (Les Employés) denigration of the bureaucrat has been a national sport. At regular intervals publicists, journalists, and jurists devote themselves to bitter attacks on the plethora of public officials, their dilatoriness, their red tape, their brusqueness, their abuse of office.

But the French have two peculiarities. First, the officials themselves are as caustic as the public about themselves and their work. Commenting on the difference between working in a public and a private concern in France, one author says, 'In private industry the official will be very well aware of the absence of that freedom of speech and attitude which is considered to be one of the characteristic features of public service. To criticize, to discuss, to interpret instructions, to run down the administration in which you are serving, are games well suited to the Frenchman's subtle spirit. But industry will not stand for them.'[2] Unfortunately the French public is not well aware of this habit, which in some ways is more sympathetic than the high seriousness of the Swedish or German official.

But in France both public and officials can afford to adopt this scathing tone of criticism because in fact the French public services are very good. This attitude has some of the curious characteristics of a man's feelings towards the armed service in which he has served. A Frenchman allows himself liberties of criticism he will not accept from a foreigner. Even the ordinary citizen is self-consciously aware of France's 'civilizing mission' in the world, and takes it as perfectly natural that his administration should be the model for other countries. He demands

[1] A typical example is: 'Suisse, ta liberté f . . . le camp,' in *Curieux*. March 17, 1955.

[2] M. Abadie: 'Carrière d'Etat ou carrière privée.' *Promotions*, 1956. p. 49.

(and obtains) a very high standard from his public services, be they railways, postal services, street cleaning or administrative jurisprudence. The fact that they are good is, however, no reason why the official should be trusted. The Frenchman would prefer to believe that they are good only as a result of his perpetual complaint that they are bad. 'La méfiance est une donnée fondamentale de la psychologie française.'[1]

In Italy and Spain scepticism and distrust are not counter-balanced by the secret pride of the French. In both countries there is some fear in the citizen who has dealings with the administration. The Italian also considers his public services to be venal and sporadically corrupt.[2] He believes they are sometimes manipulated for private advantage and used as arenas for political manœuvring. The services are regarded as inefficient, dogmatic and obscurantist. A plague of ministerial circulars descends on local authorities from Rome; no one will take responsibility for them; they are drafted so as to be unintelligible to the ordinary subordinate official, and sometimes they state the law incorrectly.[3] Ministries are suspected of modifying laws they do not like by simply issuing interpretative instructions down through the official hierarchy.[4]

This attitude is partly the result of the traditions of Italian government through the centuries. In fact many higher Italian civil servants are men of considerable capacity and some devotion to duty. But they do not live in a simple atmosphere, and the heritage of past days, and the political pressures of the present make it difficult for them to build a public service sheltered from the storms of public life. For instance, one author justifies retaining the administrative guarantee which allows legal proceedings against prefects or mayors only after permission from the Consiglio di Stato on the grounds that everyone who votes against the mayor will naturally be his enemy, and be only too anxious to take advantage of the numerous openings in the criminal code for obstructing him in

[1] R. Grégoire: 'Les caractéristiques fondamentales du travail dans la fonction publique.' ITAP conference, 1953.

[2] M. La Torre: 'Malcostume amministrativo.' In *Amministrazione Italiana*, 1954. p. 56. Also U. Fragola: 'Note sulla moralità amministrativa.' ibid. 1953. p. 909.

[3] U. Fragola: 'La piaga delle circolari.' op. cit.

[4] G. Bardi: Ibid. p. 124

the course of his duties.[1] This is exaggerated, but it contains a grain of truth. But the Italian, with innate humanism, is equally likely in an unguarded moment to argue that the minor official is a poor devil, underpaid and overworked.

Corruption and inefficiency are also to be found in Spanish public services. It seems to be more unusual than in Italy at the highest levels of administration. In local government Barcelona is a joke of quite a different order from Naples, and several American industrialists have learnt that leaving bulky envelopes with senior ministerial officials is not always the best method of doing business. Some Spanish officials have a pride and sternness which compares favourably with other countries. But Spanish public administration is irrevocably handicapped by miserably low salaries which force officials to find other jobs or sources of income to obtain a living wage. At the higher levels the financial problem is eased by holding two or three government posts at the same time, so doubling or trebling the basic salary. Lower down, however, officials have to seek part-time jobs in private business. It is not therefore surprising that abuses occur, or that some officials in central ministries accept retainers from private firms for ensuring their business smooth passage.

The need to grease the wheels in this way is to a considerable extent the result of the watertight compartments within which each central ministry works. The ministry of Finance and the ministry of Commerce are frequently in conflict at the field level. The ministry of Commerce imposes a tax on certain articles according to its own rules, and then the customs department decides that according to its rules a tax cannot be levied in this way. The complete stalemate that ensues can only be resolved by reference to Madrid. In these conditions the value of a delegate within the ministries is clear enough.

Finally, Belgium and Norway, which are also in a more subdued way 'republican' in temperament, regard their public services with that half contemptuous, half patronising indifference the British have for their local government officials. In Belgium the influence and potential prestige of the small

[1] M. La Torre: 'La garenzia amministrativa.' *Amministrazione Italiana*. 1953. pp. 589–602.

number of higher civil servants tends to be submerged under the massive weight of the trade unions. In a syndicalised public service there is not much mutual respect, and not much sympathy between the different grades of the services. Prestige declines when public officials themselves consider their job is just like any other.

The public official is naturally affected by the way the public regards him. He inevitably acquires characteristics which the public expects of him. If he is treated with respect he will carry himself with conscious dignity; if with distrust he will become defensively aggressive. In every country the public official is in social terms a typical member of the middle class. But he has special strengths and failings which he acquires from the nature of his profession, and these tend to mark him off from his fellow citizens of comparable social status.

Excluding the industrial workers, the public service epitomises the various levels of the middle class.[1] The clerical official representing the lower middle-class, the executive official the middle middle-class, the administrative official the upper middle-class. Even when their salary scales do not fully correspond to their position in society, the different grades of public service adopt the social customs and outlooks of their appropriate social grading.

There are very few reliable statistics on the social origins of public officials in western Europe, and it is not possible to prove that public service is a factor in social mobility. The scanty material available suggests that the majority of officials recruited in each class of the public service come from their corresponding social class, and that the remainder come from the social class immediately below. This is, of course, what would reasonably be expected.[2]

In Sweden, for instance, where social group I only accounts for 5% of the population, 52% of all higher officials come from this group.[3] Similar figures are quoted for France and Ger-

[1] This question is dealt with in broad terms in: Fritz Croner: *Tjänstemannakåren i det moderna samhället*. Uppsala, 1951.

[2] In France the annual reports from the ENA contain fairly full information about candidates, but these are not related to the rest of the French public service for which there are no figures.

[3] Sten-Sture Landström: *Svenska Ambetsmäns Sociala Ursprung*. Uppsala, 1954.

many.[1] In certain branches there is clearly even more social weighting; indeed, 30% of the Swedish diplomatic corps are members of the nobility. In all three countries there are two traditions which are worth noting in this respect. The first is the tradition of the administrative family, whereby one son of a member of the higher civil service follows in his father's footsteps. Some administrative families can be traced over three or four generations. The second tradition is the gradual social climb from one generation to another within the public service: the great-grandfather a peasant or small farmer, the grandfather an elementary school teacher, the father a pastor, secondary school teacher or executive-class official, the son a senior official.

The final jump is clearly the most difficult. It is obviously easier to go from the clerical-worker level to the executive-class level, than from the executive class to the administrative class. In the German gehobener Dienst, for example, 60% have come from the working class or lower middle class, which represents an improvement in social status; the remaining 40% were already established there as children of secondary school teachers, members of the gehobener Dienst, pastors, and so on.[2]

Three points are quite certain. First, social class in the public service does not work in reverse. The sons of members of the administrative class are to all intents and purposes never found lower down the scale. Unless they can join at their father's level they diverge into another profession. Second, the working class is under-represented at all levels of the administration in comparison with the proportion of the population it represents. For instance, only 10% of the Swedish higher officials came from it.[3] Third, the agricultural population is also under-represented. This seems to be due in France to parental

[1] C. Brindillac: 'Les hauts fonctionnaires': *Esprit*, June, 1953. pp. 862–6.

W. Bohr: 'Nachwuchsklage und Nachwuchssorgen beim gehobenen Verwaltungsdienst.' In *Die Verwaltungspraxis*, Heft 3, 1952. Mainz.

I am indebted to the Land Ministry of the Interior in Stuttgart for a survey of social origins for officials in Württemberg-Baden on this point.

R. Bottomore: 'La mobilité sociale dans la haute administration française.' In *Cahiers Internationaux de Sociologie*, vol. XIII, 1952.

[2] W. Bohr: op. cit.

[3] Swedish social democrats are rightly disturbed at this figure after twenty years of social democratic government. See: *Demokratin inom statsförvaltningen.* Paper and discussion at 19th. Socialist Party Congress.

opposition to education.[1] The same is probably true also in Switzerland, Holland and Denmark. In Spain and Italy the possibilities of education for the agricultural population, even those above the subsistence level, are too restricted to give peasant children any reasonable chance of success. Where educational facilities do exist in Italy, however, advantage is not taken of them. The German-speaking population of the South Tyrol, for instance, continually complains at the small proportion of officials in the area who are natives. The simple truth is that no more than a handful of the farming population will consent to secondary or higher education for their children, and those that do so oppose entry into public service.

But if the public official is socially representative of the various grades of the middle class, and as a citizen behaves and thinks much as his social equals, his professional ways of thought are quite distinctive, imposed on him by the nature of his duties.

This ambivalent attitude is mainly to be found amongst those public officials who have functions without parallel outside the public service. But these, being mostly senior officials, affect the general ethos of their service despite their relatively small numbers. And the attitudes they inculcate are surprisingly similar in all European public services.

The work of senior officials, their social class and their duty to society make them conservative, and their first preference is to keep the peace and maintain the status quo. Yet they sympathise with efforts to clear up the worst or most noticeable abuses in the fields of government which are their direct concern. They, frequently more so than politicians, are aware of the black spots in society, even though their knowledge may be second-hand; and this instinct for improvement has been responsible for many minor social and industrial reforms throughout Europe. The sentiment is more commonly found in the newer fields of government than in the traditional branches of defence, law and order, foreign affairs and finance. The instinct to improve is, moreover, most frequently confined to the official's special field. This rather schizophrenic attitude of progressive conservatism is a characteristic of the senior civil servant.

[1] C. Brindillac: op. cit.

Most senior officials suspect that they are more disinterested, intelligent and far-sighted than the other people engaged in government. Very few senior officials are fundamentally anti-parliamentarian, but they generally regard parliament with some reticence as only too likely to interfere in matters it does not understand. This is not so much authoritarianism as the attitude of the professional menaced by the enthusiastic amateur.

They are conscious of civic virtuousness in themselves, and are keenly aware of their responsibilities for protecting the state against the depredations of others. They normally prefer, for instance, to deal with large-scale organizations, for the interests of these are generally interwoven with the interests of the state; their representatives can usually appreciate the larger view even when they disagree with it, and they have a surer and more intellectual approach to what is politically and economically feasible. The single-track, single-minded economic pressure group and 'the little men' are generally so rapacious, so narrow, and show so little regard for broader considerations that the official is offended as a citizen, as a guardian of state interests, and as a man of intelligence.

The senior official's attitude to the public is also affected by popular misconceptions about the nature of bureaucracy and administration. The public considers it has an inalienable right to efficiency, impartiality, and rationality. No doubt the official would like to offer all these things, but he has to deal with a world which is neither efficient, rational or equitable.

For instance, the Dutch administration in recent years has been responsible for the allocation of land reclaimed from the sea. Any competent administrator could put forward various criteria of selection: for instance, proved ability to farm comparable lands, priority for the landless, or for people returned from the East Indies, or even for those successful in a ballot, as is done in southern Italy. In fact public and political pressure eventually forced allocation to groups according to the relative strength of parties in parliament: 35% for catholics, 45% for protestants, 20% for the rest. Even when this was agreed to, the administration had still to face religious demands for denominational schools. Efficiency and economy clearly recommended that people of the same religion be grouped into communities needing only one school. But social peace and public policy were advanced as reasons for mixed communities of different religions, and this view carried the day. Each new community now needs two schools. The Dutch administrator involved in these negotiations is hardly likely to take seriously the dictum 'that among several alternatives involving the same expenditure the one should always be selected which leads to the greatest accomplishment of administrative objectives; and among several alternatives that lead to the same accomplishment the one should be selected which involves the least expenditure.'[1]

Furthermore, every senior official knows that full impartiality and equality of treatment is impossible. Any administration which followed a policy of rigorous impartiality would damage the fabric of government. Not because there would be trouble from people who consider themselves more equal than others—though this sometimes happens—but simply because the primary duty of an administration is to put first things first. Some people, some firms, some interests are of incomparably greater importance than others.[2] Rigorous equality of treatment would mean that the administration treated all demands impersonally, according to strict rules of priority and precedence. The essence of administration is that most people believe it to be impersonal, while those who are really important know how to operate the informal machinery which ensures priority. The key to this arrangement is that only a few people know how to work it, and that only those who know how to work it know that the arrangement exists.

In many other fields public demands are incompatible. Most people want security but resent controls; they want social services but complain of the size of public services; they want high standards of integrity in officials but object to good salary scales.[3] The relations between the public and the

[1] H. Simon: *Public Administration.* New York, 1951. p. 60.

[2] To the extent that one German speaks of '. . . der Pluralismus oligarchischer Herrschaftsgruppen' (W. Weber: *Spannungen und Kräfte in Westdeutschen Verfassungs-system.* Stuttgart, 1951). It has also been suggested that the federal and Länder governments are faced with these groups in a way reminiscent of the 14th. and 15th. century emperors faced with the Landesfürsten and the Ständen (Theodor Eschenburg: *Der Beamte in Partei und Parlament.* Frankfurt a/M, 1952. p. 193).

[3] For an excellent example of this attitude, see: 'Wandlungen in der Wirtschaft.' In *Schweizerische Beamtenzeitung.* Berne, March 5, 1955. Also R. Zorn: 'Zum Beamtenproblem.' In Bayerische *Beamtenzeitung.* February and March, 1952.

official are often marred by inconsistencies of which the official is aware and the public is not. Public opinion may be inspired, but, like woman, it reaches truth by instinct rather than reason.

Many problems concerning training, recruitment, control, and conditions of service have been touched upon in the course of this book. No country has a perfect public service, and it would not be difficult to suggest reforms for every country.

But if one views western Europe as a whole, three major questions stand out.

First, in every country the increase in public services has not been accompanied by sufficient serious thought as to the best way to absorb them into the structure of the modern state. There are not always advantages in clarity, but there are always disadvantages in confusion. The haphazard creation of semi-public, public, quasi-private and partly autonomous bodies complicates law, operation, and control. Many of them could easily be absorbed into the traditional ministerial structure of administration as boards or departments attached to ministries. Many others could be adapted to the German system of öffentliche Anstalt which has proved capable of absorbing banks, insurance companies and electricity undertakings.

Second, clarification in this field might help to disentangle some of the acuter problems of public service law. There is no sensible reason why a postman should be a civil servant and a gas inspector or railway driver a private law employee. Nor is there any serious reason why the vast mass of manipulative, clerical and, often, executive staff employed in public administration, whose duties are exactly comparable with those in private employment, should not be engaged on private law contracts. A much more rigorous distinction in public administration between public officials and private law employees would do two things. It would simplify public service law and introduce into personnel matters an element of flexibility which is lacking in many countries. It would also permit serious consideration to be given to the general unification of the public services. This is particularly important at higher levels. All branches of the public service, ministries as much as industrial public enterprises, need a proper balance between administrator, manager, and technician. If the latter sometimes lack high-class administrators, ministries certainly lack technical competence in scientific, industrial and economic fields.

Third, the recent awareness of the need for better government public relations has gone no further than communicating to the public what the public service concerned is doing rather than why it is doing it. Only in Sweden are any effective measures taken to ensure the maximum publicity for government business; the preamble to the law on the press enjoins the government to do this explicitly on the grounds of public education. No other country in Europe makes a positive effort of this kind, but the pathological secretiveness of British government is matched only in Spain and Portugal. In the other countries the attitude of politicians and civil servants, the nature of the law, and a serious press ensure a steady flow of informed comment on government affairs. But everywhere there is room for improvement. The attitude dates from the time when government business was the concern of the monarch himself, or of a very small group of political and administrative leaders convinced that they were innately more intelligent, better bred and more profoundly patriotic than the rest of the population. There are three reasons why a government should withhold information from the public: because a matter is genuinely secret; because the government's actions or motives would look disreputable; because it does not trust the public.

In fact very few matters genuinely need to be secret. This may be true of a few military dispositions or statistics, some scientific data, some financial programmes. But most national secrets are, in fact, not being kept from foreign countries, but from the public at home. To take an extreme case: any senior official in the Swiss department of military affairs knows that 'Mr Jones' is the head of the British secret service, or that the French SDECE is responsible for espionage and not counter-espionage. Some fifty-page top-secret defence documents contain no information not already known to any academic specialist in the subject. It is clear from memoirs, foreign office papers and cabinet minutes when they are finally published, that only a fraction of the material classified as secret is genuinely confidential. So much secrecy is no more than a habit, a desire for self-importance, a Holstein complex.

Secrecy as regards internal policies too often simply reflects a government's desire to look more respectable than it is. It is not to protect the integrity of a realm but to save the face of a political party. It is very convenient to wrap up a shady deal in the robe of Tiresias. Unfortunately for the politician he needs the connivance of the civil servant; unfortunately for the public the civil servant considers it his duty to co-operate. A menial mind should not be a qualification for high administrative office. As the German public service found under Hitler, what an official tolerates as a civil servant he has to pay for as a citizen. There comes a time when a civil servant should stand on his rights as a man rather than his dignity as a servant. The civil servant too often suffers from the optical illusion that the public is a herd of Gadarene swine. He sees politicians stampeded into unwise policies by the pressure of the public. It may be that no public can be trusted, but since no government in Europe, outside Sweden, has ever tried it, the evidence is incomplete. Public stampedes, to judge from the past, have always been caused by lack of information, or twisted information, not by a surfeit.

In the last hundred years in Europe there have been repeated attempts to abolish arbitrary powers: of judges by codifying law, of politicians by writing constitutions, of public officials by creating administrative courts. Arbitrary power has now been replaced by anonymous power, and anonymous power is the antonym of public administration.

Bibliography

This bibliography follows the main divisions of the book: the Historical Introduction and the four Parts. It is not possible, without excessive duplication, to break the Parts down into their respective chapters: the overlap between the subjects treated in each Part is too great. The books and articles listed in the bibliography have been chosen because they provide the essential preliminary reading for any further study of particular topics. Certain standard works are, of course, useful for all aspects of public law and government, and these are listed first. They are not subsequently listed under the separate Parts. In addition much material can be gleaned by an assiduous study of the better academic reviews published in Europe. These also are listed separately.

GENERAL TEXT BOOKS

CAETANO, M.: *Manual de Direito Administrativo*. 4th ed. Coimbra, 1957.

FORSTHOFF, E.: *Lehrbuch des Verwaltungsrechts*. Berlin, 1951.

GASCON Y MARIN, J.: *Tratado de Derecho Administrativo*. 13th ed. Madrid, 1955.

HECKSCHER, G.: *Svensk Stats Förvaltning i Arbete*. Stockholm, 1952.

DE LAUBADERE, A.: *Traité Elémentaire de Droit Administratif*. Paris, 1953.

MERIKOSKI, V.: *Précis du Droit Public de la Finlande*. Helsinki, 1954.

NEEHOV, M.: *Overzicht van de Administratieve Rechtspraak hier te Lande*. 2nd ed. Hague, 1948.

ORLANDO, V. E.: *Principi di Diritto Amministrativo*. Revised ed. by S. Lessona. Florence, 1952.

PETERS, H.: *Lehrbuch der Verwaltung*. Berlin, 1949.

ROLLAND, L.: *Précis de Droit Administratif*. 9th ed. Paris, 1947.

RUCK, E.: *Schweizerisches Verwaltungsrecht*. Zürich, 1934. 2 vols.

SANDULLI, A. M.: *Manuale di Diritto Administrativo*. 2nd ed. Naples, 1954.

VON TUREGG, K. E.: *Lehrbuch des Verwaltungsrechts*. 2nd revised ed. Berlin, 1954.

WALINE, M.: *Traité de Droit Administratif*. 6th ed. Paris, 1956.

WIGNY, P.: *Principes Généraux du Droit Administratif Belge.* Brussels, 1948.

WILKIN, R.: *L'Organısation Administrative de la Belgique.* Liege, 1950.

ZANOBINI: *Corso di Diritto Amministrativo.* 6th ed. Milan, 1948–50.

REVIEWS

ZOR	*Zeitschrift für Oeffentliches Recht.* (Vienna.)
RISA	*Revue International des Sciences Administratives.* (Brussels.)
CCE Reports	*Rapports Annuels du Conseil Central de l'Economie.* (Brussels.)
RA	*Revue Administrative.* (Paris.)
RDP	*Revue du Droit Public et de la Science Politique.* (Paris.)
Prom.	*Promotions.* (ENA, Paris.)
Et. & Doc.	*Etudes et Documents, Conseil d'Etat.* (Paris.)
R uS	*Recht und Staat.* (Tübingen.)
OV	*Die Oeffentliche Verwaltung.* (Stuttgart.)
J uV	*Justiz und Verwaltung.* (Hamburg.)
BBZ	*Bayerische Beamtenzeitung.* (Munich.)
Riv. Amm.	*Rivista Amministrativa della Repubblica Italiana.*
R. Dir. Pubb.	*Rivista Trimestrale di Diritto Pubblico.* (Milan.)
N. Rass.	*Nuova Rassegna di Legislazione, Dottrina e Giurisprudenza.* (Florence.)
Cor. Amm.	*Il Corriere Amministrativo.* (Empoli.)
Amm. It.	*L'Amministrazione Italiana.*
Riv. C.C.	*Rivista della Corte dei Conti.* (Rome.)
RAP	*Revista de Administración Pública.* (Madrid.)
VSJ	*Verhandlungen des Schweizerischen Juristenvereins.* (Basle.)
ZSR	*Zeitschrift für Schweizerisches Recht.* (Basle.)
SBZ	*Schweizerische Beamtenzeitung.* (Berne.)

HISTORICAL INTRODUCTION

General

BARKER, E.: *The Development of Public Services in Western Europe, 1660–1930.* Oxford, 1944.

BLOCH, M.: *La Société Féodale: la transformation des liens de dépendance.* Paris, 1940.

FINER, H.: *Theory and Practice of Modern Government.* Revised ed. New York, 1949.

IISA: *Enquête sur le recrutement et le fonctionnement des agents du cadre administratif supérieur.* RISA, 1937.

JOLOWICZ, H. F.: *Revivals of Roman Law. Journal of the Warburg and Courtauld Institutes*, vol. XV. London, 1952.

KERN, F: *Kingship and Law in the Middle Ages*. Translated from the German. Oxford, 1948.

ed. WHITE, L. D.: *The Civil Service in the Modern State*. Chicago Univ., 1930. (Symposium.)

ed. WHITE, L. D.: *Civil Service Abroad*. London, 1935. (Symposium.)

Austria

ADAMOVICH, L.: *Grundriss des Oesterreichischen Verfassungsrechts*. Vienna, 1947.

FELLNER, T.: *Die Oesterreichische Zentralverwaltung*. Vienna, 1907.

GEBHARD, L.: *Deutsche und Oesterreichische Organisation der inneren Verwaltung*. Munich, 1927.

HARTUNG: *Zur Frage nach den burgundischen Einflüssen in Oesterreich*. Vienna, 1921.

HELLBLING, E. C.: *Oesterreichische Verfassungs- und Verwaltungsgeschichte*. Vienna, 1956.

ed. HUGELMANN, K. G.: *Das Nationalitätenrecht des alten Oesterreichisch*. Vienna, 1934.

KANN, R. Z.: *The Multi-national Empire: nationalism and national reform in the Hapsburg Monarchy, 1848–1918*. Colombia Univ., 1950. 2 vols.

MAYRHOFER, E.: *Handbuch für den Politischen Verwaltungsdienst*. 5th ed. Vienna, 1898–1902.

RODE, W.: *Wien und die Republik*. Vienna, 1920.

RODE, W.: *Oesterreichs Beamtenpyramide*. Vienna, 1927.

ed. WALTER, F.: *Die Oesterreichische Zentralverwaltung*. Vienna, 1950.

Belgium

CRABBE, V.: *Les commissions de réforme administrative en Belgique*. Institut Belge des Sciences Administratives. Brussels, 1954.

DIDESHEIM, R.: *La formation et le recrutement du cadre administratif supérieur*. RISA, 1939.

France

BERTHELEMY, H.: *Droit Administratif*. 7th ed. Paris, 1913.

BLOCH, M.: *Dictionnaire de l'Administration Française*. 5th ed. Paris, 1905. 2 vols.

CHARDON, H.: *L'Administration de la France: les fonctionnaires de gouvernement, le Ministère de la Justice*. Paris, 1908.

CORMENIN, M. DE: *Droit Administratif*. 5th ed. Paris, 1840. 2 vols.

DE LAUNAY, L.: 'La vie brève d'une école d'Etat: Ecole d'Administration, 1848–9'. *Revue des Deux Mondes*, 15 April, 1937.

DUGUIT, L.: *Les Transformations du Droit Public*. Paris, 1913.
DUGUIT, L.: *Traité de Droit Constitutionnel*. 3rd ed. Paris, 1927. 5 vols.
ESMEIN, A., & GENESTAL: *Histoire du Droit Français*. 15th ed. Paris, 1930.
GODECHOT, J.: *Les Institutions de la France sous la Révolution et l'Empire*. Paris, 1951.
HAAS, C. P. M.: *L'Administration de la France*. Paris, 1861. 4 vols.
HARMIGNIE: *L'Etat et ses Agents*. Louvain, 1911.
HAURIOU, M.: *La Jurisprudence Administrative de 1892 à 1929*. 2nd ed. Paris, 1931. 3 vols.
HAURIOU, M.: *Précis de Droit Administratif*. 8th ed. Paris, 1914. (First published 1892.)
HUGUES, P. D.: *La Guerre des Fonctionnaires*. Paris, 1912.
JEANNENY, J.: *Associations et Syndicats de Fonctionnaires*. Paris, 1908.
LEPOINTE, G.: *Histoire des Institutions du Droit Public Français au XIXe. Siècle*. Paris, 1953.
MACAREL, M.: *Cours d'Administration et de Droit Administratif professé à la Faculté de Droit de Paris*. 1st ed. Paris, 1842.
OLIVIER-MARTIN, F.: *Précis d'Histoire du Droit Français*. Paris, 1945.
RAGON, M.: *Le CGT et la fonction publique*. RA, 1939.
SHARP, W. R.: *The French Civil Service*. New York, 1931.
VIOLLET, P.: *Histoire des Institutions Politiques et Administratives de la France*. Paris, 1890. 3 vols.
VIVIEN: *Etudes Administratives*. 3rd ed. Paris, 1859.

Germany

BLACHLY, F., & OATMAN, M.: *The Government and Administration of Germany*. John Hopkins, 1928.
BLUNTSCHLI, J. C.: *Lehre vom Modernen Staat*. Stuttgart, 1875. (Vols. I–III, *Theory of the State*, vol. I.)
BRAUN, O.: *Von Weimar zu Hitler*. New York, 1940.
BRECHT, A.: *Prelude to Silence: the end of the German Republic*. Oxford, 1944.
DORWART, R. H.: *The Administrative Reforms of Frederick William I of Prussia*. Harvard, 1953.
DITTMAR, W. R.: *The Government of the Free State of Bavaria*. New York, 1934.
EMERSON, R.: *State and Sovereignty in Modern Germany*. Yale Univ. 1928.
ESCHENBURG, T.: *Das Problem der Neugliederung der Deutschen Bundesrepublik*. Frankfurt, 1950.
FRIEDENSBURG, R.: *Die Weimarer Republik*. Berlin, 1946.
GENGLER, L. F.: *Die Deutschen Monarchisten*. Kulmbach, 1932.
GERBER, C. F. VON: *Grundzüge des Deutschen Staatsrechts*. Leipzig, 1865.

GERLACH, H. VON: *Meine Erlebnisse in der Preussischen Verwaltung.* Berlin, 1919.

GNEIST, H. R.: *Der Rechtstaat.* Berlin, 1872.

GROSSER, A.: *Administration et Politique en Allemagne Occidentale.* Paris, 1954.

HAUSSHERR, H.: *Verwaltungseinheit und Ressorttrennung vom Ende des 17. bis zum Beginn des 19. Jahrhunderts.* Berlin, 1953.

HEINZEN, K.: *Die Preussische Burokratie.* Darmstadt, 1845.

JELLINEK, W.: *Allgemeine Staatslehre.* 1900.

LABAND, P.: *Das Staatsrecht des Deutschen Reichs.* 5th ed. Berlin, 1913.

ed. LITCHFIELD, E. H.: *Governing Post-war Germany.* Cornell Univ. 1953.

LOTZ, A.: *Geschichte des Deutschen Beamtentums.* Berlin, 1909.

MEIER, E. VON: *Französische Einflüsse auf die Staats- und Rechtsentwicklung Preussen; 19 Jahrhundert.* Leipzig, 1908.

MAYER, O.: *Deutsches Verwaltungsrecht.* Leipzig, 1895. 2 vols.

PERTHES: *Der Staatdienst in Preussen.* Berlin, 1835.

SCHNEIDER, H.: *Der Preussische Staatsrat, 1817–1918.* Berlin, 1952.

SCHRODER, R.: *Lehrbuch der Deutschen Rechtsgeschichte.* Leipzig, 1919.

SEELEY, J. R.: *Life and Times of Stein.* Cambridge, 1878. 2 vols.

SMALL, A.: *The Cameralists.* Chicago, 1909.

STEIN, L. VOM: *Die Verwaltungslehre.* Stuttgart, 1866.

UDERSTADT, E. R.: *Die Ostpreussische Kammerverwaltung, ihre Unterbehörden und Lokalorgane.* Königsberg, 1911.

Holland

MAURITS DE BRAUW, W.: *De Departementen van Algemeen Bestuur in Nederland sedert de Omwenteling van 1795.* Utrecht, 1864.

Italy

ASSEMBLEA COSTITUENTE: *Relazione della commissione per studi attinenti alla reorganizzazione dello Stato.* Rome, 1946.

COMMISSIONE PARLAMENTARE DI INCHIESTA *sull'ordinamento delle amministrazione di stato e sulle condizione del personale.* Rome, 1922.

JEMOLO, C. A.: *Sull'ordinamento della pubblica amministrazione in Italia.* Riv. Dir. Pubb., 1919.

MIGLIO, G.: *Le Origini della Scienza dell'Amministrazione.* Milan, 1957.

MINGHETTI, M.: *I Partiti Politici e la Ingerenza loro nella Giustizia e nell'Amministrazione.* Bologna, 1881.

PERSICO, F.: *Le Rappresentanze Politiche e Amministrative.* Naples, 1942.

PRESIDENZA DEL CONSIGLIO DEI MINISTRI: *Stato dei lavori per la riforma della pubblica amministrazione, 1948–53.* Rome, 1953. 3 vols.

PRESUTTI, E.: *Principii Fondamentali di Scienza dell'Amministrazione.* Milan, 1910.

RANELETTI, O.: *Il sindicalismo della pubblica amministrazione. Annali della R. Università di Macerata*, vol. II. 1927.

SPAVENTA, R.: *Burocrazia, Ordinamenti Amministrativi e Fascismo*. Milan, 1928.

Spain

DISCURSOS *leidos para commemorar el primero centenario de Don Juan Bravo Murillo*. Madrid, 1952.

FABREGAS DE PILAR, J.: *Políticos y Funcionarios*. Madrid, 1932.

JORDANA, L.: *El Consejo de Estado Español y las Influencias Francesas a lo largo de su Evolucion*. Madrid, 1954.

OLIVAN, A.: *De la Administración Publica con relación a España*. First published 1843, new ed. by E. Garcia de Enterria, Madrid, 1954.

Sweden

HESSLEN, G.: *Public Administration in Sweden*. Swedish Institute, Stockholm, 1954. (Contains a list of approximate Swedish-English equivalents of common terms and titles in public administration.)

Switzerland

BIAUDET, J-C.: *Les Origines de la Constitution Fédérale de 1848*. Lausanne, 1949.

BRIDEL, M.: *L'Esprit et la Destinée de la Constitution Fédérale de 1848*. Lausanne, 1949.

ESCHER, H.: *Schweizerisches Bundesbeamtenrecht*. Zürich, 1903.

PART ONE

General

ed. FRIEDMANN, W.: *The Public Corporation*. London, 1954. (Symposium.)

LANGROD, G.: *L'Entreprise Publique en Droit Administratif Comparé*. RA, 1956, No. 2.

MEYER, P.: *Administrative Organisation*. London, 1957.

Belgium

ed. INSTITUT BELGE DES SCIENCES ADMINISTRATIVES: *La réforme du statut des agents de l'Etat*. Brussels, 1954. 2 vols.

REED, T. H.: *Government and Politics in Belgium*. New York, 1924.

SECRETARIAT PERMANENT DU RECRUTEMENT: *Le recrutement du personnel de l'Etat Belge*. Mimeo. Brussels, 1952.

SECRETARIAT PERMANENT DU RECRUTEMENT: *Rapports annuels*. Brussels, starting 1950. (Also in *Moniteur Belge*.)

TALLOEN, L.: *Notes sur la formation professionnelle en Belgique.* Mimeo. IISA, Brussels, 1955.

VALLES, A. DE: *La formation du personnel administratif.* IISA, Brussels, 1954.

VAN DE MEULEN, J.: *La gestion des bourgemestres-fonctionnaires en Belgique.* RISA, 1939.

Denmark

HARDER, E.: *Le Droit Municipal en Danemark.* RISA, 1952, No. 3.

INDENRIGEMINISTERIUM: *Lov om Landkommunernesstyrelse.* July 6, 1950. Copenhagen.

France

AMNEDGAUD & COUDE DU FORESTO: *Proposition de résolution au Conseil de la République, pour la réforme des méthodes de financement et de gestion des entreprises de droit public,* etc. Paris, 1954.

BONNAUD DELAMARE, R.: *Du recrutement et des débouchés des cadres supérieurs du ministère de l'Intérieur. Rapport à l'Assemblée Générale de l'Association du Corps Préfectoral.* July, 1952.

CHASSAING: *Les problèmes du personnel.* RA, July–Aug., 1948.

DIRECTION DE LA FONCTION PUBLIQUE: *Rapport sur le fonctionnement de la Direction de la Fonction Publique: bilan 1945–51.* Paris, 1952.

ed. LA DOCUMENTATION FRANCAISE: *Présidence du Conseil: L'Organisation gouvernementale, administrative et judiciaire de la France.* Paris, 1952.

ECOLE NATIONALE D'ADMINISTRATION: *Recruitment and training for the higher civil service in France.* Paris, 1956.

ECOLE NATIONALE D'ADMINISTRATION: *Concours d'entrée et scolarité.* Paris, 1945 and 1946 special, then annually.

ECOLE NATIONALE D'ADMINISTRATION: *Epreuves et statistiques des concours.* Paris, 1947 onwards.

ECOLE NATIONALE DES PONTS ET CHAUSSEES: *Règlement intérieur.* Paris, 1956.

ECOLE NATIONALE DES PONTS ET CHAUSSEES: *Programme des Cours.* Paris, annually.

ECOLE NATIONALE SUPERIEURE DES MINES DE PARIS: *Notice sur l'organisation de l'école et programme des cours.* Paris, annually.

ECOLE POLYTECHNIQUE: *Livre du Centenaire.* Paris, 1895. 3 vols.

ECOLE POLYTECHNIQUE: *Règlement Intérieur et Programme des Cours.* Paris, annually.

EISENMANN, C.: *Centralisation et Décentralisation. Esquisse d'une théorie générale.* Paris, 1948.

FUSILIER, R.: *Le statut du personnel des entreprises nationalisées comparé au statut des agents de la fonction publique.* RDP, May, 1956.

GARDELLINI, R., & COUAILLIER, P.: *L'intervention de l'Etat dans le domaine économique*. RA, 1952.

GENDARME, R.: *L'Expérience Française de la Nationalisation Industrielle et ses Enseignements Économiques*. Paris, 1950.

GIELEN, V.: *Das Elitekorps der französischen Staatsverwaltung*. OV, May, 1958.

LAVERGNE, B.: *Le Problème des Nationalisations*. Paris, 1946.

MALLET, D.: *Pour une vraie réforme des administrations centrales*. RA, 1954. No. 42.

MEJAN, F.: *Le perfectionnement des cadres supérieurs de l'administration en France*. In Actas of 10th Congress of IISA, 1956.

MINISTERE DE L'INTERIEUR: *Rapports d'ensemble presentés par l'Inspection Générale des Services Administratifs*. Paris, annually.

PROVOST, C.: *La Sélection des Cadres*. Paris, 1949.

PUGET, H.: *L'administration en matière économique*. RA, 1953.

REYMOND, J-E.: *'Hauts fonctionnaires'*. RA, 1954.

RIVET, H.: *A propos du 'loyalisme'*. RA, 1953.

SABATIER, J.: *L'avenir de l'ENA*. Promotions, Jan., 1952.

SALLET, R.: *Der diplomatische Dienst: seine Geschichte und Organisation in Frankreich, Gross Britanien und den Vereinigten Staaten*. Stuttgart, 1953.

TIZIER, G.: *Le formation des cadres supérieurs de l'Etat en Grande Bretagne et en France*. Paris, 1948.

Germany

BOHR, W.: *Die Ausbildung für den gehobenen Verwaltungsdienst*. Mimeo, Stuttgart, 1954.

BRINTZINGER, O. L.: *Problematik der gegenwärtigen und zukünftigen Verwaltungsausbildung*. OV, in 2 parts, Feb., 1957.

BUHR, F.: *Ubersicht über die soziale Herkunft der gehobenen Dienst in Württemberg, 1957*. Mimeo, Stuttgart, 1957.

EMMERIG, E. & BACHOF, O.: *Ein neues Polizeigesetz in Bayern*. OV, Feb., 1955.

FISCHERHOH, H.: *Oeffentliche Versorgung mit Wasser, Gas, Elektrizität und öffentliche Verwaltung*. OV, May, 1957.

HELMREICH, K.: *Die neue Bayerische Gemeindeordnung und die Gemeindebeamten*. BBZ, Feb., 1952. Munich.

INNENMINISTERIUM: BADEN-WURTTEMBERG: *Soziologische Struktur der Beamten des Innenministeriums, Baden-Württemberg*. Mimeo, Stuttgart, 1954.

INNENMINISTERIUM: BADEN-WURTTEMBERG: *Ausbildung der Inspektoren in Württemberg*. Mimeo, Stuttgart.

JUSTIZMINISTERIUM: HESSE: *Juristischen Ausbildungsordnung für Hesse*. Wiesbaden, 1951.

JUSTIZMINISTERIUM: RHEINLAND-PFALZ: *Justizausbildungsordnung: Rheinland-Pfalz*. Koblenz, 1948.

KRANZ, H. & WAGNER, A.: *Sind Richter Beamte?* OV, March, 1955.

LANDESPERSONALAMT: HESSE: *Rechtliche Stellung und Organisation des Landespersonalamtes und der Landespersonalkommission*. Wiesbaden.

MULLER, H.: *Die Verstaatlichung der Vollzugspolizei—eine politische Notwendigkeit*. OV, Feb.–Mar., 1955.

OEFFENTLICHE VERWALTUNG: *Verwaltungsreform in den Ländern der Bundesrepublik Deutschland*. Special number, June, 1956.

RAUMER, K.: *Ausbildungs- und Prüfungsordnung für den höheren Justiz- und Verwaltungsdienst*. Munich, 1953.

RODER, K.: *Der Wirtschaftswissenschaftler im höheren Verwaltungsdienst: zur Frage der Ausbildung für den höheren Verwaltungsdienst*. OV, Jan., 1956.

ROETDORF, F.: *Die Einheit der Verwaltung auf der Kreisebene*. OV, Apr., 1958.

SCHAFER, H.: *Die bundeseigene Verwaltung*. OV, Apr., 1958.

SCHEUNER, U.: *Die Einheit des Deutschen Rechtstandes und die Frage der juristischen Ausbildung*. OV, July, 1955.

SIGRIST, H. & RODING, H.: 'Selection and training for the German Foreign Service.' *Indian Quarterly*, New Delhi. July–Sept., 1956.

TURK & DORRHOFER: *Neuzeitliche Methoden der Personalauslese*. Frankfurt, 1950.

WEINMANN: *Die Preussische Ausbildungsordnung für Juristen*. Berlin, 1927.

Holland

DAUMERIE, T.: *Le centenaire de la loi communale Néerlandaise*. RISA, 1951, No. 4.

MARIS, A. G.: *Le 'Waterstaat'*. RISA, 1951.

VAN POELJE, G. & SMIT, J.: *The training of higher grade officials in the Netherlands*. In Actas of 10th Congress of IISA, 1956.

Italy

AMENDOLA, M.: *Gli studi e le realizzazioni per la riforma della pubblica amministrazione*. Riv. Dir. Pubb. 1952.

COSMO, G.: *Le partecipazioni economiche dello stato. Quaderno di Cultura e Storia Sociale*. Jan. 1953.

COSMO, G.: 'State participation in business concerns in Italy.' *Quarterly Review of Banca Nazionale del Lavoro*. Rome, Oct., 1951.

LA MALFA: *Relazione sulla riorganizzazione delle partecipazioni economiche dello Stato*. Rome, 1952.

LENTINI, A.: *L'Amministrazione Locale*. Como, 1953.

LUCIFREDI, R.: *Sul ministero delle partecipazioni statali. Discorso alla Camera dei Deputati*. April 18, 1956. Rome.

MAZZAGLIA, A.: *Trasferimento e decentramento di funzioni dello stato.* Amm. It. 1954.

ROSSI, E.: *Lo Stato Industriale.* Bari, 1953.

SEPE, O.: *Il disegno di legge sulle attribuzioni del Governo e sull'ordinamento della Presidenza del Consiglio dei Ministri.* Riv. Dir. Pubb. 1957.

SEPE, O.: *Gli enti locali e il decentramento dei servizi del Ministero degli Interni.* N. Rass. 1954. No. 19.

STAMMATI, G.: *Corsi di perfezzionamento tecnico per i funzionari dell'amministrazione finanziaria.* Riv. Amm. March, 1953.

Portugal

COSTA, A.: *Organizacão politica e administrativa de nacão.* 5th ed. Lisbon, 1944.

Spain

ENTERRIA, E. G. DE: *La actividad industrial y mercantil de los municipios.* RAP, 1955. No. 17.

FRAGA IRIBARNE, M.: *Así se gobierna España.* Madrid, 1952.

PRESIDENCE DU GOUVERNEMENT: (Sec. Gen. Tech.): *L'Organisation administrative de l'Etat Espagnol.* Madrid, 1957.

LEY DE REGIMEN LOCAL: *Texto articulado.* December 16, 1950. Madrid.

Sweden

ARNESON, B. A.: *The Democratic Monarchies of Scandinavia.* London, 1949.

EKLESIASTIKDEPT: *Arbetsordning för Kungl. Skolöverstyrelsen.* October 27, 1952. Stockholm.

EKLESIASTIKDEPT: *Instruktion för Skolöverstyrelsen, N661.* Oct. 3, 1952. Stockholm, 1952.

INRIKESDEPARTEMENTET: *Polisutbildningskommitté 1948: Rekrytering och Utbildning av Polispersonal.* Stockholm, 1952.

INRIKESDEPARTEMENTET: *Sekretessen vid förundersökning i brottmål.* Stockholm, 1955.

LANDSTROM, S-T.: *Svenska Ambetsmäns sociala ursprung.* Uppsala, 1954.

PHILIP, D.: *L'administration centrale suédoise.* RA, 1954. No. 42.

SOCIALDEMOKRATISKA ARBETAREPARTIET: *De Samhälleliga Företagsformerna.* Stockholm, 1952.

WIJKMAN, G.: *Statens Organisationsnämnd och dess verksamhet. In Departement och Nämnder,* 1954.

Switzerland

LOBSIGER, E.: *Die berüfliche Ausbildung des Staatsbeamten in der Schweiz.* Paper read at conference of IISA, 1951.

RAPPARD, W. E.: *La Constitution Fédérale de la Suisse*. Neuchâtel, 1948.

SAUSER-HALL, G.: *Guide Politique Suisse*. Lausanne, 1947.

PART TWO

Belgium

BERTA, J. & VANDEVEL, E.: *Codes des lois politiques et administratives*. 5th ed. Brussels, 1950.

CAMU, A.: *La réforme administrative en Belgique*. RISA, 1938.

CRABBE, V.: *Les commissions de réforme administrative en Belgique*. IISA, 1954.

ed. IISA: *La réforme du statut des agents de l'Etat*. Brussels, 1950. 2 vols.

SEELDRAYERS, E-P.: *La notation des fonctionnaires et ses exigences*. RISA, 1952. No. 3.

SEELDRAYERS, E-P.: *Le premier rapport de la 'Commission Philippart'*. RISA, 1952. No. 1.

STATUT des. agents du Ministère des Affaires Etrangères et du Commerce Extérieur. January 11, 1954 and April 25, 1956. Brussels.

VAN DEN DRIES, J.: *Etude sur la formation des échelles de traitement*. RISA, 1953. No. 4.

VERSPECHT, J.: *Des agents de l'Etat, leur statut administratif*. Mimeo. Brussels, 1951.

Denmark

ed. ANDERSEN, U. & FEDDERS, H. C.: *Tjenestemands Loven*. Copenhagen, 1954.

France

BIZE, P.: *Le problème de la spécialisation du personnel*. RA, 1953.

CARCELLE, P. & MAS, G.: *Les pensions et le budget*. RA, 1952.

CARCELLE, P. & MAS, G.: *Le réemploi des retraités de l'Etat et des services publics*. RA, 1952. In 2 parts.

CARCELLE, P. & MAS, G.: *Les pensions de l'Etat*. RA, 1952.

CARCELLE, P. & MAS, G.: *Les traitements et la situation matérielle des fonctionnaires*. RA, 1949.

CHAVANON, C.: 'Les fonctionnaires et la fonction publique'. *Cours à l'Institut d'Etudes Politiques*. Paris, 1950–1.

COLIN, J.: *Le régime des pensions pour ancienneté de services des fonctionnaires et agents non-titulaires de l'Etat*. RA, 1952.

COLIN, J.: *Cumul d'emplois—cumul de rémunérations*. RA, 1953.

DEBRE, M.: *La Mort de l'Etat Républicain*. Paris, 1948.

DIRECTION DE LA FONCTION PUBLIQUE: *Rapport sur le fonctionnement de la Direction de la Fonction Publique: bilan, 1945–51*. Paris, 1951.

DUBAS, J.: *La notation des fonctionnaires*. Mimeo. Fondation Nationale des Sciences Politiques. April, 1947.

GREGOIRE, R.: *La Fonction Publique*. Paris, 1954.

MARTIN, M.: *La Fonction Publique: étude de droit public comparé*. Paris, 1943.

MEJAN, F.: *Il faut étendre aux premiers les garanties disciplinaires désormais accordées aux seconds*. RA, 1952.

PRESIDENCE DU CONSEIL: *Réforme de la Fonction Publique*. Paris, 1945.

SESEGAS, C.: *Les Droits et les Obligations des Fonctionnaires*. Paris, 1953.

STATUT GENERAL DES FONCTIONNAIRES: *Loi*, October 14, 1946.

STATUT GENERAL du personnel des communes et des établissements publics communaux. *Loi*, April 28, 1952.

TUNC, R.: *Le secret professionnel et les relations administratives*. RA, May–June, 1948.

Germany

ANSCHUTZ, G.: *Beamten und die revolutionären Parteien*. Berlin, 1931.

BAYERISCHE LANDTAG: *Verordnung über die Anwendung der Dienststrafordnung auf Kommunalbeamte vom Juli 15, 1953. Bayerische Gesetz- und Verordnungsblatt, Jul. 30, 1953.*

BENDIX, L.: *Das Streitrecht der Beamten*. Berlin, 1922.

BUNDESRAT SEKRETARIAT: *Entwurf: Gesetz zur Sicherung des einheitlichen Gefüges der Bezüge im öffentlichen Dienst*. Bonn, 1954.

GEIB, E.: *Probleme des Schleswig-Holsteinischen Beamtengesetzentwurfs*. OV, Feb.–Mar. 1955.

INNENMINISTERIUM: BADEN-WURTTEMBERG: *Beamtengesetz für Baden-Württemberg* (*7 Beilagen*). Nov. 19, 1946. Stuttgart, 1946.

INSTITUT ZUR FORDERUNG OEFFENTLICHER ANGELEGENHEITEN: *Neues Beamtentum: Beitrage zur Neuordnung des öffentlichen Dienstes*. Frankfurt, 1951.

KAISER, J. H.: *Der Politische Streik*. Berlin, 1955.

ed. LITTMANN, G. & WOLF, K.: *Hessisches Beamtenrecht*. Wiesbaden, 1952.

MINISTERIALBLATT: *Durchführung des Bundesbeamtengesetzes und des Gesetzes zu Artikel 131 G.G.* Bonn, Jun. 12, 1954.

RAUMER, K.: *Der Beamtenanwärter*. B.B. Feb. 1952.

ed. SARTORIUS, C.: *Beamtengesetz, Jul. 14, 1953. Bundesgesetzblatt, Teil I, Jul. 17, 1953.*

SOMMERSBACH, H.: *Die Gehorsamspflicht der Deutschen Reichs- und Staatsbeamten*. Griefswald, 1903.

WACKE, G.: *Das Gesamt-Personalrecht des öffentlichen Staatsverwaltung*. OV, Apr. 1958.

WICHERT, E.: *Deutsches Beamtengesetz*. Bonn, 1952.

Holland

ALGEMEEN RIJKSAMBTENAREN REGLEMENT: June 12, 1931 (*Staatsblad No. 284*). *Staatsdrukkerij*, Hague. (With amendments up to Jan. 1956.)

AMBTENARENWET: Hague, 1929.

WET *Rechtsherstel Overheidspersoneel*, 1946. Zwolle, 1953.

Italy

AMENDOLA, A.: *Per la riforma della legislazione sui dipendenti statali.* Riv. Dir. Pubb. 1953.

BENNATI, A. & GIAMBATTISTA, E. DI: *Il nuovo statuto e la carriera degli impiegati civili dello stato.* Naples, 1956.

CAMERA DEI DEPUTATI: Doc. 7. No. 1. *Messagio alle camere del Presidente della Repubblica, a norma dell'articolo 74 della costituzione trasmesso alla Presidenza il 21 Novembre, 1953; proroga della legge 14 Febbraio, 1953, No. 49, relativa ai diritti e compensi dovuti al personale dagli Uffici dipendenti dai Ministri delle Finanze e del Tesoro e della Corte dei Conti.* Rome.

CATALDI, G.: *La réforme administrative en Italie.* RISA, Brussels, 1953. No. 1.

COMMISSIONE PARLAMENTARE *di inchiesta sull'ordinamento delle amministratione di stato e sulle condizione del personale.* Rome, 1922.

CORIGLIONI, U.: *Il pensionato e il suo stato di disagio.* Amm. It. Sept. 1953.

GUICCIARDI, E.: *Esercizio di funzioni pubblici e interesse personale nei collegi amministrativi.* Riv. Amm. 1948.

LA TORRE, M.: *La responsabilità degli amministratori e impiegati degli enti locali.* Riv. C.C. 1934.

PRESIDENZA DEL CONSIGLIO DEI MINISTRI: *Stato dei lavori per la riforma della pubblica amministrazione (1948–53).* Rome, 1953. 3 vols.

Spain

MEDINA, L. & MARAÑON, M.: *Leyes Administrativas de España.* 2 vols. Madrid, 1957.

JORDANA, L.: *La seguridad social de los funcionarios públicos en España.* Las Ciencias, Madrid.

MINISTERIO DE LA GOBERNACION: *Reglamento de funcionarios de administración local.* Madrid, 1953.

USERA, G. DE: *Legislación de Hacienda Española.* Madrid, 1947.

Sweden

HERLITZ, N.: *Die gegenwärtige Lage der Verwaltung und der Stand der*

Verwaltungswissen schaftlichen Forschung in den Scandinavischen Ländern. VA, Oct. 1957.

SANDLER, A. & EKMAN, E.: *Government, Politics and Law in the Scandinavian countries.* Minnesota Univ. 1954.

Switzerland

ARRETE DU CONSEIL FEDERAL *concernant la classification des fonctions.* Berne, 29 Jan. 1954.

KAUFMANN, O.: *Die Verantwortlichkeit der Beamten und die Schadenersatzpflicht des Staates im Bund und Kantonen.* VSJ, 1953.

STATUT DES FONCTIONNAIRES: *Loi Fédérale,* Jun. 30, 1927 with amendments of Jun. 24, 1949. Berne.

CONSEIL FEDERAL: *Message à l'Assemblée Fédérale à l'appui d'un projet de loi sur le statut des fonctionnaires fédéraux (1868).* Berne, Jul. 18, 1924.

ORDONNANCE *sur les rapports de service des fonctionnaires de l'administration générale de la confédération.* Berne, Sept. 26, 1952.

ORDONNANCE *sur les rapports de service des fonctionnaires des Chemins de Fer Fédéraux.* Berne, Sept. 26, 1952.

ORDONNANCE *sur les rapports de service des employés de l'administration générale de la confédération.* Berne, Sept. 29, 1952.

OTT, H.: *Théorie juridique de la fonction publique fédérale.* Lausanne, 1915.

REGLEMENT *concernant la Commission du Personnel.* Berne, Dec. 21, 1954.

PART THREE

Austria

SPANNER, H.: *Die Verwaltungsgerichtsbarkeit in Oesterreich.* OV, Oct. 1955.

Belgium

CONSEIL D'ETAT: *Loi et Arrêtés essentiels. Moniteur Belge,* Jan. 9, 1947. Brussels.

ILLIGEMS, M.: *Le régime et le contrôle financier en Belgique.* Mimeo. IISA, Brussels, 1951.

PUGET, H.: *Le Conseil d'Etat Belge. Etudes et Documents.* Paris, 1949.

VELGE, H.: *Le Conseil d'Etat.* Brussels, 1947.

VELGE, H.: *Le contentieux administratif en Belgique.* RISA, 1935.

Denmark

FOLKETINGETS OMBUDSMANDS *beretning.* Copenhagen, annually 1955 onwards.

LOV *om Folketingets Ombudsmand.* No. 203. June 11, 1954. Copenhagen.

FORFATNINGSKOMMISSIONEN: *Betænkning,* 1946. Copenhagen, 1953.

GRUNDLOV OG TRONFØLGELOV: Copenhagen, 1953.

France

ALIBERT, J.: *Le Contrôle Juridictionnel de l'Administration au Moyen du Recours pour Excès de Pouvoir*. Paris, 1926.

BATBIE, A.: *Traité Théorique et Pratique de Droit Public et Administratif*. 2nd ed. Paris, 1885. 3 vols.

CARCELLE, P. & MAS, G.: *Le contrôle de l'Etat sur les finances publiques*. RA, 1953.

CASSIN, R.: *L'évolution récente des juridictions administratives en France*. RISA, 1953. No. 4.

CONSEIL D'ETAT: *Livre jubiliaire*. Paris, 1949.

DUEZ, P.: *Les Actes de Gouvernement*. Paris, 1934.

GUILLIEN, R.: *Les commissaires du gouvernement près les juridictions administratives et, spécialement, près le Conseil d'Etat français*. RDP, Apr.–Jun. 1955.

HAMSON, C. J.: *Executive Discretion and Judicial Control: an aspect of the French Conseil d'Etat*. London, 1954.

LAFERRIERE, J.: 'Le recours contre le silence de l' administration.' *Revista de Drept Public*. Bucharest, 1931.

LAMPUE, P.: *Le développement historique du recours pour excès de pouvoir depuis ses origines jusqu'au début du XXe. siècle*. RISA, 1954. No. 2.

LANGROD, G.: *Procédure administrative et droit administratif*. RISA, 1956. No. 3.

LANGROD, G.: 'Quelques réflexions méthodologiques sur la comparaison en science juridique.' *Revue International de Droit Comparé*. 1957. No. 2.

LAUBADERE, A. DE: *Les Réformes Administratives de 1953*. Paris, 1954.

LETOURNEUR, M. & MERIC, J.: *Conseil d'Etat et Juridictions Administratives*. Paris, 1955.

LEY, A.: *Les transformations de la comptabilité publique*. RISA, 1951.

MARTIN, M.: *Le Conseil d'Etat*. Paris, 1952.

MINISTERE DES FINANCES: *Commission de Vérification des Comptes des Entreprises Publiques*. Paris, annually 1949 onwards.

POMME DE MIRIMONDE: *Le Cour des Comptes*. Paris, 1947.

SOUTY, P.: *Recueil de Jurisprudence en Matière Administrative*. 4th ed. Paris, 1949.

TROTOBAS, L.: *Précis de Science et Législation Financières*. 9th ed. Paris, 1947.

Germany

ARENDT, W.: *Prüfung privatrechtlicher Gesellschaften durch die Rechnungshöfe*. OV, Apr. 1957.

ENTSCHLIESSUNG *der 'gemischten Kommission' zu Entwurf der Verwaltungsgerichtsordnung*. OV, Mar. 1955.

FEUCHTE: *Aufgaben und Stellung der Verwaltungsgerichtsbarkeit. Staatsanzeiger für Baden-Württemberg*. Stuttgart. Aug. 1954.

FISCHER-MENSCHAUSEN, H.: *Das Finanzverfassungsgesetz*. OV, Mar. 1956.

FLEINER, F.: *Institutionen des Deutschen Verwaltungsrechts*. 8th ed. Tübingen, 1928.

FRIEDERICH-MENGER, C.: *Rechtssatz, Verwaltung und Verwaltungsgerichtsbarkeit. Prolegomena zu einer Lehre von den Möglichkeiten und Grenzen des verwaltungsgerichtlichen Rechtsschutzes*. OV, Oct. 1955.

ed. GENZER, W. E. & EINBECK, W.: *Die Uebertragung rechtsetzender Gewalt im Rechtstaat*. Frankfurt, 1952.

GOLZ, G.: *Finanzkontroll der Rechnungshof bei Unternehmen des Bundes und der Länder*. OV, Aug. 1956.

INSTITUT ZUR FORDERUNG OEFFENTLICHER ANGELEGENHEITEN: *Bundesrecht und Bundesgesetzgebung*. Frankfurt, 1950.

KOLLMANN, O.: *Verwaltung und Verwaltungsgerichtsbarkeit*. OV, Jan. 1955.

MAETZEL, W. B.: *Die verwaltungsgerichtliche Anfechtung von Ablehnungsbescheiden*. OV. Jul. 1955.

MEYER, G.: *Deutsches Verwaltungsrecht*. 4th. ed. Tübingen, 1915.

NAUMANN, R.: *Der Entwurf der Finanzgerichtsordnung*. OV, Mar. 1958.

PENTZ, A.: *Die neuen Haftungsbestimmungen des Beamtenrechtsrahmengesetzes und des Bundesbeamtengesetzes*. OV, Jul. 1958.

SCHOEN, X.: *Die Grenzen der Verwaltungsgerichtsbarkeit*. OV, Mar. 1955.

ed. WOLFF, E.: *Beitrage zum Oeffentlichen Recht*. Tübingen, 1950.

ed. WOLFF, E.: *Beitrage zur Rechtforschung*. Tübingen, 1950.

Holland

HUART, F. J. A.: *Le contentieux administratif aux Pays Bas*. RISA, Brussels, 1935.

PUGET, H.: *Le Conseil d'Etat Néerlandais. Etudes et Documents*. Paris, 1948.

Italy

ALLEGRINI, A.: *La Corte dei Conti e la riforma della Repubblica Italiana*. N. Rass. 1952.

AMATUCCI, G.: *Corte dei Conti*. Riv. C.C. 1953.

BENVENUTI, F.: *L'Istruzione nel Processo Amministrativo*. Padua, 1953.

BONNAUDI, E.: *L'evoluzione del potere esecutivo e gli atti di potere politico del governo*. Riv. Amm. 1949.

GALEOTTI, S.: *The Judicial Control of Public Authorities in England and in Italy*. London, 1954.

GENNARO, G. DE.: *Il rapporto contabile pubblico e contabili di diritto e di fatto*. Riv. C.C. 1953.

LEGGI AMMINISTRATIVI: *Concerning Consiglio di Stato, Giunta Provinciale*

Amministrative, Corte dei Conti, Corte Costituzionale, Avvocato dello Stato. No. 897. Pirola, Milan, 1952.

LENTINI, A.: *L'Amministrazione Locale*. Como, 1953.

LESSONA, S.: *La Gustizia Amministrativa*. Bologna, 1953.

MINISTERO DEGLI INTERNI: *Funzionamento della Giunta Provinciale Amministrativa in sede giurisdizionale e dei Consigli di Prefettura*. Ministerial Circular, 1953.

ORTONA, A.: *Corte dei Conti*. Riv. C.C. 1949.

PUGET, H.: *Le Conseil d'Etat Italienne*. RISA, 1952.

SEPE, O.: *Il disegno di legge sull'azione amministrativa. Corriere Amministrativo*. Jan. 15, 1957.

SEPE, O.: *Il controllo della Corte dei Conti sugli enti sovvenzionati*. Florence, 1955.

SOLMI, G.: *La responsabilità contabile dei pubblici funzionari*. Amm. It. Jan. 1953.

Spain

GONZALEZ PEREZ, J.: *La reforma de la jurisdicion contencioso administrativa*. RAP, May–Aug. 1955. Madrid.

RODO, L. L.: *Le recours contentieux administratif en Espagne*. RISA, 1953. No. 1.

Sweden

HERLITZ, N.: *Le droit administratif Suédois*. RISA, 1953. No. 3.

JUSTITIEDEPT: *Instruktion för Riksdagens Justitieombudsman*. No. 4. Mar. 14, 1941. Stockholm, 1941.

JUSTITIEDEPT: *Betänkende angående Justitiekanslerns, Justitieombudsmannens och Militieombudsmannens allmänna ämbetsställning*. Stockholm, 1939.

JUSTITIEOMBUDSMANNENS AMBETSBERATTELSE, Stockholm, annually.

KOMMITTEN ANG. DET ALLMANNAS SKADESTANDSANSVAR: *Utkast till lag om skadestånd i offentlig verksamhet*. Stockholm, 1954.

LAGERGREN, B.: *Le Conseil d'Etat en Suède*. RISA, 1949, No. 1.

MILITIEOMBUDSMANNENS AMBETSBERATTELSE, Stockholm, annually.

STATSLIGARE *för Budgetåret 1954–5* (2 parts). Stockholm, 1954 (annually).

UTRIKESDEPT: *The committee system in the Swedish Riksdag*. Stockholm.

UTRIKESDEPT: *The Swedish budgetary system*. Stockholm.

Switzerland

GEERING, W.: *Das Verfahren vor Bundesgericht in verwaltungsrechtlichen Streitigkeiten*. Geneva, 1945.

GRAFF, P.: *La responsabilité des fonctionnaires et de l'Etat pour le dommage causé à des tiers, en droit fédéral et en droit cantonal*. Basle, 1953.

HUBER, H.: *Die Verfassungsbeschwerde: vergleichende und kritische Betrachtungen. Juristische Studiengesellschaft*, Karlsruhe, Heft 9, 1954.

IMBODEN, M.: *Der Schutz vor staatlicher Willkür*. Zürich, 1945.

IMBODEN, M.: *Der nichtige Staatakt*. Zürich, 1944.

IMBODEN, M.: *Das Gesetz als Garantie rechtstaatlicher Verwaltung. Basler Studien zur Rechtswissenschaft*. Helf 38, 1954. Basle.

IMBODEN, M.: *Erfahrungen auf dem Gebiet der Verwaltungsrechtsprechung in den Katonen und im Bund*. VSJ, 1947.

LOI *sur la responsabilité des autorités et des fonctionnaires publics* (implementing article 17 of the Constitution). Berne, May 19, 1951.

NEF, H.: *Sinn und Schutz verfassungsmässiger Gesetzgebung und rechtmässiger Verwaltung im Bunde*. ZSR, Heft 4, 1950.

OTT, H.: *La Justice Administrative Fédérale*. Lausanne, 1904.

PANCHAUD, A.: *Les garanties de la Constitutionalité et de la légalité en droit fédéral*. ZSR, vol. 69, 1950.

PROCEDURE FEDERALE: *Organisation judiciaire, procédure civile, procédure pénale. Chancellerie Fédérale*. Berne, 1949.

SCHNEIDER, P.: *Beamtenverantwortlichkeit und Staatshaftung im Schweizerischen Recht*. OV, Sept. 1955.

SCHWEIZERISCHER BUNDESGERICHT: *Bericht an die Bundesversammlung über seine Geschäftsführung im Jahre 1954*. Berne, Feb. 8, 1955.

PART FOUR

Austria

HEITERER-SCHALLER, P.: *Die gegenwärtige Lage der Verwaltung in Oesterreich*. VA, Oct. 1957.

Belgium

CRABBE, V.: *Une erreur dans le statut syndical des agents de l'administration étatique Belge*. RISA, 1952. No. 4.

CRABBE, V.: *Balzac et l'administration*. RISA, 1954.

CRABBE, V.: *Syndicalisme et fonction publique en Belgique*. RISA, 1953.

CRABBE, V.: *Considérations sur la bureaucratie: ses causes sociologiques et ses motifs politiques. Revue de l'Institut de Sociologie*. Brussels, 1955.

LECLERCQ, J.: *Les conseil économiques nationaux en Belgique, en France et aux Pays Bas: étude comparative*. Brussels, 1954.

France

ABADIE, M.: *Carrière d'Etat ou carrière privée?* Promotions. 1956. No. 37.

ARDANT, G.: *Technique de l'Etat*. Paris, 1954.

BIZE: *Le problème de la déformation professionelle: ses effets sur l'efficacité*. RA, 1952.

BOTTOMORE, T.: *La mobilité sociale dans la haute administration française. Cahiers Internationaux de Sociologie.* Vol. XIII, 1952. Paris.

BRINDILLAC, C.: *Les hauts fonctionnaires.* Esprit, June, 1953.

CAHEN, G.: *Les Fonctionnaires: leur Action Corporative.* Paris, 1911.

CATHERINE, R.: *Fonction Publique: vingt-quatre libres propos.* Paris, 1952.

CATHERINE, R.: *Cabinets et services.* RA, 1953.

DEBRE, M.: *La République et son Pouvoir.* Paris, 1950.

ECOLE POLYTECHNIQUE: *Annuaire, containing notes on present positions of students.* Annually, Paris.

FAVARELLE, R.: *Le fonctionnairisme. Revue de Paris,* Sept.–Oct. 1901.

GINGEMBRE, L.: *Le syndicalisme patronal et l'administration.* RA, 1949.

GREGOIRE, R.: *Les caractéristiques fondamentales du travail dans la fonction publique.* ITAP Conference, Nov. 30, 1953. Paris.

GUILLAUME, M.: *Considérations juridiques sur la grève des services publics. Cahiers Chrétiens.* Paris, Apr. 1954.

HAMON, L.: *Gouvernement et intérêts particuliers.* Esprit, Jun. 1953.

JOUVENEL, R. DE: *Le République des Camarades.* 16th ed. Paris, 1914.

LAUZANNE, S.: *La République de la papérasserie. Revue de Paris,* May-Jul. 1929.

LELONG, P.: *Politique et Fonction Publique. Thesis, Institut d'Etudes Politiques,* Paris, 1952.

MAZE, J.: *Le Système: 1943–51.* Paris, 1953.

MER, G.: *Le Syndicalisme des Fonctionnaires.* Paris, 1930.

PAPON, M.: *L'Ere des Responsables.* Tunis, 1954.

RAGON, M.: *Le CGT et la fonction publique.* RA, 1950.

WILLIAMS, P.: *Politics in Post-war France.* London, 1954.

WURMSER, L.: *Le milieu administrative en France et à l'étranger.* RA, 1951.

Germany

ARON, R.: *La Sociologie Allemande Contemporaine.* Paris, 1950.

BOHR, W.: *Nachwuchsklage und Nachwuchssorgen beim gehobenen Verwaltungsdienst. Verwaltungspraxis.* Heft 3, 1952.

BUHR, F.: *Ubersicht über die soziale Herkunft der gehobenen Dienst im Württemberg.* Mimeo. Stuttgart, 1937.

ESCHENBURG, T.: *Der Beamte in Partei und Parlament.* Frankfurt, 1952.

FLEINER, F.: *Beamtenstaat und Volksstaat.* Tübingen, 1916.

GROSSER, A.: *Administration et Politique en Allemagne Occidentale.* Paris, 1954.

HAUSSLEITER, O.: *Verwaltungs soziologische Denken in Deutschland.* OV, Jan. 1958.

HECKEL, H.: *Die Rolle der Juristen in der Fachverwaltung.* OV, Jan. 1958.

INNENMINISTERIUM: BADEN-WURTTEMBERG: *Soziologische Struktur des Innenministeriums, Baden-Württemberg.* Mimeo. Jul. 1954.

INSTITUT ZUR FORDFRUNG OEFFENTLICHER ANGELEGENHEITEN: *Ratgeber von Parlament und Regierung.* Frankfurt.

INSTITUT ZUR FORDERUNG OEFFENTLICHER ANGELEGENHEITEN: *Neues Beamtentum: Beitrage zur Neuordnung des öffentlichen Dienstes.* Frankfurt, 1951.

KOTTGEN, A.: *Das Deutsche Berufsbeamtentum und die parlamentarische Demokratie.* Berlin, 1928.

LAUBE, H.: *Verwaltungstaktik—Menschenkunde, Menschenführung.* OV, Dec. 1955.

LECHNER, H. & HULSHOFF, K.: *Parlament und Regierung.* Berlin, 1953. (*Textsammlung des Verfassungs-, Verfahrens- und Geschäftsordnungsrechts der obersten Bundesorgane.*)

LOFFLER, M.: *Darf die Verwaltung in das Grundrecht der Pressefreiheit eingreifen?* OV, Dec. 1957.

MAINHOLZ, H.: *Ministerialburokratie.* BBZ, Mar. 1952.

MOLL, R.: *Dürfen die Bezüge der Wahlbeamten herabgesetzt werden?* OV, Apr. 1957.

NAWIASKY, H.: *Die Stellung der Berufsbeamtentums im parlamentarischen Staat. Recht und Staat,* No. 37. Tübingen, 1925.

NOSKE, G.: *Erlebtes aus Aufstieg und Niedergang einer Burokratie.* Offenback-Main, 1947.

OPLER, K. & PELDRAM, E. R.: *Die Neugestaltung des öffentlichen Dienstes.* Frankfurt, 1950.

RANTZAU, J. A. VON: *Glorification of the State in German Historical Writing.* In German History, some new views, ed. H. Kohn, London, 1954.

RITTER, G.: *Europa und die Deutsche Frage. Betrachtung über die geschichtliche Eigenart des Deutschen Staatdenkens.* Munich, 1947.

SCHEUMER, U.: *Das parlamentarische Regierungssystem in der Bundesrepublik: Probleme und Entwicklungslinien.* OV, Sept. 1957.

SCHWEIGER, K.: *Die Verwaltungs Vereinfachung.* OV, Aug. 1955.

WEBER, W.: *Spannungen und Kräfte in Westdeutschen Verfassungssystem.* Stuttgart, 1951.

ZORN, R.: *Die Als-Ob Demokratie.* Mannheim, 1953.

Holland

GOES VAN NATERS, DE JOUGH, DE VRIES & SENS: *Ambtenaar en Politiek.* Hague, 1948.

VAN PRAAG, P.: *The role and function of the trade unions in and towards politics.* Mimeo. Hague, 1954.

Italy

FRAGOLA, U.: *La piaga dei circolari.* N. Rass. 1952.

FRAGOLA, U.: *Note sulla moralità amministrativa.* Amm. It. Nov. 1953.

LA TORRE, M.: *La garenzia amministrativa.* Amm. It. July–Aug. 1953.

LA TORRE, M.: *Malcostume amministrative.* Amm. It. Jan. 1954.

LA TORRE, M.: *Crisi del diritto amministrativo—e rapporti tra giuristi e amministratori.* Amm. It. Jan. 1954.

PERSICO, F.: *Le rappresentanze politiche e amministrative.* Naples, 1942.

PRESUTTI, E.: *Lo Stato Parlamentare ed i suoi Impiegati Amministrativi.* Naples, 1899.

TAGLIACOZZO: *Studi sul Movimento Operaio in Italia: 1861–1925.* Rome, 1937.

Spain

BOLETINO OFFICIAL DE ESTADO: *Escalafón del Cuerpo de Abogados del Estado, 1955.* Madrid, 1956.

ELORRIAGA, G.: *Ensayo sobre la Vocación Política.* Madrid, 1958.

ENTERRIA, E. G. DE: *Aspectos de la Administración Consultiva.* Madrid, 1958.

SOLIS, J.: *L'Experience Syndicale Espagnole.* Madrid, 1954.

SOLIS, J.: *Nuestro Sindicalismo.* Madrid, 1955.

Sweden

CRONER, F.: *Tjänstemannakåren in det Moderna Samhället.* Uppsala, 1951.

KALVESTEN, A-L.: *The social structure of Sweden.* Mimeo. Stockholm, 1951.

LAGERGREN, B.: *Les secrétaires généraux des cabinets ministériels en Suède.* RISA, 1949, No. 1.

LANDSTROM, S-S.: *Svenska Ambetsmäns sociala ursprung.* Uppsala, 1954.

REHN, G.: *Fördelningen av ett statens upplysningsanslag vid folkomröstningar.* Stockholm, 1954.

SOCIALDEMOKRATISKA ARBETAREPARTIET: *Demokratin inom statsförvaltningen. Betänkande avgivet till 19e. Kongress, 1952.* Stockholm, 1952.

TCO: *The Central Organisation of Salaried Employees in Sweden.* Stockholm, 1953.

TCO: *Styrelsens och Revisorernas Berättelser för ar 1954.* Stockholm, annually.

UTRIKESDEPT: *The Committee System in the Swedish Riksdag.* Stockholm.

Switzerland

AFFEAC: *Statut de l'Association des fonctionnaires et employés fédéraux des administrations centrales.* Berne, 1950.

AFFEAC: *Que veut l'Affeac?* Berne, 1955.

CRONER, F.: *Tjänstemän och Tjänstemannaproblem i Schweiz. TCO's Skriftserie, N°. 4.* Boras, 1954.

HUBER, H.: *Recht, Staat und Gesellschaft.* Berne, 1954.

IMBODEN, M.: *Die gegenwärtige Lage der Verwaltung in der Schweiz.* VA, Oct. 1957.

SCHWEIZERISCHES GEWERKSCHAFTSBUND: *Die Schweizerischen Gewerkschaftsverbände im Jahre 1953.* Berne, annually.

SOLOVEYTCHIK, G.: *Switzerland in Perspective.* Oxford, 1954.

UNION FEDERATIVE DU PERSONNEL DES ADMINISTRATIONS ET DES ENTREPRISES PUBLIQUES: *Statut, Apr. 26, 1950.* Berne.

ed. WECKERLE: *The Trade Unions in Switzerland. Swiss Federation of Trade Unions.* Berne, 1947.

Index

A

Abogados del Estado, 150, 283
Abuse of power, 207, 212, 219, 252, 253
Actes d'autorité, 35, 37, 213
Actes de gestion, 37, 213
Actes de gouvernement, 196, 213, 215, 218, 231, 234
Administrative courts, 28, 41, 185 seq., 199 seq., 206 seq.
Administrative law, 185, 187 seq., 196–8, 206 seq.
Administrative Procedure Act (Austria), 268
Administrative Staff College, 128
Administrative tribunals, 185, 211
Advanced courses, 124–30
Aerarium, 10
Algemeen Comite van Overheids-personeel, 301
Allied High Commission in Germany, 109
Alsace, 31
Ambtenarencentrum, 301
Amsterdam, 63, 69
Anfechtungsklage, 224–5
Angestellten, 53, 146, 296–7
Anstalt, *see* Oeffentliche Anstalt
Appeals, 162–3, 172, 211, 214, 215, 221, 227, 231, 262
Architects, 77, 94
Arnhem, 69
Assemblée Fédérale, 51, 221
Attitudes, officials', 24–5, 92–3, 107–8, 126, 135, 141, 173, 208, 295, 315
Audit, 262–3
Auditeurs, 203
Auditorium, 11
Augustus, 10
Ausiliarios, 146
Austria:
  Administrative Procedure Act, 268
  history of control, 190
  history of administration, 21–2, 30, 40
  politics, 284, 288
  public opinion, 310
  recruitment, 76

B

Balzac, 312
Banca Nazionale del Lavoro, 59
Bank of France, 266, 283
Barcelona, 314
Basle, 311
Bavaria, 67, 102, 103, 105, 191, 224, 225, 285, 309
Beamten, 52, 66–7, 77, 108, 146, 162, 288, 296–7, 310
Beamtengesetz, 133
Belgium:
  administrative courts, 197–8, 201, 204, 208, 212–15
  control, history of, 41, 188, 189, 196–8
  discipline, 134, 163
  history of administration, 29, 41
  local government, 65, 68–9, 71–2
  pensions, 153–7
  police, 64
  politics, 284, 287, 291
  promotion, 171, 172, 174
  public opinion, 314–15
  rating, 176
  recruitment, 76, 77–9, 83, 86–8
  security of tenure, 146
  statute of civil service, 133
  trade unions, 37–8, 42, 79, 297–9
  training, 113–14
Bereitschaftspolizei, 62
Berlin, 201
Bern, 67
Berthelémy, H., 35
Bezirk, 22, 30, 66, 103, 202
Bezirksausschuss, 191
Bezirksverwaltungsgericht (Berlin), 201
Bismarck, 31
Blanco case, 54, 238
Bluntschli, 34
Boards, *see* Royal Boards
Bond Hogere Politie-ambtenaren, 302
Bourgmestre, 68–9
Breviarum Alaricianum, 13
Britain:
  administrative courts, 192–3, 195, 196 (*see also* Legal profession)
  attitudes, 208, 280

Britain—*contd.*
Board of Inland Revenue, 150
centralisation, 73
civil service (class), 76, 77
discipline, 163
duties, 143–4
Franks Committee, 196
National Insurance Tribunals, 185
nationalised industries, 55, 56
Official Secrets Act, 137
police, 64
promotion, 165, 173, 174
recruitment, 77, 83, 86, 92–4
security of tenure, 32
security programme, 151, 161
technocrats, 97–8
transfer, 150
Bundesdisziplinar Anwalt, 162
Bundesdisziplinarhof, 162–3
Bundesdisziplinarkammern, 161–2
Bundesrechnungshof, 260
Bundestag, 148
Bundesverwaltungsgericht, 162, 201, 226–8
Burgermeester, 69–70
Bürgermeister, 66, 174
Burgundy, 21

C

Cameralistics, 23
Camu, L., 78
Cantons, 84, 194, 220, 221
Cartel des syndicats indépendants des services publics, 298
Casuali, 136
Catholics, 284–5, 298, 301
Central Organisation of Graduate Workers (Sweden), 304
Centrale générale des services publics, 298
Centrale van Hogere Rijksambtenaren, 301
Centralisation, 19, 20–1, 22, 30, 61–2, 64, 68, 72–3, 77–8
Centralpersoneeldienst, 79–80
Centre des Hautes Etudes Administratives (CHEA), 128–30
Chambre de recours, 134, 163, 298
Character, 93–4, 167
Christelijke Politiebond, 302
Cinecittà, 59
Civil servant, *see* Official
Codified law, 25, 29
Cogne works, 59
Collosenzen, 300
Colonial Service, 94
Comes rerum privatarum, 11
Comes sacrarum largitionum, 11
Comités paritaires de consultation syndicale, 298
Commission de la verification des comptes, 261, 265–7
Commission de consultation syndicale, 298
Commissione di disciplina, 135
Commissioner of the Queen (Holland), 69–73
Commissions administratives paritaires, 134, 163, 172
Commissions d'avancement, 172
Committees, 18, 27, 291–4
Commune, 27, 66, 67, 68, 69–70
Concordia, 14
Conditions of service, 133 seq.
Confédération des syndicats chrétiens, 298
Conseil de direction, 172
Conseil d'Etat (French), 28, 41, 81, 120, 148, 151, 186–7, 188, 190, 191, 199, 203, 213, 229–41, 269
Conseil d'Etat (Belgian), 197–8, 201, 204, 213–15, 299
Conseil de préfecture, 188, 199, 203
Conseil Fédéral, 138, 163, 168, 194, 220, 222
Conseil National, 194
Conseil Supérieur de la Magistrature, 148
Consejo de Aragón, 17
Consejo de Cabinete, 20
Consejo de Cruzada, 17
Consejo de Estado, 17, 202
Consejo de Hacienda, 17
Consejo de la Inquisición, 17
Consejo Real, 17
Consejo Supremo de la Guerra, 17
Consiglio di Prefettura, 200, 202, 262
Consiglio di Stato, 148–9, 159, 189, 191, 204, 215–19, 262
Consiglio superiore della pubblica amministrazione, 134, 135
Constantine, 9
Control:
financial, 260 seq.
history of, 186 seq.
theory of, 181–6, 267–70.
(*See also* Administrative courts, Ombudsman, Parliament)
Co-optation, 24
Copenhagen, 64
Corps:
Diplomatic, 74, 77, 97–8, 146
grands, 81, 82, 120, 266, 280
Prefectoral, 81, 120, 146
Technical, 28, 74, 81, 95–7, 146
Corpus Juris, 9, 13
Corruption, 139–40, 207, 275, 295, 314
Corte dei Conti, 215, 261–3
Council of the Realm (Sweden), 18–19
Councils, elected, 67, 68, 71–2

Cour de Cassation, 190
Cour des Comptes, 81, 120, 231, 260, 265, 266
Court of Impeachment (Sweden), 248
Courts, 183–4, 188, 189, 190, 192, 193, 196, 210, 213, 220, 224, 232, 233, 238, 248, 249, 252, 253, 254, 256, 260, 268–9 (*see also* Administrative courts)
Crispi, 280, 286
Cromwell, Thomas, 19
Crown, 16–17, 22–3, 26, 27, 30, 44, 186, 197–8, 208–12, 213, 214, 215, 242, 245, 246–7, 254, 264, 276–7, 308
Cuerpos especiales, 150
Cuerpos tecnicos, 146

D

Dale, 136
Damages, 207, 210, 214, 223, 224, 232–3, 234, 238–40
Decentralisation, 71–3
Denmark:
  administrative courts, 208, 257–8
  control, *see* Administrative courts *and* Ombudsman
  history, 31, 41
  local government, 65
  Ombudsman, 208, 255–9
  police, 63–4
  politics, 277, 288, 291
  promotion, 173
  recruitment, 83
  security of tenure, 145
  training, 100, 101, 114, 125
Députation permanente, 68
Deputazione provinciale, 200
De Rerum Novarum, 301
Détournement de pouvoir, 225, 237–8
Dicey, 41, 192
Diocletian, 9, 11
Diplomatic Corps, *see* Corps
Direction de la Fonction Publique, 82, 91, 134
Disciplinary codes, 160–3
Disciplinary Courts, 159 seq.
Discipline, 32, 38, 158–63, 164, 168, 202, 258
Discretion, 181, 236–7, 242 (*see also* Actes de gouvernement, Abuse of power)
Dismissal, 31, 37, 38, 160, 161, 163, 252, 253
Doctors, 77, 94
Duguit, L., 35–6, 44, 137
Duties, 136 seq.

E

Eastern Marches League, 273
Echevins, 68
Ecole de préparation aux carrières administratives, 113
Ecole Libre des Sciences Politiques, 42, 81
Ecole Nationale d'Administration (ENA), 42, 82, 83, 88–94, 97, 111, 115–24, 130, 203
Ecole Nationale des Douanes, 114
Ecole Nationale des Mines, 74, 96–7, 110–11
Ecole Nationale Supérieure des Ponts et Chaussées, 74, 96–7, 110–11
Ecole Polytechnique, 28, 29, 74, 96–7, 110, 111
Einaudi, 136
Eindhoven, 70
Eisenbahnverband, 304
Elections, 287–9
Electricité de France, 233
Engineers, *see* Technocrats
Enseñada, Marquis de la, 20
Equity, 215
Esmein, 35
Etablissement public, 54
Examinations, 24, 79, 82–3, 86, 87, 88, 89–92, 96, 103, 105–6, 119, 122, 170–1, 204

F

Fault, 159, 239–40
Faute de service, 239–40
Faute personnelle, 239–40
Federal Administrative Court, *see* Bundesverwaltungsgericht
Federal Polytechnic (Switzerland), 95
Federal state, 62, 64, 65–6, 67, 84–5, 101, 191, 220–3, 226–8
Financial courts, 260–3, 265–7
Finland:
  administrative courts, 244
  control, *see* Administrative courts, Ombudsman, Justitiekansler
  Justitiekansler, 246–7
  ministries, 65
  Ombudsman, 255
  pensions, 153–7
  politics, 288, 294
  rating, 177
  recruitment, 83
  security of tenure, 145
Fiscus, 10
Fisher, Warren, 282
Fiskalerna, 245
Fleiner, 311
Föderativverband, 305–6
Folketingets Ombudsmandsudvalg, 257
Foreign Service, *see* Corps
Fouché, 61

France:
administrative courts, 200, 203, 208, 231–41
control, *see* Administrative courts
financial, 260, 265–7
history of, 28, 41, 190, 197–8
discipline, 134, 159, 161, 163
duties, 141, 143
history, 13, 16, 17, 20–1, 25–30, 32, 35–7, 41–2
local government, 65
nationalised industries, 54–6
pay, 55
pensions, 153–7
police, 62–3
post office, 55
politics, 280, 284, 288, 291
promotion, 74, 171, 172, 174
public opinion, 33, 308, 312–13
railways, 54, 55
rating, 175
recruitment, 74, 76, 77, 80–3, 86, 88–94, 95–7
rights, 140
security of tenure, 146, 148, 159
social structure, 28–9, 122–3, 315–16
statute, 42, 55, 133
Frankfurt, 23
Frankfurt Constitution, 1848, 190
Franks Committee, 185–6, 196
Frederick William I, 22, 183
Freemasonry, 285–6

G

Geheimer Rat, 21
Gendarmerie, 63, 64
Gerber, 33
Gerichtsverfassungsgesetz, 223
Germany:
administrative courts, 201, 202–3, 208, 223–8
Bundesbeamtengesetz, 133
control:
financial, 260
history of 187, 190–2, 194–5
discipline, 157, 158, 161–3
duties, 141
history 16, 17, 18, 22–5, 29, 31–2, 33–4, 38–9
Länder, 54, 62, 64, 66, 77, 83, 101 seq., 150, 194, 201, 202, 223, 224, 226–7, 288
local government, 53, 65–7
officials' attitudes, 24–5, 107, 108, 228
pensions, 153–7
police, 62, 64
politics, 273, 275, 280, 284, 287, 288, 290
promotion, 167, 169, 171, 173
public opinion, 25, 33, 308–10
railways, 51–2
rating, 176–7
recruitment, 74, 76, 77, 83, 84–5, 95
rights, 140
security of tenure, 147–9
social class, 315–16
Giunta provinciale amministrativa, 200, 202, 215
Gladden, 136
Gneist, 35, 190
Gothenburg, 280
Governing bodies of public service, 133–6
Government Accounting Office, (Sweden), 264
Governor, provincial, 68–73
Greffier provincial, 72
Grosse Staatsprüfung, 105–6, 108
Guardia di Finanza, 125
Gubernien, 22

H

Halle, 23
Hamburg, 201
Hammarskjöld, L., 193
Hauriou, 35
Hegel, 33
Heine, 33, 308
Hesse, 66, 104, 105, 191
Hewart, Lord, 195
Hitler, 40, 275
Hochschule für Verwaltungswissenschaften, Speyer, 104–5, 128
Hofkammer, 21, 22
Hofkanzlei, 21
Hofrat, 21
Holland:
administrative courts, 201, 204, 208
Commissioner of the Queen, 69–73
control, history of, 187
history, 41
local government, 65, 68–70
officials' attitudes, 208
pay, 76
police, 64
politics, 69, 284, 288, 291, 293, 318–19
promotion, 168
public opinion, 310–11, 318
Raad van Staate, 186, 188, 208–12
rating, 175–6
recruitment, 77, 79–80, 83, 95
trade unions, 300–2
training, 127
Waterstaat, 52, 95
Hungary, 22, 30
Hurwitz, S., 256, 257

I

Idoneità, 170–1
Imboden, 311
Imperium, 14, 15, 16, 25, 36
Industrial workers, 146
Inspection Générale des Finances, 28, 81, 120, 123, 283
Inspection Générale des Mines, 28, 81
Inspection Générale des Ponts et Chaussées, 28, 81
Instituto de Estudios de Administración Local, 125
Instituto per la Ricostruzione Industriale, 58–60
Instituts d'Études Politiques, 82, 122
Intendent de Hacienda, 20
Interessi legittimi, 200
Italy:
  administrative courts, 200, 202, 204, 208, 215
  Consiglio di Stato, 148–9, 215–19
  Corte dei Conti, 215, 261–3
  control:
    financial, 261–3
    history of 185, 187, 189, 190, 191
  discipline, 134–5
  duties, 142–3
  history, 14, 29, 32, 34, 38–9, 42
  Instituto per la Ricostruzione Industriale (IRI), 58–60
  local government, 65
  local officials, 65–8
  pay, 136
  pensions, 153–7
  police, 62–3
  politics, 280, 284, 291, 295
  promotion, 170–1, 173
  public opinion, 313–14, 317
  recruitment, 76, 77, 83, 86, 95
  regions, 65
  security of tenure, 146, 148
  state holdings, 57–61
  statute, 42, 133
  trade unions, 37–8, 300
  training, 125, 126–7

J

Jefe de Administración, 171
Jefe de Negociado, 170
Jellinek, 34
Jews, 285
Josef II, 22
Judges, 104, 107, 147–9, 202–5, 228, 253
Judiciary, *see* Courts, Judges
Juristenmonopol, 109, 290
Justi, 16
Justice déléguée, 186, 197, 198, 214
Justice retenue, 186, 197, 198, 214
Justinian, 9
Justitieombudsman, 245 seq.
Justitiekansler, 245 seq.
Justizstaat, 183–6

K

Kreis, 22, 30, 66, 103, 202
Kreisausschuss, 191
Kreistag, 66
Kriegs-und-Domänen Kammer, 22

L

Laband, 34
Laferrière, E., 36
La Malfa, 58
Län, 72
Länder, 54, 62, 64, 66, 77, 83, 101 seq., 150, 194, 201, 202, 223, 224, 226–7, 288
Landesverwaltungsgericht, 201
Landrat, 66, 174
Landskamreren, 72
Landsorganisation (LO), 303–4
Landssekreteraren, 72
Legal profession, 109, 192–3, 195–6, 228, 253–4, 290
Legality, 206, 212–13, 217, 218, 219, 221, 224, 225, 230, 235–7, 242, 243, 247, 248, 262
Legatii, 10
Legislative process, 290–1
Letrados del Estado, 150
Letrados del Tribunal de Cuentas, 150
Letter of Instruction (Sweden), 50–1
Lex regia, 9, 15
Lex Romana Visigothorum, 13
Liability, 207, 210, 223, 238–41
Limburg, 69
Local government, 21, 24–5, 26, 53, 61–73, 85, 279, 314
Louis the Pious, 14
Loyalty, 39–40, 151
Loyseau, 16
Luleå, 64
Lutheran Church, 251, 285

M

Magister militum, 11
Magister officiorum, 11
Maître des Requêtes, 203
Maria Theresa, 21
Marseilles, 63
Maximilian I, 21–2
Maximus, 11
Mayor, 27, 66, 67
Mecklenburg, 191
Merit, 24, 26, 164 seq.
Merito, 191, 200, 219
Meyer, O., 34

Militieombudsman, 248 seq.
Ministerial cabinets, 279–81, 284
Ministerialrat, 169
Ministries, 48 seq.
Ministry of Agriculture, 48, 283, 285
Ministry of Commerce, 48, 314
Ministry of Communications, 49
Ministry of Defence, 48, 49
Ministry of Education, 48, 285
Ministry of Finance, 28, 48, 49, 113, 125–7, 150, 265, 266, 283, 314
Ministry of Foreign Affairs, 27, 48, 49, 283
Ministry of Health, 48, 156
Ministry of the Interior, 27, 48, 62, 63, 64, 68, 69, 70, 72, 77, 103, 150, 161, 202, 284
Ministry of Justice, 27, 48, 49, 62, 77, 103, 249, 257, 283, 285
Ministry of the Middle Class, 284
Ministry of National Insurance, 48
Ministry of Pensions, 48
Ministry of Police, 61
Ministry of Population, 284
Ministry of Public Works, 150, 284
Ministry of Social Affairs, 48, 49, 243, 258
Ministry of State Holdings, 60–1
Ministry of Transport, 48, 265
Monnet, 282
Montesquieu, 187
Morant, 282
Myrdahl, 282

N

Naples, 63, 314
Napoleon, 25–30, 186–7, 188
Nation, 25, 30, 186
National Insurance Tribunals, 185
National Union of Civil Servants (Sweden), 304
Nationale, Das, 274
Nationalisation, 55, 56, 233, 265–7
Nederlandsche Politiebond, 302
Negligence, 159, 160–3, 232, 248
Nepotism, 164, 167
Nord Rhein-Westfalen, 106
Norway:
  local government, 65
  public opinion, 314
  recruitment, 83
  security of tenure, 145

O

Obedience, 141–4
Oberbürgermeister, 66
Oberlandesgerichtspräsident, 103
Oberregierungsrat, 169
Oberverwaltungsgerichtshof, 191
Oeffentliche Angestellten, 53
Oeffentliche Anstalt, 53–4, 66, 320
Official Secrets Act, 137
Official, public:
  attitudes of, 24–5, 107, 108, 208, 228, 321
  definition of, 55, 66, 71, 72, 73, 89
  local, 47, 65, 67, 68, 72, 73
  state, 47, 52, 61 seq., 65 seq., 71, 73
Ombudsman, 208, 245–59, 269
Opler, 308
Opus Dei, 285
Orlando, 34

P

Pan-German Movement, 273
Pantouflage, 283–4
Paris de Bollardière, General, 143
Parliament, 41, 51, 182, 193, 195, 206, 247, 248, 249, 255, 256, 257, 263–4, 270, 275, 287, 288, 289–95, 309
Parteistreitigkeit, 221, 224
Patrimonium, 10, 25
Patronage, 31, 279
Pay, 43–4, 55, 135, 136, 149, 311, 314
Pensions, 153–7, 263
Perthes, 34
Piedmont, 32, 189
Poland, 31
Polders, 52–3
Police, 61 seq., 258, 302
Police powers, 12, 47, 67, 71–3
Politics:
  and civil servants, 273 seq., 281, seq.
  and parties, 284–6
  and posts of confidence, 31, 151–2, 275–9, 280
  (*See also* Attitudes, Elections, Legislative process, Ministerial cabinets, Parliament, Trade unions)
Polizia Armada, 63
Polizeistaat, 183–6, 195
Portugal:
  duties, 141
  local government, 65, 67
  ministries, 49
  officials' attitudes, 321
  police, 62
  politics, 284, 287, 288
  recruitment, 83
  security of tenure, 151
Posts and telegraphs, 49, 50, 51, 55
Praepositus sacri cubuculi, 11
Prefect, 10–12, 29, 67, 68–73, 188, 200, 287
Prefectoral Corps, 81, 146.
Prerogative power, *see* Crown, Actes de gouvernment
Primicerius notariorum, 11
Privy Councils, 17, 18–19, 20

Profession, 43, 134, 178, 281, 296–7, 306
Promotion, 151, 164–78
Protection, from vexatious prosecution, 159, 259
Protestant League, 273
Prot.-Christelijke Centrale, 301
Province 22–3, 71–3
Prussia, 16, 17, 18, 22–5, 31–2, 51, 74, 102, 183, 190–1
Pubblica Sicurezza, 63
Public interest, 216, 226, 234
Public official, *see* Official
Public opinion, 25, 33, 219–20, 222–3, 269–70, 308 seq.
Public power, 16, 26, 27, 33, 34, 36, 233
Public services, *see* Services
Publicity of public acts, 34

R

Raad van Staate, 186, 188, 201, 204, 209–12
Railways, 49, 50, 51, 54, 55, 265, 299, 305
Rating, 174–8
Rechtstaat, 183–6, 311
Recruitment, 74 seq.
Referendar, 103, 104, 105, 107
Referendari, 204
Régie, 54
Regierungsinspektoranwärter, 106
Regierungspräsident, 64, 103, 106
Regeringsrätten, 201, 204, 241–4
Renault works, 54
Revisionsekreterare, 253–4
Rheinland-Pfalz, 104, 105–6
Ribertet, 19
Richelieu, 21
Ricorso straordinario, 217
Rights, 136 seq.
Riksdag, 246 seq., 263
Riksgäldskontoret, 263
Rijkspolitievereniging, 302
Ritter, 309
Roman law, 9–12, 15
R.K. Centrale, 301
Royal Boards (Sweden), 18–19, 49–51, 84

S

Saar, 104
St. Gall, 113
St. Michael association, 302
Saint Pierre, Abbé de, 18
Sardinia, 65
Saxony, 51, 191
Schleswig-Holstein, 106
Schools, 41, 99–100, 104–5, 110–11, 115–24, 125–7, 286
  training, 99 seq.
SDECE, 321
Secrecy, 137, 321
Secrétaire Général, 72
Secrétariat Permanent de Recrutement, 78–9, 87, 134, 171
Secretaries of State, 19–21
Secretario del Despacho Universal, 20
Security of tenure, 145 seq.
Seniority, 164 seq.
Servant, civil, *see* Official
Service d'administration generale, 78–9, 134
Services:
  local, 47, 61 seq.
  national, 47 seq.
  public, 13, 15, 16–17, 18, 26–7, 34, 36, 47–8, 51–3, 54–7, 61, 95–6, 97, 232, 320
Sicily, 65, 204
Social class, 24, 28–9, 42, 122–3, 315–20
South Tyrol, 65, 317
Sovereignty, 15–16, 32 seq.
Spain:
  administrative courts, 202–5
  control, history of, 187
  cuerpos especiales, 150
  cuerpos tecnicos, 146
  duties, 141
  history, 13, 17, 20, 29, 38–9
  local government, 65, 67
  local officials, 68
  officials' attitudes, 321
  pay, 136, 314
  pensions, 153–7
  police, 62–3
  politics, 283, 284, 285
  promotion, 170, 171, 173
  public opinion, 313, 314, 317
  recruitment, 83, 95
  security of tenure, 146, 151
  trade unions, 37–8
  training, 100, 125
Stadion, 30
Stadtverwaltungsgericht (Berlin), 201
State, theories of, 9–10, 14, 15–17, 25–6, 27, 32–8
Statsrevisorer, 264
Statutes, 41, 42, 55, 82, 87, 133–4, 136
Statut générale de la fonction publique, 133
Stein, Baron vom, 24, 25
Steuerräte, 22
Strikes, 137
Student clubs, 286
Supreme Administrative Court (Sweden), 184, 193–4, 201, 241–4
Supreme Public Service Court (Finland), 244
Suspension, 160, 161
Sûreté Nationale, 63

Sweden:
administrative courts (*see* Supreme Administrative Court)
control:
financial, 263–4, 268
history of, 184, 193
discipline, 159, 160–1
history, 18–19, 32, 41
local government, 65, 68, 71–3
ministries, 49, 84
Ombudsman, 245–55
pay, 76, 135, 149
police, 64–5
politics, 276–7, 285, 291, 293, 294
promotion, 165, 168
public opinion, 269–70
rating, 177
recruitment, 83, 84
rights, 133
Royal Boards, 18–19, 49–51, 84
security of tenure, 145, 149
social class, 315–16
Supreme Administrative Court, 184, 193–4, 201, 241–4
trade unions, 303–5
Swissair, 304
Switzerland:
administrative courts, 200, 208, 219–22
cantons, 62, 64, 65, 67, 85
control, history of, 194
discipline, 163
duties, 138
history, 34–5
local government, 65, 67
ministries, 49
officials' attitudes, 311
pay, 311
pensions, 153–7
police, 62, 64
politics, 287, 294
promotion, 168
public opinion, 219–20, 222–3, 311–12
railways, 51
rating, 177
recruitment, 83, 85–6, 95
statute, 133
trade unions, 299, 304–7
training, 100, 112–13
Syndical state, 37–8, 172, 296–8, 315

T

Talma, 301
Technocrats, 95–7
Tecnicos, 146
Thuringia, 191
Tjänstemännens Central organisation (TCO), 303–4
Trade unions, 37–9, 40, 42, 78, 79, 80, 137, 279, 296 seq.
Training, 24, 28, 41–2, 99 seq.
Transfer, 149–50
Tribunal Administratif, 199, 203, 231
Tribunal des Conflits, 190, 233, 238
Tribunal Fédéral, 163, 194, 200, 220–2
Tribunal Suprema, 202

U

Ulpian, 9
Unestablished officials, 146–7
Universities, 23, 24, 76, 83, 86, 88, 92, 95, 103, 125, 141, 147, 286
Untätigkeitsklage, 225–6

V

Val d'Aosta, 59, 65
Verband des Personals Oeffentlicher Dienst, 304
Vereinigtebӧhmisch-Oesterreichische Hofkanzlei, 22
Verwaltungsgerichtshof, 191, 201
Vicarii, 10
Vienna, 40, 310
Vivien, 36

W

Warning, 160, 161
Waterstaat, 52–3, 95
Wehrbeauftragter, 245
Weimar Republic, 39, 284
Widows, 156–7
Württemberg-Baden, 67, 104, 174, 191, 201, 225

Z

Zurich, 311